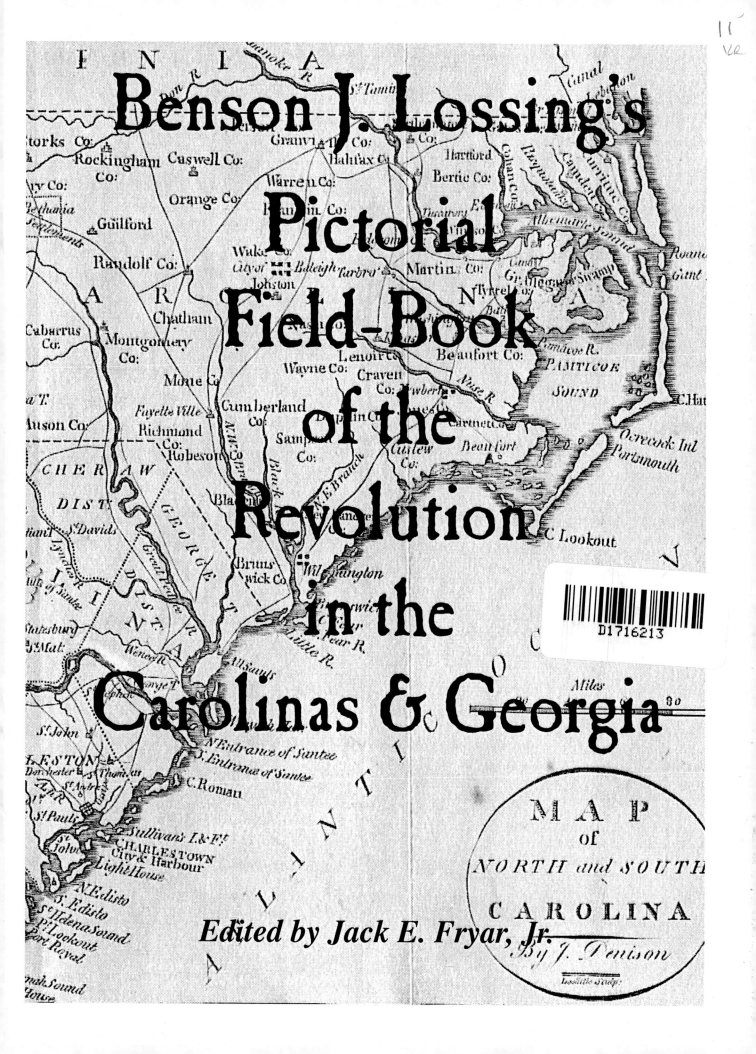

Benson J. Lossing's
Pictorial
Field-Book
of the
Revolution
in the
Carolinas & Georgia

Edited by Jack E. Fryar, Jr.

Original publication: 1850
This edition: 2004

Published in the United States of America by Dram Tree Books,
a JEF Publications company.

Publisher's Cataloging-in-Publication Data
(Provided by Quality Books, Inc.)

Lossing, Benson John, 1813-1891
    [Pictorial field-book of the Revolution. Selections]
    Benson J. Lossing's pictorial field-book of the
Revolution in the Carolinas & Georgia / edited by Jack
E. Fryar, Jr. - 1st ed.
    p. cm
    Reprint of selections from the 1850 ed.
    ISBN 0-9723240-4-6

    1. United States-History-Revolution, 1775-1783
2. North Carolina-History-Revolution, 1775-1783
3. South Carolina-History-Revolution, 1775-1783
4. Georgia-History-Revolution, 1775-1783.   I. Fryar,
Jack E.   II. Title: Pictorial field-book of
the Revolution in the Carolinas & Georgia

E208 L883 2004   973.3
                        QB104-200515

10 9 8 7 6 5 4 3 2 1
Dram Tree Books
2801 Lyndon Avenue
Wilmington, N.C. 28405-3045
(910) 538-4076
dramtreebooks@ec.rr.com

*Discounts available
for educators.
Call or e-mail for terms.*

Contents

Chapter XVI - 81

Chapter XVII - 113

Chapter XX - 219

Chapter XXI - 243

A Note About This Edition...

Twelve years before the guns of Charleston signaled the opening salvo of the Civil War by firing on Fort Sumter, Benson John Lossing conceived of a book that would tell the story of our first civil war, the American Revolution. In that earlier conflict, the people of the thirteen colonies found themselves divided over the question of independence from Great Britain. Before the issue was decided, each of the rebellious colonies would witness acts of bravery and sacrifice, cruelty and nobility, heroism and cowardice, and even more than a little treachery. Lossing, an editor, illustrator and historian, set out to record those stories before they faded into the oblivion of time. He covered more than 8,000 miles in each of the thirteen original states and Canada, recording the story of the war from eyewitnesses and their offspring. The result is a book of monumental girth and value. The two volumes that comprise Lossing's *Pictorial Field-Book of the Revolution* recount virtually every clash between the Americans and Great Britain in the war. Simply put, if a Yank and a Redcoat even threw rocks at each other from opposite sides of a stream, chances are it's recorded in Lossing's work.

Benson J. Lossing

This book deals specifically with those parts of Lossing's book that focus on the war in the Carolinas and Georgia. Most grade school history books seem to focus primarily on the events that took place north of the Mason-Dixon Line. As a result, virtually everyone knows the story of Lexington and Concord, Paul Revere's ride, Valley Forge and Bunker Hill. But it was in the South that the decisive battles of the war were fought. The first American victory of the war came in 1776, at a murky little tributary in modern Pender County, North Carolina, called Moores Creek. In a brief but ferocious fight, militiamen under Alexander Lillington and Richard Caswell smashed a superior force of Scotch Highlanders. The result was that the British were kept out of the South for another four years, until Major James H. Craig occupied Wilmington, N.C. as part of Cornwallis' campaign of 1781. In the murky swamps of the South Carolina Low Country, Francis Marion waged a guerrilla war that would distract British men and supplies from other battlefields and become a case study for future soldiers even today. Daniel Morgan and Nathaniel Greene would make names for themselves at places called The Cowpens and King's Mountain. Charleston, S.C. would for the first time (but not the last time) in its history learn what it was to be a military target and suffer an enemy occupation. British commander Charles Lord Cornwallis would win a battle but perhaps lose a war at Guilford Courthouse. Camden. Eutaw Springs. Ninety-Six. Savannah. The list of names goes on and on. In a very real sense, the British gambled everything on the outcome of the war in the southern colonies, and much of that gamble came in America's southernmost three colonies. This book excerpts Benson J. Lossing's remarkable chronicle of what happened there.

Those readers with access to original copies of Lossing's book will note there are design differences between his book and this one. The content of the two works are the same. Every sentence Lossing wrote in the original is included here. The main differences are that footnotes in the original book are endnotes coming after each chapter here, and we've omitted Lossing's original introduction, in which he talks mostly about the discovery of America and the explorers who did the discovering. Also, the illustrations found in the original are reproduced here at a larger size, in most cases. Dates are presented in the narrative in a different manner than Lossing did in his original, too. In Lossing's original book, he had a lot of material to get into a finite number of pages. Since this volume deals with only a portion of the original's content, there is room to enlarge the illustrations for better enjoyment by the reader. Having said all of that, we at Dram Tree Books hope you enjoy this remarkable chronicle of America's first civil war - a world war, in fact - as it happened in North Carolina, South Carolina and Georgia.

Jack E. Fryar, Jr. - Editor
Wilmington, N.C.
November 2004

he story of the American Revolution has been well and often told, and yet the most careless observer of the popular mind may perceive that a large proportion of our people are but little instructed in many of the essential details of that event, so important for every intelligent citizen to learn. Very few are ignorant of the more conspicuous circumstances of that period, and all who claim to be well-informed have a correct general knowledge of the history of our war for independence. But few even of that intelligent class are acquainted with the location of the various scenes depicted by the historian, in their relation to the lakes and rivers, towns and cities, whose names are familiar to the ears of the present generation. For example: the citizen of Saratoga may have a thorough knowledge of the memorable places in his own vicinage, and of the incidents which have hallowed them, yet how puzzled he would be if asked to tell the inquiring stranger, or his more inquisitive children, upon what particular stream, or lofty height, or broad plain, or in what mountain gorge, occurred the battles of Rocky Mount, King's Mountain, Eutaw Springs, or the Cowpens. These are places widely known in their respective districts, and the events connected with them form as important links in the chain of circumstances which were developed in the progress of the colonies toward independence, as the surrender of Burgoyne and his army upon the plain at Saratoga. Among this class, claiming to be generally informed, but ignorant in many particulars, especially in relation to the character and situation of localities, the writer places himself; and to an appreciation of the necessity of a more thorough knowledge of these places, and of the men who are identified with the Revolution, the reader is partially indebted for the pages which follow this confession.

To obtain this accurate chorographical knowledge of our early history as a confederation of states, was not the only incentive to undertake a journey to the battle-fields and other localities hallowed by the events of the Revolution. My limited observation had perceived many remaining physical vestiges of that struggle. Half-hidden mounds of old redoubts; the ruined walls of some stronger fortification; dilapidated buildings, neglected and decaying, wherein patriots met for shelter or in council; and living men, who had borne the musket and knapsack day after day in that conflict, occasionally passed under the eye of my casual apprehension. For years a strong desire was felt to embalm these precious things of our cherished household, that they might be preserved for the admiration and reverence of remote posterity. I knew that the genius of our people was the reverse of antiquarian reverence for the things of the past; that the glowing future, all sunlight and eminence, absorbed their thoughts and energies, and few looked back to the twilight and dim valleys of the past through which they had journeyed. I knew that the invisible fingers of decay, the plow of agriculture, and the behests of Mammon, unrestrained in their operations by the prevailing spirit of our people, would soon sweep away every tangible vestige of the Revolution, and that it was time the limner was abroad. I knew that, like stars at dawn which had beamed brightly through a long night, the men of old were fast fading away, and that relics associated with their trials and triumphs would soon be covered up forever. Other men, far more competent than myself to use the pen and pencil, appeared indisposed to go out into the apparently shorn and unfruitful field upon which I looked with such covetous delight, except to pick up a grain here and there for special preservation. I knew that the vigorous reapers who had garnered the products of that broad field, must have let fall from their full hands many a precious ear loaded with choice grain, and I resolved to go out as a gleaner, carefully gather up what they had left behind, and add the winnings to their store. Like the servants of Boaz, when Ruth followed the reapers, they seem to have "let fall also some of the *handfuls* of purpose for me, that I might glean them," for I found a far greater abundance than hope had promised. I have "gleaned in the field until even, and beat out that I have gleaned," and here is my "ephah of barley."

In the arrangement of a plan for presenting the result of these labors to the public in an acceptable form many difficulties were perceptible. Other histories of our Revolution had been written, embellished, and read; what could be produced more attractive than they? The exciting literature of the day, ranging in its intoxicating character from the gross pictures of sensual life drawn by the French writers of fiction, to the more refined, but not less intoxicating works of popular and esteemed novelists, so cheaply published and so widely diffused, has produced a degree of mental dissipation throughout our land, destructive, in its tendency, to sober and rational desires for imbibing useful knowledge. Among the young, where this dissipation is most rife, and deleterious in its effects, it seemed most desirable to have the story of our Revolution known and its salutary teachings pondered and improved, for they will be the custodians of our free institutions when the active men of the present generation shall step aside into the quiet shadows of old age. Next to tales of love and gallantry, the young mind is most charmed by the narratives of the traveler. The woof of our history is too sacred to be interwoven with the tinsel filling of fiction, and we should have to high a regard for truth to seek the potential aid of its counterfeit in gaining audience in the ear of the million; but to the latter tase we may consistently pay court, and in behalf of sober history, use its power in disputing for the preference with the tourist. As my journey was among scenes and things hallowed to the feelings of every American, I felt a hope that a record of the pilgrimage, interwoven with that of the facts of past history, would attract the attention, and win to the perusal of the chronicles of our Revolution many who could not be otherwise decoyed into the apparently arid and flowerless domains of mere history. I accordingly determined to make the record of the tour to the important localities of the Revolution a leading feature in the work. Here another difficulty was encountered. So widely scattered are those localities, and so simultaneous were many of the events, that a connected narrative of the journey must necessarily break up the chronological unity of the history, and, at times, produce some confusion. To give incidents of the journey, and sketches and descriptions of the scenery and relics as they appear at present, in fragmentary notes, would deny to the work the charm of a book of travel, and thus almost wholly remove the prime object in view in giving such narrative. The apparently less objectionable course was chosen, and the history was broken into fragments, arranged, in the exhibition, in accordance with the order in which each locality was visited, the fragments individualized as much as possible, yet always maintaining a tie of visible relationship with the whole. The apparent difficulties in the way of the student which this plan suggests, are removed by the aid of a complete Analytical Index at the close of the work, while the narrative of the tour remains unbroken, except by the continually recurring appendices of history. How far this arrangement shall accomplish the desired result the candid judgment of the reader must determine.

To collect the pictorial and other materials for this work, I traveled more than eight thousand miles in the Old Thirteen States and Canada, and visited every important place made memorable by the events of the war; yet, in all that long and devious journey, through cities and villages, amid mountains and vast pine forests, along rivers and over fertile plantations, from New England to Georgia, with no passport to the confidence, no claim to the regard of those from whom information was sought, except such as the object of my errand afforded, and communing with men of every social and intellectual grade, I never experienced an unkind word or cold repulsion of manner. On the contrary, politeness always greeted my first salutation, and, when the object of my visit was announced, hospitality and friendly services were freely bestowed.

Every where the memorials of our Revolution are cherished with devotional earnestness, and a feeling of reverence for these things abounds, though kept quiescent by the progressive spirit of the age. To those who thus aided and cheered me in my enterprise, I here proffer my sincere thanks. I can not name them all, for they are too numerous, but they will ever remain cherished "pictures on memory's wall."

It has been said that "diligence and accuracy are the only merits which a historical writer may ascribe to himself." Neither labor nor care has been spared in the collection of materials, and in endeavors to produce a work as free from grave errors as possible. It has imperfections; it would be foolish egotism to assert the contrary. In the various histories of the same events many discrepancies appear; these I have endeavored to reconcile or correct by documentary and other reliable testimony; and if the work is not more accurate than its predecessors, it is believed to be equally so with the most reliable. Free use has been made of the available labor of others in the same department of literature, always accrediting the source from whence facts were derived. I have aimed to view men and events with an impartial eye, censuring friends when they deserved censure, and commending enemies when truth and justice demanded the tribute. The historical events recorded were those of a family quarrel concerning vital principles in jurisprudence; and wisely did a sagacious English statesman console himself, at the close of the war, with the reflection, "We have been subdued, it is true, but, thank Heaven, the brain and the muscle which achieved the victory were nurtured by English blood; Old England, upon the Island of Great Britain, has been beaten only by Young England, in America."

In the pictorial department, special care has been observed to make faithful delineations of fact. If a relic of the Revolution was not susceptible of picturesque effect in a drawing, without a departure from truth, it has been left in its plainness, for my chief object was to illustrate the *subject*, not merely to embellish the *book*. I have endeavored to present the features of things as I found them, whether homely or charming, and have sought to delineate all that fell in my way worthy of preservation. To do this, it was necessary to make the engravings numerous, and no larger than perspicuity demanded, else the work would be filled with pictures to the exclusion of essential reading matter.

The plans of military movements have been drawn chiefly from British sources, for very few were made by the engineers in the Continental service. These appear to be generally correct, so far as they represent the immediate movements of the armies in actual conflict; but the general topographical knowledge possessed by those engineers, was quite defective. I have endeavored to detect and correct their inaccuracies, either in the drawings or in the illustrative descriptions.

With these general remarks respecting the origin and construction of the work, it is submitted to the reading public. If a perusal of its pages shall afford as much pleasure and profitable knowledge as were derived from the journey and in the arrangement of the materials for the press, the effort has not been unfruitful of good results. With an ardent desire that it may prove a useful worker in the maintenance of true patriotism,

I Dedicate to the VIRTUOUS these Volumes Spirit of LIBERTY.

OF THE REVOLUTION IN THE CAROLINAS & GEORGIA

Chapter XIV

"Carolina! Carolina! Heaven's blessings attend her;
While we live we will cherish, and love, and defend her;
Though the scorner may sneer at, the witlings defame her.
Our hearts swell with gladness whenever we name her.

Though she envies not others this merited glory,
Say, whose name stands the foremost in Liberty's story?
Though too true to herself e'er to crouch to oppression,
Who can yield to just rule more loyal submission?
            Hurrah! hurrah! the Old North State forever!
            Hurrah! hurrah! the good old North State!"
                                        - *William Gaston*

The settlement of the Scotch refugees at Cross Creek (now Fayetteville), at the head of navigation on the Cape Fear River, is an important point to be observed, in considering the history of the progress of free principles in North Carolina. These settlers formed a nucleus of more extensive immigrations subsequently. They brought with them the sturdy sentiments of the Covenanters, and planted deeply in the interior of that province the acorns of civil freedom, which had grown to unyielding oaks, strong and defiant, when the Revolution broke out. The sentiment of loyalty, kindred to that of patriotism, was an inherent principle in their character, and this was first displayed when Donald M'Donald called upon his countrymen to remember their oath of allegiance to King George and his successors, and to assist the royal governor in quelling rebellion in 1776. But as that rebellion assumed the phase of righteous resistance to tyranny, many of those who followed their chief to Moore's Creek, under the banner of the house of Hanover, afterward fought nobly in defense of the principles of the Covenanters under the stars and stripes of the Continental Congress. Other immigrants, allied to them by ties of consanguinity and religious faith, had already planted settlements along the Cape Fear and its tributaries, and in the fertile domain between the Yadkin and Catawba; and in those isolated regions, far removed from the petty tyrannies of royal instruments, they inhaled the life of freedom from the pure mountain air, and learned lessons of independence from the works and creatures of God around them. These were chiefly Presbyterians from the north of Ireland, commonly called Scotch-Irish, or the descendants of that people already in Virginia. Their principles bore the same fruit in Carolina, as in Ulster two centuries earlier; and long before the Stamp Act aroused the Northern colonies to resistance, the people of Granville, Orange, Mecklenburg and vicinity, had boldly told the governor upon the coast that he must not expect subservience to unjust laws upon the banks of the rivers in the upper country. **1** There was another class of emigrants whose religious principles tended to civil freedom. These were the *Unitas Fratrum* – the Moravians – who planted settlements in North Carolina in the middle of the last century (1749.). These, with other German Protestants, were firmly attached, from the commencement, to the principles which gave vitality to our Declaration of Independence a quarter of a century afterward. **2** We will not stop to examine the philosophy of religious influence in the formation of our civil government. It is a broad and interesting field of inquiry, but not within the scope of this work; yet so deeply are the principles of the various phases of Protestantism – the Puritans, the Scotch-Irish, **3** and the Huguenots – impressed upon the Constitutions of every state in our union, that we must not, we can not, lose sight of the fact that the whole superstructure of our laws and government has for its basis the broad postulate of religious freedom asserted by the Puritans and the Covenanters. – *FREEDOM OF CONSCIENCE IN MATTERS OF BELIEF – FREEDOM OF ACTION ACCORDING TO FAITH – FREEDOM TO CHOOSE TEACHERS AND RULERS IN CHURCH AND STATE.*

Two years after the settlement of the Highlanders under the general direction of Neil M'Neil, the first printing-press was brought into the province, from Virginia, by James Davis, and set up at Newbern in 1749. This was an important event in the political history of the province. Hitherto the laws had been in manuscript, and it was difficult for the people to obtain knowledge, even of the most essential enactments. In the course of 1751, the printing of the first revisal of the acts of the Assembly was accomplished, and by the multiplication of copies, the people generally became acquainted with the laws, and learned their rights and duties. It was not until 1764 that a periodical paper was published in North Carolina, and then the want of good postal arrangements, and, indeed, the character of the paper itself, made it of little service as a messenger with news. The same year another paper was commenced, much superior in its character, and from that time the influence of the press and popular education began to be felt in that state. **4**

In expectation of hostilities between the French and English in America, all of the colonies turned their attention to the subject of defenses, and pecuniary resources. Magazines were established in the different counties of North Carolina, two or three forts were erected, and emissions of bills of credit were authorized by the Legislature. When hostilities commenced, and Governor Dinwiddie asked the other colonies to assist in driving the French from the Ohio, North Carolina was the only one that responded promptly, by voting a regiment of four hundred and fifty menon in March, 1754, and an emission of paper money wherewith to pay them. This movement was made at the instigation of Governor Rowan. These troops marched to Virginia under Colonel James Innes, of Hanover; but by the time they reached Winchester, the appropriation for their pay being exhausted, they were disbanded, and only a few of them followed Washington toward the Monongahela.

The following year (1755), North Carolina voted forty thousand dollars as further aid toward "repelling the encroachments of the French." Arthur Dobbs, an aged Irishman of "eminent abilities," was then governor, but his usefulness was impaired by attempting to exercise undue authority, and in too freely bestowing offices upon his relatives and countrymen. He was a thorough aristocrat, but his feelings became much softened by surrounding democratic influences, and he held the office until succeeded by William Tryon, in 1766. Dobbs attended the meeting of colonial governors convened at Alexandria by Braddock, in April, 1755. Impressed with the importance of frontier defenses against the Indians, he recommended the erection of forts on the Yadkin. Governor Glenn, of South Carolina, at the same time caused forts to be erected on the borders of the Cherokee country along the Savannah River. With the exception of occasional Indian hostilities, and a sort of "anti-rent" outbreak, **5** nothing disturbed the tranquillity of the province from that period, until two or three years after the signing of the treaty of peace at Paris, in 1763.

The passage of the Stamp Act produced great uneasiness in the public mind in North Carolina, as well as in the other provinces. Already the extortions of public officers in the exaction of fees for legal services had greatly irritated the people, and they regarded the requirements of the Stamp Act as a more gigantic scheme for legal plunder. The first published murmurs, as we have seen, was at Nut Bush in June, 1765, then in Granville county. At about the same time, the inhabitants of Edenton, Newbern, and Wilmington, assembled in their respective towns, and asserted their hearty concurrence in the sentiments expressed by the people of the

Seal and signature of Tryon. 6

Northern colonies unfavorable to the Stamp Act. During the summer and autumn, denunciations of the measure were boldly expressed at public meetings, notwithstanding the presence of Tryon, the lieutenant governor. Tryon had been acting governor and commander-in-chief of the province from the death of Governor Dobbs, on the first of April of that year, and now began his career of misrule in America. He was appointed governor toward the close of the year. This was the same Tryon, afterward governor of New York, whom we have already met at the conflagrations of Danbury, Continental Village, and other places. Haughty, innately cruel, fond of show, obsequious when wishing favors, and tyrannical when independent, he was entirely incompetent to govern a people like the free, outspoken colonists of the Upper Carolinas.

Fearing a general expression of the sentiments of the people, through their representatives, on the subject of the odious act, Tryon issued a proclamation on October 25 proroguing the Assembly, which was to meet on the thirtieth of November, until the following March. This act incurred the indignation of the people; and when, early in January, the sloop of war Diligence arrived in Cape Fear River, having stamps on board for the use of the province, the militia of New Hanover and Brunswick, under Colonels Ashe and Waddell, marched to the village of Brunswick, 7 and notified the commander of their determination to resist the landing of the stamps. Earlier than this, Colonel Ashe, who was the speaker of the Lower House, had informed Tryon that the law would be resisted to the last. Tryon had issued his proclamation on January 6, 1766, directing the stamp distributors to make application for them, but the people were too vigilant to allow these officials to approach the vessel. Taking one of the boats of the Diligence, and leaving a small party to watch the movements of the sloop, the remainder of the little army of volunteers proceeded to Wilmington. Having placed a flag in the boat, they hoisted it upon a cart, and with the mayor (Moses John De Rosset, Esq.) and principal inhabitants, paraded it through the streets. At night the town was illuminated, and the next day a great concourse of people, headed by Colonel Ashe, proceeded to the governor's house and demanded William Houston, the stamp master. Houston appeared, and going to the market-place, he voluntarily took a solemn oath not to perform the duties of his office. The populace, satisfied with their triumph, gave three cheers, conducted him back to the governor's house, and then dispersed.

Tryon was alarmed at this demonstration of the popular temper, and endeavored to conciliate the militia of New Hanover, at a general muster in February 1766, by treating them to a barbacued ox and a few barrels of beer. The insulted people cast the ox into the river, poured the beer upon the ground, and mocked the governor. The officers of the Diligence espoused the cause of the chief magistrate, and a general fight ensued. The riot continued several days, and during the excitement one man was killed. **8** The Stamp Act was repealed shortly afterward, and the province became comparatively tranquil.

For several years previous to the Stamp Act excitement rebellion had been ripening among the people in the western counties. The rapacity of public officers, and the corrupt character of ministers of justice, weighed heavily upon the property and spirits of the people. The most prominent evils complained of were the exorbitant charges of the clerks of the Superior Courts, whereby those courts had become instruments of oppression; and oppressive taxes exacted by the sheriffs, and the outrages committed by those officers when their authority was questioned in the least. These evils every where existed, and every petition of the people (who began to assemble for consultation) for redress appeared to be answered by

Front view of Tryon's Palace

increased extortions. At length the inhabitants resolved to form a league, take power into their own hands, and regulate matters. **9** Herman Husband, "one of those independent Quakers who was taught in the honest school of William Penn, and refused to pull off his hat and bow before the minions of despotism," **10** a man of grave deportment, superior mind, and of great influence, **11** but evidently without education, **12** drew up a written complaint. It was carried to Hillsborough, during the sitting of the court in October 1766, by a number of firm men, who requested the clerk to read it aloud. The preamble asserted that "The Sons of Liberty would withstand the Lords in Parliament," and it set forth that evils of great magnitude existed. It recommended a general meeting of delegates, appointed by each militia company in Orange county, to be held at some suitable place, where there was no liquor, to "judiciously inquire whether the freemen of this county labor under any abuse of power," &c., &c. The proposition being considered reasonable, a meeting was appointed to be held at Maddock's Mills, on the Eno, two or three miles west of Hillsborough. The meeting was held on the tenth of October, but not many delegates attended. They discussed various topics fairly and dispassionately. Another meeting was held on the fourth of April following (1767), at the same place, and the resolutions passed at that time were almost equivalent to a declaration of independence of the civil power of the state. From that time THE REGULATION was a permanent and powerful body. **13**

It was at about this time that the pride and folly of Governor Tryon led him to make a demand upon the Assembly for an appropriation of twenty-five thousand dollars for the purpose of building a palace at Newbern "suitable for the residence of a royal governor." To obtain this appropriation, Lady Tryon, and her sister Esther Wake, **15** both beautiful and accomplished women, used all the blandishments of their charms and society to influence the minds of the burgesses. Lady Tryon gave princely dinners and balls, and the governor finally succeeded in obtaining, not only the first appropriation asked, but another of fifty thousand dollars, to complete the edifice. It was pronounced the most magnificent structure in America. The pride of the governor and his family was gratified; the people, upon whom the expense was laid, were highly indignant.

The inhabitants of North Carolina were now thoroughly awakened to the conviction that both the local and the imperial government, were practically hostile to the best interests of the colonists. The taxes hitherto were very burdensome; now the cost of the palace, and an appropriation to defray the expenses of running the dividing line between their province and the hunting-grounds of the Cherokees, made them insupportable. **16** The rapacity of public officers appeared to increase, and the people saw no prospect of relief. Current history reports that, among the most obnoxious men, who, it was alleged, had grown rich by extortionate fees, **17** was Edmund Fanning, a lawyer of ability. He was regarded as a coworker with the government; haughty in demeanor, and if common report spoke truth, was immoral. The people, excited by their leaders, detested him, and avoided no occasion to express their displeasure. His first open rupture with the Regulators was in the spring of 1768 (April 27). Tryon issued a proclamation, half menacing and half persuasive, evidently intended to awe the REGULATION and persuade the other inhabitants to avoid that association. He sent his secretary, David Edwards, to co-operate with Fanning in giving force to the proclamation among the people. They directed the sheriff to appoint a meeting of the vestry-men of the parishes and the leading Regulators, to consult upon the public good and settle all differences. Fair promises dispelled the suspicions of the Regulators, and their vigilance slumbered while awaiting the day of meeting on May 20, 1768. They were not yet fully acquainted with the falsity of their governor, or they would never have heeded the fair words of his proclamation. They were soon assured of the hollowness of his professions; for, while they were preparing, in good faith, to meet government officers in friendly convention, the sheriff, at the instigation of Fanning, proceeded, with thirty horsemen, to arrest Herman Husband and William Hunter, on a charge of riotous conduct. These, the most prominent men among the Regulators, were seized and cast into Hillsborough jail on May 1, 1768. The whole country was aroused by this treachery, and a large body of the people, led by Ninian Bell Hamilton, a brave old Scotchman of three-score-and-ten years, marched toward Hillsborough to rescue the prisoners.

Fanning and Edwards, apprised of the approach of Hamilton, were alarmed, and released the prisoners just as the people reached the banks of the Eno, opposite Hillsborough. Fanning, with a bottle of rum in one hand, and a bottle of wine in the other, went down to the brink of the stream, urged Hamilton not to march into the town, and asked him to send a horse over that he might cross, give the people refreshments, and have a friendly talk. Hamilton was not to be cajoled by the wolf in sheep's clothing. "Ye're nane too gude to wade, and wade ye shall, if ye come over!" shouted Hamilton. Fanning did wade the stream, but his words and his liquor were alike rejected. **18** Edwards then rode over, and solemnly assured the people that if they would quietly disperse, all their grievances should be redressed. The confiding people cried out, "Agreed! agreed!" and, marching back toward Maddock's Mills, they held a meeting at George Sally's the next day, May 21, 1768, to consult upon the public good. They drew up a petition, and sent Rednap Howell and James Hunter to lay it before the governor, at Brunswick. It was most respectful, yet Tryon, in imitation of his royal master, haughtily spurned it. He commanded the deputies to return to their houses, warn their associates to desist from holding meetings, disband the association, and be content to pay the taxes! He then graciously promised them to visit Hillsborough within a month, and listen to the complaints of the people.

Tryon and some of his council met at Hillsborough early in July. He issued a proclamation, which, for a moment, deceived the people into a belief that justice was about to bear rule, and that the infamous system of extortion was to be repressed. They were again deceived. Instead of mediator, the governor appeared as a judge; instead of defending the oppressed, he encouraged the oppressors. He went into Mecklenburg, raised a large body of troops, and marched from Salisbury to Hillsborough with the parade of a conqueror. But this display did not frighten the people. He sent the sheriff to collect the taxes; that officer was driven back to Hillsborough by the excited populace. The governor was execrated for his false and temporizing conduct, and a general rising of the Regulators was apprehended. From the eleventh of August until the twenty-second of September, when Husband and others would be tried before the Superior Court, the militia were held in readiness to oppose any insurgents, and Tryon remained until the trials were over.

Maurice Moore

On the opening of the court, three thousand people from the surrounding country encamped within half a mile of the town, but, true to a promise they had made **19** not to obstruct the course of justice, they were quiet. Husband was acquitted; Hunter and two others were heavily fined and imprisoned; while Fanning, who was tried under seven indictments for extortion, and was found guilty, was fined one penny on each! **20** The judges upon the bench, on this occasion, were Martin Howard, chief justice, and Maurice Moore and Richard Henderson, associates. The governor, perceiving the indignation of the populace at this mockery of justice, speedily issued a proclamation of a general pardon to all the Regulators except thirteen whom he considered as the principal leaders. **21** By this act of apparent clemency he hoped to pacify the disturbed public mind. Satisfying himself that quiet would now prevail, he returned to his palace at Newbern, neither a wiser nor a better man.

Edmund Fanning

vs

Abraham Smith

Fanning's Autograph

For almost two years comparative quiet prevailed; not the quiet of abject submission on the part of the people, but the quiet of inactive anarchy. The sheriffs dared not enforce their claims, and the evident impuissance of government made the Regulators bold. Finally, many unprincipled men, who espoused their cause in order to benefit by change, committed acts of violence which all good patriots deplored. The records of the Superior Court at Hillsborough show evidence of a lawlessness, in 1770, quite incompatible with order and justice; and yet, from the character of some of the men engaged in breaking up the court at the September term of that year, it must be inferred that sufficient cause existed to warrant, in a great degree, their rebellious proceedings. **22** An excited populace gathered there at the opening of the court, and committed acts which Husband and Howell, and their compatriots, would doubtless have prevented, if in their power. But reason and prudence are alike strangers to a mob. Not content with impeding the course of justice by driving the judge from the bench and the advocates from the forum, the Regulators severely beat a lawyer in the street, named John Williams, and dragged Fanning out of the court-house by his heels, beat him with rods, and kept him in confinement during the night. On the following morning, when they discovered that the judge had escaped, they beat Fanning again, demolished his costly furniture, and pulled down his house. They intended to burn it, but the wind was high, and they apprehended the destruction of other property. **23** These proceedings were highly disgraceful, and the harsh treatment of Fanning was condemned by all right-minded men.

Fanning pays, costs but loses nothing

Yorke's Autograph

When this violence was completed, they repaired to the court-house, and appointed a schoolmaster of Randolph county, named Yorke, clerk; chose one of their number for judge; took up the several cases as they appeared upon the docket, and adjudicated them, making Fanning plead law; and then decided several suits. As the whole proceedings were intended as a farce, their decisions were perfectly ridiculous, while some of the "remarks" by Yorke were vulgar and profane. **24**

Judge Henderson, who was driven from the bench, called upon Tryon to restore order in his district. The governor perceived that a temporizing policy would no longer be expedient, and resolved to employ the military force to subdue the rebellious spirit of the Regulators. He deferred operations, however, until the meeting of the Legislature, in December. Herman Husband was a member of the Lower House, from Orange, and there were others in that body who sympathized with the oppressed people. Various measures were proposed to weaken the strength of the Regulators; and among others, four new counties were formed of portions of Orange, Cumberland, and Johnson. **25** Finally, when the Legislature was about to adjourn without authorizing a military expedition, information came that the Regulators had assembled in great numbers at Cross Creek (modern Fayetteville), with the intention of marching upon Newbern, having heard that their representative (Husband) had been imprisoned. **26** The Assembly immediately voted two thousand dollars for the use of the governor. The alarmed chief magistrate fortified his palace, and placed the town in a state of defense. He also issued a proclamation on February 7, 1771, and orders to the colonels of the counties in the vicinity, to have the militia in readiness. These precautions were unnecessary, for the Regulators, after crossing the Haw, a few miles above Pittsborough, to the number of more than one thousand, met Husband on his way home, and retraced their steps.

The governor soon issued another proclamation, prohibiting the sale of powder, shot, or lead, until further notice. This was to prevent the Regulators supplying themselves with munitions of war. This measure added fuel to the flame of excitement, and finally, the governor becoming again alarmed, he made a virtual declaration of war, through his council. That body authorized him to raise a sufficient force to march into the rebellious districts and establish law and order. The governor issued a circular on March 19, 1771, to the colonels, ordering them to select fifty volunteers from their respective regiments and send them to Newbern. With about three hundred militia-men, a small train of artillery, some baggage wagons, and several personal friends, Tryon left Newbern on the twenty-fourth of April. On the fourth of May he encamped on the Eno, having been re-enforced by detachments on the way. **27** General Hugh Waddel was directed to collect the forces from the western counties, rendezvous at Salisbury, and join the governor in Orange (now Guilford) county. While he was waiting at Salisbury for the arrival of powder from Charleston, a company of men assembled in Cabarras county, blackened their faces, intercepted the convoy with the ammunition, between Charlotte and Salisbury, routed the guard, and destroyed the powder.

General Waddel crossed the Yadkin on the morning of May 10, 1771, intending to join Governor Tryon. He had advanced but a short distance, when he received a message from a body of Regulators, warning him to halt or retreat. Finding that many of his men were averse to fighting, and that others were favorable to the Regulators, and were thinning his ranks by desertions, he retreated across the Yadkin, hotly pursued by the insurgents. They surrounded Waddel's small army, and took several of them prisoners, after a slight skirmish. The general and a few followers escaped to Salisbury.

Tryon, informed of the disaster of Waddel, broke up his camp on the Eno, crossed the Haw just below the Falls on May 13., and pressed forward toward the Allamance, where he understood the Regulators were collecting in force on the Salisbury Road. He encamped very near the scene of Colonel Pyles's defeat in 1781, within six miles of the insurgents, just at sunset, and during the night sent out some scouts to reconnoiter. **28** On the fifteenth he received a message from the Regulators, proposing terms of accommodation, and demanding an answer within four hours. **29** He promised a response by noon the next day. At dawn the following morning (May 16) he crossed the Allamance, a little above the present site of Holt and Carrigan's cotton factory, and marched silently and undiscovered along the Salisbury Road, until within half a mile of the camp of the Regulators, where he formed his line in battle order. Dr. Caldwell, who was there, with many of his parishioners, now visited the governor a second time, and obtained a renewal of a promise made the night before to abstain from bloodshed; but Tryon demanded unconditional submission. Both parties advanced to within three hundred yards of each other, when Tryon sent a magistrate, with a proclamation, ordering the Regulators to disperse within an hour. Robert Thompson, an amiable, but bold, outspoken man, who had gone to Tryon's camp to negotiate, was detained as a prisoner. Indignant because of such perfidy, he told the governor some plain truths, and was about to leave for the ranks of the Regulators, when the irritated governor snatched a gun from the hands of a militia-man and shot Thompson dead. Tryon perceived his folly in a moment, and sent out a flag of truce. The Regulators had seen Thompson fall, and, deeply exasperated, they paid no respect due to a flag, and immediately fired upon it. **30** At this moment Dr. Caldwell rode along the lines and urged his people and their friends to disperse; and had an equal desire to avoid bloodshed guided the will of Tryon, valuable lives might have been spared. But he took counsel of his passions, and gave the word "Fire!" The militia hesitated, and the Regulators dared them to fire. Maddened with rage, the governor rose in his stirrups and

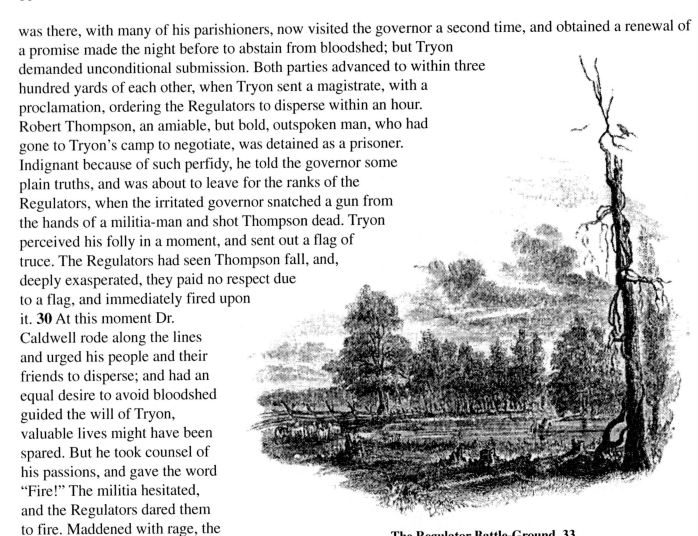

The Regulator Battle-Ground. 33

shouted "Fire! fire on them, or on me!" A volley ensued, and the cannons were discharged with deadly effect. The fire was returned, and the governor's hat was pierced by a musket-ball. He sent out a flag of truce, but the bearer immediately fell. Some young men among the Regulators rushed forward and took possession of the cannons. They did not know how to manage them, and, soon abandoned them. The military now fired with vigor, and the Regulators fell back to a ledge of rocks on the verge of a ravine, not, however, until their scanty supply of ammunition was exhausted. They had no acknowledged leader; **31** for as soon as it was evident that blood would be shed, Herman Husband, the soul of the agitation, declared that his peace principles as a Quaker would not allow him to fight, and he rode off, and was not seen again in North Carolina until the close of the Revolution. Charity must stretch her mantle to cover this delinquency of the leader of the Regulators; for why should he have urged the people to assemble for resistance unless they were to fight? All was confusion when the conflict began, and each fought for life and liberty in his own way. Although they, were defeated in that early conflict – that first battle of our war for independence – they were not subdued, and many of the survivors were among the most determined opposers of Cornwallis a few years later. Nine of the Regulators and twenty-seven of the militia fell in that conflict, and a great number on both sides were wounded. **32** Tryon, in his report, said, "The loss of our army in killed, wounded, and missing, amounted to about sixty men."

The admitted excesses of the Regulators afford no excuse for the cruelty of Tryon after the battle on the Allamance. With the implacable spirit of revenge, he spent his wrath upon his prisoners, and some of his acts were worthy only of a barbarian. **34** Having rested a few days near the battle-ground, he went on as far as the Yadkin, and, after issuing a proclamation on May 17, 1771, of pardon to all who should lay down their arms and take the oath of allegiance before the tenth of July, except a few whom he named, he made a circuitous route through Stokes, Rockingham, and Guilford counties, back to Hillsborough, exhibiting his prisoners in chains in the villages through which he passed. He exacted an oath of allegiance from the people; levied contributions of provisions; chastised those who dared to offend him; and at Hillsborough he offered a large reward for the bodies of Husband and other Regulators, "dead or alive." **35** On his march he held courts-martial for trying civil cases, burned houses, and destroyed the crops of inoffensive people. At Hillsborough he held a court-martial for the trial of his prisoners. Twelve were condemned to suffer death; six were reprieved, and the others were hung on June 9, 1771, among whom was Captain Messer, whose life had been spared a few days before by the intercession of his little child. His thirst for revenge satiated, Tryon returned to his palace at Newbern, where he remained but a short time, having been called to the administration of affairs in the province of New York. Josiah Martin succeeded him as governor, and acted with judgment. He so conciliated the Regulators that many of them were firm Loyalists when the governor was finally driven away by the Whigs.

The movements of the Regulators and the result of the battle on the Allamance, form an important episode in the history of our Revolution. Their resistance arose from oppressions more personal and real than those which aroused the people of New England. It was not wholly the abstract idea of freedom for which they contended; their strife consisted of efforts to relieve themselves of actual burdens. While the tea-duty was but a "pepper-corn tribute," imposing no real burden upon the industry of the people in New England, extortion in every form, and not to be evaded, was eating out the substance of the working-men in North Carolina. Implied despotism armed the New Englanders; actual despotism panoplied the Carolinians. Each were equally patriotic, and deserve our reverent gratitude. The defeat on the Allamance did not break the spirit of the patriots; and many, determined no longer to suffer the oppressions of extortioners, abandoned their homes, with their wives and children, went beyond the mountains, and began settlements in the fertile valleys of Tennessee. As Mr. Bancroft, in a letter to the Honorable David L. Swain, happily expressed it, "Like the mammoth, they shook the bolt from their brow, and crossed the mountains."

While the Regulator movement planted deep the seeds of resistance to tyranny, the result of the battle on the Allamance was disastrous in its subsequent effects. The people, from whom Tryon wrung an oath of allegiance, were conscientious, and held a vow in deep reverence. Nothing could make them swerve from the line of duty; and when the hostilities of the Revolution fully commenced, hundreds, whose sympathies were with the patriots, felt bound by that oath to remain passive. Hundreds of men, with strong hearts and hands, would have flocked around the standards of Gates and Greene, in Guilford, Orange, and the neighboring counties, had not their oath been held too sacred to be violated, even when it was evident that the king could no longer protect them. Loyalty to conscience, not opposition to the principles of the Revolutionists, made these men passive; for their friends and neighbors on the other side of the Yadkin, where Tryon's oath was not exacted, were among those who earliest cast off their allegiance to the British crown.

The course of Governor Martin was generally so judicious, that the people of North Carolina were not very restive, while the Northern colonies were all on fire with rebellion in 1774. Yet sympathy for the people of Boston, suffering from the effects of the Port Bill, was general and sincere, and the inhabitants of Wilmington and other towns made large contributions for their relief. When the final decision was to be made respecting allegiance to, or independence of the British crown, very many remained loyal, and the ardent Whigs required the full exercise of all their zeal to leaven the inactive population of the state. The efficient machinery of corresponding committees was put in operation early. In December, 1773, the resolution of the House of Burgesses, of Virginia, recommending the appointment of committees of correspondence, was received by the Assembly of North Carolina and approved of. A committee was appointed, and instructed to be vigilant and industrious in the performance of their duties. **36** Governor Martin was then in New York, and the duties of his office devolved upon James Hasell, the president of the council. Hasell was rather favorably inclined toward republicanism, and opposed the patriots only so far as his official duty demanded action. The proceedings of that short session were quite offensive to the governor and most of his council, as representatives of the imperial government, and the amity of the provincial legislation was disturbed. The governor soon returned home, and prorogued the Assembly until March following (1774), that the members might "reflect upon their proceedings, learn the sentiments of their constituents, and adopt a more loyal course." When they again met, strengthened by the approval of their constituents, they were firmer than ever in their opposition to some of the measures of government; and that the sincerity and courage of those who professed patriotic proclivities might be tested, the Yeas and Nays were taken upon the adoption of an important bill. **37** A committee was appointed to address the king, and on the twenty-fifth of March the Assembly was again prorogued. Four days afterward, it was dissolved by the governor's proclamation; an act considered unconstitutional, and which highly offended the people.

During the summer of 1774, a majority of the inhabitants, in primary meetings assembled, openly avowed their approval of a Continental Congress, as proposed by Massachusetts. A general meeting of delegates from the several towns was proposed to be held at Newbern on the twenty-fifth of August. On the thirteenth of that month, the governor issued his proclamation, disapproving of the district meetings, and requiring the people to forbear sending delegates to the general convention. The people did not heed his proclamation, and the delegates met on that day. John Harvey, of Perquimans, the late speaker of the Assembly, was chosen moderator. The council convened by the governor, seeing the gathering of the people's representatives, decided that "nothing could be done." The convention expressed its firm loyalty to the king; claimed only the common rights of Englishmen; asserted the doctrine that they ought not to be taxed without their own consent; reprobated the tea and other duties; expressed great sympathy for the people of Massachusetts; condemned the Boston Port Bill, as a "cruel infringement of the rights and privileges of the people," and other measures of government as unrighteous; signed a non-importation agreement, and expressed their hearty approval of the proposition for a general Congress. This approval was further manifested by the choice of deputies to represent the province in the Continental council. **38**

Pursuant to the recommendations of the general Congress when it convened in September, contributions were raised in all parts of the province for the relief of the people of Boston; and committees of safety were appointed in every county and chief town, to see that the articles of association adopted by the Congress were signed and faithfully observed. Activity every where prevailed among the Whigs during the winter; and when Governor Martin fixed the day for the assembling of the Legislature as April 5, 1775., John Harvey, who presided over the convention at Newbern several months before, now summoned those delegates to meet as a Provincial Congress on the same day. Governor Martin attempted, by proclamation, to prevent the meeting of the deputies, but in vain. The two bodies, composed chiefly of the same men, met at the same time, and Harvey was called upon to preside over both. The governor attempted to keep the two Assemblies distinct. He besought the legal Assembly to discountenance the irregular convention of the other deputies, chosen by the people, and expressed his determination to use all the means in his power to counteract their treasonable influence. He denounced the Continental Congress as "seditious and wicked," "highly offensive to his majesty," and in firm but respectful language urged the people to remember their allegiance and to faithfully maintain it. His appeals were of no avail, for both Assemblies were too intimately allied in sentiment to act in opposition to each other. Both bodies concurred in approving of the proceedings of the Congress of 1774, and in appointing delegates to a new one, to meet in Philadelphia in May following on May 10, 1775. The governor, perceiving the Assembly to be intractable, consulted his council, and by their recommendation dissolved it, by proclamation, on the eighth of April.

Governor Martin and the representatives of the people were now fairly at issue. The latter organized a Provincial Congress, and, assuming the functions of government, sent forth an address to the people, recommending the adoption of measures for resistance, similar to those pursued in other colonies. After transacting some other business for the public good, they quietly separated. As soon as the deputies had departed, the governor, perceiving the tide of public opinion setting strongly against him, became alarmed, and sought to intimidate the people, and at the same time to protect his person, by placing some cannon in front of the palace. He dispatched messengers to the Highlanders at Cross Creek, upon whose loyalty he relied, and others were sent into the more westerly districts to promise the Regulators exemption from the punishments to which they were still liable for past misdeeds, if they would assist the king's government against its opposers. These promises had great effect, and, strange as it may seem,

many of the Regulators were active Loyalists. About this time, a letter which the governor had sent to General Gage at Boston, soliciting a supply of arms and ammunition, was intercepted. The people were greatly exasperated, and the Committee of Safety of Newbern seized and carried off six of the cannons which had been placed in front of the palace. From every quarter the governor heard of hostile preparations, and becoming alarmed for his personal safety, he fled to Fort Johnson, on the Cape Fear River, near Wilmington on June 14, 1775, whence he sent forth a menacing proclamation on June 16. **39**

At the beginning of July, preparations for a servile insurrection on the Tar River were discovered. This plot was disclosed to Thomas Rispess, a former member of the Assembly from Beaufort, by one of his slaves. It was generally supposed that Governor Martin was an accessory in inducing the slaves to rise and murder their masters. **40** Fired with indignation by this opinion, the exasperated people determined to demolish Fort Johnson, lest the governor should strengthen it, and make it a place of reception for a hostile force and insurgent negroes. Under Colonel John Ashe, a body of about five hundred men marched to the fort, when it was ascertained that the governor had fled to the sloop of war Cruiser, lying in the river, and that Collett, the commander of the fortress, had removed all the small arms, ammunition, and part of the artillery, to a transport hired for the purpose. The militia immediately, set fire to the buildings, and demolished a large portion of the walls of the fort. **41** The Committee of Safety of Wilmington, at the same time, publicly charged the governor with fomenting a civil war, and endeavoring to excite an insurrection among the negroes. They declared him an enemy to his country and the province, and forbade all persons holding any communication with him. While these events were transpiring on the coast, the people of Mecklenburg county, over the Yadkin, met by representatives, and, by a series of resolutions, virtually declared themselves independent of the British crown, and established republican government in that county. This important movement will be considered in the next chapter.

Pursuant to a resolve of the late convention, delegates from the several towns in the state were summoned to meet in Provincial Congress at Hillsborough, on the twentieth of August, 1775. When this summons appeared, Governor Martin, yet on board the Cruiser, issued a long proclamation, in which he stigmatized the incendiaries of Fort Johnson as traitors to the king; pronounced the proceedings of the Wilmington committee as base and scandalous; denounced the movement in Mecklenburg in May; **42** warned the people not to send delegates to Hillsborough; denounced Colonels Ashe **43** and Howe as rebels; and offered the king's pardon for all past outrages to those who should return to their allegiance. The people defied the governor's threats, and mocked his proffers of forgiveness; and on Sunday, the twentieth of August, every county and chief town in the province had a delegate in Hillsborough. They organized on Monday, **44** when one hundred and eighty-four deputies were present. One of their first acts was to declare their determination to hold the aegis of popular power over the Regulators, who were liable to punishment, and had not been cajoled into submission by the governor's promises. They also declared the governor's proclamation to be a "false, scurrilous, malicious, and seditious libel," and tending to stir up tumult and insurrections, dangerous to the peace of the king's government." It was then directed to be burned by the common hangman. They also provided for raising and equipping a military force of one thousand men for the defense of the liberties of the province. This force was divided into two regiments. The command of the first regiment was given to Colonel James Moore (one of Tryon's officers when he marched against the Regulators), of New Hanover; the second to Colonel Robert Howe, of Brunswick. In addition to this regular force, a battalion of ten companies, of fifty men each, was directed to be raised in each district, to be called minute-men, their uniform to be a hunting-shirt, leggings or spatterdashes, and black gaiters. To pay these troops and other expenses of the government, the Provincial Congress directed the emission of bills of credit to the amount of $150,000, for the redemption of which a poll tax was levied for nine years, commencing in 1777. The deputies closed their labors by agreeing to an address to the inhabitants of the British empire (which was drawn up by William Hooper), and in organizing a provisional government. **45** The Congress adjourned on the nineteenth of September, 1775.

The provincial council met for the first time on the eighteenth of October following, and appointed Cornelius Harnett, of Wilmington, president. **46** Already the Continental Congress had adopted measures for the defense of the province. The two battalions of five hundred men each were attached to the Continental army, and the committees of safety were requested to employ all the gunsmiths in the colony, that might be procured in making muskets. Two Gospel ministers were sent by the provincial council to explain to the Highlanders and others the nature of the quarrel with the mother country, and endeavor to win them to the patriot cause. In the mean while, Governor Martin had busy emissaries among the Highlanders and Regulators, endeavoring to unite them in favor of the king. This was an object of great importance; for if he could embody a strong force of Loyalists in the heart of the province, he could easily keep the sea-board quiet, especially after the arrival of Sir Henry Clinton with troops from the North, then daily expected. He had also received intelligence that Sir Peter Parker, with a strong squadron, bearing Lord Cornwallis with a considerable force, would sail for America at the beginning of 1776. These anticipations gave the governor pleasing hopes for the future.

While Lord Dunmore, as we have seen, was making a demonstration against the lower counties of Virginia, **47** Governor Martin prepared to strike a blow against the patriots in North Carolina. He gave Donald M'Donald, an influential Highlander at Cross Creek, a commission of brigadier general, and with it a large number of copies of a proclamation, with a blank left for the date, which commanded all the king's loyal subjects in North Carolina to join his standard. M'Donald had discretionary powers concerning the distribution of these proclamations. While Colonel Robert Howe, with North Carolina troops, was absent at Norfolk, in Virginia, whither he had gone to assist Colonels Woodford and Stevens against Dunmore, M'Donald set up the royal ensign at Cross Creek on February 1, 1776 (now Fayetteville), and issued some of the proclamations. The loyal-hearted Scotchmen, not fully comprehending the nature of the difficulties, obeyed blindly; and in a few days more than one thousand of them, with many timid Regulators, in all fifteen hundred strong, gathered around the standard of the Highland chief. M'Donald was a brave veteran, and had fought valiantly for the Pretender on the field of Culloden, and his influence over his countrymen was very great.

At Cross Creek lived Flora M'Donald, the noble and beautiful girl who saved the life of Charles Edward, after the defeat of the troops at Culloden. **48** She was now the wife of Allan M'Donald, and it is said used all her influence in bringing her countrymen to the standard of the Scotch general. Her husband took a captain's commission under him, and was one of the most active officers in the engagement which speedily ensued.

As soon as Colonel James Moore, of Hanover, was apprised of the gathering of the Loyalists to the banner of M'Donald, he marched with his regulars and a detachment of New Hanover militia (in all about eleven hundred men), toward Cross Creek, and encamped about twelve miles south of the Highlander's head-quarters February 15, 1776. He fortified his camp, and by scouts and spies cut off all communication between M'Donald and Governor Martin. The Loyalist general, feeling the necessity of dislodging the patriots, marched toward their camp. When within four miles, he halted, and sent the governor's proclamation, and a friendly but firm letter to Moore, urging him to prevent bloodshed by joining the royal standard; at the same time threatening him, in case of refusal, with the treatment due to rebels against the king. After some delay, during which he sent an express to Colonel Caswell, Moore replied, that he was engaged in a holy cause, from which he could not be seduced. He besought M'Donald to prevent bloodshed by signing the Test proposed by the Provincial Congress, and menaced him with the same treatment which the general proposed to award to the patriot colonel and his followers. M'Donald was not prepared to put his threats into execution, for he was advised of the rapid gathering of the minute-men around him. Informed, in the mean while, of the expected arrival of Sir Henry Clinton and Lord William Campbell in the Cape Fear River, M'Donald resolved to avoid an engagement that might prove disastrous, and attempt to join the governor and his friends at Wilmington. At midnight he decamped, with his followers, crossed the Cape Fear, and pushed on at a rapid pace, over swollen streams, rough hills, and deep morasses, hotly pursued by Colonel Moore. On the third day of his march, he crossed the South River (one of the principal tributaries of the Cape Fear), from Bladen into New Hanover, and as he approached Moore's Creek, a small tributary of that stream, **49** he discovered the gleaming of fire-arms on February 26, 1776. He had come upon the camp of Colonels Caswell **50** and Lillington, **51** near the mouth of the Creek, who, with the minute-men of Dobbs, Craven, Johnston, and Wake counties, and battalions from Wilmington and Newbern, in all about one thousand strong, were out in search of the Tory army. **52** The situation of M'Donald (who was now very ill) was perilous in the extreme. The strong minute-men of the Neuse region, their officers wearing silver crescents upon their hats, inscribed with the stirring words, "Liberty or Death," were in front; and Colonel Moore, with his regulars, were close upon his rear. To fly was impossible; to fight was his only alternative.

Both parties were encamped in sight of each other during the night. A professed neutral informed Colonel Lillington of the intended movements of the enemy in the morning, and he and Caswell took measures accordingly. During the night, they cast up a breast-work, removed the planks from the bridge across Moore's Creek, and disposed their forces so as to command the passage and the roads on each side. The patriots lay upon their arms all night, ready, at a signal, to meet the foe. At early dawn, bagpipes were heard, and the notes of a bugle, ringing out upon the frosty air, called the eighteen hundred Loyalists to arms. In a few minutes they rushed forward to the attack, led on by Captain M'Leod, for General M'Donald was too ill to leave his tent. Finding a small intrenchment next the bridge quite empty, they concluded the Americans had abandoned the post. They had advanced to within thirty paces of the breast-work, when the Whigs, though unused to war, arose from their concealment, bravely confronted the foe, and for ten minutes the contest was fierce and bloody. Captain M'Leod was killed at the beginning of the battle. Captain John Campbell, the next in command, soon fell, mortally wounded. At that moment, Lieutenant Slocum, of the patriot army, with a small detachment, forded the stream, penetrated the swamp on its western bank, and fell with vigor upon the rear of the Loyalists. **53** The Scotchmen were routed and dispersed, and many of them were made prisoners. Among the latter were General M'Donald, and also the

lodged. Cornwallis used it for an office, during his tarryings in Hillsborough, after driving General Greene out of the state. After sketching this, we visited the office of the Clerk of the Superior Court, and made the fac similes and extracts from its records. We next visited the head-quarters of Cornwallis, a large frame building situated in the rear of Morris's Hillsborough House, on King Street. Generals Gates and Greene also occupied it when they were in Hillsborough, and there a large number of the members of the Provincial Congress were generally lodged. The old court-house, where the Regulators performed their lawless acts, is no longer in existence. I was informed by Major Taylor, an octogenarian on whom we called, that it was a brick edifice, and stood almost upon the exact site of the present court-house, which is a spacious brick building, with steeple and clock. The successor of the first was a wooden structure, and being removed to make room for the present building, was converted into a place of meeting for a society of Baptists, who in 1849 yet worship there. Upon the hill near the Episcopal church, and fronting King Street, is the spot where the Regulators were hung. The residence of Governor Tryon, while in Hillsborough, was on Church Street, a little west of Masonic Hall. These compose the chief objects of historic interest at Hillsborough. The town has other associations connected with the Southern campaigns, but we will not anticipate the revealments of history by considering them now.

At one o'clock I exchanged adieus with the kind Dr. Wilson, crossed the Eno, and, pursuing the route traversed by Tryon on his march to the Allamance, crossed the rapid and now turbid Haw, **62** just below the falls, at sunset. I think I never traveled a worse road than the one stretching between the Eno and the Haw. It passes over a continued series of red clay hills, which are heavily wooded with oaks, gums, black locusts, and chestnuts. Small streams course among these elevations; and in summer this region must be exceedingly picturesque. Now every tree and shrub was leafless, except the holly and the laurel, and nothing green appeared among the wide-reaching branches but the beautiful tufts of mistletoe which every where decked the great oaks with their delicate leaves and transparent berries. Two and a half miles beyond the Haw, and eighteen from Hilisborough, I passed the night at Foust's house of entertainment, and after an early breakfast, rode to the place where Colonel Pyle, a Tory officer, with a considerable body of Loyalists, was deceived and defeated by Lieutenant-colonel Henry Lee and his dragoons, with Colonel Pickens, in the spring of 1781. Dr. Holt, who lives a short distance from that locality,
kindly accompanied me to the spot and pointed out the place where
the battle occurred; where Colonel Pyle lay concealed in a pond,
and where many of the slain were buried. The place of conflict
is about half a mile north of the old Salisbury highway, upon
a "plantation road," two miles east of the Allamance, in
Orange county. Let us listen to the voices of history and
tradition.

In February, 1781, General Greene, then in
command of the American army at the South,
accomplished a wonderful and successful retreat across
North Carolina into Virginia, closely pursued by Lord
Cornwallis. This memorable retreat we shall consider
presently. When Cornwallis was certified that Greene had
escaped across the Dan with all his force, baggage, and
stores, he ordered a halt on February 14, 1781, and, after
refreshing his wearied troops, moved slowly back to
Hilisborough, and there established his head-quarters. **63**
His object was partially accomplished; he had not captured
the "rebel army," but he had driven it from the Carolinas,
and he now anticipated a general rising of the Tories, to
assist him in crushing effectually the remaining

Republicanism at the South. Although driven across the Dan, Greene had no idea of abandoning North Carolina to the quiet possession of the enemy. In the fertile and friendly county of Halifax, in Virginia, his troops reposed for a few days, and then they were called again to the field of active exertion. He resolved to recruit his thinned battalions, and as soon as possible recross the Dan and confront Cornwallis.

Among the most active and efficient officers engaged in the Southern campaigns was Henry Lee, **64** at this time lieutenant colonel, in command of a corps of choice cavalry. He was in Greene's camp when that general issued his orders to prepare for recrossing the Dan into the Carolinas. His patriot heart leaped for joy when the order was given, and he was much gratified when himself and General Pickens, who commanded a body of South Carolina militia, with Captain Oldham and two companies of Maryland veteran militia, were directed on February 18, 1781, to repass the Dan and reconnoitre the front of Cornwallis, for he burned to measure strength with the fiery Tarleton. They were sent by Greene to interrupt the intercourse of Cornwallis with the country surrounding his army at Hillsborough, and to suppress every attempt of the Loyalists to join him in force. This proved necessary, for the British commander issued a proclamation on the twentieth of February, 1781, inviting the Loyalists to join his standard at Hillsborough.

Lieutenant-colonel Lee crossed the Dan on the eighteenth, and was followed by Pickens and Oldham. He sent out his scouts, and early on the morning of the nineteenth he was informed by them that Tarleton and his legion were out toward the Haw reconnoitering, and offering protection to the Loyalists who were desirous of marching to Cornwallis's camp. Lee and Pickens pushed on to gain the great road leading from Hillsborough to the Haw. They ascertained that Tarleton had passed there the day before, and was probably then on the western side of the Haw. The next day, February 21, the Americans crossed the Haw, and were informed that the Loyalists between that and the Deep River were certainly assembling to join the earl. They also learned from a countryman (a sort of passive Tory named Ephraim Cooke) that Tarleton's force consisted of most of his cavalry, four hundred infantry, and two light field pieces; and that he was encamped about four miles distant with all the carelessness of confident security. Lee determined to surprise him, and placed his little army in battle order for a quick march. They reached the designated spot too late, for Tarleton had left and proceeded a few miles further, to the plantation of Colonel William O'Neil, whose memory, if common report speaks true, deserves a greater share of the odium of his countrymen than the most bitter Tory, for by his avaricious acts while claiming to be a Whig, he drove many of his neighbors to join the ranks of the Loyalists. **65** Two of Tarleton's officers, who were left behind, were captured.

Lee now resolved to employ stratagem. His legion greatly resembled that of Tarleton, and he made the country people believe that his was a detachment sent by Cornwallis to re-enforce that officer. The two prisoners were commanded to favor the deception, under the penalty of instant death. The legion took the van in the march on February 25, 1781, with Lieutenant-colonel Lee at the head, preceded, at the distance of a few hundred yards, by a scout. The officer of the van soon met two well-mounted young men, who, believing him to belong to a British re-enforcement, promptly answered an inquiry by saying that they were "rejoiced to fall in with him, they having been sent forward by Colonel Pyle, the commander of quite a large body of Loyalists, to find out Tarleton's camp, whither he was marching with his followers." A dragoon was immediately sent to Lee with this information, and was speedily followed by the young men, who mistook "Legion Harry" for Tarleton, and, with the greatest deference, informed him of the advance of Colonel Pyle. Lee dispatched his adjutant to General Pickens to request him to place his

Pyle's Pond

riflemen (among whom were those of Captain Graham, **66** who had just joined him) on the left flank, in a place of concealment in the woods, while he himself should make an attempt to capture the deceived Loyalists. Lee also sent one of the duped young men, with the dragoon who escorted them, to proceed to Colonel Pyle with his compliments, and his request "that the colonel would be so good as to draw out his forces on the side of the road, so as to give convenient room for Lee's much wearied troops to pass by without delay to their right position." The other young countryman was detained to accompany Lee himself, whom he supposed to be Tarleton. The van officer was ordered to halt as soon as he should perceive the Loyalists. This order was obeyed; and presently the young man who had been sent to Colonel Pyle, returned with that officer's assurance that he was "happy to comply with the request of Colonel Tarleton." It was the intention of Lee, when his force should obtain the requisite position to have the complete advantage of Colonel Pyle, to reveal his real name and character, demand the immediate surrender of the Tories, and give them their choice, to return quietly to their homes, after being disarmed, or to join the patriot army. Thus far every thing had worked favorably to Lee's humane design.

Lee's cavalry first approached the Loyalists, who, happily for the furtherance of the plan, were on the right side of the road; consequently, the horsemen following Lee were obliged to countermarch and confront the Loyalists. As Lee approached Colonel Pyle, the Loyalists raised the shout, "God save the king!" He rode along the Tory column (who were also mounted, with their rifles on their backs), and, with gracious smiles, complimented them on their fine appearance and loyal conduct. As he approached Pyle and grasped his hand (the signal for his cavalry to draw when he should summon the Tories to surrender), the Loyalists on the left discovered Pickens's militia, and perceived that they were betrayed. They immediately commenced firing upon the rear-guard of the American cavalry, commanded by Captain Eggleston. **67** That officer, as a matter of necessity, instantly turned upon the foe, and this movement was speedily followed by the whole column. A scene of dreadful slaughter followed, for the Loyalists, taken by surprise, could not bring their rifles to bear before Lee had struck the fatal blow. Colonel Pyle commanded four hundred Loyalists; ninety of them were killed in that brief moment, and a large portion of the remainder were wounded. A cry for mercy arose from the discomfited Tories, but the hand of mercy was stayed until the red arm of war had placed the Americans beyond danger. **68** Colonel Pyle was badly wounded, and fled to the shelter of a small pond, which was environed and deeply shaded by a fringe of oaks, persimmons, hawthorns, crab-trees, and black jacks, trellised with the vines of the muscadine. Tradition says that he laid himself under the water, with nothing but his nose above it, until after dark, when he crawled out, made his way home, and recovered. The place of his concealment is yet known as "Pyle's Pond," of which the engraving is a correct view, as it appeared when I visited the spot on January 2, 1849. It is on the verge of a cultivated field, of some six acres, half a mile northwest from the Salisbury road. Its dense fringe is gone, and nothing indicates its former concealment but numerous stumps of the ancient forest.

Lee and Pickens did not pursue the retreating Loyalists; but, anxious to overtake Tarleton, who was at Colonel O'Neil's, upon the Greensborough road, three miles northward, he resumed his march, notwithstanding it was almost sunset. He halted within a mile of O'Neil's, and encamped for the night, where they were joined by Colonel Preston and three hundred hardy mountaineers from Virginia, who had hastened to the support of Greene. At ten o'clock in the morning, the Americans formed for attack, when it was ascertained that Tarleton, alarmed by the exaggerated stories of some of the survivors of Pyle's corps, who made their way to his camp, had hastened to obey the orders of Cornwallis, just received, and was moving toward the Haw. The Americans pursued him as far as that river, when they halted, and Tarleton, after a narrow escape at the ford, returned in safety to Hilisborough. "Fortune, the capricious goddess," says Lee, "gave us Pyle, and saved Tarleton." **70**

Chapter XIV
Endnotes

1 In the upper part of the state, in the vicinity of the route traversed by the armies of Cornwallis and Greene during the memorable retreat of the latter, there were above twenty organized churches, with large congregations, and a great many preaching places. All of these congregations, where the principles of the Gospel independence had been faithfully preached by M'Aden, Patillo, Caldwell, M'Corkle, Hall, Craighead, Balch, M'Caule, Alexander, and Richardson, were famous during the struggle of the Revolution, for skirmishes, battles, loss of libraries, personal prowess, individual courage, and heroic women. In no part of our republic was purer patriotism displayed, than there.

2 The Moravians purchased a tract of one hundred thousand acres between the Dan and the Yadkin Rivers, about ten miles eastward of the Gold Mountain. They gave to their domain the name of Wachovia, the title of an estate belonging to Count Zinzendorf, in Austria – See Martin, ii., 57. Much earlier than this, in 1709, a colony of Swiss and Germans, under Baron De Graffenreidt, settled on the Neuse and Cape Fear Rivers. They founded a city, and called it New Berne (at present Newbern), after Berne, in Switzerland.

3 Henry the Eighth of England forced the people of Ireland to accept the rituals of the Reformed Church. Elizabeth, his daughter, pursued the same policy, and reaped the abundant fruit of trouble brought forth by the discontents of the Irish people. In consequence of the failure of a rebellion against the authority of James the First, in the province of Ulster, at the beginning of the seventeenth century, nearly six counties, embracing half a million of acres, became the property of the king, by confiscation. Thither James sent Protestant colonies from England and Scotland (chiefly from the latter), hoping thereby to fix the principles of the reformation there, and thus to subdue the turbulence of the people. The Scotch settlers retained the characteristic traits of their native stock, but were somewhat molded by surrounding influences. They continued to call themselves Scotch, and, to distinguish them from the natives of Scotland, they received the name of Scotch-Irish. From the beginning they were Republicans. They demanded, and exercised the privilege of choosing their own ministers and spiritual directors, in opposition to all efforts of the hierarchy of England to make the choice and support of their clergy a state concern. From the descendants of these early Republicans came the Scotch-Irish immigrants who settled in the interior of North Carolina. – See History of Religious Principles and Events in Ulster Province.

4 The first periodical paper, called The North Carolina Magazine, or Universal Intelligencer, was published by Davis, at Newbern, on a demi sheet, in quarto pages. It was filled with long extracts from the works of theological writers, or selections from British magazines. The second newspaper was called the North Carolina Gazette and Weekly Post Boy. It was printed at Wilmington, by Andrew Stewart, a Scotchman, and contained intelligence of current events. The first number was published in September, 1764. The Assembly that year passed an act for the erection of a school-house at Newbern; the first legislative movement in the province in favor of popular education. The Cape Fear Mercury was established by Adam Boyd, in October, 1767. Boyd was a zealous patriot, and was an active member of the Committee of Safety, of Wilmington.

5 The outbreak alluded to is known as the Enfield Riot. It occurred in 1759. Extortion had become rife in every department of government. Deputy-surveyors, entry-takers, and other officers of inferior grade, became adepts in the chicanery of their superiors. The people finding their complaints unavailing, and that Corbin, who had the chief direction of the land-office, was increasing his fees without authority, resolved to redress their grievances themselves. Fourteen well-mounted men crossed the Chowan, a few miles above Edenton, by night, seized Corbin, took him to Enfield, and kept him there until he gave a bond in forty thousand dollars, with eight sureties, that he would produce his books within three weeks and return all his illegal fees. As soon as released, he commenced suits against four of the men who seized him, and they were committed to Enfield jail. The next day an armed posse cut down the prison doors, and released them. Corbin was obliged to discontinue his suits and pay the costs. In Mecklenburg county, in May, 1765, a number of people, with their faces blackened, forcibly compelled John Frohock, a surveyor, to leave the lands of George A. Selwyn, who possessed large tracts in that county, and who had sent him there to survey them.

6 William Tryon was a native of Ireland, and was educated to the profession of a soldier. He was an officer in the British service. He married Miss Wake, a relative of the Earl of Hillsborough, secretary for the colonies. Thus connected, he was a favorite of government, and was appointed lieutenant governor of North Carolina, in 1765. On the death of Governor Dobbs, he succeeded him in office, and exercised its functions until called to fill the same office in New York, in 1771. The history of his administration in North Carolina is a record of extortion, folly, and crime. During his administration in New York, the Revolution broke out, and he was the last royal governor of that state, though nominally succeeded in office in 1780 by General Robertson, when he returned to England. His property in North Carolina and in New York was confiscated. The public acts of Governor Tryon, while in America, are recorded upon various pages of these volumes.

7 The village of Brunswick, once a flourishing town, but now a desolation, was situated upon a sandy plain on the western side of the Cape Fear, on New Inlet, in full view of the sea, fifteen miles below Wilmington. It enjoyed considerable commerce; but Wilmington, more eligibly situated, became first its rival, and then its grave-digger. Little now remains to denote the former existence of population there, but the grand old walls of "St. Philip's Church, of Brunswick," which was doubtless the finest sacred edifice in the province at the time of its erection, about one hundred years ago. I am indebted to Frederick Kidder, Esq., of Boston, who visited the ruins in 1851, for the accompanying drawing and general description of the present appearance of the church. It is situated within a thick grove of trees, chiefly pines, about an eighth of a mile from the river bank, and its massive walls, built of large English bricks, seem to have been but little effected by time. They exhibit "honorable scars" made by cannon-balls hurled from British ships in the Cape Fear to cover the landing of Cornwallis, when, in the spring of 1776, he desolated the plantation of Colonel Robert Howe, and other Whigs in the neighborhood of that patriot's estate. The edifice is seventy-five feet in length from east to west, and fifty-four feet in width. The walls are about three feet in thickness, and average about twenty-eight feet in height. The roof, floor, and windows have long since perished; and where the pulpit stood, upon its eastern end, a vigorous cedar spreads its branches. Nine of these green trees are within its walls, and give peculiar picturesqueness to the scene. On the top of the walls is flourishing shrubbery, the

Ruins of St. Philip's Church

product of seeds planted by the winds and the birds. Around the church are strewn the graves of many of the early settlers, the names of some of whom live in the annals of the state. The view here given is from the east. About a quarter of a mile northeast from the church, are remains of the residence of Governor Tryon at the time of the Stamp Act excitement.

8 Martin, 210-12. The man who was killed was Thomas Whitechurst, a relative of Mrs. Tryon. He fell in a duel with Simpson, master of the sloop of war Viper, who took the side of the colonists. Simpson was tried for murder and acquitted. Tryon charged Chief-justice Berry with partiality, and severely reprimanded him. The judge was very sensitive, and, under the impression that he was to be suspended from office, committed suicide in the most horrible manner.

9 Those who associated for the purpose assumed the name of REGULATORS, and the confederacy was called THE REGULATION.

10 North Carolina Weekly Times.

11 Caruthers, 120.

12 The deficiency in Husband's education, and his ignorance of the proper construction of language, is evinced in a pamphlet prepared chiefly by himself, entitled "An Impartial Relation of the first Rise and Cause of recent differences in Public Affairs," which was printed for the "compiler" in 1770. The only copy of this rare and curious pamphlet which I have seen is in the possession of the Reverend Francis Hawks, D. D., L. L. D, of New York City.

13 These resolutions were drawn by Herman Husband. The signers agreed to form an association to regulate public affairs in Orange county. They resolved to pay no more taxes until satisfied that they were legal; to pay officers no more fees than the strict letter of the law required, unless forced to, and then to show open resentment; to be cautious in the selection of representatives, and to petition the governor, council, king, and Parliament for a redress of grievances; to keep up a continual correspondence with each other; to defray all necessary expenses; all differences in judgment to be submitted to the whole REGULATION, the judgment of the majority to be final; and closed by a solemn oath or affirmation to "stand true and faithful to this cause, until we bring things to a true regulation." These REGULATORS were also styled "Sons of Liberty."

14 This picture of the palace I made from the original drawings of the plan and elevation, by John Hawks, Esq., the architect. These drawings, with others of minor details, such as sections of the drawing-room, chimney-breasts for the council-chamber and dining-hall, sewers, &c., are in the present possession of a grandson of the architect, the Reverend Francis L. Hawks, D. D., L. L. D., rector of Calvary Church, in the city of New York, to whose courtesy I am indebted for their use. With the drawings is the preliminary contract entered into by the governor and the architect, which bears the private seal of Tryon and the signatures of the parties, from which I made the fac simile printed upon page 361. The contract is dated January 9th, 1767, and specifies that the main building should be of brick, eighty-seven feet front, fifty-nine feet deep, and two stories in height, with suitable buildings for offices, &c., and was to be completed by the first day of October, 1770. For his services, Mr. Hawks was to receive an annual salary of "three hundred pounds proclamation money." The view here given was the north front, toward the town. The center edifice was the palace. The building on the right was the secretary's office and the laundry; that upon the left was the kitchen and servant's hall. These were connected with the palace by a curviform colonnade, of five columns each, and covered. Between these buildings, in front of the palace, was a handsome court. The rear of the building was finished in the style of the Mansion-House in London. The interior of the palace was elegantly finished. "Upon entering the street door," says Ebenezer Hazzard, in his journal for 1777, when he visited it, "you enter a hall in which are four niches for statues." The chimney-breasts for the council-chamber, dining-hall, and drawing-room, and the cornices of these rooms, were of white marble. The chimney-breast of the council-chamber was the most elaborate, being ornamented by two Ionic columns below, and four columns, with composite capitals, above, with beautiful entablature, architrave, and friese.* Over the inner door of the entrance-hall or ante-chamber was a tablet, with a Latin inscription, showing that the palace was dedicated to Sir William Draper, Ü "the Conqueror of Manilla;" and also the following lines, in Latin, which were written by Draper, who was then on a visit to Governor Tryon:

> *"In the reign of a monarch, who goodness disclos'd,*
> *A free, happy people, to dread tyrants oppos'd,*
> *Have to virtue and merit erected this dome;*
> *May the owner and household make this their loved home –*
> *Where religion, the arts, and the laws may invite*
> *Future ages to live in sweet peace and delight"*

The above translation was made by Judge Martin, the historian of North Carolina, who visited the edifice in 1783, in company with the unfortunate Don Francisco de Miranda. That gentleman assured Martin that the structure had no equal in South America. á The palace was destroyed by fire about fifty years ago, and the two smaller buildings, only, remain.

---

* Among the colonial documents at Raleigh is an account of this chimney-piece. The paper bears the date of December 6, 1769. It is one of several manuscripts deposited there by Dr. Hawks, which he found among his grandfather's papers.

Ü Sir William was an excessively vain man. Upon a cenotaph, at his seat at Clifton Down, near Bristol, England, he had this inscription placed: "Here lies the mother of Sir William Draper."

á History of North Carolina, ii., 226.

---

15 Wake county was so named in honor of this accomplished lady. Afterward, when party zeal changed the name of Tryon county, and it was proposed to alter that of Wake also, the gallantry of the Assembly overruled their feelings of hostility to the governor and his family, and the name was retained.

16 The appropriations made by the province on account of the French and Indian war had founded a heavy public debt. These, with the palace debt and the appropriation for the boundary commission, together with the unredeemed bills and treasury-notes, amounted to almost half a million of dollars. This burden upon the common industry became greater in consequence of the depreciation of the paper money of the colony in the hands of the people, at least fifty per cent. at the period in question. To sink this public debt, a poll tax of about a dollar and a half was levied upon every male, white and black, between the ages of sixteen and sixty years. This bore heavily upon the poor, and awakened universal discontent. The running of the western boundary line was an unnecessary measure, and the people were convinced that Tryon projected it for the purpose of gratifying his love of personal display. Commissioners were appointed, and at a time of profound peace with the Indians on the frontier, Tryon marched at the head of a military force, "ostensibly to protect the surveyors." He made such a display of himself before the grave sachems and warriors of the Cherokees, that they gave him the just, though unenviable title of "The great wolf of North Carolina!"

17 The legal fee for drawing a deed was one dollar. Many lawyers charged five dollars. This is a single example of their extortion. Thomas Frohock, who held the office of clerk of the Superior Court in Salisbury,

was another extortioner, who was detested by the people. He frequently charged fifteen dollars for a marriage license. When we consider the relative value of money at that time, it was equal to forty or fifty dollars at the present day. Many inhabitants along the Yadkin dispensed with the license, took each other "for better, or for worse," unofficially, and considered themselves as married, without further ceremony.

18 Dr. Caruthers, in his Life of Caldwell, has preserved the two following verses of a doggerel poem of eight stanzas, composed on the occasion:

> *"At length their head man they sent out*
> *To save their town from fire:*
> *To see Ned Fanning wade Eno,*
> *Brave boys, you'd all admire.*
> *With hat in hand, at our command,*
> *To salute us every one, sir,*
> *And after that, kept off his hat,*
> *To salute old Hamilton, sir."*

19 The governor had demanded that twelve wealthy men should meet him at Salisbury, on the twenty-fifth of August, and execute a bond, in the penalty of $5000, as security that the Regulators should keep the peace during the trials. This request was refused, but a promise to abstain from violence was made and faithfully kept.

20 Statement of Herman Husband. Record of the Superior Court at Hillsborough.

21 The names of these "outlaws" were James Hunter, Ninian Bell Hamilton, Peter Craven, Isaack Jackson, Herman Husband, Matthew Hamilton, William Payne, Malichi Tyke, William Moffat, Christopher Nation, Solomon Goff and John O'Neil. These were some of the "Sons of Liberty" of western North Carolina.

22 While in Hillsborough, in January, 1849, I was permitted by the Clerk of the Superior Court, to make the following extracts from the old records: "Monday, September 24th, 1770. Several persons styling themselves Regulators, assembled together in the court-yard, under the conduct of Herman Husband, James Hunter, Rednap Howell, William Butler, Samuel Divinny, and many others, insulted some of the gentlemen of the bar, and in a riotous manner went into the court-house and forcibly carried out some of the attorneys, and in a cruel manner beat them. They then insisted that the judge (Richard Henderson being the only one on the bench) should proceed to the trial of their leaders, who had been indicted at a former court, and that the jury should be taken out of their party. Therefore, the judge finding it impossible to proceed with honor to himself, and justice to his country, adjourned the court till to-morrow at ten o'clock, and took advantage of the night, and made his escape." The court, of course, did not convene on the next day, and instead of a record of judicial proceedings, I found the following entry: "March term, 1771. The persons styling themselves Regulators, under the conduct of Herman Husband, James Hunter, Rednap Howell,* William Butler, and Samuel Divinny, still continuing their riotous meetings, and severely threatening the judges, lawyers, and other officers of the court, prevented any of the judges or lawyers attending. Therefore, the court continues adjourned until the next September term." These entries are in the hand-writing of Fanning.

---

* Rednap Howell was from New Jersey, and was a brother of Richard Howell a patriot of the Revolution, and governor of that state. Like his brother (who wrote the ode of welcome to Washington printed on page 38 in the original text), he was endowed with poetic genius, and composed about forty songs during the Regulator movements. He taught school somewhere on the Deep River, and was a man of quite extensive

influence. Like Freneau, at a later day, he gave obnoxious officials many severe thrusts. He thus hits Frohock and Fanning:

> *Says Frohock to Fanning, to tell the plain truth,*
> *When I came to this country I was but a youth;*
> *My father sent for me; I wa'nt worth a cross,*
> *And then my first study was to steal for a horse.*
> *I quickly got credit, and then ran away,*
> *And hav'n't paid for him to this very day*
> *Says Fanning to Frohock, 'tis a folly to lie;*
> *I rode an old mare that was blind of an eye;*
> *Five shillings in money I had in my purse,*
> *My coat it was patched, but not much the worse;*
> *But now we've got rich, and 'tis very well known*
> *That we'll do very well if they'll let us alone."*

In a song which became very popular, Howell thus lampooned Colonel Fanning:

> *"When Fanning first to Orange came,*
> *He looked both pale and wan;*
> *An old patched coat upon his back –*
> *An old mare he rode on.*
> *Both man and mare wa'n't worth five pounds,*
> *As I've been often told,*
> *But by his civil robberies*
> *He's laced his coat with gold."*

In 1771, a pamphlet was published in Boston, entitled "A Fan for Fanning, and a Touch for Tryon; containing an Impartial Account of the Rise and Progress of the so-much-talked-of Regulators in North Carolina. By Regulus." In this pamphlet, Tryon and Fanning were sufficiently scorched to need a "fan."

---

23 Fanning's house was upon the site of the present Masonic Hall, a handsome brick building within a grove on King Street. On the opposite side of the street is his office, too much modernized for a drawing of it to possess any interest.

EDMUND FANNING was a native of Long Island, New York, son of Colonel Phineas Fanning. He was educated at Yale College, and graduated with honor in 1757. He soon afterward went to North Carolina, and began the profession of a lawyer at Hillsborough, then called Childsborough. In 1760, the degree of L. L. D. was conferred upon him by his alma mater. In 1763, he was appointed colonel of Orange county, and in 1765 was made clerk of the Superior Court at Hillsborough. He also represented Orange county in the Colonial Legislature. In common with other lawyers, he appears to have exacted exorbitant fees for legal services, and consequently incurred the dislike of the people, which was finally manifested by acts of violence. He accompanied Governor Tryon to New York, in 1771, as his secretary. Governor Martin asked the Legislature to indemnify Colonel Fanning for his losses; the representatives of the people rebuked the governor for presenting such a petition. In 1776, General Howe gave Fanning the commission of colonel, and he raised and commanded a corps called the King's American Regiment of Foot. He was afterward appointed to the lucrative office of surveyor general, which he retained until his flight, with other Loyalists, to Nova Scotia, in 1783. In 1786 he was made lieutenant governor of Nova Scotia, and in 1794 he was appointed governor of Prince Edward's Island. He held the latter office about nineteen years, a part of which time he was also a brigadier in the British army, having received his commission in 1808. He married in Nova Scotia, where some of his family yet reside. General Fanning died in London, in 1818, at the age of about eighty-one years. His widow and two daughters yet (1852) survive. One daughter, Lady Wood, a widow, resides near London with her mother; the other, wife of Captain Bentwick Cumberland, a nephew of Lord Bentwick, resides at Charlotte's Town, New Brunswick. I am indebted to John Fanning Watson, Esq., the Annalist of Philadelphia and New York, for the portrait here given.

Edmund Fanning

General Fanning's early career, while in North Carolina, seems not to have given promise of that life of usefulness which he exhibited after leaving Republican America. It has been recorded, it is true, by partisan pens, yet it is said that he often expressed regrets for his indiscreet course at Hillsborough. His after life bore no reproaches, and the Gentlemen's Magazine (1818), when noting his death, remarked, "The world contained no better man in all the relations of life."

24 The facsimiles here given of the writing of Fanning and Yorke are copies which I made from the original in the old record book. The first shows the names of parties to the suit entered by Fanning on the record. The mock court, of course, decided in favor of the defendant, Smith, and opposite these names and the record of the verdict, Yorke wrote, with a wretched pen, the sentence here engraved: "Fanning pays cost, but loses nothing." He being clerk of the court, and the lawyer, the costs were payable to himself, and so he lost nothing. Yorke was a man of great personal courage, and when, a few years later, the war of the Revolution was progressing, he became the terror of the Loyalists in that region. An old man on the banks of the Allamance, who knew him well, related to me an instance of his daring. On one occasion, while Cornwallis was marching victoriously through that section, Yorke, while riding on horseback in the neighborhood of the Deep River, was nearly surrounded by a band of Tories. He spurred his horse toward the river, his enemies in hot pursuit. Reaching the bank, he discovered he was upon a cliff almost fifty feet above the stream, and sloping from the top. The Tories were too close to allow him to escape along the margin of the river. Gathering the reins tightly in his hands, he spurred his strong horse over the precipice. The force of the descent was partially broken by the horse striking the smooth sloping surface of the rock, when half way down. Fortunately the water was deep below, and horse and rider, rising to the surface, escaped unhurt. It was a much greater feat than Putnam's at Horse Neck.

25 These were Guilford, Chatham, Wake, and Surrey.

26 Tryon, who feared and hated Husband, procured the preferment of several charges against him, and he was finally arrested, by order of the council, and imprisoned for several days. The charges, on investigation, were not sustained, and he was released.

27 Colonel Joseph Leech commanded the infantry, Captain Moore the artillery, and Captain Neale a company of rangers. On his way to the Eno, he was joined by a detachment from Hanover, under Colonel John Ashe, another from Carteret, under Colonel Craig; another from Johnston, under Colonel William Thompson; another from Beaufort, under Colonel Needham Bryan; another from Wake, under Colonel Johnson Hinton; and at his camp on the Eno, he was joined by Fanning, with a corps of clerks, constables, sheriffs, and other materials of a similar kind. The signatures given here, of two of Tryon's officers on this occasion, I copied from original committee reports to the Colonial Legislature, now in possession of the Reverend Dr. Hawks. Some of these officers were afterward active patriots. Several other signatures of North Carolina men given in this work, I copied from the same documents.

28 Colonel Ashe and Captain John Walker, who were out reconnoitering, were caught by the Regulators, tied to a tree, severely whipped, and detained as prisoners. The great body of the Regulators in camp censured this cruelty and disclaimed approval.

29 The Reverend David Caldwell, D. D., of Orange, many of whose congregation were with the Regulators, was the messenger on this occasion, and received from Tryon the most positive assurances that no blood should be shed unless the insurgents should be the first aggressors. Dr. Caldwell was a pure patriot, and during the war which ensued a few years later, himself and family were great sufferers for "conscience' sake."

30 Tradition currently reported that Donald Malcolm, one of Governor Tryon's aids, and who was afterward a very obnoxious under-officer of the customs at Boston, was the bearer of the flag. When the firing commenced, he retreated with safety to his person, but had the misfortune to have the buttons of his small clothes leave their fastenings. Trumbull, in his M'Fingall, with rather more wit than modesty, notices the circumstance in four lines.

31 Captain Montgomery, who commanded a company of Mountain Boys, was considered the principal leader, if any might be called by that name. He was killed by the second fire of the cannon, when most of the Regulators fled. James Pugh, a young gunsmith from Hillsborough, and three others, shielded by a ledge of rocks on the edge of a ravine, did great execution with rifles. Pugh fired while the others loaded, and he killed fifteen men. He was made prisoner, and was one of six who were hung at Hillsborough.

32 Martin, Williamson, Caruthers, Foote.

33 This view is from the south side of the Salisbury Road, which is marked by the fence on the left. The belligerents confronted in the open field seen on the north of the road, beyond the fence. Between the blasted pine, to which a muscadine is clinging, and the road, on the edge of a small morass, several of those who were slain in that engagement were buried. I saw the mounds of four graves by the fence. where the sheep, seen in the picture, are standing. The tree by the road side is a venerable oak, in which are a few scars produced by the bullets.

34 Among his victims was a young carpenter of Hillsborough, named James Few. He was the sole support of his widowed mother, and had suffered greatly, it is said, at the hands of Fanning. Young Few alleged that he had not only made him feel the curse of his exactions, but had actually seduced a young girl who was his betrothed. Driven to madness, he joined the Regulators, was taken prisoner, and was hung on the night after the battle, without trial, and without witnessing friends.* Justice to the dead, and a regard for the truth of history, demand the acknowledgment that this story, like the apocryphal one that the Regulators cut off Fanning's ears, Ü needs confirmation, and rests solely upon uncertain tradition. It is further related that Tryon destroyed the property of Few's mother when he reached Hillsborough!

Captain Messer, who was made prisoner, was sentenced to be hanged the day after the battle. His wife, informed of his intended fate, hastened to him with her, little son, a lad ten years old. She pleaded for her husband's life in vain. Messer was led to execution, while his wife lay weeping upon the ground, her boy by her side. Just as Messer was to be drawn up, the boy went to Tryon and said, "Sir, hang me, and let my father live." "Who told you to say that?" said the governor. "Nobody," replied the lad. "And why," said the governor, "do you ask that?" "Because," the boy replied, "if you hang my father, my mother will die, and the children will perish." The heart of the governor was touched, and he said, "Your father shall not be hanged to-day." Messer was offered his liberty if he would bring Husband back. He consented, and his wife and children were kept as hostages. He returned in the course of a few days, and reported that he overtook Husband in Virginia, but could not bring him. Messer was immediately bound, and, after being exhibited with the other prisoners, was hung at Hillsborough.

---

* Foote's Sketches of North Carolina, pages 61, 62.

Ü See Johnson's Traditions and Reminiscences of the Revolution, page 573.

---

35 Husband fled to Pennsylvania, and settled near Pittsburgh. He went to North Carolina on business soon after the close of the war, but did not remain long. In 1794 he was concerned in the "Whisky Insurrection," in Western Pennsylvania, and was appointed on the Committee of Safety with Brackenridge, Bradford, and Gallatin. Husband was arrested, and taken a prisoner to Philadelphia, where he was pardoned, through the interposition of Dr. Caldwell who happened to be there, Dr. Rush, and the North Carolina senators. He met his wife on his return home, and died at an inn before he reached his own neighborhood. Husband was a member of the Pennsylvania Legislature for some years.

36 The committee consisted of John Harvey (speaker of the Assembly), Robert Howe (afterward a general in the Continental army), Cornelius Harnett, William Hooper (one of the signers of the Declaration of Independence), Richard Caswell, Edward Vail, John Ashe, Joseph Hewes (another signer), and Samuel Johnson.

JOHN HARVEY was an active citizen in public life, before the war of the Revolution began. He was a member of the Colonial Legislature for a number of years, and in 1766 succeeded John Ashe as speaker of the House. He presided with dignity for three years, and at the close of each session received the unanimous thanks of the House for his impartiality. He early espoused the patriot cause; was active in the first Revolutionary movements in his state, but died before the struggle had advanced far toward a successful issue.

37 A bill for the establishment of Superior Courts upon a new basis, which was calculated to remove the powers of the judiciary further from the control of the people.

38 William Hooper, of the county of Orange, Joseph Hewes, of the town of Edenton, and Richard Caswell, of the county of Dobbs were chosen deputies. They were instructed to carry out the principles embodied in the preamble and resolutions adopted by the convention, the substance of which is given in the text.

39 To this proclamation the General Committee of Safety of the District of Wilmington, as appears by their proceedings, issued an answer, denying many of its allegations, and proclaiming the governor to be "an instrument in the hands of administration to rivet those chains so wickedly forged for America." This answer was drawn up and adopted in the session of the committee, at the court-house in Wilmington, on the twentieth of June, 1775.

40 In a letter to Lewis Henry de Rosset, the governor endeavored to vindicate himself, and denied all knowledge of the matter. He said in his letter, "that nothing could justify such a measure but the actual and designed rebellion of the king's subjects, and the failure of all other means to maintain his government." From these expressions and the language held in a pamphlet, entitled Taxation no Tyranny, written by the celebrated Dr. Johnson, together with the conduct of Lord Dunmore, of Virginia, it was evident that the inciting of the slaves to massacre their masters was a part of the programme of ministers for crushing the rebellion.*

---

* "The slave should be set free," said Johnson; "an act which the lovers of liberty must surely commend. If they are furnished with arms for defense and utensils of husbandry, and settled in some simple form of government, within the country they may be more honest and grateful than their masters."

---

41 Fort Johnson was on the west side of the Cape Fear River, two miles above its mouth, where the present town of Smithville, the capital of Brunswick county, is situated. There is now a fortress and small garrison there.

42 An account of the proceedings in Mecklenburg were published in the Cape Fear Mercury.

43 This was the same officer who accompanied Tryon to the Allamance, and was flogged by the Regulators. He resigned his commission as colonel of the militia of Hanover, under the king, and espoused the patriot cause. We shall meet him in the field hereafter.

44 The members of the Provincial Congress assembled in the Presbyterian Church, which stood where the present place of worship of that denomination, in Hillsborough, is located.

45 A provincial council was established, composed of two persons duly chosen by the delegates of each district, and one by the whole Congress.* A Committee of Safety, composed of a president and twelve members, were chosen for each district; the freeholders were also directed to choose a committee. The provincial council and the committees of safety exercised the functions of government in the management of civil and military affairs. Secret committees of correspondence were also organized. Premiums were voted for the manufacture of saltpetre, gunpowder, cotton and woolen cards, pins, needles, linen and woolen cloth, and for the erection of rolling and slitting mills, furnaces for the manufacture of steel and iron, paper-mills, salt-works, and for refining sulphur.

* Samuel Johnson, Cornelius Harnett, Samuel Ashe, Abner Nash, James Coor, Thomas Jones of Edenton, Whitmill Hill, William Jones, Thomas Jones of Halifax, Thomas Person, John Kinchen, Samuel Spencer, and Waightstill Avery, composed this first provincial council. They were to meet quarterly.

46 In the Wilmington Chronicle, August 21, 1844, there appeared a very interesting memoir of CORNELIUS HARNETT, which I have condensed. Mr. Harnett was a native of England, and was born on the twentieth of April, 1723. The precise time when became to America is not known. He was a man of wealth and consideration, before circumstances brought him into public life. He was among the earliest in North Carolina in denouncing the Stamp Act and kindred measures, and from that period until his death he was extremely active in public affairs. He resided upon Hilton plantation, about one mile from the center of Wilmington, where he owned a large estate, and was a gentleman of leisure. He represented the borough of Wilmington in the Provincial Assembly, in 1770-71, and was chairman of the most important committees of that body. From one of the reports of a committee of which Harnett was chairman, I copied the accompanying signature of the patriot. In 1772, Mr. Harnett, with Robert (afterward General) Howe, and Judge Maurice Moore, constituted a committee of the Assembly to prepare a remonstrance against the appointment, by Governor Martin, of commissioners to run the southern boundary line of the province. In 1773, Josiah Quincy, the young and ardent patriot of Boston, while traveling in the South for his health, passed a night at Wilmington, at the residence of Mr. Harnett, whom he denominated "the Samuel Adams of North Carolina" (except in point of fortune). "Robert Howe, Esq., Harnett, and myself," he wrote, "made the social triumvirate of the evening." The plan of "Continental Correspondence" was a subject for discussion that evening, and Quincy returned to Boston, feeling that with such men as Pinckney, Rutledge, Gadsden, and Harnett, as leaders, the South would co-operate with Massachusetts in resistance.

In December, 1773, Mr. Harnett was placed on the Committee of Correspondence for Wilmington district. In that sphere he was the master-spirit of the Revolution upon the Cape Fear and its vicinity. In the Provincial Congress of 1775, he represented his old constituents; and when a provincial council was appointed to fill the vacancy in government caused by the abdication of Martin, he was made its president, and became, in that capacity, actual governor of North Carolina. He was a member of the Provincial Congress which assembled at Halifax in the spring of 1776, and was chairman of the committee appointed to consider the usurpations, &c., of the imperial government. He submitted a report on the twelfth of April, which contained a resolution empowering the delegates of North Carolina in the Continental Congress, to use their influence in favor of a Declaration of Independence. When, in the spring of 1776, Sir Henry Clinton, with a British fleet, appeared in the Cape Fear River, that commander honored Harnett and Robert Howe, by excepting them in his offer of a general pardon to those who should return to their allegiance, as published in his proclamation issued to the people of North Carolina from the Pallas transport. They were considered arch-rebels. When, on the twenty-second of July, 1776, the Declaration of Independence arrived at Halifax, Harnett read it to a great concourse of citizens and soldiers. When he concluded, the latter crowded around him, took him upon their shoulders, and bore him in triumph through the town. In the autumn, he was on a committee for drafting a State Constitution, and a Bill of Rights; and to his liberal spirit the people were indebted for the claim in the first document, guaranteeing the privilege of enjoying the public offices and emoluments to Dissenters and Churchmen, equally. Under the new Constitution, Richard Caswell was made the first governor of the state, and Harnett was one of his council. He was afterward elected to fill his place in the Continental Congress, and Cornelius Harnett's name is attached to the "articles of confederation and perpetual union." When the British afterward held possession of the country around the Cape Fear, Harnett was made prisoner, and died while a captive. His remains lie buried in the northeast corner of the grave-yard attached to St. James's Church, in Wilmington, and at the head and foot of his grave are two upright slabs of brown stone. On the one at the head is inscribed. "CORNELIUS HARNETT, Died, 1781, aged 58 years."

Harnett's House . Ü

Ü This sketch is from a pencil drawing made in 1851 by Mr. Charles Burr. It is situated about a mile and a half from the center of Wilmington, on the northeast branch of the river. I am informed by Edward Kidder, Esq., of Wilmington, through whose kindness this and several other drawings in his vicinity have been procured for my work, that it has never been altered since Mr. Harnett occupied it. This is a view of the south point.

---

47 See page 328 in original text.

48 The Pretender, while a fugitive among the Highlands of Scotland, was discovered by his enemies, and fled in an open boat to South Uist, an island on the west coast, where he found refuge with Laird M'Donald. His pursuers discovered his retreat, and three thousand English soldiers were sent to search every nook and dell, crag and cottage upon the island. A cordon of armed vessels surrounded South Uist, so that escape appeared impossible. But escape from the island was necessary for the safety of the prince. Lady M'Donald proposed that he should put on the garb of a servant-woman, and, in company with a lady as waiting-maid, leave the island. Who had the courage? Flora M'Donald, from Millburg, a beautiful girl just from school at Edinburgh, was there on a visit. Her step-father was then on the island, in command of a corps of soldiers searching for the prince. Regardless of the certain displeasure of her father and the extreme peril of the undertaking, Flora acceded to the proposal of Lady M'Donald to save the prince; and that very night, in company with a trusty officer, she went among the crags of Carradale, to the cave where the royal fugitive was concealed. Great was the astonishment and delight of the prince when he was informed of the plan for his escape. Within a day or two, Flora procured a passport from her unsuspecting step-father for herself, a young companion, a boat's crew, and Betsey Bourke, an Irish woman, whom Flora pretended she had procured as a spinster for her mother. The prince, attired as Betsey Bourke, embarked with Flora and her companions, on the twenty-eighth of June, 1746, for the Isle of Skye. A furious tempest tossed them about all night, and a band of soldiers prevented their landing in the morning. They finally landed near the residence of Sir Alexander M'Donald, where the prince was concealed in the cavity of a rock, for the laird was his enemy, and his hall was filled with soldiers seeking the fugitive. Flora touched the heart of Lady M'Donald, and by her aid the prince and the maiden made a safe journey of twelve miles on foot, to Potarce. There they parted forever, the prince to escape to France, Flora to be soon afterward carried a prisoner to London and cast into the Tower. The story of her adventure excited the admiration of all classes, and as she was not a partisan of the Pretender, nor of his religious faith, the nobility interfered in her behalf. The father of George the Third visited her in prison, and so much was he interested in her that he procured her release. While she remained in London, her residence was surrounded by the carriages of the nobility; and Lady Primrose, a friend of the Pretender, introduced her to court society. When presented to the old King George the Second, he said to her, "How could you dare to succor the enemy of my crown and kingdom." Flora replied with great simplicity, "It was no more than I would have done for your majesty, had you been in like situation." A chaise and four were fitted up for her return to Scotland, and her escort was Malcolm M'Leod, who often said afterward, "I went to London to be hanged, but rode back in a chaise and four with Flora M'Donald." Four years afterward she married Allan, the son of the Laird M'Donald, and became mistress of the mansion where the prince passed his first night in the Isle of Skye. In 1775, Flora and her husband, with several children, arrived among their countrymen in North Carolina. Full of loyalty, she encouraged her countrymen to rally in defense of the royal cause. After suffering much, they embarked in a sloop-of-war for Scotland. On the voyage, the vessel was attacked by a French cruiser, and the brave Flora, who was on deck during the action, was severely wounded in the hand. They reached their country, where Flora lived until the fifth of March, 1790. She was buried in the cemetery of Killmuir, in the Isle of Skye; her shroud was the sheet in which the prince slept while under her guidance; and three thousand persons stood and wept as her coffin was let down into the grave.

49 Moores Creek runs from north to south, and empties into the South River, about twenty miles above Wilmington.

50 I am indebted to the Honorable David L. Swain, late governor of North Carolina, and now president of the University at Chapel Hill, for the following sketch of the public life of Richard Caswell. Governor Swain married a grand-daughter of Governor Caswell; and from among the family papers in his possession, he sent me the subjoined interesting autograph letter, written by Caswell, to his son, from Philadelphia.*

Richard Caswell was born in Maryland, August 3, 1729. In 1746, he was induced, by unsuccessful mercantile speculations of his father, to leave his home, and seek his fortune in the then colony of North Carolina. Bearing letters to Governor Johnston from the governor of Maryland, he soon received employment in one of the public offices. Subsequently, he was appointed deputy surveyor of the colony, and was clerk of the County Court of Orange in 1753. He finally settled himself in Dobbs (now Lenoir) county, where he married Mary Mackilwean, who bore him a son, William. He afterward married Sarah, the daughter of William Herritage, an eminent attorney, under whom he had studied law. He had obtained a license, and practiced the profession with great success. In 1754 he was chosen a member of the Colonial Assembly from Johnston county, which he continued to represent till 1771. In this and the preceding year, he was made the speaker of the House of Commons. He was also colonel of the militia of his county, and, as such, commanded the right wing of Governor Tryon's forces at the battle of Allamance, May 16, 1771.

In 1774, he was one of the delegates to Congress, with William Hooper and Joseph Hewes, and was continued in this office in 1775. In September of this year, having been appointed treasurer of the Southern District of North Carolina, he resigned his seat in Congress. The estimate formed by his contemporaries of Caswell's merits in this affair, is clearly shown in the resolve passed by the Provincial Congress, on the thirteenth of April, "that the thanks of this Congress be given to Colonel Richard Caswell and the brave officers and soldiers under his command, for the very essential service by them rendered this country at the battle of Moore's Creek;" and by the further fact that, on the twenty-second of the same month, the same body appointed him "brigadier general of the militia for the District of Newbern." In November of the same year, he was chosen president of the Provincial Congress, which framed the Constitution of the state, and, in December, was elected the first governor under it. This office he held during the stormy and perilous period of 1777, 1778, and 1779. He refused to receive any compensation for his services beyond his expenses. In 1780 he led the troops of North Carolina, under General Gates, and was engaged in the disastrous battle at Camden. In 1782 he was chosen speaker of the Senate, and controller general, and continued to discharge the duties of both offices till 1784, when he was again elected governor of the state, and re-elected in 1785 and 1786, when he ceased to be eligible under the Constitution. The Assembly of 1787 elected him a delegate to the convention which was to meet at Philadelphia in May of that year, to form a Federal Constitution, and conferred on him the extraordinary power, in case of his inability to attend, to select his successor. William Blount was selected by him, and his name is appended to that instrument. In 1789 he was elected senator from Dobbs county, and also a member of the convention which, in November, ratified the Federal Constitution. When the General Assembly met, he was chosen speaker of the Senate. But his course was run. His second son, Richard, had been lost on his passage by sea from Charleston to Newbern, and the father certainly entertained the opinion that he had been taken by pirates and carried to Algiers, or murdered. This and other events threw a cloud over his mind, from which he seems never to have recovered. While presiding in the Senate, on the fifth of November, he was struck with paralysis, and after lingering speechless till the tenth, he expired, in the sixtieth year of his age. His body was, after the usual honors, conveyed to his family burial-place in Lenoir, and there interred. As a statesman, his patriotism was unquestioned, his discernment was quick, and his judgment sound; as a soldier, his courage was undaunted, his vigilance untiring, and his success triumphant. Mrs. Anne White, Governor Caswell's last remaining child, died at Raleigh, on the twentieth of September, 1851, in the eighty-fourth year of her age.

---

* Letter of Governor Caswell. I print the subjoined letter of Governor Caswell entire, because it gives an interesting view of the excitement which prevailed it the time, and the manner in which the delegates to the Continental Congress were carefully escorted on their way to Philadelphia.

"Philadelphia 11th May 1775.

"MY DEAR SON. – By a gentleman Bound to Tar River, I now write to inform you that after I parted with you at Halifax, Mr. Hewes & myself proceeded on our Journey as follows; Sunday evening we arrived at Petersburg in Virginia where we met the express with an acc't of a Battle between the King's Troops & the Bostonians. The next day we crossed James River & Lodged at Hanover Court House, where we had an Acco't of 1500 Men being under Arms to proceed to Williamsburg in Order to Oblige Lord Dunmore to return some powder he had taken out of the Magazine & Lodged on Board of a Man-of-War in James River. What was done in that matter we have not since Heard. The next day we were constantly meeting Armed men who had been to Escort the Delegates for Virginia, on their way towards this place. We Lodged that night at Port Royal and were only 2 or 3 Hours after the Virginia Gentn. The next day we got down to Potowmack side before the Boats returned that had carried the Virginians over. Here were part of the Militia of three Counties under Arms, & in the Uniforms of Hunting Shirts. They received us, and Conducted us on the return of the Boats, to the water's edge with all the Military Honors due to General Officers. We then crossed the River, and learned at the Ferry on Maryland side that a Company of Independents in Charles County had attended the Virginia Delegates from thence under Arms. We proceeded and overtook them at Port Tobacco, where, indeed, the Independents made a Most Glorious Appearance. Their Company consisted of 68 Men beside officers, all Genteelly drest in Scarlet & well equiped with Arms, & Warlike Implements, with drum & Fife. Sentinels were placed at the doors & Occasionally relieved during the Time we stayed there. The next Morning we all set out together, & were Attended by the Independents to the Verge of their County, where they delivered us to another Company of Independents in Prince George's; they in like Manner to a Second, and that to a Third, which brot us thro' their County. We Lodged that night at

Marlborough & the next day tho' we met with a Most Terrible Gust of Lightning, thunder, wind, Hail & rain, Arrived at Baltimore, at the entrance of which Town we were received by four Independent Companies who Conducted us with their Colours Flying, drums Besting and Fife's playing, to our lodgings at the Fountain Tavern (Grants). The next day we were prevailed on to stay at Baltimore, where Coll Washington, Accompanied by the rest of the Delegates, reviewed the Troops. They have four Companies of 68 men each, Compleat, who go throh their Exercises extremely Clever. They are raising, in that Town, three other Companies which they say will soon be full. We were very Genteelly entertained here in the Court House. The next day we Breakfasted at my old Master Cheynes & dined at Susquehannah; crossed the River & Lodged at the Ferry House. As I had in some Measure been the cause of the Virginia Gentn going round the Bay by reccommending that road, & being the only person In Company acquainted with the road, I was Obliged to keep with them so that I did not call on any of my relations. I sent George to Jos. Dallams where he left the Letters I brot for our Friends, and was informed my Grand Mother & all Friends were well except Mrs Dallam who had been poorly some Time – the next day we got to Wilmington where we fell In with Several of the Maryland Delegates, & came all into the City to Dinner, on the 9th Instant. Yesterday the Congress met Agreeable to Appointment, & this day it was Resolved that they enter upon the Consideration of American Grievances on Monday next. Here a Greater Martial Spirit prevails, if possible, than I have been describing in Virginia and Maryland. They have 28 Companies Compleat, which make near 2000 Men, who March out to the Common & go thro' their Exercises twice a day regularly. Scarce any thing but Warlike Musick is to be heard in the Streets. There are several Companies of Quakers only, and many of them beside enrolled in other Companies promiscuously. 'Tis said they will, in a few days, have 3000 Men under Arms ready to defend their Liberties. They are raising Men in New York & all the Northern Governments. The Yorkers, I am told by their Delegates, are determined to Defend their Liberties, & since the action between the Kings Troops and the Provincials, scarcely a Tory is to be found amongst them. I herewith inclose you a paper In which is a List of the Killed and Wounded of the Kings Troops. But 'tis said this is not Genuine, a much greater number being Actually Killed. On the side of the Bostonians 37 were Killed outright 4 are missing & I forget the number of Wounded; I think thirty odd. Thus you have the fullest Account I am able to give of these matters, and as the Accot is so long, 'twill not be in my power to Communicate the same to any other of my Countrymen and friends but throh you. You may therefore remember me in the Strongest manner to Your Uncles, Capt Bright, and others of my particular Friends. Shew them this Letter, and tell them it will be a Reflection on their Country to be Behind their neighbours; that it is Indispensibly necessary for them to arm and form into a Company or Companies of Independents. When their Companies are full, 68 private Men each, to elect Officers, Viz a Capt. 2 Lieuts an Ensign & Subalterns, And to meet as often as possible & go thro' the exercise. Recieve no man but such as can be depended on, at the same Time reject none who will not discredit the Company. If I live to return I shall most Chearfully Join any of my Countrymen even as a rank & file man. And as in the Common cause I am here exposed to Danger, that or any other difficulties I shall not shun whilst I have any Blood in my Veins, But freely offer it in Support of the Liberties of my Country. Tell your Uncles (the Clk & Sherf) it may not he prudent for them so far to engage yet awhile in any Company as to risk the loss of their offices. But you, my Dear Boy, must become a soldier & risk your life in Support of those invaluable Blessings which once lost, Posterity will never be able to regain. Ü Some men, I fear, will start objections to the enrolling of Companies & exercising the Men, & will say it will be acting against Government. That may be answered "that it is not so." That we are only Qualifying ourselves and preparing to defend our Country & Support our Liberties. I can say no more at present. But that May God*

Almighty protect you all & his Blessing Attend your good endeavor, is the Ardent prayer of My Dear Child Your Affectionate Father.

"P.S. – only shew this letter to such as I have described above, & dont let it be Copied. Consult Capt Bright &c.

"Mr William Caswell."

---

* This was Mrs. Smith, the grandmother also of Governor William Paca, of Maryland, one of the signers of the Declaration of Independence. She lived to the remarkable age of ninety-one years.

Ü I am informed by Governor Swain, that this boy entered the service in less than four months afterward, and before he had attained his majority, as an ensign. He was a lieutenant in 1776, and in 1777 was promoted to captain, and commanded a company at the battle on the Brandywine. In 1781 he was a brigadier, his father, at the same time, being a major general, and his younger son a colonel in active service struggling to counteract the operations of Major Craig at Wilmington.

---

51 I am indebted to Miss Margaret H. Lillington, a great grand-daughter of General Lillington, for the materials of the following brief sketch of the public career of that officer:

JOHN ALEXANDER LILLINGTON, was the son of Colonel George Lillington, an officer in the British service, who, after being engaged in an expedition against the French in the West Indies, settled upon the island of Barbadoes, and became a member of the Royal Council in 1698. In that capacity he remained during the latter part of the reign of William and Mary, and the beginning of that of Queen Anne. His son, the subject of this memoir, captivated by the glowing accounts given of the Carolina country, emigrated thither, and settled within the present limits of New Hanover county.

The fine mansion delineated in the engraving, and known as Lillington Hall, is yet standing. It was built in 1734. Its location is near the great road leading from Wilmington to Newbern, on the northeast branch of the Cape Fear River, about thirty miles above Wilmington. When the "Hall" was erected, that part of Carolina was a wilderness, and the savannah or grassy opening where it stands, in the midst of vast pine forests, made it an oasis in the desert.

John Alexander inherited the military tastes of his father, and when the notes of preparation for the Revolutionary contest was heard all over the land, his skill was brought into requisition. His patriotic principles were early made known; and when the war broke out, we find him a member of the Wilmington Committee of Safety, and a colonel of militia. In the first battle fought at the South (Moore's Creek Bridge), described in the text, Colonel Lillington was conspicuous, with his neighbor and friend, Colonel Richard Caswell. Soon after this decisive battle, Colonel Lillington was promoted to brigadier. He served under General Gates in the Carolinas, in 1780. His son, Colonel John Lillington, also served with honor during this campaign. The silver crescents which each wore on his hat during the war are preserved by the family, and I am indebted to Miss Lillington for the opportunity of making a drawing of the one worn by the general. These crescents bear the initials of the names of the respective owners, and each has the motto, "LIBERTY OR DEATH," engraved upon it. The sketch is about half the size of the original.

General Lillington remained in service until the close of the war, when he retired to his estate at Lillington Hall. Near his mansion repose the remains of the general and his son. Over the grave of the

Lillington Hall

former is a marble slab, bearing the following Inscription: "Sacred to the memory of General JOHN ALEXANDER LILLINGTON, a soldier of the Revolution. He commanded the Americans in the battle of Moore's Creek, fought the twenty-seventh day of February, 1776, and by his military skill and cool courage in the field, at the head of his troops, secured a complete and decisive victory. To intellectual powers of a high order he united an incorruptible integrity, devoted and self-sacrificing patriotism. A genuine lover of liberty, he periled his all to secure the independence of his country, and died in a good old age, bequeathing to his posterity the remembrance of his virtues." Near his grave is that of his son, with a stone bearing the following inscription: "Sacred to the memory of Colonel JOHN LILLINGTON, son of General John Alexander Lillington; a patriot and soldier of the Revolution, he served his country faithfully during the entire war."

"General Lillington," writes Miss L., "is represented as a man of Herculean frame and strength. There are no portraits of him extant. Some few of his old slaves still remain (1852), who were children, of course, at the time, who can remember some of the events of the Revolution. It would be interesting to one unacquainted with the patriarchal relations of master and slave, to see how their aged faces kindle with enthusiasm when they speak of the kindness of 'Old Master,' and of 'Massa Jackie comin' hum from college in Philadelphia to help his father fight the British.' " On account of his uniform kindness to all, the fine mansion of General Lillington was saved from the torch by the interposition of many of his Tory neighbors.

52 Colonel Lillington, with the Wilmington battalion of minute-men, arrived at the bridge about four hours before Caswell, with his larger force, made his appearance. Caswell, who was the senior officer, took command of the whole patriot army.

53 Mrs. Ellett relates a noble instance of female heroism which this battle developed. The wife of Lieutenant Slocum, whose home was sixty miles distant from the scene of conflict, had dreamed, after her husband and his neighbors had departed with Caswell, that she saw him lying dead upon the ground. She awoke in great distress, arose, saddled a horse, and rode at full gallop in the direction the troops had taken. Through that thinly-settled and swampy country she pressed on, and at nine o'clock in the morning she heard the firing. As she came near the battle-ground, she saw a body lying in her husband's cloak, but it proved to be another man, who was wounded. She alighted, washed his face, bound up his wounds, and was administering comfort to another wounded man, when Caswell and her astonished husband came up. With true womanly feeling, she interceded for the life of the prisoner, attended to the wounded Loyalists through the day, and at midnight started for home. She did not tell her husband of her dream until his return. She rode one hundred and twenty-five miles in less than forty hours, and without one interval of rest! A mother's love, for she "wanted to see her child," impelled her to return with speed. The Carolinas were full of such heroic women as Mary Slocum when the storm of the Revolution swept over them. – See Mrs. Ellett's Domestic History of the Revolution, page 46; Women of the Revolution, i., 317-321.

54 The patriots captured thirteen wagons, three hundred and fifty guns and shot-bags, about one hundred and fifty swords and dirks, and fifteen hundred excellent rifles. – Gordon, ii., 37.

55 The Provincial Congress issued a manifesto on the twenty-ninth of April, respecting the Loyalists, in which they averred, "We have their security in contemplation, not to make them miserable. In our power, their errors claim our pity; their situation disarms our resentment. We shall hail their reformation with increasing pleasure, and receive them among us with open arms. . . . . . We war not with helpless females whom they have left behind; we sympathize in their sorrow, and wish to pour the balm of pity into the wounds which a separation from husbands, fathers, and the dearest relations has made. They are the rightful pensioners upon the charity and bounty of those who have aught to spare from their own necessities for the relief of their indigent fellow-creatures; to such we recommend them." Had such noble sentiments governed Cornwallis and his officers when they subdued the Carolinas, a few years later, they might have made their victory permanent. General M'Donald and his son, who held a colonel's commission, were granted liberal paroles of honor; and, during the summer, the general and twenty-five of his fellow-prisoners were exchanged at Philadelphia.

56 Governor JOSIAH MARTIN was a soldier by profession, and, in 1770, had risen to the rank of major in the British army. When Tryon was transferred to New York in 1771. Martin was appointed governor of North Carolina, and was the last royal chief magistrate of that colony. He was a man of considerable ability, urbane in manners, and sincerely desirous of promoting the best interests of the colony. After going to New York with Sir Henry Clinton, when driven from the colony, he joined the army, under Cornwallis, and was in the battle near Camden, where Gates was defeated. He was with Cornwallis in Carolina as late as April, 1781, when impaired health caused him to leave. He went to New York, spent a part of the summer at Rockaway, on Long island, and then sailed for England. He died in London, in July, 1786. Samuel Martin, who fought a duel with the celebrated John Wilkes in 1763, was the governor's brother. His father was Colonel Samuel Martin, of Virginia, who lost a large estate by confiscation. Judge Martin, the historian of North Carolina, computes the population of that state, when Governor Martin fled and the royal power ended, at one hundred and fifty thousand, more than one fifth of whom were slaves.

57 Gordon, ii., 36, 37; Foote, 143-145: Martin, ii., 380-384. On the fifth of May, 1776, Sir Henry Clinton issued a proclamation from the Pallas sloop of war, which declared North Carolina in a state of rebellion, ordered all Congresses to be dissolved, and offered pardon to all penitents, except the arch-rebels Cornelius Harnett and Robert Howe. The people laughed at him. Fired with indignation, he vented his spite upon the property of Colonel Howe. On the twelfth, he sent Cornwallis and a marauding party of nine hundred men on shore, who ravaged Howe's plantation in Brunswick, treated some women at his house with brutality, burned some mills in the neighborhood, and then returned to the ships. Despairing of success in that quarter, Clinton sailed with the British fleet of thirty vessels for New York.

58 The following gentlemen were appointed brigadiers: Richard Caswell, of Newbern; John Ashe, of Wilmington; Thomas Person,* of Hillsborough; Griffith Rutherford, of Salisbury, Edward Vail, of Edenton; and Allen Jones, of Halifax.

---

* Thomas Person had been one of the leading Regulators, and exceedingly active against the royal government. He was for many years a member of the State Senate. Person Hall, of the university at Chapel Hill, North Carolina, was so named to commemorate a munificent donation which he made to that institution.

---

59 The following gentlemen were appointed state officers under the Republican Constitution: RICHARD CASWELL, governor; JAMES GLASGOW, secretary of state; CORNELIUS HARNETT, THOMAS PERSON, WILLIAM DAY, WILLIAM HAYWOOD, EDWARD STARKEY, JOSEPH LEECH, and THOMAS EATON, counselors of state.

60 The committee consisted of William Hooper, Joseph Hewes, and Thomas Burke. The seal then adopted continues to be that of the state. The two figures represent respectively LIBERTY and PLENTY. Liberty holds the Constitution in one hand, and in the other a staff; with the cap of freedom, indicating the security of liberty by the Constitution. Clasped by one arm, Plenty holds a small bundle of wheat ears, and with the other supports an overflowing cornucopia, indicating the generous fertility of the soil of North Carolina.

61 This view is from the piazza of the Union Hotel. The building is of logs, covered with clap-boards. When James Monroe (afterward President of the United States) visited the Southern army in 1780, as military commissioner for Virginia, he used this building for his office while in Hillsborough.

62 The Haw River (which derives its name from the abundance of hawthorns in that region) rises in Rockingham and Guilford counties, and in Chatham county unites with the Deep River, and forms the northwest branch of the Cape Fear.

63 Cornwallis remained in Hilisborough about ten days. While a detachment of his army lay at the Red House, a short distance from the town, they occupied the Church of Hugh M'Aden, the first located missionary in North Carolina. Supposing M'Aden (then a short time in his grave) to have been a rebel, because he was a Presbyterian, the British burned his library and papers. His early journal escaped the flames. – Foote, 273.

64 Henry Lee was born at the family seat, in Stratford, on the twenty-ninth of January, 1756. He was educated at Princeton College, where he graduated in 1773. Fond of active life, and imbued with a military spirit, he sought and obtained the command of a company, in Colonel Bland's regiment of Virginia volunteers, in 1776. He joined the Continental army in September, 1777, where he soon attracted the favorable notice of Washington. He was promoted to the rank of major, in command of a separate corps of cavalry. On the sixth of November, 1780, Congress promoted him to lieutenant colonel, and ordered him to join the Southern army under General Greene, where his career was marked by great skill and bravery. His military exploits and the honors conferred upon him by Congress, are noticed in various places in this volume. In 1786, he was appointed a delegate to Congress, which position he held until the adoption of the Constitution. In 1791, he succeeded Beverly Randolph as governor of Virginia, and remained in office three years. He commanded the forces, by appointment of Washington, which were sent to quell the whisky insurrection in Pennsylvania. He was a member of Congress in 1799, and was chosen to pronounce a funeral oration at Washington, on the occasion of the death of the first president. He wrote his Memoirs of the War in the Southern Department of the United States, in 1808. He was active in quelling a mob in Baltimore in 1814, and from wounds received at that time he never fairly recovered. Toward the close of 1817, he repaired to the West Indies for the benefit of his health, but without success. Returning, he stopped at Cumberland Island, near St. Mary's, in Georgia, to visit Mrs. Shaw, the daughter of General Greene, where he died on the twenty-fifth of March, 1818, at the age of sixty-two years. The names of Lee, Marion, Morgan, Sumter, and Pickens form a brilliant galaxy in the Southern firmament of our Revolutionary history.

65 See Caruthers's Life of Caldwell, page 213.

66 The father of the late Secretary of the Navy.

67 Captain Eggleston was one of the most efficient cavalry officers in Lee's legion, during the campaigns further south the same year. We shall meet him hereafter.

Chapter XV

"Cornwallis led a country dance;
    The like was never seen, sir;
Much retrograde, and much advance,
    And all with General Greene, sir.
They rambled up and rambled down.
    Joined hands, and off they ran, sir;
Our General Greene to old Charlestown,
    And the earl to Wilmington, sir." 1

"There was Greene in the South; you must know him –
    Whom some called a "Hickory Quaker;"
But he ne'er turned his back on the foeman,
    Nor ever was known for a Shaker."
               – William Elliott

I left the place of Pyle's defeat toward noon, and, following a sinuous and seldom-traveled road through a forest of wild crab-apple trees and black jacks, crossed the Allamance at the cotton-factory of Holt and Carrigan, two miles distant. 2 Around this mill quite a village of neat log-houses, occupied by the operatives, were collected, and every thing had the appearance of thrift. I went in, and was pleased to see the hands of intelligent white females employed in a useful occupation. Manual labor by white people is a rare sight at the South, where an abundance of slave labor appears to render such occupation unnecessary; and it can seldom be said of one of our fair sisters there, "She layeth her hands to the spindle, and her hands hold the distaff." 3 This cotton-mill, like the few others which I saw in the Carolinas, is a real blessing, present and prospective, for it gives employment and comfort to many poor girls who might otherwise be wretched; and it is a seed of industry planted in a generous soil, which may hereafter germinate and bear abundant fruit of its kind in the midst of cotton plantations, thereby augmenting immensely the true wealth of the nation.

At a distance of two miles and a half beyond the Allamance, on the Salisbury road, I reached the Regulator battle-ground; and, in company with a young man residing in the vicinity, visited the points of particular interest. The rock and the ravine from whence James Pugh and his companions did such execution with their rifles, are now hardly visible. The place is a few rods north of the road. The ravine is almost filled by the washing down of earth from the slopes during eighty years; and the rock projects only a few ells above the surface. The whole of the natural scenery is changed, and nothing but tradition can identify the spot.

While viewing the battle-ground, the wind, which had been a gentle and pleasant breeze from the south all the morning, veered to the northeast, and brought omens of a cold storm. I left the borders of the Allamance, and its associations, at one o'clock, and traversing a very hilly country for eighteen miles, arrived, a little after dark, at Greensborough, a thriving, compact village, situated about five miles southeast from the site of old Guilford Court House. It is the capitol of Guilford county, and successor of old Martinsburg, where the court-house was formerly situated. Very few of the villages in the interior of the state appeared to me more like a Northern town than Greensborough. The houses are generally good, and the stores gave evidences of active trade. Within an hour after my arrival, the town was thrown into commotion by the bursting out of flames from a large frame dwelling, a short distance from the court-house. There being no fire-engine in the place, the flames spread rapidly, and at one time menaced the safety of the whole town. A small keg of powder was used, without effect, to demolish a tailor's shop, standing in the path of the conflagration toward a large tavern. The flames passed on, until confronted by one of those broad chimneys, on the outside of the house, so universally prevalent at the South, when it was subdued, after four buildings were destroyed. I never saw a population more thoroughly frightened; and when I returned to my lodgings, far away from the fire, every bed in the house was packed ready for flight. It was past midnight when the town became quiet, and a consequently late breakfast delayed my departure for the battle-field at Guilford Court House, until nine o'clock the next morning.

A cloudy sky, a biting north wind, and the dropping of a few snow-flakes when I left Greensborough, betokened an unpleasant day for my researches. It was ten o'clock when I reached Martinsville, once a pleasant hamlet, now a desolation. There are only a few dilapidated and deserted dwellings left; and nothing remains of the old Guilford Court House but the ruins of a chimney, depicted on the plan of the battle. Only one house was inhabited, and that by the tiller of the soil around it. Descending into a narrow, broken valley, from Martinsville, and ascending the opposite slope to still higher ground on the road to Salem, I passed among the fields consecrated by the events of the battle at Guilford, on March 15, 1781, to the house of Mr. Hotchkiss, a Quaker, who, I was informed could point out every locality of interest in his neighborhood. Mr. Hotchkiss was absent, and I was obliged to wait more than an hour for his return. The time passed pleasantly in conversation with his daughter, an intelligent young lady, who kindly ordered my horse to be fed, and regaled me with some fine apples, the first fruit of the kind I had seen since leaving the James River. While tarrying there, the snow began to fall thickly, and when, about noon, I rambled over the most interesting portion of the battle-ground, and sketched the scene, the whole country was covered with a white mantle. Here, by this hospitable fireside, let us consider the battle, and those wonderful antecedent events which distinguished General Greene's celebrated RETREAT.

After the unlucky battle near Camden, where General Gates lost the laurels he had obtained at Saratoga, Congress perceived the necessity of appointing a more efficient commander for the army in the Southern Department, and directed General Washington to make the selection. The commander-in-chief appointed General Nathaniel Greene on October 30, 1780, late the quarter-master general, who immediately proceeded to his field of labor. 4 Passing through Delaware, Maryland, and Virginia, he ascertained what supplies he was likely to obtain from those states; and leaving the Baron Steuben to direct the defense of Virginia, and to raise levies and stores for the Southern army, he proceeded to Hillsborough, the seat of government of North Carolina. Governor Nash received him with joy, for the dangers which menaced the state were imminent. After remaining there a few days, he hastened on to Charlotte, the head-quarters of the army. General Gates received him with great respect, and on the day after his arrival he took formal command of the army (Dec. 3, 1780). Gates immediately set out for the head-quarters of Washington (then in New Jersey, near the Hudson), to submit to an inquiry into his conduct, which had been ordered by Congress on October 5, 1780. From that time until the commencement of his retreat from the Carolinas, Greene was exceedingly active in the arrangement of the army, and in wisely directing its movements.

His first arrangement was to divide his army into two detachments, the largest of which, under himself, was to be stationed opposite Cheraw Hill, on the east side of the Peedee River, in Chesterfield District, upon a small stream called Hick's Creek, about seventy miles to the right of Cornwallis, who was then at Winnsborough, in Fairfield District. The other, composed of about one thousand troops, under General Morgan, was placed some fifty miles to the left, near the junction of the Broad and Pacolet Rivers, in Union District. Cornwallis sent Colonel Tarleton, with a considerable force, to disperse the little army of Morgan, and soon the memorable battle of the Cowpens occurred on January 17, 1781, in which the Americans were victorious. Tarleton, with the remnant of his troops, retreated precipitately to the main army of Cornwallis, who was then at Turkey Creek; and Morgan, in the evening of the same day, crossed the Broad River, and moved, by forced marches, toward the Catawba, to form a junction with the division of General Greene.

When Cornwallis heard of the defeat of Tarleton and the direction that Morgan had taken, he resolved on pursuit, with the hope of regaining the prisoners taken at the Cowpens, and of demolishing the Americans before they could reach the Catawba. He was joined on the eighteenth by General Leslie and his troops, from Camden. To facilitate his march, he ordered all the superfluous baggage and wagons to be destroyed on January 25, at Ramsour's Mills, on the south fork of the Catawba. 5 In the mean while, General Greene had been apprised of the battle and the result, and on the same day when Cornwallis commenced pursuit, he ordered Brigadier Stevens to march with his Virginia militia (whose term of service was almost expired) by way of Charlotte, to take Morgan's prisoners and conduct them to Charlottesville, in Virginia. Greene, anxious to confer with Morgan personally, left the camp on the Pedee, under the command of General Huger and Colonel Otho H. Williams, and started, with one aid and two or three mounted militia, for the Catawba (Jan. 28). On the route he was informed of Cornwallis's pursuit, and immediately sent an express to Huger and Williams to break up the camp, and march with all possible dispatch to form a junction with Morgan's light troops at Salisbury or Charlotte. Greene reached Sherrard's Ford, on the Catawba, on the thirty-first, where he had an interview with Morgan, and directed his future movements.

The pursuit by Cornwallis had been keen and untiring. He had kept between the Broad and the Catawba Rivers, and his sole efforts were to reach the fords toward which Morgan was pressing, in time to cut him off. Morgan's march was equally rapid, and he crossed the Catawba at the Island Ford, on the northern border of the present Lincoln county, with his prisoners and baggage on January 28, 1781, two hours before the arrival of the British van-guard, under Brigadier-general O'Hara. It was sunset, and the earl, confident of his prey, postponed further pursuit until morning. This delay was fatal to his success. Rain fell copiously during the night, and in the morning the Catawba was brimful, and entirely unfordable. Thus it remained for forty-eight hours; and in the mean while Morgan's prisoners were sent forward to a place of safety, and measures were adopted to dispute the passage of the river with the British. Had the flood in the river happened a few hours earlier, Morgan's little army must have been lost. The event was properly marked by the friends of liberty as the tangible interposition of Providence. The arrival of Greene, at this juncture, was equally providential; for Morgan had resolved upon a line of retreat which must have proved fatal. Greene interposed counter orders, and the whole army was saved.

When the waters subsided, Cornwallis resumed his pursuit. Lieutenant-colonel Webster, with a small detachment, moved toward Beattie's Ford, to give the impression that the British army would cross there;

husband of Flora. The Loyalists lost seventy men in killed and wounded; the Americans had only two wounded, and one of them survived. **54** Colonel Moore arrived soon after the engagement ended, and that evening the men of the united forces of the patriots slept soundly upon the field of their victory.

Cornwallis's Office.

The effect of this defeat of the Loyalists was of vast importance to the Patriot cause in North Carolina. It exhibited the courage and skill of the defenders of liberty, and completely broke the spirit of the Loyalists. It prevented a general organization of the Tories, and their junction with the forces under Sir Henry Clinton, which arrived in the Cape Fear in May, upon which the royal power in the South depended for vitality. The opposers of that power were encouraged, and the timid and wavering were compelled to make a decision. The kindness extended to the prisoners and their families won the esteem of all, and many Loyalists were converted to the Republican faith by the noble conduct of the victors. **55** The plans of the governor, and of Sir Henry Clinton and Lord William Campbell, were, for the time, completely frustrated, and Martin **56** soon afterward abdicated government, and took refuge on board the Bristol, the flag-ship of Sir Peter Parker. **57** Royal government in North Carolina now ceased forever, and a brighter era in the history of the state was opened.

The provincial council now labored vigorously in the elaboration of measures for the defense of the colony, and the maintenance of liberty. A strong military establishment was organized, and in each district a brigadier general was appointed, with an efficient corps of field-officers. **58** On the eighteenth of December, 1776, a state government was formed under a Constitution, **59** and, a few days afterward, a device for a great seal of the commonwealth was presented by a committee appointed for the purpose, and adopted. **60** In all their actions, the Carolinians exhibited the aspect of men determined to be free, and conscious that hope for reconciliation with the mother country was vain. A blow had been struck

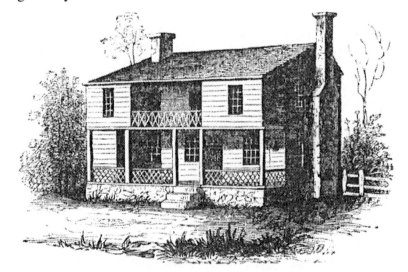

Cornwallis's Head-Quarters.

which marked out the bright line of future operations. There could no longer be hesitation, and the line between Whigs and Tories was as distinctly drawn as that of the twilight between the day and the night.

The siege of Charleston, and other events of the war which speedily followed the battle on Moore's Creek, will be detailed hereafter. From this time until the close of the Revolution, the military history of North Carolina is identified with that of the whole confederacy. From the time of the battle on Moore's Creek until Cornwallis and his army overran the Carolinas, there were no regularly organized bands of Loyalists in the "Old North State."

Here let us close the chronicle for a day, and ride on toward the fertile region of the Allamance, after glancing at noteworthy objects in Hillsborough.

I employed the first morning of the new year (Jan. 1, 1849), in visiting places of interest at Hillsborough, in company with the Reverend Dr. Wilson. The first object to which my attention was called was a small wooden building, represented in the engraving above, situated opposite the hotel where I was while Cornwallis, decamping at midnight with the main body, moved rapidly toward Cowan's Ford, six miles below. This was a private crossing-place, and the earl supposed he would thus elude the vigilance of Greene and Morgan. It was a miscalculation, as numerous camp-fires assured him when he approached the ford, a little before dawn on February 1, 1781. General Davidson, the commander in Salisbury District, who had arrived the day before with three hundred North Carolina militia, was sent by Greene, who was

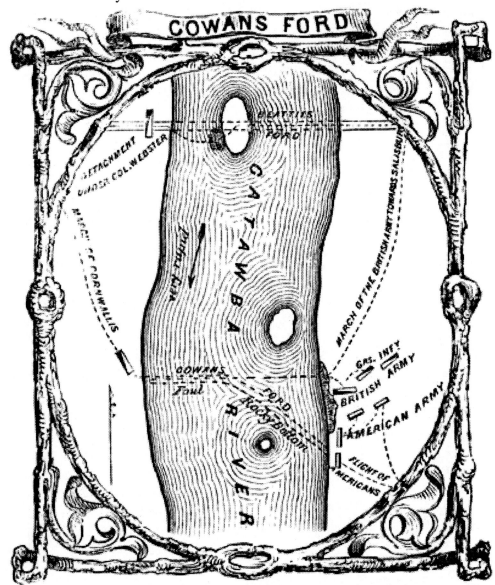

quartered at Salisbury, **6** to guard the ford and dispute its passage if attempted. Neglecting to place his main body near the river, so as to make an imposing appearance, he did not deter Cornwallis from proceeding to cross. The current was rapid, the stream in many places waist-deep, and almost five hundred yards wide, yet the brave Britons, led on by General O'Hara, plunged into the stream, and in the face of a severe fire from Captain Graham's' **7** riflemen, who were posted at the ford, pressed forward to the opposite bank. **8** The British reserved their fire until they had gained the shore, and then, pouring a few volleys into the ranks of Graham, soon dispersed them. While ascending the bank, Colonel Hall, of the British army, was killed. General Davidson was stationed half a mile from the ford, with the main body of the militia. Hearing the firing, he hastened to the spot, with Colonel William Polk and the Reverend Thomas M'Caule. They arrived just as the Americans were about to flee. Davidson was the last upon the ground, and as he turned to follow his troops he was shot dead by a rifle ball. **9** The militia were entirely routed; and all the fords being abandoned, Cornwallis, with the whole royal army, crossed the Catawba without further molestation. **10** The militia reassembled at Tarrant's tavern, about ten miles distant. Tarleton, who had been sent with his cavalry in pursuit, hastened to their rendezvous, made a furious charge, broke through their center, killed quite a number, and dispersed the whole. A heavy rain had injured their powder, and they were not prepared to fight. The loss of General Davidson, and the total dispersion of the militia, greatly dispirited the patriots in that region, and Toryism again became bold and active.

Now fairly commenced the great race between Greene and Cornwallis; the goal was the Dan, the prize the possession of the Carolinas.

General Greene had hoped, by guarding the fords on the Catawba with the light troops under Morgan, to prevent the passage of the British army until Huger and Williams should arrive with the other divisions of the American forces. The passage at Cowan's Ford destroyed these hopes, and Morgan and his light troops retreated precipitately toward the Yadkin. The detachment of Lieutenant-colonel Webster crossed at Beattie's Ford, and joined Cornwallis the next day (Feb. 2), on the road to Salisbury, five miles from the crossing-place. The royal army rested at Salisbury **11** that night, and the next morning started in pursuit of Greene and Morgan. These officers did not await the dawn, but passed the Yadkin at Trading Ford (see cut below), while Cornwallis was slumbering; and when, on the morning of the third, the earl hastened to strike a fatal blow on the banks of that stream, the Americans were beyond his reach, and Providence had again placed an impassable barrier of water between them. Another copious rain in the mountains had swollen the Yadkin to a mighty river. The horses of Morgan had forded the stream at midnight, and the infantry passed over in bateaux at dawn. These vessels were secured on the east shore of the Yadkin, and Cornwallis was obliged to wait for the waters to subside before he could cross. Again he had the Americans almost within his grasp. A corps of riflemen were yet on the west side when O'Hara, with the van-guard, approached, but these escaped across the river, after a smart skirmish of a few minutes. Nothing was lost but a few wagons belonging to the Whigs who were fleeing with the American army, with their effects.

Trading Ford. 12

Greene now pushed on toward Guilford Court House, where he arrived on February 7, 1781. He had dispatched an order to Huger and Williams to march directly to that point, and join him there. This order was promptly obeyed, and these officers, with their commands, arrived there on the same day with Greene and Morgan. Lieutenant-colonel Lee and his legion, who had been on an expedition to Georgetown, seventy-five miles below Cheraw, overtook them on their march, and that gallant corps was now added to the concentrated strength of the Americans. The army, lying at rest **13** on the slopes around Martinsville, was mustered on the eighth, and amounted to about two thousand men, including five hundred militia. Of this number nearly two hundred were superior cavalry. The army of Cornwallis in pursuit, was between two thousand five hundred and three thousand strong, of which three hundred were mounted men.

Perceiving no prospect of the falling of the river, for the rain continued, Cornwallis marched as rapidly as possible up the western side of the Yadkin to the shallow ford near the present village of Huntsville, in Surrey county, where he crossed. There he was informed of the junction of the two divisions of the American army, and the hope of keeping them separate was extinguished. An attempt to intercept their march toward Virginia, and compel Greene to fight or surrender, was now the chief object of the earl's solicitude. Upon the success of this undertaking depended not only the maintenance of his power in the Carolinas, but perhaps the actual existence of his army. He knew the inferiority of the American army in numbers, and being assured that the rivers which lay between Greene and Virginia were too much swollen to be forded, and the ferries too wide apart to furnish a sufficient number of boats at one point to transport the retreating army across, he felt confident of success. His lordship was now within twenty-five miles of

Greene, at Guilford, and nearer the shallow fords of the Dan than he was; and on the ninth of February, 1781, he resumed his march with vigor, to gain a position in front of the Americans.

Greene, also aware of the inferiority of his forces, called a council of war on February 9, when it was resolved to avoid a battle, and retreat as rapidly as possible across the Dan into the friendly districts of Virginia. A light army, designed to maneuver in the rear of the Americans and in front of the pursuers, was formed out of Lee's legion, the regular battalion of infantry under Colonel Howard, the cavalry under Colonel Washington, and a small corps of Virginia riflemen under Major Campbell, in all about seven hundred men, the flower of the Southern army. General Morgan, who was worn down by fatigue, and tortured by rheumatism, expressed a desire to quit the service. Greene was embarrassed, for he was at a loss how to supply the place of the brave partisan, and wished him to command the light corps just organized.

Morgan declined, and Greene bestowed the honor upon his deputy adjutant general, Colonel Otho Holland Williams, a brave young officer of the Maryland line, who proved himself worthy of the confidence of his commander. 14 Williams entered upon his command on the morning of the tenth, and on that day the whole army moved toward the Dan at a point seventy miles from Guilford Court House.

The two armies moved in lines almost parallel with each other, Greene on the right, and Cornwallis on the left. Colonel Williams, with his light corps, took an intermediate road, to watch the movements of the enemy. Lee's "partisan legion," which maneuvered in the rear, was often in sight of O'Hara's van-guard. Great vigilance was necessary at night to prevent a surprise, and so numerous were the patrols, that each man on the march enjoyed only six hours sleep in forty-eight. Williams always moved at three o'clock in the morning, so as to get a sufficient distance in advance to partake of breakfast, the only meal they were allowed each day. Cornwallis was equally active, and both armies made the extraordinary progress of thirty miles a day.

On the morning of the thirteenth, while a portion of the light troops were eating breakfast at a farm-house, they were informed by a friendly countryman, who came from his plow for the purpose, that the British army had left their direct route, and were only four miles in the rear, upon the road they were marching. Lee dispatched Captain Mark Armstrong, one of the most efficient of his cavalry officers, to reconnoiter, and his whole camp was soon in commotion. Lee, with a considerable force, concealed himself in a wood, to await the approach of the British van. Soon a sharp firing was heard, and Captain Armstrong came dashing by where Lee was posted, with some of Tarleton's cavalry, under Captain Miller, in hot pursuit. Lee instantly gained the road, and made such a fierce charge upon the pursuers that he completely broke their ranks, killing a large number. Captain Miller was made prisoner, and narrowly escaped hanging, for Lee charged him with the murder of his bugler, a lad of eighteen, who, while hastening to Williams, was overtaken and sabred by the British cavalry. 15 Lee was about to hang him upon a tree, when the British van appeared, and Miller was sent on to General Greene as a prisoner of war. In this skirmish eighteen of the British dragoons were killed; the Americans lost only the little bugler. The dead were buried by Cornwallis, an hour afterward.

In the course of the day another encounter occurred. Lee's troops had been deprived of their morning meal, which was half cooked when the countryman gave the alarm. By taking a road shorter and more secluded than the one passed by Williams, he hoped to gain time to dine at a well-stocked farm. He did not apprehend a surprise, for the road was only a by-way. He stationed a few videttes, however, to watch, and well he did. Just as the horses were about to partake of their provender, and the soldiers of corn bread and bacon, the videttes fired an alarm and came dashing toward the main body. Battle or flight was the alternative. Before them was a swollen stream spanned by a single bridge; to gain and hold this, was an object of vital importance to Lee. His infantry were ordered to run and take possession of it, while the cavalry prepared to cover a retreat. The van of the British were surprised at this meeting, not being aware of the proximity of their foe, and while halting to receive orders, Lee's troops had an opportunity to pass the bridge. The British soon followed, and across a cultivated plain both parties sped with all their might. The Americans had the strongest and fleetest horses, and, ascending a hill to its summit, they entered upon the great road leading to Irwin's Ferry, on the Dan. All day long O'Hara, with the van of the British army, continued in pursuit, and was frequently in sight of Lee's legion; sometimes within rifle-shot. Thus again escaped this right arm of the Southern army. Vigilance – sleepless vigilance alone, under Providence, preserved it.

The night that succeeded was dark, cold, and drizzly. Cornwallis and his whole army were directly in the rear of the Americans, and now was his only chance for striking an effective blow, for another day, and Greene might be beyond the Dan. The British commander resolved to push forward with the hope of overtaking his prey before morning. Williams and the wearied troops of Lee were compelled to do the same to avoid an encounter. They were ignorant of the position of Greene, and felt great anxiety for his safety. At eight o'clock, they were much alarmed by the apparition of camp fires, a mile in advance, supposing it to be the camp of Greene, and that Cornwallis would inevitably overtake him. Williams prepared to confront and annoy the enemy while Greene should escape. This sacrifice was unnecessary, for the camp fires were those Greene had lighted two nights before, and had been kept burning by friendly people in the neighborhood. With glad hearts the light troops pressed forward, until assured that the enemy had halted for the night, when they lighted fires, laid down, and slumbered for three or four hours.

Only forty miles now intervened between Cornwallis and the Dan. His rest was brief, and before dawn he was again in pursuit. The roads, passing through a red clay region, were wretched in the extreme, yet the pursued and the pursuers pushed forward rapidly. It was the last stake for the prize, and eagerly both parties contended for it. During the forenoon, only a single hour was allowed by the belligerents for a repast. At noon a loud shout went up from the American host; a courier, covered with mud, his horse reeking with sweat, brought a letter to Colonel Williams from Greene, announcing the joyful tidings that he had *crossed the Dan safely at Irwin's Ferry on the preceding day* (Feb. 13, 1781). That shout was heard by O'Hara, and Cornwallis regarded it as ominous of evil. Still he pressed forward. At three o'clock, when within fourteen miles of the river, Williams filed off toward Boyd's Ferry, leaving Lee to maneuver in front of the enemy. Williams reached the shore before sunset, and at dark was landed upon the north side. Lee sent his infantry on in advance, and at twilight withdrew with his cavalry, and galloped for the river. When he arrived, his infantry had just passed in boats with safety. The horses were turned into the stream, while the dragoons embarked in bateaux. At nine o'clock, Lieutenant-colonels Lee and Carrington (the quarter-master general **16**), embarked in the last boat, and before midnight the wearied troops were in deep slumber in the bosom of Virginia. During the evening Cornwallis heard of the passage of Greene, and the escape of Williams and his light troops. The Dan was too much swollen to be forded; every boat was moored upon the northern shore, and for the third time a barrier of water interposed between the pursuer and pursued. The prize was lost, and with a heavy heart Cornwallis moved slowly back toward Hillsborough, after resting his wearied troops for a day. He had but one hope left, the promised general rising of the Tories in North Carolina, now that the "rebel army" was driven out of the state. Greene encamped in the rich and friendly district of Halifax county, in Virginia, and there his wearied troops reposed after one of the most skillfully conducted and remarkable retreats on record. **17** Upon this movement all eyes were turned, and when the result was known the friends of liberty every where chanted a loud alleluiah.

As we have observed, Greene soon prepared to recross the Dan, and attempt to retrieve his losses in Carolina. We have considered the first movements toward the accomplishment of this object – the expedition of Lee and Pickens beyond the Haw, the defeat of Pyle, and the retreat of Tarleton to

Hillsborough. The success of this enterprise, the arrival in camp of General Stevens, with six hundred Virginia militia, and the necessity of making a demonstration before the Tories should rise, caused Greene to break up his camp after a few days of repose. He recrossed the Dan on February 23, 1781, and this event being made known, completely dispirited the Loyalists who were disposed to join the royal army. The recruiting service stopped, and the friends of government, awed by the fate of Pyle's corps, stood still. The situation of Cornwallis was full of peril. The country around Hillsborough was speedily stripped of provision by his army, **18** and he found it expedient to fall back and take a new position upon the south side of the Allamance, west of the Haw on February 27. On the same day, Lee and Pickens, with their respective forces, joined the main body of the American light infantry, and the whole corps crossed the Haw, a little below the mouth of Buffalo Creek. Greene, with the main army augmented by the North Carolina militia, crossed above Buffalo Creek the next morning (Feb. 28), and encamped between Troublesome Creek and Reedy Fork. It was an ineligible place; and, hoping to gain time for all his expected re-enforcements to come in, Greene constantly changed his position, and placed Colonel Williams and his light corps between the two armies, now within a score of miles of each other. Tarleton occupied the same relative position to the British army, and he and Williams frequently menaced each other. Finally, the latter having approached to within a mile of the British camp, Tarleton attacked him on March 2, 1781, and a brief but warm skirmish ensued. This encounter was sustained, on the part of the Americans, chiefly by Lee's legion and Preston's riflemen. About thirty of the enemy were killed and wounded. The Americans sustained no loss. In the mean while, Greene's constant change of position, sometimes seen on the Troublesome Creek, and sometimes appearing near Guilford, gave the impression that his force was larger than it really was, and Cornwallis was much perplexed. Well knowing that the American army was augmenting by the arrival of militia, he resolved to bring Greene to action at once. Under cover of a thick fog, he crossed the Allamance on March 6, hoping to beat up Williams's quarters, then between that stream and Reedy Fork, and surprise Greene. Williams's vigilant patrols discovered the approach of the enemy at about eight o'clock in the morning, on the road to Wetzell's Mill, an important pass on the Reedy Fork. Lee's legion immediately maneuvered in front of the enemy, while Williams withdrew his light troops and other corps of regulars and militia across the stream.**19** A covering party, composed of one hundred and fifty Virginia militia, were attacked by Lieutenant-colonel Webster, with one thousand British infantry and a portion of Tarleton's cavalry. The militia boldly returned the-fire, and then fled across the creek. The British infantry followed, **20** and met with a severe attack from Campbell's riflemen and Lee's infantry. Webster was quickly re-enforced by some Hessians and chasseurs, and the whole were supported by field-pieces planted by Cornwallis upon an eminence near the banks of the stream. The artillery dismayed the militia, which Williams perceiving, ordered them to retire. He followed with Howard's battalion, flanked by Kirkwood's Delaware infantry and the infantry of Lee's legion, the whole covered by Washington's cavalry. **21** The day was far spent, and Cornwallis did not pursue. In this skirmish the Americans lost about fifty killed and wounded.

As soon as Greene heard of the approach of Cornwallis, he fell back across the head waters of the Haw with the main army, determined not to risk an engagement until the arrival of re-enforcements, now fast approaching. In the mean while he changed his position daily, and Cornwallis, who, unwilling to wear down his army by useless attempts to strike the Americans in detail, had retired slowly to Bell's Mills on the Deep River, about thirteen miles below the present Jamestown, could gain no positive information concerning him. **22** At length, while encamped at Speedwell's iron-works, on Troublesome Creek, northeast of Guilford, Greene was joined by a brigade of militia from Virginia, under General Lawson; two from North Carolina, under Generals Butler and Eaton; and four hundred regulars, raised for eighteen months on March 10. He now felt strong enough to grapple with the earl, and the light corps of Colonel Williams was incorporated with the main army.**23** Crossing the Haw and Reedy Fork, Greene encamped in battle order near Guilford Court House on March 13. The movements of the two generals during the ten preceding days were of great interest. They were contending for a prize of the greatest value. One false step by either party would have been his ruin. None were more interested spectators than the Tories, from whom Cornwallis fondly anticipated aid. When Greene invited battle, they were utterly amazed, and not one dared lift his arm in defense of the king, the issue being so doubtful.

Cornwallis, in the mean while, had advanced from Deep Reep River toward New Garden (Quaker) meeting-house. Perceiving Greene's disposition to fight, he gladly prepared to meet him. It was an event he had been trying to accomplish for more than six weeks. Sending his baggage back to Bell's Mills, on the evening of the fourteenth, under a proper escort, he moved forward at dawn the next morning (March 15), with twenty-four hundred men, chiefly veterans. The vigilant Lee, with his legion, was near New Garden meeting-house when the van of the British army, consisting of cavalry, some light infantry, and yagers, under Lieutenant-colonel Tarleton, **24** approached. Desirous of drawing them as far from the royal army, and as near Greene's as possible, Lee ordered a change of front, and a slow retreat. Hoping to produce a route, Tarleton and his cavalry pressed forward upon Armstrong, who was now in the rear, but with little effect. They made a second charge, and emptied their pistols, when Lee, with the troops of Rudolph and Eggleston, advanced upon Tarleton. The moment Tarleton saw the whole cavalry of the legion pressing upon him, he sounded a retreat; for he well knew the superiority of the horses of the Americans. **25** Only one front section of the British cavalry met the shock, and these were all dismounted, and most of the horses were prostrated. Some of the dragoons were killed, and others made prisoners. The Americans lost neither man nor horse. Tarleton, with the remainder of his corps, withdrew in great haste, and sought to gain the main army. Lee did not pursue, but endeavored to cut off Tarleton's retreat. While pushing forward with eager hope, he met the British van-guard, in the midst of the lofty oaks at the meeting-house. They instantly displayed, and gave his cavalry a terrible volley. Lee ordered a retreat, when his infantry came running up, and delivered a well-directed fire. This was followed by a volley from Campbell's riflemen, who had taken post on the left of the infantry, and a general action ensued. It had continued but a few minutes, when Lee, perceiving that the main body of the British was approaching, ordered a general retreat; his cavalry falling in the rear, to cover the infantry and riflemen. **26** During this skirmish, Greene prepared for battle.

From Guilford Court House southward, the ground slopes abruptly, terminating in a broken vale, through which winds a small stream. At the time of the engagement, there were pretty broad clearings around the court-house, which extended southward along the great Salisbury road. On either side of the road, and crossing it at some distance from the court-house, was a forest of lofty oaks. Within the southern border of this forest, and concealed behind a fence and some dwarf trees, lay the North Carolina forces *(B)*, militia and volunteers, and some riflemen, the whole under Generals Butler and Eaton. They were strongly posted, and much was expected of them. Within the woods, about three hundred yards in the rear of the first line, the second line *(C)* was formed. It was composed of the Virginia militia, under Generals Stevens and Lawson; **27** the right flank of Stevens, and the left flank of Lawson, resting on the road. The Continental infantry, consisting of four regiments, were drawn up near the court-house, in the field, on the north side of the road, about four hundred yards in the rear of the Virginians. The two Continental regiments of Virginia were commanded by Colonel Greene and Lieutenant-colonel Hewes, under Brigadier Huger, and composed the right. The two Maryland regiments, led by Colonel Gunby and Lieutenant-colonel Ford, were under Colonel Williams, and composed the left. The remainder of the troops, under Greene, lay near the court-house. Only Gunby's regiment were experienced soldiers; the remainder were new recruits. Lieutenant-

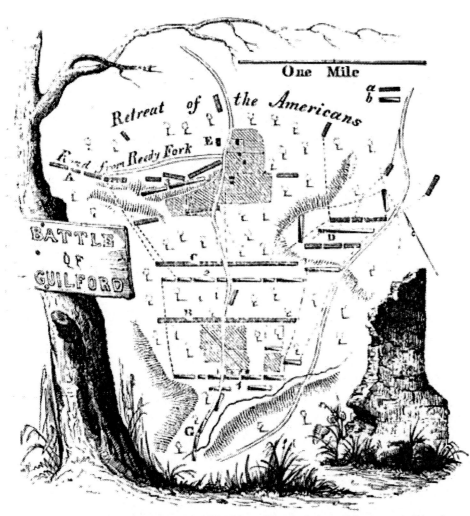

colonel Washington, with his cavalry, the old Delaware corps, under Captain Kirkwood, and Colonel Lynch with a battalion of Virginia militia, were posted on the right; Lieutenant-colonel Lee, with his legion, and the Virginia riflemen, under Colonel Campbell, were posted on the left, each being ordered to support the respective flanks. Captain Singleton, with two six pounders, took post in the road, a little in advance of the front line, and the remainder of the artillery (only two pieces) were with the rear line, near the court-house.

Such was the disposition of the Americans for battle when the royal army, under Cornwallis, approached. It was about noon; the sun was unclouded, and the air was cool, but not cold. They could be seen for more than a mile, defiling *(G)* from the Salisbury road into the open fields, and presented a gorgeous spectacle; their scarlet uniforms and burnished arms strongly contrasting with the somber aspect of the country, then barren of leaves and grass. Having formed their line, they approached slowly and steadily, chiefly in solid column *(1)*, to the contest. As soon as the van appeared, Singleton opened a cannonade upon it, but with little effect. Lieutenant M'Leod, commanding the British artillery, pressed forward along the road, and

NOTE. – Explanation of the Plan. – The shaded parallelograms, A, B, and C, and others not lettered, represent American troops; the half shaded ones the British troops. G, the British columns advancing along the road from the direction of the New Garden meeting-house. 1. Their first position, in battle order. B, the first American line, consisting of North Carolina militia, posted at the head of a ravine, in the edge of a wood. C, the second American line, of Virginia militia. A, the American right wing, extending along the road to Reedy Fork, to its junction with the main road, near the court-house. E, the Maryland and Virginia Continentals, under Huger and Williams. 2. The second position of the British, after the retreat of the Carolinians. 3. The third position of the British, endeavoring to gain Greene's right. D, severe conflict between Leslie with the Hessians and the Americans. E, Guilford Court House. The broken chimney in the corner of the map represents all that is left of the old court-house.

returned the fire, also with little effect. The battle now commenced. Although Cornwallis knew his inferiority of numbers, and the great advantages of Greene's position, he boldly began what he had so long sought an opportunity for – a general battle with his antagonist. He had brave and veteran troops. The 71st (Fraser's Highland regiment), with the Hessian regiment of Bose, formed his right, under General Leslie; his left consisted of the 23d and 33d regiments, under the command of Lieutenant-colonel Webster. The royal artillery, led by M'Leod, and supported by the light infantry of the guards and the yagers, moved along the road in the center. Lieutenant-colonel Norton, with the first battalion of the guards, supported the right, and Brigadier O'Hara, with the grenadiers and second battalion of guards, supported the left.

After a brisk cannonade of nearly half an hour, Singleton, pursuant to orders, fell back to the second line, when Leslie, with the guards in the center, the Hessians on the extreme left, and Webster's brigade, with Norton's battalion, on the right, immediately advanced upon the North Carolinians, who were concealed behind a fence in the edge of the wood. When the British were within rifle shot, the Carolinians commenced a desultory fire upon them. The British pressed steadily forward, and when at a proper distance, discharged their guns, and with a loud shout rushed forward to a bayonet charge. The North Carolinians wheeled and fled in great confusion, though not a man had been killed, or even wounded. Only a few of General Eaton's men were exempt from the panic, and these, falling back upon Lee's legion and Campbell's riflemen, maintained their ground well. Butler and Eaton, with Colonel Davie, the commissary general, endeavored, but in vain, to rally the fugitives. Throwing away their muskets, knapsacks, and even canteens, they rushed through the woods like frightened deer, until far beyond the point of danger. **28** Had the first line done its duty, the result of the battle must have been far different; for the few that remained with Campbell, together with his corps, maintained their position so manfully that Leslie was obliged to order Lieutenant-colonel Norton into line for his support. The cowardly flight of the Carolinians left Lee's legion exposed to the danger of being cut off from the main body. The Virginians of the second line, upon whom the first had partially retreated, did their duty nobly, **29** until, being hard pressed by the British, the right of that line, under General Lawson, wheeled round upon the left, and retreated in confusion, back to the line of regulars. Lieutenant-colonel Webster, with the British left, now advanced across the open fields, in the face of a terrible fire from the Americans, and gallantly attacked their right, while Leslie and Bose were in fierce conflict with the American left. The whole of the British infantry were now engaged in action. The Virginians, under Stevens and Lawson, combated vigorously with Webster, while supported on the right by Washington and his cavalry. That officer sent Lynch's battalion of riflemen to fall upon the flank of Webster. Perceiving this, O'Hara, with the grenadiers and second battalion of guards, hastened to the support of the left. Webster immediately turned the 33d regiment upon Lynch, and relieved his flank from annoyance. O'Hara, advancing at that instant with the remainder of the left, with fixed bayonets, aided by the 71st, under Leslie, compelled first Lawson's and then Stevens's brigade to give way, and the second line of the Americans was broken up.

In the mean while, the action on the right *(D)*, between the regiment of Bose and the riflemen, and the legion infantry, was unremitting. The portion of the British force thus engaged could not be brought to bear upon the third line of the Americans, now well supported by Colonel Washington at the head of his cavalry, and Captain Kirkwood with his brave Delawares. Greene felt hopeful, and, riding along the lines, exhorted his battalions to stand firm, and give the final blow which would secure victory. Webster pressed forward over the ground lately occupied by the Virginia militia *(C)* to attack the right wing of the Continentals. There stood Colonel Gunby and Lieutenant-colonel Howard, with the first Maryland regiment, ready to do battle. The British, with great courage, rushed forward, and engaged in a close fire. The Marylanders, nobly sustained by Howe's Virginia regiment and Kirkwood's Delawares, received the shock so valiantly, that Webster recoiled and fell back across a ravine, where, upon an elevation, he awaited the arrival of the remainder of his line. Very soon Lieutenant-colonel Stuart, with the first battalion of guards, followed by two other small corps, swept across the open fields, and attacked the second Maryland regiment, under Colonel Ford, which was supported by Captain Finley with two six pounders. Colonel Williams expected to observe bravery on the part of his second regiment, like that of the first, and hastened toward it to combine his whole force in repelling the attack, but he was disappointed. It gave way at the first shock, fled, and abandoned the two field-pieces to the enemy. Stuart pursued, when Gunby, who had been left free by the recession of Webster to the other side of the ravine, wheeled upon him, and a very severe conflict ensued. Lieutenant-colonel Washington, who was upon the flank of the Continentals, pressed forward with his cavalry, and Stuart was soon compelled to give way. With sword in hand, followed by his cavalry, and Howard and his infantry with fixed bayonets, Washington furiously charged the British, and put them to flight. **30** Stuart was slain by Captain Smith of the first Maryland regiment, the two field-pieces were retaken, and great slaughter ensued. The whole of Stuart's corps would have been killed or made prisoners, had not Cornwallis, who came down from his post where the Salisbury road enters the wood a little south of the court-house, ordered M'Leod to draw up his artillery and pour grape-shot upon the pursuers. This cannonade endangered friends as well as foes, for it was directed in the face of the flying guards. It was effectual, however; and Washington and Howard, perceiving two regiments of the enemy, one on the right, and the other on the left, approaching, withdrew to the line of Continentals.

When Webster perceived the effect of Stuart's attack upon Ford, he recrossed the ravine, and fell upon Hawes and Kirkwood. The 71st and 23d (the two regiments discovered by Washington) were soon connected in the center by O'Hara, who, though severely wounded, kept his horse, and, rallying the remnant of the guards, filled up the interval between the left and right wing. The fierce contest upon the British right

View of the Battle-ground

still continued, with some advantage to the enemy. Norton, believing Bose's regiment sufficient to maintain the conflict, joined the 71st, in preparation for a final blow upon the Continentals. Lee's legion infantry and Campbell's riflemen immediately attacked Bose with new vigor. Bose and his major, De Buy, fought gallantly, and by example encouraged their men. Leaving Campbell to continue the contest, Lee hastened, with his infantry, to rejoin his cavalry, whom he had left on the flank with the Continentals. On his way, he found Norton with the guards upon the eminence occupied by Lawson's brigade. He attacked Norton, and driving him back upon Bose, withdrew with Campbell, and joined the Continentals near the court-house. The flight of the North Carolinians, the retreat of the second Maryland regiment, the scanty supply of ammunition, and the junction of the two wings of the British army, convinced Greene that there was no hope of success in a conflict with Webster, who was now pressing forward in good order, with a prospect of speedily turning the American right. He had resolved, before the battle, not to risk the annihilation of his army, and he now determined to retreat before it should be too late. Ordering the brave veteran Colonel Greene, with his Virginia regiment, to take post in the rear, and cover a retreat, the Americans withdrew in regular order, leaving their artillery behind, for almost every horse had been slain. The 71st and 23d British regiments, supported by Tarleton's cavalry, commenced a pursuit; but Cornwallis, unwilling to risk such a movement, soon recalled them. **31** Thus ended the battle at Guilford Court House; a battle, in its effects highly beneficial to the cause of the patriots, though resulting in a nominal victory for the British army. Both of the belligerents displayed consummate courage and skill, and the flight of the North Carolinians from a very strong position is the only reproach which either army deserved. It doubtless caused the loss of victory to the Americans. Marshall justly observes, that "no battle in the course of the war reflects more honor on the courage of the British troops than that of Guilford." Greene had a much superior force, and was very advantageously posted. The number of the Americans engaged in the action was quite double that of the British. The battle lasted almost two hours, and many brave men fell upon that field of carnage. 33 The British claimed the victory; it was victory at fearful cost and small advantage. **34** In some degree, the line of the Scotch ballad might be applied to the combatants,

"They baith did fight, they baith did beat, and baith did rin awa'."

The Americans retreated in good order to the Reedy Fork, and crossed that stream about three miles from the field of action. Tarrying a short time to collect the stragglers, they retired to Speedwell's iron-works, on Troublesome Creek, ten miles distant from Guilford. Cornwallis remained upon the battle-ground that night, burying the dead. The next morning he proceeded as far as New Garden meeting-house. On March 18, 1781, he issued a proclamation boasting of his complete victory, calling upon the Loyalists to join him in restoring good government, and offering pardon to the rebels. Had he remained, this proclamation might have given confidence to the Tories, but the very next day (March 19) he decamped, leaving behind him between seventy and eighty wounded British officers and soldiers in the New Garden meeting-house, which he used for a hospital. He also left behind him all the American prisoners who were wounded, and retreated as speedily as possible southward, toward Cross Creek (Fayetteville), evidently afraid that Greene would rally his forces and attack him. Greene, supposing the earl would advance, had made preparations to confront him; as soon as he was informed of his retreat, he eagerly commenced a pursuit on March 20, after writing a letter to the Quakers at New Garden, desiring them to take care of the sick and wounded of both parties. Notwithstanding heavy rains and wretched roads, Greene pressed after his lordship with great alacrity, as far as Ramsay's Mills, on the Deep River, in Chatham county. On the way, frequent skirmishes occurred between the light troops of the two armies, and Greene arrived at the earl's encampment, on the Deep River, only a few hours after Cornwallis had left it.

Before leaving Winnsborough, Cornwallis sent an order to Lieutenant-colonel Balfour, who commanded at Charleston, to dispatch a competent force by water to Wilmington, to hold that post as a depot for supplies for the royal army in North Carolina. Balfour detached Major Craig upon that service, who drove the American militia from Wilmington, and took possession of it on the same day when General Davidson was killed at Cowan's Ford. After the battle at Guilford Court House, Cornwallis, observing the backwardness of the Loyalists in that vicinity, and the scarcity of provisions, determined to fall back to Cross Creek, where, he knew, had been a population of loyal Scotchmen, and there make his head-quarters, not doubting that his army could be easily supplied with stores, by water, from Major Craig at Wilmington. In these expectations the earl was bitterly disappointed. The Loyalists were comparatively few, a large portion having been changed to either active or passive Whigs; provisions were very scarce, and no communication could be had with Major Craig. Greene was in eager pursuit, and the earl had no alternative but to continue his march to Wilmington. This he performed along the southwestern side of the Cape Fear, and arrived at Wilmington on the seventh of April (1781). He had got so much the start of Greene, that the latter relinquished pursuit at Ramsay's Mills (March 28), where he resolved to allow his troops to repose and recruit, as far as circumstances would allow. Greene dismissed all of the militia except a few North Carolinians, yet he could not afford his army such comforts as he desired. **35**

At the suggestion of Lieutenant-colonel Lee, Greene resolved to march back into South Carolina and take post at Camden with the main army, while the light troops should join Marion on the Pedee, and beat up all the British posts between Camden and Ninety-Six, and Charleston. Pursuant to this plan, he left Ramsay's and marched toward Camden, to confront Lord Rawdon, then in command there. Cornwallis soon afterward marched into Virginia, while Greene and his brave partisan allies of the South regained all that had been lost in previous conflicts.

Let us here leave the two commanders and their armies for a time, and resume our journey toward King's Mountain and the Cowpens. We shall meet them both frequently, in our future journeys in the Carolinas and Georgia.

I left the Guilford battle-ground and the hospitable cottage of Mr. Hotchkiss, at noon, the snow falling fast. At four miles distant, on the Salisbury road, I reached the venerable New Garden meeting-house, yet standing within the stately oak forest where Lee and Tarleton met. It is a frame building with a brick foundation. It was meeting-day, and the congregation were yet in session. Tying Charley to a drooping branch, I entered softly. A larger number than is usually present at "week-day meetings" had congregated,

New Garden Meeting House

for a young man of the sect from Randolph county, thirty miles distant, and a young woman of Guilford, had signified their intentions to declare themselves publicly, on that day, man and wife. They had just risen before the elders and people when I glided into a seat near the door, and with a trembling voice the bridegroom had begun the expression of the marriage vow. His weather-bronzed features betokened the man of toil in the fields, and strongly contrasted with the blonde and delicate face, and slender form of her who, with the downcast eyes of modesty, heard his pledge of love and protection, and was summoning all her energy to make her kindred response. I had often observed the simple marriage ceremony of the Quakers, but never before did the beauty of that ritual appear so marked with the sublimity of pure simplicity.**36**

At the close of the meeting, I learned from one of the elders that a Friend's boarding-school was near, and, led by curiosity, I visited it. The building is of brick, spacious, and well arranged. It was under the superintendence of Thomas Hunt, a son of Nathan Hunt, an eminent Quaker preacher. An incidental remark concerning my relationship with Quakers, made while conversing with the wife of the superintendent, caused her to inquire whether I had ever heard of her father-in-law. I replied in the affirmative, having heard him preach when I was a boy, and expressed the supposition that he had long ago gone to his rest. "Oh no," she replied, "he is in the adjoining room," and leading the way, I was introduced to the patriarch of ninety-one years, whose voice, still vigorous, I had listened to when I was a lad of twelve years. He remembered well when the New Garden meeting-house was built, and resided in the neighborhood when the wounded and dying, from the field of Guilford, were brought there. Although physical infirmities were weighing heavily upon him, his mind appeared clear and elastic. When I was about departing, and pressed his hand with an adieu, he placed the other upon my head and said, "Farewell! God's peace go with thee!" I felt as if I had received the blessing of a patriarch indeed; and for days afterward, when fording dangerous streams and traversing rough mountain roads, that uttered blessing was in my mind, and seemed like a guardian angel about my path. Gloomy unbelief may deride, and thoughtless levity may laugh in ridicule at such an intimation, but all the philosophy of the schools could not give me such exquisite feelings of security in the hands of a kind Providence as that old man's blessing imparted.

The storm yet continued, and the kind matron of the school gave me a cordial invitation to remain there until it should cease; but, anxious to complete my journey, I rode on to Jamestown, an old village situated upon the high southwestern bank of the Deep River, nine miles from New Garden meeting-house, and thirteen miles above Bell's Mills, where Cornwallis had his encampment before the Guilford battle. The country through which I had passed from Guilford was very broken, and I did not reach Jamestown until sunset. It is chiefly inhabited by Quakers, the most of them originally from Nantucket and vicinity; and as they do not own slaves, nor employ slave labor, except when a servant is working to purchase his freedom, the land and the dwellings presented an aspect of thrift not visible in most of the agricultural districts in the upper country of the Carolinas.

I passed the night at Jamestown, and early in the morning departed for the Yadkin. Snow was yet falling gently, and it laid three inches deep upon the ground; a greater quantity than had fallen at one time, in that section, for five years. Fortunately, my route from thence to Lexington, in Davidson county, a distance of twenty miles, was upon a fine ridge road **37** a greater portion of the way, and the snow produced but little inconvenience. Toward noon, the clouds broke, and before I reached Lexington (a small village on the west side of Abbott's Creek, a tributary of the Yadkin), at half past two in the afternoon, not a flake of snow remained. Charley and I had already lunched by the margin of a little stream, so I drove through the village without halting, hoping to reach Salisbury, sixteen miles distant, by twilight. I was disappointed; for the red clay roads prevailed, and I only reached the house of a small planter, within a mile of the east bank of the Yadkin, just as the twilight gave place to the splendors of a full moon and myriads of stars in a cloudless sky. From the proprietor I learned that the Trading Ford, where Greene and Morgan crossed when pursued by Cornwallis, was only a mile distant. As I could not pass it on my way to Salisbury in the morning, I arose at four o'clock, gave Charley his breakfast, and at earliest dawn stood upon the eastern shore of the Yadkin. The air was frosty, the pools were bridged with ice, and before the sketch was finished, my benumbed fingers were disposed to drop the pencil. I remained at the ford until the east was all aglow with the radiance of the rising sun, when I walked back, partook of some corn-bread, muddy coffee, and spare-ribs, and at eight o'clock crossed the Yadkin at the great bridge, on the Salisbury road. **38** The river is there about three hundred yards wide, and was considerably swollen from the melting of the recent snows. Its volume of turbid waters came rolling down in a swift current, and gave me a full appreciation of the barrier which Providence had there placed between the Republicans and the royal armies, when engaged in the great race described in this chapter.

From the Yadkin the roads passed through a red clay region, which was made so miry by the melting snows that it was almost eleven o'clock when I arrived at Salisbury. This village, of over a thousand inhabitants, is situated a few miles from the Yadkin, and is the capital of Rowan county, a portion of the "Hornet's Nest" of the Revolution. It is a place of considerable historic note. On account of its geographical position, it was often the place of rendezvous of the militia preparing for the battle-fields; of various regular corps, American and British, during the last three years of the war; and especially as the brief resting-place of both armies during Greene's memorable retreat. Here, too, it will be remembered, General Waddell had his head-quarters for a few days, during the "Regulator war." I made diligent inquiry, during my tarry in Salisbury, for remains of Revolutionary movements and localities, but could hear of none. **39** The Americans, when fleeing before Cornwallis, encamped for a night about half a mile from the village, on the road to the Yadkin; the British occupied a position on the northern border of the town, about an eighth of a mile from the court-house. I was informed that two buildings, occupied by officers, had remained until two or three years ago, when they were demolished. Finding nothing to invite a protracted stay at Salisbury, I resumed the reins, and rode on toward Concord. The roads were very bad, and the sun went down, while a rough way, eight miles in extent, lay between me and Concord. Night approached, brilliant and frosty; the deep mud of the road soon became half frozen, and almost impassable, and I was beginning to speculate upon the chances of obtaining comfortable lodgings short of the village, when a large sign-board by the way-side indicated a place of entertainment, and relieved my anxiety. Such an apparition is so rare in the upper country of the Carolinas, where the traveler must depend upon the hospitality of the planters, that it is noteworthy. Passing through a lane, I came to the spacious mansion of Mr. Martin Phifer, one of the largest planters in Cabarras county. It is in the midst of one of the finest districts of North Carolina for the production of upland cotton. Practical observations upon that great staple of the South was the chief topic of our evening's conversation, which was protracted to the "small hours of the morning;" and I left his hospitable abode a wiser man than when I entered it. Mr. Phifer is a grandnephew of John Phifer, one of the leading patriots of Mecklenburg, whose remains lie buried at the Red Hills, three miles west of Concord. A rough, mutilated slab covers the grave of the patriot. Tradition avers that when the British army was on its march from Charlotte to Salisbury, a fire was built upon the stone by the soldiers, in contempt for the patriot's memory.

Departing from the post-road, a little distance from Mr. Phifer's, I traversed a nearer, though a rougher route to Charlotte than through Concord, passing that village about three miles to the westward, close by the Red Hills. The scenery through this whole region is extremely picturesque. Wooded hills, deep ravines, broad cultivated slopes and uplands, and numerous water-courses, present diversified and pleasing pictures at every turn of the sinuous road. In summer, when the forests and fields are clad, the roads hard, and the deep shades of the ravines and water-courses desirable, I can not imagine a more agreeable tour for a traveler of leisure than that portion of my journey from the Roanoke to the Cowpens, across the Broad River, back to the eastern side of the Catawba, and so down to the verge of the low country, near Camden. In the vicinity of Concord are the head-waters of several tributaries of the Yadkin and Catawba, and between that village and Charlotte I crossed the Coddle, Stony, and Mallard Creeks, and one of the main branches of Rocky River. The latter, which is a considerable tributary of the Yadkin, is here a small stream, but very turbulent, and broken into numerous cascades. I reached Charlotte at half past three o'clock, having traveled only twenty-one miles since morning.**40** It was Saturday, January 6, 1849, and I eagerly coveted the Sabbath's rest, after a week of excessive toil. Charley, too, was jaded, and needed repose; for a large portion of the circuitous journey from Hillsborough hither had been through a region abounding in red clay, saturated with rains and melting snows.

Charlotte has historical notoriety, chiefly on account of its being the place where a convention of patriots assembled in 1775, and by a series of resolutions virtually declared themselves and those they represented free and independent of the British crown. To this event I particularly directed my inquiries, but was singularly unsuccessful. Two gentlemen, to whom I had letters of introduction from President Polk, were absent. I called upon another, whom he named, but could not obtain information of much value. Being an entire stranger, I knew not unto whom to apply, and I left Charlotte on Monday, with feelings of disappointment not to be expressed. Since my visit, I have received varied and important information from James W. Osborne, Esq., superintendent of the Branch Mint, and others in that vicinity, which compensates me, in a measure, for my failure.

By the merest accident, I ascertained that the mill upon Sugar Creek, two or three miles south of Charlotte, and known as Bissell's, was formerly the property of Colonel Thomas Polk, one of the active patriots in that section. Early on Monday morning, I rode down to the mill. Informed that it had been materially altered since the Revolution, I did not stop to sketch the locality. It is an interesting spot, for there a portion of Cornwallis's army was encamped, and the mill was used during the cantonment there, to supply his troops with flour.

Let us glance at the historical events which render Charlotte famous in our annals. While public sentiment in North Carolina and its sister colonies was making rapid strides toward a bold resistance to augmenting oppressions, the people of Mecklenburg and vicinity, between the Yadkin and the Catawba, were neither indifferent nor inactive, notwithstanding their distance from the sea-board. There was no printing-press in the upper country; and as no regular post traversed that region, a newspaper was seldom seen there among the people. They were in the habit of assembling at stated places to hear printed hand-bills from abroad read, or to obtain verbal information of passing events. Charlotte was a central point for these assemblages, and there the leading men in that section often met at Queen's Museum or College, the Faneuil Hall of North Carolina, to discuss the exciting topics of the day. These meetings were at first irregular, and without system. It was finally agreed that Thomas Polk, a large property-holder in the vicinity of Charlotte, colonel of the militia of Mecklenburg, a man of great excellence of character, extensive knowledge of the people around him, and deservedly popular, should be authorized to call a convention of the representatives of the people whenever circumstances should appear to require it. **41** It was also agreed that such representatives should consist of two from each captain's company, to be chosen by the people of the several militia districts, and that their decisions, when thus legally convened, should he binding upon the people of Mecklenburg. This step was in accordance with the recommendation of the eleventh article of the American Association, adopted by the first Continental Congress, and now generally acted upon throughout the colonies.

When Governor Martin made an attempt to prevent the assembling of a Provincial Congress at Newbern in April 1775, the people were much exasperated, for they remembered his arbitrary proceedings in dissolving the last Provincial Legislature, after a session of four days, and before any important business had been transacted. The excitement throughout the province was intense. While the public mind was thus inflamed, Colonel Polk issued a notice to the elected committee-men of the county, to assemble in the courthouse **42** at Charlotte toward the close of May. On what precise day they first met, can not now be positively determined. They appointed Abraham Alexander, **43** an esteemed citizen, who had served them in the Colonial Legislature, chairman, and Dr. Ephraim Brevard, **44** a scholar and unwavering patriot, clerk or secretary. According to tradition, intelligence of the affairs at Lexington and Concord, in Massachusetts, was received during the session of the delegates, and added greatly to the excitement among the people, who had assembled in great numbers around the court-house, eager to know the resolves of their representatives within. The principal speakers on the occasion were Dr. Brevard, Reverend Hezekiah J. Balch, William Kennon (a lawyer of Salisbury), and Colonel Polk. The first three gentlemen were appointed a committee to prepare suitable resolutions, and on the thirty-first of May, 1775, the following preamble and resolves were unanimously adopted: **45**

"*Whereas*, By an address presented to his majesty by both Houses of Parliament in February last, the American colonies are declared to be in a state of actual rebellion, we conceive that all laws and commissions confirmed by or derived from the authority of the king and Parliament are annulled and vacated, and the former civil Constitution of these colonies for the present wholly suspended. To provide in some degree for the exigencies of this county in the present alarming period, we deem it proper and necessary to pass the following resolves, viz.

I. That all commissions, civil and military, heretofore granted by the crown to be exercised in these colonies, are null and void, and the Constitution of each particular colony wholly suspended.

II. That the Provincial Congress of each province, under the direction of the great Continental Congress, is invested with all legislative and executive powers within their respective provinces, and that no other legislative or executive power does or can exist at this time in any of these colonies.

III. As all former laws are now suspended in this province, and the Congress has not yet provided others, we judge it necessary for the better preservation of good order, to form certain rules and regulations for the internal government of this county, until laws shall be provided for us by the Congress.

IV. That the inhabitants of this county do meet on a certain day appointed by the committee, and, having formed themselves into nine companies (to wit: eight for the county, and one for the town), do choose a colonel and other military officers, who shall hold and exercise their several powers by virtue of the choice, and independent of the crown of Great Britain, and former Constitution of this province.

V. That for the better preservation of the peace and administration of justice, each of those companies do choose from their own body two discreet freeholders, who shall be empowered each by himself, and singly, to decide and determine all matters of controversy arising within said company, under the sum of twenty shillings, and jointly and together all controversies under the sum of forty shillings, yet so as their decisions may admit of appeal to the convention of the selectmen of the county, and also that any one of these men shall have power to examine and commit to confinement persons accused of petit larceny.

Signers of the Mecklenburg Resolves

Abra'm Alexander — *Eph. Brevard*

Thos. Polk — *Adam Alexander*

David Reese — *Jno. McKnitt Alexander*

Hez. Alexander — *John Phifer*

Robt. Irwin — *Richd. Barry*

Will Kennon

Benjamin Patton — *John Foard*

John Davidson — *William Graham*

John Flenniken — *Waightstill Avery*

Charles Alexander

Henry Downs — *Robt. Harris*

Ezra Alexander — *Neill Morrison*

James Harris

VI. That those two selectmen thus chosen do jointly and together choose from the body of their particular company two persons to act as constables, who may assist them in the execution of their office.

VII. That upon the complaint of any persons to either of these selectmen, he do issue his warrant directed to the constable, commanding him to bring the aggressor before him to answer said complaint.

VIII. That these select eighteen selectmen thus appointed do meet every third Thursday in January, April, July, and October, at the court-house in Charlotte, to hear and determine all matters of controversy for sums exceeding forty shillings, also appeals; and in case of felony to commit the persons convicted thereof to close confinement until the Provincial Congress shall provide and establish laws and modes of proceeding in all such cases.

IX. That these eighteen selectmen thus convened do choose a clerk, to record the transactions of said convention, and that said clerk, upon the application of any person or persons aggrieved, do issue his warrant to any of the constables of the company to which the offender belongs, directing said constable to summon and warn said offender to appear before said convention at their next sitting, to answer the aforesaid complaint.

X. That any person making complaint, upon oath, to the clerk, or any member of the convention, that he has reason to suspect that any person or persons indebted to him in a sum above forty shillings intend clandestinely to withdraw from the county without paying the debt, the clerk or such member shall issue his warrant to the constable, commanding him to take said person or persons into safe custody until the next sitting of the convention.

XI. That when a debtor for a sum above forty shillings shall abscond and leave the county, the warrant granted as aforesaid shall extend to any goods or chattels of said debtor as may be found, and such goods or chattels be seized and held in custody by the constable for the space of thirty days, in which time, if the debtor fail to return and discharge the debt, the constable shall return the warrant to one of the select men of the company, where the goods are found, who shall issue orders to the constable to sell such a part of said goods as shall amount to the sum due. That when the debt exceeds forty shillings, the return shall be made to the convention, who shall issue orders for sale.

XII. That all receivers and collectors of quit-rents, public and county taxes, do pay the same into the hands of the chairman of this committee, to be by them disbursed as the public exigencies may require, and that such receivers and collectors proceed no further in their office until they be approved of by, and have given to this committee good and sufficient security for a faithful return of such moneys when collected.

XIII. That the committee be accountable to the county for the application of all moneys received from such public officers.

XIV. That all these officers hold their commissions during the pleasure of their several constituents.

XV. That this committee will sustain all damages to all or any of their officers thus appointed, and thus acting, on account of their obedience and conformity to these rules.

XVI. That whatever person shall hereafter receive a commission from the crown, or attempt to exercise any such commission heretofore received, shall be deemed an enemy to his country; and upon confirmation being made to the captain of the company in which he resides, the said company shall cause him to be apprehended and conveyed before two selectmen, who, upon proof of the fact, shall commit said offender to safe custody, until the next sitting of the committee, who shall deal with him as prudence may direct.

XVII. That any person refusing to yield obedience to the above rules shall be considered equally criminal, and liable to the same punishment as the offenders above last mentioned.

XVIII. That these resolves be in full force and virtue until instructions from the Provincial Congress regulating the jurisprudence of the province shall provide otherwise, or the legislative body of Great Britain resign its unjust and arbitrary pretensions with respect to America.

XIX. That the eight militia companies in this county provide themselves with proper arms and accouterments, and hold themselves in readiness to execute the commands and directions of the General Congress of this province and this committee.

XX That the committee appoint Colonel Thomas Polk and Dr. Joseph Kennedy to purchase three hundred pounds of powder, six hundred pounds of lead, and one thousand flints, for the use of the militia of this county, and deposit the same in such place as the committee may hereafter direct.

Signed by order of the Committee.

EPHRAIM BREVARD, Clerk of the Committee."

These resolutions, which not only substantially declared the people of Mecklenburg, represented by the convention, free and independent of the British crown, but organized a civil government upon a republican basis, were read to the assembled multitude from the courthouse door, and were received with loud acclaims of approbation. It is said that they were read to fresh gatherings of the people several times during the day, and were always greeted with cheers.

These resolutions formed the closing proceedings of the convention, and having provided for the transmission of the resolutions to the Provincial Congress of North Carolina, to meet in Hillsborough in August, and to the Continental Congress, then in session at Philadelphia, it adjourned. Captain James Jack, of Charlotte, was the appointed messenger, and a few days after the adjournment of the convention, he proceeded to Philadelphia, and placed the papers in his charge, in the hands of Caswell, Hooper, and Hewes, the delegates in Congress from North Carolina. **47** These gentlemen, perhaps considering the movement premature or too radical, did not make the proceedings public. They still hoped for reconciliation with the mother country, and were willing to avoid any act that might widen the breach. They addressed a joint letter to the people of Mecklenburg, complimenting them for their patriotism, recommending the strict observance of order, and expressing their belief that the whole continent would soon follow their example, if the grievances complained of were not speedily redressed. For the same prudential reasons, the Provincial Congress at Hillsborough declined taking any immediate action upon their bold proceedings. **48** But for this hesitation, growing out of a sincere desire to preserve the integrity of the British realm, the world would long ago have conceded to the people of Mecklenburg, in North Carolina, the distinguished honor of making a Declaration of Independence of the British crown, thirteen months previous to the Federal declaration by the Continental Congress. That honor has not only been withheld, but the fact denied by men presumed to have positive information upon all subjects connected with Revolutionary events. Documentary evidence has settled the question beyond cavil. **49**

Charlotte was the point to which Gates retreated, with a few followers, after the disastrous battle near Camden, in August, 1780, and soon afterward it became the scene of actual hostilities. After refreshing his army at Camden, and adopting further measures for keeping down the spirit of rising rebellion in South Carolina, Cornwallis moved, with his forces, toward Charlotte on September 8, 1780, for the purpose of giving encouragement to the timid loyalists between the Yadkin and the Catawba; to assist Major Ferguson, who was then across the Broad River attempting to embody the militia in the service of the king; to awe the Republicans, who were in the ascendant in Mecklenburg, Rowan, and vicinity; in fact, to conquer North Carolina before Congress could organize another army at the South. Cornwallis reached Charlotte toward the close of the month, where he expected to be joined by Ferguson and his Loyalists. But he was doomed to disappointment; that officer was soon afterward killed, and his whole force was broken up in a severe battle on King's Mountain (Oct. 7). Cornwallis was diligent in issuing his proclamations, in which he denounced "the rebels;" offered pardon to those who should seek it, and protection to persons and property to those who would accept it. Gates, in the mean while, had retired, with the remnant of his army, to Salisbury, and soon proceeded to Hillsborough. Hundreds, who were stanch patriots, came forward and accepted protection from Cornwallis, for they saw no alternative but that, and the ruin of their families and estates. Among them was Colonel Ephraim Polk, who thereby incurred the suspicions of his countrymen; but when the danger was over, he renounced the forced allegiance. Non-conformity would have insured the destruction of all his property; he accepted a protection, and saved his estate. Colonel Thomas Polk was also under a cloud of distrust for a short season. **50**

When Cornwallis marched from Camden, on the east side of the Wateree, Tarleton traversed the country, with his legion, on the west side of that river. At the Waxhaws, Cornwallis halted, and there Tarleton united with the main body. On the fifth of September, Major William R. Davie **51** was appointed, by Governor Nash, colonel commandant of cavalry, and, with Major George Davidson, was very active in collecting supplies for Gates's broken army, and in repressing the depredations of the British. They had continually maneuvered in front of the approaching enemy, and fell gradually back to Charlotte as the British pressed onward. While encamped at Providence, Davie learned that some Tories and light troops were on the western bank of the Catawba, not far distant. He determined to beat up their quarters; and early on the morning of the twenty-first of September (1780), he surprised them at Captain Wahab's **52** plantation, and killed and wounded sixty, while he lost but one man wounded. He took ninety-six horses, with their equipments, and one hundred and twenty stand of arms, and returned to his camp, having marched sixty miles within twenty-four hours.

On the day of the engagement at Wahab's, Generals Sumner and Davidson, with their brigades of militia, arrived at Providence. On the advance of the British, they retreated to Salisbury, ordering Colonel Davie and Major Joseph Graham to annoy the enemy on his march. Four days afterward, Cornwallis having established a post at Blair's Mill, on Five Mile Creek, commenced his march toward Charlotte, by the Steel Creek road. Davie and Graham were on the alert, annoying him all the way. They took several of his men prisoners, in one or two skirmishes. Davie reached Charlotte at midnight on September 25, and determined to give the enemy a warm reception. He dismounted his cavalry, who were armed with swords, pistols, and muskets, and posted them in front of the court-house, under cover of a stone wall, breast high. His infantry, and Graham's volunteers were advanced eighty yards in front on each side of the street, covered by the garden inclosures of the villagers. While this arrangement was in progress, Tarleton's legion, the van of the royal army, approached. Tarleton was sick, and Major Hanger was in command. As soon as he reached the Common at the entrance of the village, and observed the Americans, Hanger's trumpeter sounded a charge. The cavalry moved slowly, while the flanking infantry attacked Graham and his party. While they were engaged, Hanger, with his cavalry, rushed toward the court-house, when Davie poured a deadly volley upon them. They recoiled, but were instantly rallied on the Common. In the mean while, the contest in the street was warmly maintained. Again the cavalry charged, and again fell back in confusion to the Common. The British infantry having gained Davie's right, he withdrew from the court-house, and formed his line on the eastern side of the town. Cornwallis had now reached the cavalry, and upbraided them for want of courage. They charged a third time, when Davie, having mounted his men, gave the enemy such a reception that they again fell back to the Common. The 71st and 33d British regiments of Webster's brigade (which fought so gallantly at Guilford nearly five months afterward) now advanced to the support of the light troops. Davie, perceiving the contest now to be very unequal, retreated toward Salisbury, leaving Cornwallis master of Charlotte. Colonel Francis Locke (who commanded at Ramsour's) and five privates were killed; and Major Graham and twelve others were wounded in this action. The British lost twelve non-commissioned officers and privates, killed; Major Hanger, two captains, and many privates, were wounded. Cornwallis remained in Charlotte until the fourteenth of October, when he retreated southward. It had been his intention to advance northward; but the loss of Ferguson and his corps, and the general lukewarmness, if not absolute hostility of the people, and the constant annoyance by the American troops, **53** caused him to retrograde, and on the twenty-ninth he established his head-quarters at Winnsborough, in Fairfield District, South Carolina, midway between the Catawba and Broad Rivers. There we shall leave the earl for the present.

The British army, while at Charlotte, lay encamped upon a plain, south of the town, on the right side of the road. Cornwallis's head-quarters were next to the southeast corner of the street from the court-house; and most of the other houses were occupied, in part, by his officers. I found no person in Charlotte yet living who remembered the British occupation and the noble deeds of the patriots; but history, general and local, fully attests the patriotism of its inhabitants during the whole war. **54** It was never visited by the British army after Cornwallis returned to Winnsborough, and only for a short time was the head-quarters of the American army, while Gates was preparing for another campaign. It was at this place General Greene took the command of the Southern army from Gates, fifty days after Cornwallis decamped (Dec. 3, 1780).

Chapter XV
Endnotes

1 These lines form a part of a song which was very popular at the close of the war, and was sung to the air of "Yankee Doodle."

2 This factory, in the midst of a cotton-growing country, and upon a never-failing stream, can not be otherwise than a source of great profit to the owners. The machinery is chiefly employed in the manufacture of cotton yarn. Thirteen hundred and fifty spindles were in operation. Twelve looms were employed in the manufacture of coarse cotton goods suitable for the use of the negroes.

3 Proverbs, xxxi., 19.

4 Nathaniel Greene was born of Quaker parents, at Warwick, in Rhode Island, in 1740. His father was an anchor smith, and in that business Nathaniel was trained. While yet a boy, he learned the Latin language, and by prudence and perseverance he collected a small library while a minor. The perusal of military history occupied much of his attention. He had just attained his majority, when his abilities were so highly estimated, that he was chosen a representative in the Legislature of Rhode Island. Fired with military zeal, and ardent patriotism, young Greene resolved to take up arms for his country, when he heard of the battle at Lexington. He was appointed to the command of three regiments in the Army of Observation, raised by his state, and led them to Roxbury. In consequence of this violation of their discipline, the Quakers disowned him. General Washington soon perceived his worth, and in August the following year, Congress promoted him from the office of brigadier of his state militia to that of major general in the Continental army. He was in the battles at Trenton, Princeton, Brandywine, and Germantown. In March, 1778, he was appointed quarter-master general, and in June was engaged in the battle of Monmouth. He resigned his office of quarter-master general in 1780, and was succeeded by Timothy Pickering. He took the command of the Southern Department, December third, 1780, and in February following made his famous retreat. He engaged in the battle of Guilford, in March, 1781, when he was defeated. In April following, he fought with Lord Rawdon, near Camden, where he was again defeated, but retreated in good order, and soon afterward captured several British posts in South Carolina. He besieged Fort Ninety-Six in May, but was unsuccessful. On the eighth of September, he gained a partial victory at Eutaw Springs, for which Congress presented him with a British standard and a gold medal. This engagement closed the war in South Carolina. He returned to Rhode Island at the conclusion of the war. He went to Georgia in 1785 to look after an estate belonging to him near Savannah. While walking one day, in June, without an umbrella, he was "sun struck," and died on the nineteenth of that month, in 1786, at the age of forty-six years. His body was buried in a vault in Savannah, on the same day, but owing to negligence in designating the one, a search for his remains, in 1820, was unsuccessful. No man living can now point out the sepulchre of that ablest of Washington's generals. On the eighth of August following, Congress adopted the following resolution: "That a monument be erected to Nathaniel Greene, Esq., at the seat of the Federal government, with the following inscription: Sacred to the memory of Nathaniel Greene, Esq., a native of the State of Rhode Island, who died on the nineteenth of June, 1786; late major general in the service of the United States, and commander of their army in the Southern Department. The United States, in Congress assembled, in honor of his patriotism, valor, and ability, have erected this monument." The Board of Treasury was directed to take action for the due execution of the foregoing resolutions.

In person General Greene was rather corpulent, and above the common size. His complexion was fair and florid; his countenance serene and mild. His health was generally delicate, but was preserved by temperance and exercise.

5 At this place a severe battle was fought on the twentieth of June, 1780, between a body of North Carolina militia and a large force of Loyalists. Early in June, General Rutherford* was in command of more than five hundred North Carolina militia, and was in the vicinity of Charlotte. Having received intelligence that the Tories were embodying in arms beyond the Catawba, in Tryon county, he issued orders to commanders in the vicinity to arouse the militia for the dispersion of those men. Ramsour's Mills, in the present county of Lincoln, on the south fork of the Catawba, was their place of rendezvous, and toward that point he marched, he having received intelligence that Lord Rawdon had retired to Camden. The Tories were assembled under Colonels John Moore and Major Nicholas Welch, to the number of almost thirteen hundred, on the twentieth of June. On Sunday, the eighteenth, having concentrated the militia of Mecklenburg, Rowan, and neighborhood, Rutherford proceeded to the Catawba, and crossed that river at the Tuckesege Ford, on the evening of the nineteenth. He dispatched a messenger to Colonel Francis Locke, of Rowan, informing him of the state of affairs, and ordering him to form a junction with him between the Forks of the Catawba, sixteen miles from Ramsour's. That officer, with the militia under several other subordinate commanders, in all about four hundred men, encamped on the nineteenth on Mountain Creek, higher up on the Catawba, above Beattie's Ford, and also sixteen miles from Ramsour's. At a council of the officers, junction with Rutherford, who was about thirty-five miles distant, was not deemed prudent, and they resolved to attack the Tories without delay. Colonel Johnson, one of their number, was dispatched to apprise General Rutherford of the situation of affairs. He reached Rutherford's camp at ten o'clock the same night.

　　　Late in the evening of the nineteenth, Colonel Locke and his companions commenced their march, and at daylight the following morning they were within a mile of the enemy's camp. The latter were upon a high hill, three hundred yards east of Ramsour's Mill, and half a mile from the present village of Lincolnton. Their position was very advantageous, and as there were but few trees upon the slope, they could fire effectually upon an approaching foe. The companies of Captains Falls, M'Dowell, and Brandon, of the patriot army, were on horseback, and led on to the attack; the footmen were under the immediate command of Colonel Locke. The Tories were surprised. Their pickets fired when the patriots appeared, and then retreated to the camp. For a moment the Tories were confused, but, recovering, they poured such a deadly fire upon the horsemen, who had pursued the pickets to the lines, that they were compelled to fall back. They rallied, and soon the action became general. Captain Hardin now gained the right flank of the Tories, while the action was warm in the center. In two instances the parties were so close that they beat each other with the buts of their guns. The Whigs soon drove the Tories from the hill, when they discovered them collected in force on the other side of the mill stream. Expecting an immediate attack, messengers were sent to urge Rutherford forward. They met him within six miles of Ramsour's, pushing on with all possible haste. Major Davie, with his cavalry, started off at full gallop, followed by Colonel Davidson's infantry. They were met within two miles of Ramsour's, with the intelligence that the Tories had retreated. Rutherford marched to the scene of action, and there encamped. The conflict was very severe, and seventy men were left dead on the ground. As all were in "citizen's dress." it was difficult to distinguish the Whigs from the Tories among the dead. It is believed that each party had an equal number killed. About one hundred men on each side were wounded. Fifty Tories were taken prisoners. A terrible voice of wail went up from that battle-field the next day, when the relatives of the slain came there in search of them.

---

* Griffith Rutherford was an Irishman by birth, brave and patriotic, but uncultivated in mind and manners. He resided west of Salisbury, in the Locke settlement, and in 1775 represented Rowan county in the Convention at Newbern. In 1776 he led a large force into the Cherokee country, and assisted the people of South Carolina in destroying their corn-fields and villages. He was appointed a brigadier by the Provincial Congress, in April, 1776. He commanded a brigade in the

battle near Camden, in August, 1780, and was taken prisoner by the British. He was exchanged, and was in command at Wilmington when that place was evacuated by the British at the close of the war. He was a state senator in 1784, and soon afterward removed to Tennessee, where he died. A county both in North Carolina and Tennessee bears his name.

---

6 Greene was quartered at Salisbury, in the house of Elizabeth Steele, a patriot of purest mold. She had heard Greene utter words of despondency, and her heart was touched. While he was at table, she brought two bags full of specie, the earnings of years of toil, and presented them to him, saying, "Take these; for you will want them, and I can do without them." Greene was grateful; and before he left her house he wrote upon the back of a portrait of the king, hanging in the room, "O George, hide thy face and mourn!" and then hung it up, with the face to the wall. That portrait, with the writing, is in the present possession of the Honorable David L. Swain, of Chapel Hill.

7 Captain Joseph Graham was an excellent specimen of those young men of Carolina who flocked to the army fighting for independence. He was born in Pennsylvania, on the thirteenth of October, 1759, and at the age of seven years accompanied his widowed mother to North Carolina. He was educated at Queen's Museum, in Charlotte, and was a spectator at the famous convention, held there in May, 1775. In May, 1778, at the age of nineteen, young Graham enlisted in the fourth regiment of North Carolina regular troops, under Colonel Archibald Lyle. Marching northward, his commander received instructions to return to Carolina, and Graham went home on furlough. He was called into active service in the autumn of that year, and accompanied General Rutherford to the banks of the Savannah, soon after the defeat of General Ashe at Brier Creek. He was with General Lincoln while maneuvering against Prevost, and was in the severe battle at Stono, in June, 1779. A fever prostrated him, and he returned home. While plowing in the field, he heard of the fall of Charleston and defeat of Buford at the Waxhaw, and, like Cincinnatus, he left the furrow to engage in public duties. He was appointed adjutant of the Mecklenburg regiment. He was engaged in active service for some time, and fought the enemy with Major Davie, at Charlotte, in the autumn of 1780. In that engagement he was cut down and severely wounded by a British dragoon. He received six sabre and three bullet wounds. These confined him in the hospital for two months. When recovered, he raised a company of mounted riflemen, and, with his fifty men, disputed the passage of the British army at Cowan's Ford. With his company, and some troops from Rowan, he surprised and captured a British guard at Hart's Mill, only a mile and a half from head-quarters at Hillsborough, and the next day was with Lee when Pyle was defeated. He was engaged in active service all that summer, and in September was appointed a major, and, with a pretty strong force, proceeded toward Wilmington to rescue Governor Burke, who had been abducted from Hillsborough by Fanning, a noted Tory, and his associates. South of Fayetteville he encountered a band of Tories, and, after a severe skirmish, defeated them. His force was only one hundred and thirty-six; that of the Tories was six hundred. It was a brilliant achievement. He was engaged in two or three other military enterprises soon afterward, when the surrender of Cornwallis caused a cessation of hostilities at the South. With this campaign, Major Graham's revolutionary services closed. In the course of four years (at the end of which he was only twenty-three years of age) he had commanded in fifteen engagements, and was greatly beloved by his companions.

Major Graham was elected the first sheriff of Mecklenburg, after the close of the war, and, in 1787, married a daughter of John Davidson, one of the members of the famous Mecklenburg Convention. By her he had twelve children, the youngest of whom, the Honorable William A. Graham, is now (1852) Secretary of the Navy of the United States. Soon after his marriage, he erected iron-works, and settled in Lincoln county, eight miles from Beattie's Ford, where he lived forty years, and died. In 1814, one thousand men were raised in North Carolina to assist the Tennessee and Georgia volunteers against the Creek Indians. Graham was urgently solicited to take the command. He consented, and received the commission of major general. He arrived with his corps just as the Creeks had submitted to Generals Jackson, Coffee, and Carroll, after the battle at the Horse Shoe. For many years after that war, General Graham was the senior officer of the fifth division of the state militia. Temperate in all things, he enjoyed remarkable health until about the time of his death, which occurred from apoplexy, on the twelfth of November, 1836, at the age of seventy-seven years. His honored remains lie in a secluded spot, near the great road leading from Beattie's Ford to Lincolnton.

8 Stedman, an eye-witness, from whose work the plan is copied, gives the following account of the passage of the river. This description illustrates the plan. "The light infantry of the guards, led by Colonel Hall, first entered the water. They were followed by the grenadiers, and the grenadiers by the battalions, the men marching in platoons, to support one another against the rapidity of the stream. When the light infantry had nearly reached the middle of the river, they were challenged by one of the enemy's sentinels. The sentinel having challenged thrice and received no answer, immediately gave the alarm by discharging his musket; and the enemy's pickets were turned out. No sooner did the guide [a Tory] who attended the light infantry to show them the ford, hear the report of the sentinel's musket, than he turned round and left them. This, which at first seemed to portend much mischief, in the end proved a fortunate incident. Colonel Hall, being forsaken by his guide, and not knowing the true direction of the ford, led the column directly across the river, to the nearest part of the opposite bank. This direction, as it afterward appeared, carried the British troops considerably above the place where the ford terminated on the other side, and where the enemy's pickets were posted, so that when they delivered their fire the light infantry were already so far advanced as to be out of the line of its direction, and it took place angularly upon the grenadiers, so as to produce no great effect." – History of the American War, ii., 328.

9 General William Davidson was born in Lancaster county, Pennsylvania, in 1746. His family went to North Carolina (Rowan county) when he was four years old. He was educated at Queen's Museum,* an institution at Charlotte, where many of the patriots of Carolina were instructed; and when the war broke out he took up arms. He was major of one of the first regiments raised in Carolina, but first saw active service in New Jersey. In November, 1779, he was detached to reenforce Lincoln at the South. In a skirmish, near Calson's Mills, a ball passed through his body, near the kidneys, but the wound was not mortal. He was appointed brigadier after the battle of Camden, in the place of General Rutherford, who was made a prisoner there. In the action at Cowan's Ford, on the first of February, 1781, he was shot through the breast, and instantly fell dead. Congress, on the twentieth of September following, ordered a monument to be erected to his memory, at a cost not exceeding $500 dollars. Ü General Davidson was a man of pleasing address, great activity, and pure devotion.

---

* This building stood upon the site of the present residence of W. J. Alexander, Esq., and was better known during the Revolution as Liberty Hall Academy. Previous to the establishment of an institution of learning here, there were but two chartered seminaries in the province; one at Edenton, and the other at Newbern. In these none but members of the Established Church were allowed to hold official station. The Presbyterians, who were very numerous, resolved to have a seminary of their own, and applied for an unrestricted charter for a college. It was granted; but, notwithstanding it was called Queen's College, in compliment to the consort of the king, and was located in a town called by her name, and a county of the same name as her birth-place, the charter was repealed in 1771 by royal decree. The triple compliment was of no avail, It continued to exist, nevertheless, and the first Legislature under the State Constitution, in 1777, gave it a charter under the title of Liberty Hall Academy. The people of Mecklenburg would not allow any preference

to be given to one religious denomination over another in the management of the affairs of the institution and with firmness they pressed forward, with a determination to maintain both religious and political freedom. These principles, ever active, made Mecklenburg, the seat of this free institution of learning – "the most rebellious county in the state" – "the Hornet's Nest." No doubt the repealing of the charter by royal authority, of this popular institution, operated powerfully in alienating the affections of the people from the parent government; for there, as in every dissenting community in America, the establishment of "the Church" as a dominant power among them, was regarded with disfavor. Episcopacy and royalty appeared to be inseparable in interest, and concurrent in aristocratic tendencies.

Ü Journals of Congress, vii., 148.

---

10 The loss on this occasion is not certainly known. Colonel Hall and three or four of the light infantry were killed, and between thirty and forty were wounded. The Americans lost Davidson, and about twenty killed and wounded. Cornwallis's horse was shot under him, and fell as soon as he got upon the shore. O'Hara's horse tumbled over with him in the water, and other horses were carried down the stream. – Lee's Memoirs, 137.

11 It is related that while at Salisbury, the British officers were hospitably entertained by Dr. Anthony Newman, notwithstanding he was a Whig. There, in presence of Tarleton and others, Dr. Newman's two little sons were engaged in playing the game of the battle of the Cowpens with grains of corn, a red grain representing the British officers, and a white one the Americans. Washington and Tarleton were particularly represented, and as one pursued the other, as in a real battle, the little fellows shouted, "Hurrah for Washington, Tarleton runs! Hurrah for Washington!" Tarleton looked on for a while, but becoming irritated, he exclaimed, "See those cursed little rebels."

12 This view of the Trading Ford, where Greene, with Morgan and his light troops, crossed the Yadkin, is from the east side of the river. It is just at the foot of an island, about a mile and a half below the great bridge on the road to Salisbury. The river is usually fordable between the island and the stakes seen in the picture; below that point the water is deep. I made this sketch just at dawn on a cold frosty morning (January 5, 1849), the moon shining brightly in the west, and the nearer stars glittering in profusion in the deep sky above.

13 Both divisions of the army were in want of rest. That of Morgan had been almost constantly in motion since the battle at the Cowpens, and had traveled one hundred and fifty miles; that of Huger had traveled one hundred miles from the camp on the Pedee, with bad wagons and poor teams, over an exceedingly wretched road. Many marched without shoes over the frozen ground, and their footsteps were marked with blood for many miles. No one can form an idea of the character of the roads in winter, at the South, where the red clay abounds, without passing over them. Until I had done so, I could not appreciate the difficulties experienced by the two armies in this race toward Virginia, particularly in the transportation of baggage wagons or of artillery.

14 OTHO HOLLAND WILLIAMS was born in Prince George county, Maryland, in 1748. His ancestors were Welsh, and came to America soon after Lord Baltimore became proprietor of the province of Maryland. He was left an orphan at twelve years of age. He was a resident of Frederick county when the war of the Revolution began, where he entered the military service as lieutenant of a rifle corps under Colonel Michael Cresap, and with that officer he went to Boston. He was afterward promoted to the command of his company. In 1776, he was promoted to major, and fought at Fort Washington with distinction. In that engagement he was wounded and captured, and for some time experienced the horrors of the provost prison of New York. He was afterward exchanged for Major Ackland, captured at Saratoga. During his captivity, he was appointed to the command of a regiment in the Maryland line. He was Gates's adjutant general during the campaign of 1780. When Gates collected the remnant of his army, scattered at Camden, the Marylanders were formed into two battalions, constituting one regiment. To Williams was assigned the command, with John Eager Howard as his lieutenant. When Greene assumed the command of the Southern army, he perceived the value of Williams, and appointed him adjutant general. In Greene's memorable retreat, and the subsequent battle at Guilford, Williams greatly distinguished himself; and at Eutaw Springs he led the celebrated charge which swept the field and gained the bloody victory. Congress promoted him to the rank of brigadier; and at the close of the war he received the appointment of collector of customs at Baltimore, which office he held until his death, which occurred on the sixteenth of July, 1794, while on his way to a watering-place for the benefit of his health.

15 The pony rode by the countryman who gave notice of the approach of the British was much jaded, and when he went back with Armstrong, Lee ordered his young bugler to change horses with the planter. Upon the jaded pony the bugler started for the ranks of Williams in advance. The attacking party, under Captain Miller, soon overtook the bugler, who, too small to carry a sword, was unarmed. The poor boy was cut down, begging for mercy. Lee saw the transaction just as he led his cavalry to the attack. He was greatly exasperated, and held Captain Miller responsible for the deed. That officer charged the cruelty upon the drunkenness of some of his men, but Lee would listen to no excuse. Miller escaped, as we have seen in the text. The bugler was left in the woods by the road side.

16 Lieutenant-colonel Edward Carrington was an exceedingly active officer. He had been detached with that portion of the Virginia regiment of artillery retained with the main army, when some of his companies had attended the Virginia line to the South, and had been taken at the surrender of Charlestown. On reaching North Carolina with De Kalb, Colonel Harrison, commander of the Virginia artillery, unexpectedly arrived and assumed the command. On account of a misunderstanding with Harrison, Carrington retired, and was afterward dispatched by Gates to superintend the examination of the Roanoke, to ascertain the readiest points of communication across it, to be used either in receiving supplies from Virginia or in retreating from North Carolina. Greene found him engaged in this service. Aided by Captain Smith of the Maryland line, he explored the Dan, and made every preparation for Greene to cross it with his army. Having completed his arrangements, he joined the army near the Yadkin, and was one of the most active of Lee's officers in the retreat to the Dan. At this time he held the office of quarter-master general of the Southern army, which office he filled with honor to himself and the service. He was afterward engaged in the siege of Yorktown, where he commanded the artillery on alternate days with Lamb and Stevens of New York. After the war, he was a representative in Congress from his native state (Virginia). When Aaron Burr was tried for treason, Colonel Carrington was the foreman of the jury. He died on the twenty-eighth of October, 1810, at the age of sixty-one years. – See Lee's Memoirs.

17 Gordon, Ramsey, Lee, Tarleton, Stedman, &c. The distance traversed by the retreating army was more than two hundred miles. It was in February, when the roads are worse than at any other season of the year, sometimes very muddy, at others frozen hard. On the day after his passage, Greene sent the following dispatch to Governor Jefferson: "On the Dan River, almost fatigued to death, having had a retreat to conduct for upward of two hundred miles, maneuvering constantly in the face of the enemy, to give time for the militia to turn out and get off our stores." Nothing of importance was lost on the way, and baggage and stores were safely crossed to the Virginia side. The condition of the army was wretched respecting clothing. The shoes were generally worn out, the body-clothes much tattered, and no more than a blanket for four men. The light corps was a little better off, yet there was only one blanket for three men. During the retreat from Guilford, the tents were never used; and Greene, in his note to Williams announcing his passage of the Dan, declared that he had not slept more than four hours since he left Guilford. The troops were allowed only one meal a day during the retreat. Before crossing, many of the North Carolina militia deserted; only about eighty remained. General Lillington (who was a colonel at the battle on Moore's Creek), was sent with his corps to Cross Creek, to awe the Tories in that quarter.

18 Stedman says *(ii., 335)*, "Such was the situation of the British army (at Hillsborough), that the author, with a file of men, was obliged to go from house to house throughout the town, to take provisions from the inhabitants, many of whom were greatly distressed by this measure, which could only be justified by extreme necessity."

19 These consisted of quite a large body of militia, under Pickens; a corps of cavalry, under Lieutenant-colonel William A. Washington; some militia and riflemen, under Colonel Campbell, the hero of King's Mountain; and regular infantry, under Colonel John Eager Howard, who distinguished himself at the Cowpens.

20 Lee says, that in the woods, near the mill, where some riflemen were stationed, was an old log schoolhouse. In this building, twenty-five of the most expert marksmen, who were at King's Mountain, were stationed by Lee, with orders not to engage in the general conflict, but to pick off officers at a distance. When Webster entered the stream, and was slowly fording its rocky bed, the marksmen all discharged their rifles at him in consecutive order, each certain of hitting him, yet not a ball touched him or his horse. Thirty-two discharges were made without effect! The hand of Providence shielded him on that day, but soon he received a fatal wound, in a battle far more fierce and bloody. – Lee's Memoirs, 164.

21 Gordon relates that Sergeant-major Perry, and Quarter-master-sergeant Lumsford, of Lee's dragoons, performed a very bold maneuver. They were separately detached, with four dragoons, to make observations. They saw sixteen or eighteen British horsemen ride into a farm-house yard in an irregular manner, and some of them dismount. The two young men joined their forces, charged the horsemen, and, in sight of Tarleton's legion, cut every man down. They then retired without a scar! – Gordon, iii., 172.

22 Cornwallis first encamped, in this retrograde march, on the plantation of William Rankin, a Whig, and then proceeded to the Plantation of Ralph Gorrel, another wealthy patriot. The family were turned out of doors, and sought shelter at a neighbor's house. The soldiers plundered and destroyed until the place was made a desolation. On Sunday, the eleventh of March, the royal army proceeded to the plantation of Reverend Dr. Caldwell, one of the most ardent Whigs in North Carolina, from the time of the Regulator movement. The doctor was then in Greene's camp, at the iron-works on Troublesome Creek. His family left the house, and retired to the smoke-house, where they remained twenty-four hours without food or a bed, exposed to the abuse and profane language of the soldiery. Cornwallis occupied the house of Mr. M'Cuistin, on the great road from the Court House to Fayetteville. Every thing but the buildings were destroyed on the plantation of Dr. Caldwell. "Every panel of fence on the premises was burned; every particle of provisions was consumed or carried away; every living thing was destroyed, except one old goose; and nearly every square rod of ground was penetrated with their iron ramrods in search of hidden treasure." By command of the officers, the doctor's valuable library and papers – even the family Bible – were burned in an oven near the house. All was made a desolation. Cornwallis had offered a reward of one thousand dollars to any one who should bring Dr. Caldwell into his camp. Dr. Caruthers, in his Life of Caldwell, gives many painful descriptions of the sufferings of this good man and his faithful Rachel. Dr Caldwell died in 1824, when in his hundredth year. His wife died in 1825, at the age of eighty-six.

23 The whole army fit for duty now consisted of 4243 foot, and 161 cavalry. It was composed of Huger's brigade of Virginia continentals, 778; Williams's Maryland brigade, and a company of Delawares, 630; infantry of Lee's partisan legion, 82; total of Continental regulars, 1490. There were 1060 North Carolina militia; 1693 from Virginia; in all, 2753. Washingtons light dragoons, 86; Lee's dragoons, 75. To these were added, the next day, 40 horse, under the Marquis of Bretagne, a French nobleman.

24 BANASTRE TARLETON was born in Liverpool, England, on the twenty-first of August, 1754. He commenced the study of the law, but when the war in America commenced, he entered the army, and came hither with Cornwallis. He served with that officer in all his campaigns in this country, and ended his military career at Yorktown, in 1781. On his return to England, the people of his native town elected him their representative in the House of Commons. In 1798, he married the daughter of the Duke of Ancaster. In 1817, he received the commission of major general, but never entered into active service. At the coronation of George the Fourth, he was created a baronet and Knight of Bath. In person, Tarleton was below the middle size, stout, strong, and heavily built. His legs were very muscular, and great activity marked all of his movements. He had a sanguinary and resentful temper, which made him unmerciful to his enemies. – See Georgian Era, London, 1833.

25 The inferiority of the horses of the British cavalry was owing to the fact that they had been taken chiefly from the plantations in South Carolina, and could not be compared in size and strength with those of Pennsylvania and Virginia, from whence came those of Lee. The momentum of the latter, when meeting, was much greater than that of the former, and, of course, in a charge they had a great advantage.

26 About forty of Tarleton's dragoons were killed in this action; and it is believed that about one hundred of the infantry were killed and wounded by the riflemen. The loss of the Americans was considerably less; the exact number was not reported. Lieutenant Snowdon, of the legion infantry, was left wounded on the field. Captain Tate, who shared in Howard's memorable charge at the Cowpens, was with Lee, and had his thigh broken.

27 These were chiefly from Augusta and Rockbridge counties, and were descendants of the Scotch-Irish, who first settled that portion of Virginia. One company was composed principally of the congregation of James Waddell, the glorious Blind Preacher of the wilderness along the eastern base of the Blue Ridge, whose person and ministration is so eloquently described in Letter VII. of Wirt's British Spy. He gave them a farewell address when they were under arms and ready to march. Many of them were left upon the field of Guilford.

28 Dr. Caruthers, speaking from tradition, says that many of the Highlanders, who were in the van, fell near the fence, from behind which the Carolinians rose and fired. Among the Carolinians were some volunteers, under Captain John Forbes, from the Allamance, consisting chiefly of his friends and neighbors. Captain Forbes fired the first gun, and in the retreat received a mortal wound. He was found by his friends thirty hours after the battle. He said that a Tory passed him, and, instead of giving him some water asked for, he kicked him, and called him a rebel. After the death of Forbes, the Tory was found one morning suspended to a tree before his own door.

29 General Stevens had posted forty riflemen twenty paces in the rear of his brigade, with orders to shoot every man who should leave his post. This had the effect to keep the cowardly in the ranks. General Stevens was shot through the thigh during this first conflict of his brigade with the British, yet he did not quit the field. When the Carolinians retreated, he had the address to prevent his own brigade being panic-stricken, by telling them that the former had been ordered to retreat after the first fire. He ordered the Virginians to open, and allow the fugitives to pass through.

30 It was at this time that Francisco, a brave Virginian, cut down eleven men in succession with his broad-sword. One of the guards pinned Francisco's leg to his horse with a bayonet. Forbearing to strike, he assisted the assailant to draw his bayonet forth, when, with terrible force, he brought down his broadsword, and cleft the poor fellow's head to his shoulders! Horrible, indeed, were many of the events of that battle; the recital will do no good, and I will forbear.

31 Ramsay, Gordon, Marshall, Lee, &c.

32 This view is from the eminence southwest of the site of old Guilford Court House, near the junction of the roads running one north to Bruce's Cross-roads, the other west to Salem. The log-house, partially clap-boarded, seen on the right, was uninhabited. It stands near the woods which intervene between Martinsville and the plantation of Mr. Hotchkiss. In the distance, near the center, is seen Martinsville, and between it and the foreground is the rolling vale, its undulations furrowed by many gulleys. In an open field, on the left of the road, seen in the hollow toward the left of the picture, was the fiercest part of the battle, where Washington charged upon the guards. Upon the ridge extending to the right, through the center of the picture, the second line (Virginians) was posted. The fence running to the right from Martinsville, down into the valley on the right, denotes the Salisbury road. The snow was falling very fast when I made this sketch, and distant objects were seen with great difficulty. Our point of view, at the old log-house, is the extreme westerly boundary of the field of controversy.

33 The British lost in killed and wounded over six hundred men, besides officers. Colonel Stuart, of the guards, and Lieutenant O'Hara (the general's brother), of the royal artillery, were killed. General O'Hara, Lieutenant-colonel Webster, Captains Schultz and Maynard, of the guards, and Captain Wilmouski and Ensign De Trott, of the Hessian regiment, were severely wounded. All but O'Hara died of the wounds received in the battle, during the march of the army to Wilmington. The whole army deeply lamented the loss of Webster, for he was one of the most efficient officers in the British service. He was the son of an eminent physician in Edinburgh, and came to America with Cornwallis. During the operations in New Jersey, in 1777, he was very active. In 1779, he had charge of Fort La Fayette at Verplanck's Point, and sustained the attack of General Robert Howe upon that post. He commanded the right wing in the battle at Camden; and, as we have seen, bore a conspicuous part in the pursuit of Greene previous to the battle in which he received his death wound. Webster was buried near Elizabeth, on the Cape Fear River, now Bladen county. Captains Goodrych, Maitland, Peter, Lord Douglas, and Eichenbrocht, who were wounded, recovered. Among the wounded was Adjutant Fox, a brother of the eminent statesman, Charles J. Fox.

The Americans lost in killed and wounded about three hundred of the Continentals, and one hundred of the Virginia militia. Among the killed was Major Anderson, of the Maryland line;, and among the wounded were Generals Stevens and Huger. Of the North Carolina militia, six were killed and three wounded, and five hundred and fifty-two missing. Of the Virginia militia, two hundred and ninety-four were missing. The missing, "as is always the case with militia after a battle," according to Lee, might be found "safe at their own firesides." By these desertions, Greene's army suffered a greater diminution than that of the British, whose loss in action was so much greater. They did not, however, desert "by thousands," as the editor of the Pictorial History of England avers.

Events such as are generally overlooked by the historian, but which exhibit a prominent trait in the character of the people of North Carolina, occurred during this battle, and deserve great prominence in a description of the gloomy picture, for they form a few touches of radiant light in the midst of the somber coloring. While the roar of cannon boomed over the country, groups of women, in the Buffalo and Allamance congregations, who were under the pastoral charge of Dr. Caldwell, might have been seen engaged in common prayer to the God of Hosts for his protection and aid; and in many places, the solitary voice of a pious woman went up to the Divine Ear, with the earnest pleadings of faith, for the success of the Americans. The battling hosts were surrounded by a cordon of praying women during those dreadful hours of contest!

34 This victory of Cornwallis was considered by many British statesmen equivalent to a defeat. In the Parliament, the intelligence of the battle produced a great sensation. Ministers were dissatisfied, and the opposition had a theme for just denunciation against the policy of government. Fox moved in committee, "That his Majesty's ministers ought immediately to take every possible measure for concluding peace with our American colonies;" and in the course of an animated debate, he declared, "Another such victory will ruin the British army." William Pitt, the successor of his father, the Earl of Chatham, inveighed eloquently against a further prosecution of the war. He averred that it was "wicked, barbarous, unjust, and diabolical – conceived in injustice, nurtured in folly – a monstrous thing that contained every characteristic of moral depravity and human turpitude – as mischievous to the unhappy people of England as to the Americans." Fox's motion was rejected by one hundred and seventy-two against ninety-nine.

35 "No magazines were opened for our accommodation," says Lee in his Memoirs; "rest to our wearied limbs was the only boon within his gift. Our tattered garments could not be exchanged; nor could our worn out shoes be replaced. The exhilarating cordial was not within his reach, nor wholesome provision in abundance within his grasp. The meager beef of the pine barrens, with corn ash-cakes, was our food, and water our drink; yet we were content; we were more than content – we were happy." – Page 189.

36 The marriage ceremony of the Quakers is very simple. The parties give notice at a monthly meeting of the society that on a certain day they intend to enter into the holy estate of matrimony. On the day appointed, they, with their friends, repair to the meeting-house, where they arise before the whole congregation and say, the bridegroom first, "I, A B, do take thee, C D, to be my wedded wife, and promise, through Divine assistance, to be unto thee a loving husband, until separated by death." The bride then repeats the same, only changing the person. A certificate of the marriage is then read by a person appointed for the purpose, and is signed by as many present as may choose to do so. These simple proceedings compose the whole marriage ceremony, which is as binding in the sight of God and man as the most elaborate formalities of priest or magistrate. The groomsman and bridesmaid are called waiters among the Quakers of New Garden.

37 These ridge roads, or rather ridges upon which they are constructed, are curious features in the upper country of the Carolinas. Although the whole country is hilly upon every side, these roads may be traveled a score of miles, sometimes, with hardly ten feet of variation from a continuous level. The ridges are of sand, and continue, unbroken by the ravines which cleave the hills in all directions for miles, upon almost a uniform level. The roads following their summits are exceedingly sinuous, but being level and hard, the greater distance is more easily accomplished than if they were constructed in straight lines over the hills. The country has the appearance of vast waves of the sea suddenly turned into sand.

38 The Yadkin rises in North Carolina, on the east of the Alleghany range, and flows east and southeast into South Carolina. A few miles below the Narrows, in Montgomery county, it receives the Rocky River, and from thence to its mouth at Winyaw Bay, near Georgetown, it bears the name of the Great Pedee.

39 An ancient stone wall exists at Salisbury, but tradition has no knowledge of its origin. It is laid in cement, and plastered on both sides. It is from twelve to fourteen feet high, and twenty-two inches thick The top of the wall is a foot below the surface of the earth at present. It has been traced for three hundred feet. Six miles from Salisbury there is a similar wall, and may connect with the other. Conjecture alone can read its history. May it not be a part of the circumvallation of a city of the mound builders?

40 Charlotte is the capital of Mecklenburg county, and contains about fourteen hundred inhabitants. It is pleasantly situated upon a rolling plain, on the east side of the Sugar or Sugaw Creek, a small tributary of the Catawba. It is in the midst of the gold region of North Carolina, and here a branch of the United States Mint is established. Eastward of Charlotte are several productive gold mines, which are now but little worked, partly on account of the more inviting field for miners in California. The first settlers in Mecklenburg county were principally the descendants of the Puritans, Scotch-Irish, and Roundheads; and, near Charlotte, the "Sugar Creek Congregation," the first on the Catawba, was established. I passed the brick meeting-house about three miles from the village, where worshiped the PARENT of the seven congregations from which came delegates to meet in political convention in 1775.* This meeting-house is the third erected by the Sugar Creek Congregation. The first stood about half a mile west from this, and the second a few feet south of the present edifice. In the second, the mother of Andrew Jackson, late president of the United States, worshiped for a-while, when she took refuge in the Sugar Creek Congregation, after the massacre of Burford's regiment, near her residence on the Waxhaw, in May, 1780. Near the site of the first church is the ancient burying-ground. Therein is the grave of Alexander Craighead, the first minister of the congregation. His only monument are two sassafras-trees, one at the head, the other at the foot of his grave, which are the living poles used as a bier for his coffin, and stuck in the ground to mark, temporarily, his resting-place. Ü

---

* These were Sugar Creek, Steel Creek, Providence, Hopewell, Center, Rocky River, and Poplar Tent. – Foote, p. 190.

Ü Ibid., p. 192.

---

41 Colonel Polk was great uncle to the late President Polk. His brother, Ezekiel Polk, whose name appears quite conspicuous in the annals of Mecklenburg county, was the president's grandfather. "The house in which President Polk is supposed to have been born," says Honorable David L. Swain, in a letter to me of recent date, "is about two hundred yards south of Sugar Creek, and eleven miles south of Charlotte, on the lands of Nathan Orr. The house shown to me is of logs, was never weather-boarded, and is covered with a decaying shingle roof. It is formed by joining two houses together."

42 The court-house was a frame building, about fifty feet square, placed upon brick pillars, ten or twelve feet in height, with a stair-way on the outside. It stood in the center of the town, at the intersection of the two principal streets, now the village green. The lower part was a market-house; the upper part was used for public purposes. Stedman says it was a "large brick building," and Lee says it was of stone. Tradition of undoubted character pronounces it such as I have described. The village at that time contained about twenty houses.

43 Abraham Alexander was a leading magistrate in Mecklenburg county, and represented it in the Colonial Legislature. At the time of the convention, of which he was appointed chairman, he was almost threescore years of age. He died on the twenty-third of April, 1786, at the age of sixty-eight years. He was buried in the old church-yard, near Charlotte, where a plain slab, with an inscription, marks his grave.

Elijah Alexander, a relative of the chairman, and who was present when the Mecklenburg Resolutions were read to the people at Charlotte, died at the residence of his son-in-law, James Osborne, Esq., in Cornersville, Tennessee, on the eleventh of November, 1850, at the age of ninety years. He voted for every president of the United States, from Washington to Taylor. His widow, to whom he was married in 1784, was yet living. in 1851.

44 Ephraim Brevard was one of the "seven sons" of his widowed mother who were "in the rebel army."* He graduated at Princeton, and, after pursuing medical studies a proper time, settled as a physician in Charlotte. His talents commanded universal respect, and he was a leader in the movements in Mecklenburg toward independence, in 1775. When the British army invaded the Southern States, Dr. Brevard entered the Continental army as a surgeon, and was taken prisoner at Charleston, in May, 1780. Broken by disease, when set at liberty, Dr. Brevard returned to Charlotte, sought the repose of privacy in the family of his friend, John M'Knitt Alexander, who had succeeded him as clerk of the Mecklenburg Committee, and there soon expired. His remains were buried in Hopewell grave-yard. No stone marks his resting-place, and "no man living," says Mr. Foote, "can lead the inquirer to the spot." He was a remarkable man, and, as the undoubted author of the Mecklenburg Declaration of Independence and Constitution of Government, deserves the reverence of all patriots. His pen was often employed in the cause of freedom, and he was probably the most accomplished writer, of his day, in Western Carolina.

Minute biographical sketches of these leading patriots of Mecklenburg, if they could be obtained, would make an exceedingly useful and entertaining volume. Of the general character of the people in that vicinity at the period of the Revolution, J. G. M. Ramsey, M. D., the historian of Tennessee, who has studied the character of the Mecklenburg patriots with great care, writes thus appreciatingly to me, under date of January 19, 1852: "In regard to the people, then residing between the Yadkin and the Catawba, it is almost impossible to conceive, at this day, the incalculable benefits the country received from their immigration and settlement in it; nor the happy influences, secular, civil, religious, and literary, they uniformly diffused in their respective neighborhoods. To these are we indebted, in a great measure, for the enterprise, industry, thrift, skill, frugality, love of order, sobriety, regard for wholesome laws, family and social government, establishment of schools, churches, and a high standard of education and training for youth, attachment to well-regulated liberty, and the representative principle in government."

---

* When Cornwallis was in pursuit of Greene, he passed near the plantation of the Widow Brevard, and ordered it to be desolated. When asked why he was so cruel toward a poor widow, he replied, "She has seven sons in the rebel army!" What higher compliment could that noble mother have received.

---

45 The following are the names of the leading patriots in Mecklenburg, and reported to have been members of the Mecklenburg Committee, who met in the Convention at Charlotte: ABRAHAM ALEXANDER, EPHRAIM BREVARD, JOHN M'KNITT ALEXANDER, ADAM ALEXANDER, HEZEKIAH ALEXANDER, EZRA ALEXANDER, CHARLES ALEXANDER, WAIGHTSTILL AVERY, HEZEKIAH J. BALCH, THOMAS POLK, JOHN FLENEKIN, JAMES HARRIS, NEIL MORRISSON, DAVID REESE, ROBERT HARRIS, senior, RICHARD BARRY, DUNCAN OCHILTREE, JOHN FORD, WILLIAM KENNON, SAMUEL MARTIN, ZACHEUS WILSON, senior, Ü BENJAMIN PATTON, ROBERT IRWIN, JOHN DAVIDSON, JOHN PFIFER, HENRY DOWNES, WILLIAM GRAHAM, MATTHEW M'CLURE, JOHN QUEARY, WILLIAM WILSON.

Ü The Wilsons were all stanch Scotch-Irish, and sturdy Republicans. The wife of Robert Wilson, a brother of Zacheus, like the Widow Brevard, had "seven sons In the rebel army," and also her husband. When Cornwallis retired from Charlotte, he halted upon Wilson's plantation, and himself and staff quartered at the house of the patriot. Mrs. Wilson was very courteous, and Cornwallis endeavored to win her to the royal cause by flattering words. Her reply deserves to be inscribed upon brass and marble: "I have seven sons who are now, or have been bearing arms; indeed, my seventh son, Zacheus, who is only fifteen years old, I yesterday assisted to get ready to go and join his brothers in Sumter's army. Now, sooner than see one of my family turn back from the glorious enterprise, I would take these boys (pointing to three or four small sons), and with them would myself enlist under Sumter's standard and show my husband and sons how to fight, and, if necessary, to die for their country!" "Ah, general," said the cruel Tarleton, "I think you've got into a hornet's nest! Never mind; when we get to Camden, I'll take good care that old Robin Wilson never gets back again." Mrs. Wilson died in Williamson county, Kentucky, on the 20th of April, 1853, aged ninety years. – See Mrs. Ellet's Women of the Revolution, iii., 347.

---

46 I am indebted to the kindness of the Honorable David L. Swain, of Chapel Hill, John H. Wheeler, Esq., author of Historical Sketches of North Carolina and James W. Osborne, Esq., superintendent of the Branch Mint at Charlotte, for the originals from which these fac similes are made.

47 It was the regular court day when Captain Jack passed through Salisbury. Mr. Kennon, a member of the convention, was in attendance there, and persuaded Jack to permit the resolutions to be publicly read. They were generally approved; but two men (John Dunn and Benjamin Boote) pronounced them treasonable, and proposed the forcible detention of Captain Jack. For this act, Dunn and Boote were arrested by some armed men sent by the committee at Charlotte for the purpose. They were first sent to Camden, in South Carolina, to be kept in confinement as "persons inimical to the country." They were afterward sent to Charleston for better security.

48 The papers were referred to a committee, who reported on the first of September. After some discussion, the Congress resolved that "the present Association ought to be further relied on for bringing about a reconciliation with the parent state." No further notice was taken of the matter, and this brilliant spark was lost in the blaze of the Federal Declaration of Independence published the following year.

49 Almost fifty years this brilliant event in Mecklenburg county remained in obscurity, and when its radiance appeared, it was believed to be only reflected light. There appeared in the Raleigh Register, April 30, 1819, a statement over the signature of J. M'Knitt, that a convention of representatives of the people of Mecklenburg county met at Charlotte, on the nineteenth and twentieth of May, 1775, and by a series of resolutions substantially declared themselves free and independent.* He alleged that Captain Jack bore those resolutions to the Continental Congress, and placed them in the hands of the delegates from North Carolina in that body, who thought them premature. Mr. M'Knitt also stated that John M'Knitt Alexander was the secretary of the convention, and that all of the original papers were destroyed when the house of that gentleman was burned in April, 1800, but that copies of the proceedings were made, one of which was sent to Dr. Hugh Williamson, of New York, who was writing a history of North Carolina, and one to General William R. Davie. Ü This statement was copied from the Raleigh Register by the Essex Register, of Massachusetts, and was brought to the notice of the venerable John Adams. Mr. Adams sent the paper to Mr. Jefferson, accompanied with the remark that he thought it genuine. On the ninth of July, 1819, Mr. Jefferson replied to Mr. Adams's letter at some length, disclaiming all knowledge of such proceedings, and giving his decided opinion that the article in the Register was a "very unjustifiable quiz." á Among his reasons for not believing the thing genuine, he mentioned the fact that no historian, not even Williamson (whose History of North Carolina was published in 1812), alluded to any such proceedings. Such was the fact, and public opinion was divided. It was singular, indeed, that such an important event should not have been mentioned by Williamson, if he believed the resolutions sent to him by Mr. Alexander to be true copies of those adopted in convention at Charlotte. Because of a similarity of expressions and sentiments in these resolutions and the Federal Declaration of Independence, Mr. Jefferson was charged with gross plagiarism, ß while the North Carolinians were charged with attempting to arrogate to themselves a glory which did not belong to them.

In 1829, Judge Martin's History of North Carolina appeared, and in vol. ii., pages 272-274, inclusive, he publishes an account of the Mecklenburg proceedings, with the resolutions. These resolutions differ materially from those which were possessed by General Davie, and published as authentic in a state pamphlet, prepared by order of the North Carolina Legislature, in 1831. Whence Judge Martin procured his copy, is not known. In 1830, a publication appeared denying the statements of the Raleigh Register in 1819, and also denying that a convention, with such results, was ever held at Charlotte. The friends of those patriots whose names appeared as members of the convention in question, very properly tender of their reputation and the honor of the state, sought for proof that such a convention, with such glorious results, was held in Charlotte. The testimonies of several living witnesses of the fact were procured, some of them as early as 1819-20, and some as late as 1830. Their certificates all agree as to the main fact that such a convention was held, but all are not explicit as to date, and some evidently point to other resolves than those referred to. These discrepancies caused doubts, and the public mind was still unsatisfied. To set the matter at rest, the Legislature of North Carolina appointed a committee to investigate the subject. The result was published in pamphlet form in 1831, and the statement made in the Raleigh Register in 1819 was endorsed as true. The certificates alluded to (which also appear in Force's American Archives, ii., 855) are published therein, together with the names of the Mecklenburg Committee appended thereto. Yet one stubborn fact remained in the way – a fact favorable to a belief in the undoubted truth and sincerity of Mr. Jefferson in his denial – namely, that in no public records or files of newspapers of the day had the resolutions of the twentieth, or an account of the convention, been discovered. Some of the most important of those of the thirty-first were published in the Massachusetts Spy in 1775. Doubt still hung over the genuineness of the published resolutions, and eminent men in North Carolina made earnest searches for further testimony, but in vain.

In 1847, the Reverend Thomas Smyth, D. D., of Charleston, published an inquiry into "The true Origin and Source of the Mecklenburg and National Declaration of Independence," in which, assuming the published resolutions, purporting to have been adopted at Charlotte, on the twentieth of May, 1775, to be genuine copies of the originals prepared by Dr. Brevard, he advances an ingenious theory, by which Mr. Jefferson is impliedly defended against the charge of plagiarism and subsequent misrepresentation. Assuming that both Jefferson and Dr. Brevard were, as students of history, familiar with the confessions, covenants, and bands (declarations and pledges) of the Presbyterian Reformers of Scotland and Ireland in the sixteenth and seventeenth centuries, he draws the conclusion that their ideas, and even their expressions, were copied from those instruments of a people struggling for religious freedom. As a proof that such forms were appealed to, he quotes Jefferson's acknowledgment (Memoirs, &c., i., 2), that to a Scotch Presbyterian tutor he was indebted for his republican bias; and his statement (p. 6) that, in preparing a resolution at Williamsburg, recommending a fast on the first of June, 1774, they "rummaged over" Rushworth "for the revolutionary precedents and forms of the Puritans of that day." Upon these premises, Dr. Smyth argues that Mr. Jefferson and Dr. Brevard doubtless drew water from the same well, without a knowledge of each other's act – a well from which copious draughts were made by the Father of our Republic.

While these inquiries were in progress, the discovery of documentary evidence settled the main question beyond cavil, and established the fact that, on the thirty-first of May, 1775, the people of Mecklenburg, in a representative convention assembled, passed resolutions equivalent in spirit to a declaration of independence, and organized a civil government upon the basis of political independence. Among the most indefatigable searchers after the truth, was the Honorable David L. Swain, late governor of North Carolina. A manuscript proclamation of Governor Martin, dated August 8, 1775, which was deposited in the archives of the state by Reverend Francis L. Hawks, D. D., was found to contain the following words: "And whereas, I have also seen a most infamous publication in the Cape Fear Mercury, importing to be resolves of a set of people styling themselves a committee for the county of Mecklenburg, most traitorously declaring the entire dissolution of the laws, government, and Constitution of this country, and setting up a system of rule and regulation repugnant to the laws, and subversive of his majesty's government," &c., &c. Here was a clue. After repeated searches at the instance of Mr. Swain, a copy of the South Carolina Gazette and Country Journal, dated "Tuesday, June 13, 1775," and containing the entire set of resolutions printed in this edition (original text has "620-21"), bearing date of May 31, 1775, was discovered by Dr. Joseph Johnson, in the Charleston Library.   These were copied, and sent to Mr. Swain, who immediately forwarded a copy to Mr. Bancroft, the historian, then the American minister at the court of St. James. Before they reached Mr. Bancroft at London, that gentleman had discovered in the State Paper Office a copy of the same South Carolina paper, containing the resolutions. This paper was sent to Lord Dartmouth, the secretary of state for the colonies, by Sir James Wright, then governor of Georgia. In a letter which accompanied the papers, Governor Wright said, "By the inclosed paper your lordship will see the extraordinary resolves of the people of Charlotte-town, in Mecklenburg county; and I should not be surprised if the same should be done every where else." These facts Mr. Bancroft communicated in a letter to Mr. Swain, written on the fourth of July, 1848.

The only question unsettled now is, Whether the Mecklenburg Committee assembled at an earlier date than the thirty-first of May, 1775, and adopted the resolutions which were in possession of General Davie, and published in the Raleigh Register in 1819. It is a question of minor historical importance, since the great fact is established beyond cavil, that more than a year previous to the promulgation of the Federal Declaration, the people of Mecklenburg declared their entire independence of the British crown, and, in pursuance of that declaration, organized a civil government.

---

* The following is a copy of the resolutions, which were in the possession of General William R. Davie, and are now in the archives of the state, at Raleigh:

"*Resolved, 1*. That whoever directly or indirectly abetted, or in any way, form, or manner, countenanced the unchartered and dangerous invasion of our rights, as claimed by Great Britain, is an enemy to this country – to America – and to the inherent and inalienable rights of man.

"*Resolved, 2*. That we, the citizens of Mecklenburg county, do hereby dissolve the political bands which have connected us to the mother country, and hereby absolve ourselves from all allegiance to the British crown, and abjure all political connection, contract, or association with that nation, who have wantonly trampled on our rights and liberties, and inhumanly shed the blood of American patriots at Lexington.

"*Resolved, 3*. That we do hereby declare ourselves a free and independent people; are, and of right ought to be, a sovereign and self-governing association, under the control of no power, other than that of our God, and the general government of the Congress; to the maintenance of which independence we solemnly pledge to each other our mutual co-operation, our lives, our fortunes, and our most sacred honor.

"*Resolved, 4*. That as we acknowledge the existence and control of no law or legal officer, civil or military, within this county, we do hereby ordain and adopt, as a rule of life, all, each, and every of our former laws; wherein, nevertheless, the crown of Great Britain never can be considered as holding rights, privileges, immunities, or authority therein.

"*Resolved, 5*. That it is also further decreed, that all, each, and every military officer in this county is hereby retained in his former command and authority, he acting conformably to these regulations. And that every member present of this delegation shall henceforth be a civil officer, viz., a justice of the peace, in the character of a 'committee-man,' to issue process, hear and determine all matters of controversy, according to said adopted laws; and to preserve peace, and union, and harmony in said county; and to use every exertion to spread the love of country and fire of freedom throughout America, until a more general organized government be established in this province."

To these resolutions, it is said, a number of by-laws were appended to regulate the general conduct of citizens.

Ü The house of Mr. Alexander was destroyed in April, 1800. The date of the earliest copy of the resolutions is September of the same year.

á Jefferson's Memoirs and Correspondence, iv., 322.

ß The chief ground upon which this charge was predicated, was the identity of expression in the last clause of the third resolution, and the closing of the Federal Declaration – "We pledge to each other our lives, our fortunes, and our most sacred honor." This charge has no weight when it is considered that this was a common parliamentary suffix. Gibbon, writing to his friend Sheffield concerning the Boston Port Bill, in 1774, said, "We voted an address of lives and fortunes, &c." See volume i. of this work (original unabridged edition), page 515.

Dr. Johnson, in his Traditions and Reminiscences of the Revolution (Charleston, 1851), gives a fac simile of a hand-bill, containing the first three of the Mecklenburg Resolutions published in the state pamphlet, together with the names ox the committee. Dr. Johnson says it is "the oldest publication of the Mecklenburg Declaration yet found in print." This is a significant fact, The hand-bill was printed by Heiskell and Brown, who established their printing-office at Knoxville, Tennessee, in 1816. This document is not now (1852) more than thirty-five years old. It was probably printed at about the time (1819) when the resolutions appeared in the Raleigh Register.

---

50 Colonel Polk was then commissary of provisions. His suspected acceptance of protection from the British was considered equivalent to a renunciation of republicanism. He was, therefore, denounced as a Tory. Among Gates's papers in the New York Historical Society is the following order, issued after Cornwallis had retreated to Winnsborough: "From a number of suspicious circumstances respecting the conduct and behavior of Colonel Thomas Polk, commissary general of provisions for the State of North Carolina. and commissary of purchases for the Continental troops, it is our opinion that the said Colonel Polk should be directly ordered to Salisbury to answer for his conduct; and that the persons of Duncan Ochiltree and William M'Aferty* be likewise brought under guard to Salisbury. Given unanimously as our opinion, this twelfth day of November, 1780."

---

* M'Cafferty, as the name is properly spelled, was a wealthy Scotchman, and was employed by Cornwallis as a guide when he left Charlotte.

---

51 William Richardson Davie was born at Egremont, near Whitehaven, England, on the twentieth of June, 1756. He came with his father to America at the age of five years, and was adopted by William Richardson, a maternal uncle, who lived near the Catawba, in South Carolina. He commenced study at Princeton, but

during the summer of 1776 entered the army as a volunteer. He resumed his studies after the battle of Long Island, graduated in the autumn of 1776, and returned to Carolina, where he commenced the study of law in Salisbury. He was elected lieutenant of a troop of horse in 1779, and was attached to Pulaski's legion. He soon rose to the rank of major. At Stono, below Charleston, he was wounded in the thigh. When he recovered, he returned to Salisbury and resumed his books. In the winter of 1780, he raised a troop of cavalry, with which he was very active in beating back the enemy, while forcing his way northward. He was in the battle at Hanging Rock; with Rutherford at Ramsour's Mills, and nobly confronted the British army at Charlotte, after a brilliant display of courage and skill at Wahab's plantation. General Greene appointed Davie commissary general of the Southern army; and he was with that officer in his Retreat, and at the battles at Guilford, Hobkirk's Hill, and Ninety-Six. In 1783, he commenced his career as a lawyer, and the same year married the daughter of General Allen Jones. He was a member of the convention which framed the Federal Constitution. He was instrumental in procuring the erection of the buildings of the University at Chapel Hill, and as grand master of the Masonic Fraternity, he laid the corner stone. He received the commission of major general of militia in 1797, and in 1798 was appointed a brigadier in the army of the United States. He was elected governor of North Carolina the same year, and in 1799 was appointed an embassador to France by President Adams. On his return, he was engaged in some Indian treaties, but on the death of his wife in 1803, he withdrew from public life. He died at Tivoli, near Landsford, in South Carolina, in December, 1820, in the sixty-fourth year of his age.

52 Captain Wahab was with Davie on this occasion, and for the first time in many months had the opportunity of embracing his wife and children. Before he was out of sight of his dwelling, he saw his dear ones driven from it by the foe, and their shelter burned to the ground, without the power to protect them.

53 Provisions soon became scarce in the British camp, for the people in the neighborhood refused a supply. In Colonel Polk's mill, two miles from the town, they found twenty-eight thousand weight of flour, and a quantity of wheat. Foraging parties went out daily for cattle and other necessaries, but so hostile were the people that Webster's and Rawdon's brigades were obliged to move, on alternate days, as a covering party. There were few sheep, and the cattle were so lean that they killed one hundred head a day. On one day, according to Stedman (who was commissary), they killed thirty-seven cows with calf. Frequent skirmishes occurred. On one occasion, the plantation of Mr. M'Intyre, seven miles north of Charlotte, on the road to Beattie's Ford, was plundered, the family having barely time to escape. While loading their wagons with plunder, a bee-hive was overturned, and the insects made a furious attack upon the soldiers. While their commander stood in the door laughing at the scene, a party of twelve patriots approached;* in a moment, the captain, nine men, and two horses lay dead upon the ground The British hastily retreated to their camp, believing that a large American force was concealed near.

---

* One of the twelve was George Graham, brother of General Joseph Graham. He was born in Pennsylvania, in 1758, and went to North Carolina, with his widowed mother, when six years of age. He was educated at Queen's Museum, and was strongly imbued with the republican principles of the Scotch-Irish of that region. He was one of the party who rode from Charlotte to Salisbury and arrested those who proposed to detain Captain Jack, as mentioned. He was active in partisan duties while the British were at Charlotte. After the war, he rose to the rank of major general of militia, and often served his country in the State Legislature. He died at Charlotte, on the twenty-ninth of March, 1826 ,in the sixty-eighth year of his age.

---

54 On one occasion, the young ladies of Mecklenburg and Rowan entered into a pledge not to receive the attentions of young men who would not volunteer in defense of the country, they "being of opinion that such persons as stay loitering at home, when the important calls of the country demand their military services abroad, must certainly be destitute of that nobleness of sentiment, that brave and manly spirit which would qualify them to be the defenders and guardians of the fair sex." – South Carolina and American General Gazette, February, 1780.

Chapter XVI

"We marched to the Cowpens, Campbell was there,
Shelby, Cleveland, and Colonel Sevier;
Men of renown, sir, like lions, so bold –
Like lions undaunted, ne'er to be controlled.
We set out on our march that very same night;
Sometimes we were wrong, sometimes we were right;
Our hearts being run in true liberty's mold,
We valued not hunger, wet, weary, or cold.
On the top of Kings Mountain the old rogue we found,
And, like brave heroes, his camp did surround;
Like lightning, the flashes; like thunder, the noise;
Our rifles struck the poor Tories with sudden surprise."
- Old Song. **1**

The Sabbath which I passed in Charlotte was exceedingly unpleasant. The morning air was keen and hazy; snow fell toward evening, and night set in with a gloomy prospect for the morrow's travel. I breakfasted by candle-light on Monday morning, and before sunrise was on the road for King's Mountain and the Cowpens. I passed the United States Branch Mint, upon the road leading from the village to the Tuckesege or Great Catawba Ford, and at the forks, about a mile from the town, halted a moment to observe the operation of raising gold ore from a mine, by a horse and windlass. This mine had not been worked for fifteen years, owing to litigation, and now yielded sparingly. The vein lies about seventy feet below the surface. This is in the midst of the gold region of North Carolina, which is comprehended within the limits of eleven counties. **2**

From Charlotte to the Catawba, a distance of eleven miles, the country is very hilly, and the roads were bad the greater portion of the way. I crossed the Catawba at the Tuckesege Ford, the place where General Rutherford and his little army passed, on the evening of the nineteenth of June, 1780, when on their way to attack the Tories at Ramsour's Mills. **4** I was piloted across by a lad on horseback. The distance from shore to shore, in the direction of the ford, is more than half a mile, the water varying in depth from ten inches to three feet, and running in quite a rapid current. In the passage, which is diagonal, two islands, covered with shrubbery and trees, are traversed. This was Charley's first experience in fording a very considerable stream, and he seemed to participate with me in the satisfaction experienced in setting foot upon the solid ground of the western shore. I allowed him to rest while I made a sketch, and then we pushed on toward the South Fork of the Catawba, almost seven miles farther. I was told that the ford there was marked by a row of rocks, occurring at short intervals across the stream; but when I reached the bank, few of them could be seen above the surface of the swift and swollen current. The distance across is about two hundred and fifty yards, and the whole stream flows in a single channel. The passage appeared (as it really was) very dangerous, and I had no guide. As the day was fast waning away, a storm seemed to be gathering, and there was not an inhabitant within a mile, I resolved to venture alone, relying upon the few rocks visible for indications of the safest place for a passage.

View at Tuckesege Ford. 3

Taking my port-folio of drawings from my trunk, and placing it beside me on the seat, and then folding my wagon-top, I was prepared to swim, if necessary, and save my sketches, if possible. Charley seemed loth to enter the flood, but once in, he breasted the stream like a philosopher. Twice the wheels ran upon rocks, and the wagon was almost overturned, the water being, in the mean while, far over the hubs; and when within a few yards of the southern shore, we crossed a narrow channel, so deep that my horse kept his feet with difficulty, and the wagon, having a tight body, floated for a moment. The next instant we struck firm ground. I breathed freer as we ascended the bank, and with a thankful heart rode on toward Falls's house of entertainment, away among the hills near the South Carolina line, twenty-six miles from Charlotte.

On account of numerous diverging ways, it was very difficult to keep in the right road from the South Fork to Falls's. I tried to reach there before dark, but the clouds thickened, and night fell suddenly. In the uncertain twilight, I missed a diverging road which I was directed to pursue, and got into the midst of a vast pine forest. Just before entering the woods, I had a glimpse of Crowder's Knob, the highest peak of King's Mountain, estimated to be three thousand feet above the level of the sea. 5 It was about twelve miles distant, and loomed up from the wilderness of pines which intervened, like some ancient castle in the dim light. For more than an hour I pursued the forest road, without perceiving the diverging one which I was directed to follow. I stopped to listen for sounds of habitation. All was silent but the moaning of the wind among the pine boughs, the solemn voice of an owl, and the pattering of the rain upon my wagon-top. For almost another hour I rode on in the gloom, without perceiving an opening in the forest, and I began to think I should be obliged to "camp out" for the night. Again I listened, and was cheered by the distant barking of a dog. I gave Charley a loose rein, and in twenty minutes an open field appeared, and the glimmer of a candle. A shout brought the master of the cottage to the door, and, in reply to my solicitation for food and shelter until morning, he informed me that a contagious disease, which had destroyed two of his family, yet prevailed in his house. He could not offer me the hospitalities of his roof and table, but he would mount his horse and guide me to Falls's, which was four miles distant. I was glad to avoid the contagion, and to reward him liberally for his kind pilotage. I ascertained that I had been within a quarter of a mile of Falls's, but, missing the "turn out," had traversed another road several miles back in the direction of Charlotte!

Mr. Falls was the postmaster, and an intelligent man, apparently about sixty years of age. It was the anniversary of the battle of New Orleans, on January 8, 1815, and as the old man had a brother killed in that engagement, it was a day always memorable to him. I was entertained with the frank hospitality so common in the Carolinas, and at my request breakfast was ready at early dawn. A more gloomy morning can not well be conceived. Snow had fallen to the depth of two inches during the night, and when I departed, a chilling cast wind, freighted with sleet, was sweeping over the barren country. King's Mountain battle-ground was fourteen miles distant, and I desired to reach there in time to make my notes and sketches before sunset. The roads, except near the water courses, were sandy and quite level, but the snow made the traveling heavy. Six miles from Falls's, I forded Crowder's Creek, a stream about ten yards wide, deep and sluggish, which rises from Crowder's Knob, and, after a course of eighteen miles, falls into the Catawba. A little beyond it, I passed a venerable post oak, which was shivered, but not destroyed, by lightning the previous summer. It there marks the dividing-line between North and South Carolina. At noon the storm ceased; the clouds broke, and at three o'clock, when I reached the plantation of Mr. Leslie, whose residence is the nearest one to the battle-ground, the sun was shining warm and bright, and the snow had disappeared in the open fields.

View at King's Mountain Battle-Ground

When my errand was made known, Mr. Leslie brought two horses from his stable, and within twenty minutes after my arrival we were in the saddle and traversing a winding way toward Clarke's Fork of King's Creek. From that stream, to the group of hills among which the battle was fought, the ascent is almost imperceptible. The whole range, in that vicinity, is composed of a series of great undulations, from whose sides burst innumerable springs, making every ravine sparkle with running water. The hills are gravelly, containing a few small bowlders. They are covered with oaks, chestnuts, pines, beaches, gums, and tulip poplars, and an undergrowth of post oaks, laurel, and sour-wood. The large trees stand far apart, and the smaller ones are not very thick, so that the march of an army over those gentle elevations was comparatively easy. Yet it was a strange place for an encampment or a battle; and to one acquainted with that region, it is difficult to understand why Ferguson and his band were there at all.

We tied our horses near the grave of Ferguson and his fellow-sleepers, and ascended to the summit of the hill whereon the British troops were encamped and fought. The battle-ground is about a mile and a half south of the North Carolina line. It is a stony ridge, extending north and south, and averaging about one hundred feet in height above the ravines which surround it. It is nearly a mile in length, very narrow upon its summit, with steep sides. From its top we could observe Crowder's Knob in the distance, and the hills of less altitude which compose the range. **7** The sun was declining, and its slant rays, gleaming through the boughs dripping with melting snows, garnished the forest for a few moments with all the seeming splendors of the mines; gold and silver, diamonds and rubies, emeralds and sapphires, glittered upon every branch, and the glowing pictures of the Arabian Nights, which charmed boyhood with the records of wondrous visions, crowded upon the memory like realities. Alas! on this very spot, where the sun-light is braiding its gorgeous tapestry, and suggesting nothing but love, and beauty, and adoration, the clangor of steel, the rattle of musketry, the shout of victory, and the groans of dying men, whose blood incarnadined the forest sward, and empurpled the mountain streams, were once heard - it was an aceldama; and there, almost at our feet, lie the ashes of men slain by their brother man! History thus speaketh of the event:

On the sixteenth of August, 1780, the Americans, under General Gates, were defeated by Cornwallis, near Camden, and dispersed. Two days afterward, Tarleton defeated Sumter at Rocky Mount, and elsewhere the American partisan corps were unsuccessful. The whole South now appeared to be completely subdued under the royal power; and the conqueror, tarrying at Camden, busied himself in sending his prisoners to Charleston, in ascertaining the condition of his distant posts at Ninety-Six and Augusta, and in establishing civil government in South Carolina. Yet his success did not impair his vigilance. West of the Wateree **8** were bands of active Whigs, and parties of those who were defeated near Camden were harassing the upper country. Cornwallis detached Major Ferguson, a most excellent officer and true marksman, of the 71st regiment, **9** with one hundred and ten regulars under the command of Captain Depuyster, and about the same number of Tories, with an ample supply of arms and other military stores. He ordered him to embody the Loyalists beyond the Wateree and the Broad Rivers; intercept the Mountain Men, **10** who were retreating from Camden, and also the Americans, under Colonel Elijah Clarke, of Georgia, who were retiring from an attack upon Augusta; endeavor to crush the spirit of rebellion, which was still rife; and, after scouring the upper part of South Carolina, toward the mountains, join him at Charlotte. Ferguson at first made rapid marches to overtake the Mountain Men, and cut off Clarke's forces. Failing in this, he proceeded leisurely, collecting all the Tories in his path, until about the last of September, when he encamped with more than a thousand men, at a place called Gilbert Town, west of the Broad River, near the site of the present village of Rutherfordton, the county seat of Rutherford, in North Carolina. **11** These were all well armed, **12** and Ferguson began to feel strong. True to their instincts, his Tory recruits committed horrible outrages upon persons and property wherever they went, and this aroused a spirit of the fiercest vengeance among the patriots. At different points, large bodies of volunteers assembled simultaneously, without concert, and placed themselves under tried leaders, the chief of whom were Colonels Campbell, of Virginia; Cleaveland, Shelby, Sevier, and M'Dowell, of North Carolina; and Lacy, Hawthorn, and Hill, of South Carolina. They all had but one object in view – the destruction of the marauders under Ferguson. They were men admirably fitted by their daily pursuits for the privations which they were called upon to endure. They had neither tents, baggage, bread, nor salt, and no Commissary Department to furnish regular supplies. Potatoes, pumpkins, roasted corn, and occasionally a bit of venison supplied by their own rifles, composed their daily food. Such were the men who were gathering among the mountains and valleys of the Upper Carolinas to beat back the invaders.

On his way to Gilbert Town, Ferguson had succeeded in capturing two of the Mountain Men. These he paroled, and enjoined them to tell the officers on the Western waters, that if they did not desist from their opposition and "take protection under his standard, he would march his army over the mountains, hang their leaders, and lay waste their country with fire and sword." **13** While Colonel Charles M'Dowell, **14** of Burke county, who, on the approach of Ferguson, had gone over the mountains to obtain assistance, was in consultation with Colonels Shelby and Sevier, the paroled prisoners arrived, and delivered their message. These officers were not dismayed by the savage threat of Ferguson, but decided that each should endeavor to raise all the men that could be enlisted, and that the forces thus collected should rendezvous at Watauga on the twenty-fifth of September. It was also agreed that Colonel Shelby should give intelligence of their movements to Colonel William Campbell, of Washington county, in Virginia, hoping that he would raise a force to assist them.

The following official report of events from the meeting of these several forces at Watauga, until the defeat of Ferguson, I copied from the original manuscript among Gates's papers. It is full, yet concise, and being official, with the signatures of the three principal officers engaged in the affair, attached, it is perfectly reliable: **15**

"On receiving intelligence that Major Ferguson had advanced up as high as Gilbert Town, in Rutherford county, and threatened to cross the mountains to the Western waters, Colonel William Campbell, with four hundred men, from Washington county, of Virginia, Colonel Isaac Shelby, with two hundred and forty men, from Sullivan county, of North Carolina, and Lieutenant-colonel John Sevier, with two hundred and forty men, of Washington county, of North Carolina, assembled at Watauga, on the twenty-fifth day of September, where they were joined by Colonel Charles M'Dowell, with one hundred and sixty men, from the counties of Burke and Rutherford, who had fled before the enemy to the Western waters. We began our march on the twenty-sixth, and on the thirtieth we were joined by Colonel Cleaveland, on the Catawba River, with three hundred and fifty men, from the counties of Wilkes and Surry. No one officer having properly a right to the command in chief, on the first of October we dispatched an express

Colonel Isaac Shelby 16

17 to Major-general Gates, informing him of our situation, and requested him to send a general officer to take command of the whole. In the mean time, Colonel Campbell **18** was chosen to act as commandant till such general officer should arrive. We marched to the Cowpens, on Broad River, in South Carolina, where we were joined by Colonel James Williams, **19** with four hundred men, on the evening of the sixth of October, **20** who informed us that the enemy lay encamped somewhere near the Cherokee Ford, of Broad River, about thirty miles distant from us. By a council of principal officers, it was then thought advisable to pursue the enemy that night with nine hundred of the best horsemen, and have the weak horse and footmen to follow us as fast as possible. We began our march with nine hundred of the best men about eight o'clock the same evening, and, marching all night, came up with the enemy about three o'clock P.M. of the seventh, who lay encamped on the top of King's Mountain, twelve miles north of the Cherokee Ford, in the confidence that they could not be forced from so advantageous a post. Previous to the attack on our march, the following disposition was made: Colonel Shelby's regiment formed a column in the center, on the left; Colonel Campbell's regiment another on the right, with part of Colonel Cleaveland's regiment, headed in front by Major Joseph Winston; **21** and Colonel Sevier's **22** formed a large column on the right wing. The other part of Cleaveland's regiment, headed by Colonel Cleaveland himself, and Colonel Williams's regiment, composed the left wing. In this order we advanced, and got within a quarter of a mile of the enemy before we were discovered. Colonel Shelby's and Colonel Campbell's regiments began the attack, and kept up a fire on the enemy, while the right and left wings were advancing to surround them, which was done in about five minutes, and the fire became general all around. The engagement lasted an hour and five minutes, the greater part of which time a heavy and incessant fire was kept up on both sides. Our men in some parts where the regulars fought, were obliged to give way a distance, two or three times, but rallied and returned with additional ardor to the attack.

The troops upon the right having gained the summit of the eminence, obliged the enemy to retreat along the top of the ridge to where Colonel Cleaveland commanded, and were there stopped by his brave men. A flag was immediately hoisted by Captain Depeyster, **23** the commanding officer (Major Ferguson having been killed a little before), for a surrender. Our fire immediately ceased, and the enemy laid down their arms (the greatest part of them charged), and surrendered themselves prisoners at discretion. It appears from their own provision returns for that day, found in their camp, that their whole force consisted of eleven hundred and twenty-five men, out of which they sustained the following loss:

Of the regulars, one major, one captain, two sergeants, and fifteen privates killed; thirty-five privates wounded, left on the ground not able to march; two captains, four lieutenants, three ensigns, one surgeon, five sergeants, three corporals, one drummer, and forty-nine privates, taken prisoners. Loss of the Tories, two colonels, three captains, and two hundred and one killed; one major, and one hundred and twenty-seven privates wounded, and left on the ground not able to march. One colonel, twelve captains, eleven lieutenants, two ensigns, one quarter-master, one adjutant, two commissaries, eighteen sergeants, and six hundred privates taken prisoners.

Total loss of the enemy, eleven hundred and five men at King's Mountain.

Given under our hands at camp.

No battle during the war was more obstinately contested than this; for the Americans were greatly exasperated by the cruelty of the Tories, and to the latter it was a question of life and death. It was with difficulty that the Americans, remembering Tarleton's cruelty at Buford's defeat, could be restrained from slaughter, even after quarter was asked. In addition to the loss of men on the part of the enemy, mentioned in the report, the Americans took from them fifteen hundred stand of arms. The loss of the Americans in killed was only twenty, but they had a great number wounded. Among the killed were Colonel Williams and Major Chronicle. Colonel Hambrite was wounded. Major Chronicle and Major Ferguson were buried in a ravine at the northern extremity of the battle-hill, where the friends of the former erected a plain monument, a few years ago,

Monument on King's Mountain

with inscriptions upon both sides. The monument is a thick slab of hard slate, about three feet high, rough hewn, except where the inscriptions are. **24**

On the morning after the battle (Oct. 8, 1780), a court-martial was held, and several of the Tory prisoners were found guilty of murder and other high crimes, and hanged. Colonel Cleaveland had previously declared that if certain persons, who were the chief marauders, and who had forfeited their lives, should fall into his hands, he would hang them. Ten of these men were suspended upon a tulip-tree, which is yet standing – a venerable giant of the forest. This was the closing scene of the battle on King's Mountain, an event which completely crushed the spirits of the Loyalists, and weakened, beyond recovery, the royal power in the Carolinas. Intelligence of the defeat of Ferguson destroyed all Cornwallis's hopes of Tory aid. He instantly left Charlotte, retrograded, and established his camp at Winnsborough on October 29, 1780, in Fairfield District, between the Wateree and Broad Rivers. It was from this point he commenced the pursuit of Morgan and General Greene, after the battle at the Cowpens, as detailed in a preceding chapter.

After making a sketch of the monument on King's Mountain, we rode back to Mr. Leslie's. It was twilight when we arrived; for we had proceeded leisurely along the way, viewing the surrounding scenery. I could perceive at almost every turn of our sinuous road the originals of Kennedy's graphic sketches in the scenery of Horse Shoe Robinson, and a recurrence to that tale at the house of Mr. Leslie awoke pleasing reminiscences connected with its first perusal. On our return, we ascertained that the grandfather of Mr. Leslie, the venerable William M'Elwees, had just arrived. His company for the evening was a pleasure I had not anticipated. He was one of Sumter's partisan corps, and fought with him at Rocky Mount and Hanging Rock. He was also in the battle at Guilford, and during the whole war was an active Whig. Mr. M'Elwees was eighty-seven years of age when I saw him in January 1849, yet his intellect seemed unclouded. His narrative of stirring incidents, while following Sumter, was clear and vivid; and when, at a late hour, the family knelt at the domestic altar, a prayer went up from that patriarch's lips, equal in fervid eloquence, both in words and accents, to any thing I ever heard from the pulpit.

A cold, starry night succeeded my visit to the battle-ground on King's Mountain, and at sunrise the next morning I was on my way to the Broad River and the Cowpens. The ground was frozen and very rough. I traversed King's Mountain in a northwesterly direction, and in the deep narrow valley at its western base crossed King's Creek, a large and rapid stream. The country over which I passed, from Leslie's to Ross's Ferry, on the Broad River, a distance of twenty-one miles, is exceedingly rough and hilly. In some places the road was deep gullied by rains; in others, where it passed through recent clearings, stumps and branches were in the way, endangering the safety of wheel and hoof. Within a mile of the ferry, I discovered that the front axle of my wagon was broken, evidently by striking a stump; but, with the aid of a hatchet and strong cord with which I had provided myself, I was enabled to repair the damage temporarily.

The sun was about an hour high when I reached the eastern bank of the Broad River, a little below the mouth of Buffalo Creek. The house of Mrs. Ross, the owner of the ferry, was upon the opposite side. For more than half an hour I shouted and made signals with a white handkerchief upon my whip, before I was discovered, when a shrill whistle responded, and in a few minutes a fat negro came to the opposite shore, and crossed, with a miserable bateau or river flat, to convey me over. The river, which is there about one hundred and twenty yards wide, was quite shallow, and running with a rapid current, yet the ferryman had the skill to "pole" his vessel across without difficulty. I was comfortably lodged at the house of Mrs. Ross for the night, and passed the evening very agreeably in the company of herself and two intelligent daughters. Here I observed, what I so frequently saw in the upper country of the Carolinas, among even the affluent planters – the windows without sashes or glass. In the coldest weather these and the doors are left wide open, the former being closed at night by tight shutters. Great light-wood (pine) fires in the huge chimney-places constantly blazing, in a measure beat back or temper the cold currents of air which continually flow into the dwellings. This ample ventilation in cold weather is universally practiced at the South. At Hillsborough and Charlotte, I observed the boarders at the hotels sitting with cloaks and shawls on at table, while the doors stood wide open!

I was now within fifteen miles of the Cowpens, and at daybreak the next morning (Jan. 11, 1849), started for that interesting locality. I was informed that the place of conflict was among the hills of Thicketty Mountain, and near the plantation of Robert Scruggs. To that gentleman's residence I directed my inquiries. After traversing a rough road, much of it, especially along the water-courses, of red clay, I began the ascent of Thicketty Mountain, upon the Mill-gap road, at the forks leading to Clarke's iron-works and Rutherfordton. Here the ground was covered with snow, and I had no means of discriminating between the beaten track of the Mill-gap way and the numerous forks. I ought to have turned to the northwest after leaving the Rutherfordton Fork half a mile, and descended the northern slope of the mountain. Instead of that, I kept along the ridge road, skirted by the forest on each side, without any indication of habitation. For an hour I slowly traversed this gradually ascending way, and almost imperceptibly approached the summit

Scene at the Cowpens

of Thicketty Mountain, until convinced that I was not in the Mill-gap road. Far to the northward, some thirty miles distant, I could see the azure range of the Blue Ridge, near the Nut-gap, where the springs of the Broad River gush out from the mountains. They were covered with snow, and from their lofty summits came a keen breeze, like that of December at the North. The day was waning, and I had no time to lose in deliberation, so I turned back and sought a lateral road, toward the west, to the settlements below. Presently I heard the crying of a child, and looking in the direction of the sound, I saw some thin blue

smoke curling among the trees near. I tied Charley to a laurel shrub, and soon discovered a log cabin, in front of which some children were at play. They fled at my approach, and the mother, a lusty mountaineer, whose husband was at work in the iron-beds which abound in that mountain, appeared astonished at the apparition of a stranger. From her I learned that I had left the Mill-gap road at least three miles back. By her direction I found it, and at about four o'clock reached the residence of Mr. Scruggs. His house is upon the Mill-gap road, and about half a mile west of a divergence of a highway leading to Spartanburg, the capital of Spartanburg District, in which the Cowpens 25 are situated. Upon the gentle hills on the borders of Thicketty Creek, covered with pine woods, within a triangle, formed by the Spartanburg and Mill-gap roads, having a connecting cross-road for a base, the hottest part of the fight occurred. The battle ended within a quarter of a mile of Scruggs's, where is now a cleared field, on the northeast side of the Mill-gap road, in the center of which was a log-house, as seen in the annexed engraving. The field was covered with blasted pines, stumps, and stocks of Indian corn, and had a most dreary appearance. 26 In this field, and along the line of conflict, a distance of about two miles, many bullets and other military relics have been found. Among other things I obtained a spur, which belonged to the cavalry of either Washington or Tarleton.

"Come listen a while, and the truth I'll relate,
How brave General Morgan did Tarleton defeat;

For all his proud boasting, he forced was to fly,
When brave General Morgan his courage did try."
- Revolutionary Song.

We have noted the disposition which General Greene made of the "shadow of an army" (less than two thousand men) which he received from Gates. Brigadier-general Daniel Morgan, **27** an exceedingly active officer, who was placed in command of the Western division, was stationed, toward the close of 1780, in the country between the Broad and Pacolet Rivers, in Spartanburg District. His division consisted of four hundred Continental infantry, under Lieutenant-colonel Howard of the Maryland line; two companies of the Virginia militia, under Captains Triplet and Tate; and the remnants of the first and third regiments of dragoons, one hundred in number, under Lieutenant-colonel William Washington. This force, at the time in question, was considerably augmented by North Carolina militia, under Major M'Dowell, and some Georgia militia, under Major Cunningham. At the close of December in 1780, Morgan and his troops were encamped near the northern bank of the Pacolet, in the vicinity of Pacolet Springs. From this camp Lieutenant-colonel Washington frequently sallied out to smite and disperse bodies of Tories, who assembled at different points and plundered the Whig inhabitants. He attacked and defeated two hundred of them at Hammond's store, and soon afterward a section of Washington's command dispersed another Tory force under Bill Cunningham. Cornwallis, who was still at Winnsborough, perceived these successes with alarm, and apprehending a design upon his important post at Ninety-Six, over the Saluda, determined to disperse the forces under Morgan, or drive them into North Carolina, before he should rally the Mountain Men in sufficient numbers to cut off his communication with Augusta. He accordingly dispatched Tarleton with his legion of horse (three hundred and fifty in number), and the foot and light infantry attached to it, the 7th regiment, and the first battalion of the 71st, with two field pieces, to force Morgan to fight, or retreat beyond the Yadkin. Tarleton's entire force consisted of about eleven hundred well-disciplined men, and in every particular he had the advantage of Morgan.

Tarleton commenced his march on the eleventh of January. The roads were in a very bad condition, and it was not until the fifteenth that he approached the Pacolet. He had crossed the Broad River near Turkey Creek, and advanced with all possible speed toward the camp of Morgan. That officer was at first disposed to dispute Tarleton's passage of the Pacolet, but, informed of the superiority of his numbers, and that a portion had already crossed above him, he retreated hastily northward, and took post on the north side of Thicketty Mountain, near the Cowpens. Tarleton passed through the place of Morgan's camp in the evening of January 16, 1781, a few hours after he had left, and leaving his baggage behind, he pressed eagerly forward in pursuit, riding all night, and making a circuit around the western side of Thicketty Mountain. Early the following morning (Jan. 17), he captured two American videttes, and learned from them the place of Morgan's encampment. At eight o'clock he came in sight of the advanced guard of the patriots, and fearing that Morgan might again retreat, and get safely across the Broad River, he resolved to attack him immediately, notwithstanding the fatigue of his troops.

The Americans were posted upon an eminence of gentle descent, covered with an open wood. They were rested, had breakfasted, and were thoroughly refreshed after their flight from the Pacolet. And now, expecting Tarleton, they were drawn up in battle order. On the crown of the eminence were stationed two hundred and ninety Maryland regulars, and on their right the two companies of Virginia militia, under Major Triplet. These composed the rear line of four hundred and thirty men, and were under the general command of Lieutenant-colonel Howard. **28** One hundred and fifty yards in advance of this line was a body of militia, about three hundred in number, all practiced riflemen, and burning with a spirit of revenge, because of the cruelties which the British and Tories had inflicted. A part of these were commanded by Captain Beatty and Samuel Hammond, of South Carolina. **29** They were commanded by Colonel Andrew Pickens, who, with his followers, had joined Morgan during the night. About one hundred and fifty yards in advance of this first line, were placed the best riflemen of the corps of M'Dowell and Cunningham. Those on the right were commanded by Cunningham, and those on the left by M'Dowell. These were directed to operate as circumstances should direct, after delivering their first fire, which was to be given when the British should be within one hundred and fifty yards. In the rear of the second line, under Howard, and behind an eminence of sufficient height to conceal them, **30** the American reserve was posted. These consisted of Washington's cavalry, and M'Call's mounted militia of Georgia, armed with sabers.

Tarleton was rather disconcerted when he found that Morgan was prepared to fight him, for he expected to overtake him on a retreat. He rode cautiously forward to reconnoiter, but the shots of the advanced corps of riflemen obliged him to retire precipitately to his lines. Yet, feeling sure of an easy victory, Tarleton quickly arranged his line in battle order upon the Spartanburg road, within three hundred yards of Morgan's first line. At this moment, Morgan, with solemn voice and sententious sentences, addressed his troops. He exhorted the militia of the first line to be steady, and fire with sure aim; and expressed his conviction that, if they would pour in two volleys at a killing distance, victory would be theirs. He addressed the second line in a similar manner, informed them that he had ordered the militia to fall back after delivering two volleys, and exhorted them not to be disconcerted by that movement. Then taking post with his line, near Lieutenant-colonel Howard, he awaited in silence the approach of the British van, already in motion. It consisted of the light troops and the legion infantry, with the 7th regiment, under Major Newmarsh. In the center of this line were the two pieces of artillery. Upon each flank was a troop of cavalry; and in the rear, as a reserve, was Major M'Arthur, with the battalion of the 71st regiment and the remainder of the cavalry. Tarleton placed himself in the first line.

It was now about nine o'clock in the morning. The sun was shining warm and bright over the summits of Thicketty Mountain, and gave brilliancy to the martial array in the forests below. At a signal from Tarleton, his advance gave a loud shout, and rushed furiously to the contest, under cover of their artillery and an incessant discharge of musketry. The riflemen, under Cunningham and M'Dowell, delivered their fire with terrible effect, and then fell back to the flanks of the first line under Pickens. The British still shouting, rushed Howard, and poured in a close fire upon the militia. These stood firm, until assailed with bayonets, when they fell back to the second line. M'Call's militia fled to their horses, while the remainder, under Pickens, took post upon Howard's right. Upon the main body Tarleton now made a vigorous charge, and was met with equal valor and determination. The contest was close and severe, and the British line began to bend, when M'Arthur, with the reserve, was ordered to advance. This movement reanimated the quailing Britons, and they plied ball and bayonet with incessant force.

While the contest was raging, M'Arthur attempted to gain the American flank under Colonel Howard. That officer perceived the movement and its intent, and instantly ordered his first company to charge the British 71st. His order was mistaken, and the company fell back. The whole line also gave way at the same moment, and Morgan ordered it to retreat to the eminence behind which the cavalry were posted. Tarleton, believing this maneuver to be a precursor of flight, ordered another charge, and, with shouts, his infantry rushed forward impetuously, in disorder. When close to Howard, that officer ordered his line to face about and give his pursuers a volley. Instantly a close and murderous fire laid many of the British line dead upon the earth, and the living, terrified by the unexpected movement, recoiled in confusion. Howard perceived the advantage of the moment, and followed it up with the bayonet. This decided the victory in favor of the Americans. At the same time, a portion of Tarleton's cavalry having gained the rear of the Americans, fell upon M'Call's mounted militia. Now was the moment for Lieutenant-colonel Washington 31 to act. With his cavalry, he struck the British horsemen a decisive blow, and drove them in confusion before him. The reserve, under M'Arthur, were too much mixed up with the main forces of Tarleton, to present a rallying point, and the whole body retreated along the Mill-gap road to the place near Scruggs's, then covered with an open wood like the ground where the conflict commenced. There the battle ended, and the pursuit was relinquished. It was near the northern border of that present open field that Washington and Tarleton had a personal conflict. In the eagerness of his pursuit of that officer, Washington had got far in advance of his squadron, when Tarleton and two of his aids, at the head of the troop of the 17th regiment of dragoons, turned upon him. An officer on Tarleton's right was about to strike the impetuous Washington with his saber, when his sergeant came up and disabled the assailant's sword-arm. An officer on Tarleton's left was about to strike at the same moment, when Washington's little bugler, too small to wield a sword, wounded the assailant with a pistol-ball. Tarleton, who was in the center, then made a thrust at him, which Washington parried, and gave his enemy a wound in the hand. 32 Tarleton wheeled, and, as he retreated, discharged a pistol, by which Washington was wounded in the knee. During that night and the following morning, the remnant of Tarleton's force reached Hamilton's Ford, on Broad River, and also the encampment of Cornwallis, at Turkey Creek, about twenty-five miles from the Cowpens. For this defeat, Tarleton's cotemporaries censured him severely. 33

The loss of the Americans in this decisive battle was about seventy men, of whom, strange to say, only twelve were killed. The British, according to Cornwallis's letter to Sir Henry Clinton, written a few days afterward, lost ten officers and ninety privates killed, and twenty-three officers and five hundred privates taken prisoners. Almost the whole of the British infantry, except the baggage guard, were killed or taken. The two pieces of artillery, **34** eight hundred muskets, two standards, thirty-five baggage wagons, and one hundred dragoon horses, fell into the possession of the Americans. **35** To the honor of the victors, it is declared that, notwithstanding the cruel warfare which Tarleton had waged had exasperated the Americans to the last degree, not one of the British was killed or wounded, or even insulted, after they had surrendered.

The defeat of the British at the Cowpens has not been inaptly compared to that of the Germans of Burgoyne's army near Bennington. The disaster, in both cases, dealt a severe blow against the success of the main army. The battle near Bennington paralyzed the energies of Burgoyne's army; the battle at the Cowpens equally affected the power of Cornwallis. He was advancing triumphantly toward the heart of North Carolina, having placed South Carolina, as he thought, in submission at his feet. The defeat of Ferguson at King's Mountain, and now of Tarleton, his favorite partisan, withered his hopes of Tory organization and co-operation. His last hope was the destruction of Greene's army by his own superior force, and for that purpose he now commenced the pursuit which we have considered in a preceding chapter, the capture of Morgan and his prisoners being his first object.

The victory of the Cowpens gave great joy to the Americans throughout the confederacy. Congress received information of it on the eighth of February (1781), and on the ninth of March that body voted an award of a gold medal to Morgan; a silver medal to Howard and Washington; a sword to Colonel Pickens; and a vote of thanks to the other officers and men engaged in the battle. **36**

It was almost sunset when I left the Cowpens to return to a house of entertainment upon the road to the Cherokee Ford, seven miles distant; for the resident there could not find a corner for me in his dwelling, nor for Charley in his stable, that cold night, "for love nor money," but generously proposed that I should send him a copy of my work when completed, because he lived upon the battle-ground. To a planter on horseback, from Spartanburg, who overtook me upon the road, I am indebted for kindness in pointing out the various localities of interest at the Cowpens; to the other for the knowledge that a small building near his house was the depository of a field-piece used by an artillery company in the vicinity, when celebrating the anniversary of the battle.

After dark, I reached the house of Mrs. Camp, where I was comfortably lodged for the night; and early the following morning, accompanied by one of her sons on horseback, I proceeded to the Cherokee Ford, on the Broad River, ten miles distant. The road was very rough most of the way, and quite hilly. At the ford, on the west side of the river, is a large iron manufactory. The ore is brought from the neighboring mountains, smelted there, and wrought into hollow-ware, nails, spikes, tacks, &c. Around the establishment quite a little village has grown up, and there, as at Matson's Ford (Conshohocken), on the Schuylkill, where hostile parties were seen during the Revolution, and all around was a wilderness, the hum of busy industry is heard, and the smiles of cultivation are seen. Here, as we have observed, the Americans, who gained the victory at King's Mountain, crossed this stream on the morning of the battle.

Before crossing the Broad River, the Eswawpuddenah of the Cherokee Indians, let us take a historical survey of the most important occurrences westward of this stream, in the beautiful country watered by the Tyger, the Ennoree, and the Saluda, and further on to the noble Savannah. Standing here upon the western selvage of civilization when the war broke out, and where the aborigines were sole masters but a few years before, let us glance, first, at the record of events which mark their conflicts with the over-reaching white race, who beat them back beyond the mountains. **37**

We have already noticed the efforts of the Corees, Tuscaroras, and other Indians of the Neuse and Cape Fear region to expel the Europeans in 1712. This conflict was soon succeeded by another, more serious in its character. For a while, the very existence of the Southern colony was menaced. The powerful nation of the Yamassees, who possessed the territory around Port Royal, where the French Huguenots first attempted settlement, had long evinced their friendship for the Carolinians, whose first settlement was in the neighborhood of the present city of Charleston, by engaging with them as allies in their wars against the Spaniards and some Indian tribes. The Spaniards at St. Augustine, who were the mortal enemies of the

Carolinians, finally succeeded in uniting the Cherokees – "the mountaineers of aboriginal America" **38** – the Muscoghees, Apalachians, and other Indian nations, in a league for the destruction of the colony. They also won the confidence of the Yamassees, and suddenly that powerful tribe appeared in arms against the Carolinians. Already the Apalachian tribes, occupying a large portion of the present State of Georgia, instigated by the Spaniards, had desolated some of the frontier settlements in 1703. Governor Moore, at the head of a body of Carolinians and friendly Indians, penetrated into the very heart of the Apalachian settlements, between the Savannah and the Alatamahaw Rivers. He laid their villages in ashes, devastated their plantations, slew about eight hundred people, and, with a large number of captives, marched back in triumph to Charleston. This invasion broke the spirit of the tribe, and made the power of the Carolinians thoroughly respected among their neighbors.

When the confederacy of the tribes of the upper country was effected, and the Yamassees lifted the hatchet against the white people in 1715, Governor Craven, who had promptly sent aid to the people of the northern provinces, as promptly met the danger at his own door. So secretly had the confederation been formed, and their plans matured, that the first blow was struck, and almost a hundred people were slain, **39** before the Carolinians were aware of danger. The Yamassees, the Muscoghees or Creeks, and Apalachians, advanced along the southern frontier, spreading desolation in their track. The Cherokees, the Catawbas, and the Congarees joined them, and the Corees, and some of the Tuscaroras, also went out upon the war-path. Almost a thousand warriors issued from the Neuse region, while those of the southern division amounted to more than six thousand. Within forty days, the Indian tribes from the Cape Fear to the St. Mary's, and westward to the Alabama, were banded together for the destruction of the colony at Ashley River.

Governor Craven, whose character was the reverse of his name, acted with the utmost energy when the confederation and its purposes were made known. He immediately proclaimed martial law; laid an embargo on all ships to prevent men or provisions from leaving the colony, and seizing arms wherever they could be found, placed them in the hands of faithful negroes, to co-operate with the white people. With twelve hundred men, white and black, he marched to confront the Indians, now approaching with the knife, hatchet, and torch, in dreadful activity. In the first encounters of his advanced parties with the enemy the Indians were victors, but Craven finally compelled them to fall back to their chief camp upon the Salk-hatchie, **40** whither the governor pursued them. Desperate were the conflicts which ensued, and for a while the victory was doubtful. The fate of the whole colony was suspended upon the result, and the Carolinians contended with all the energy of men fighting for life, home, and family. The Indians were repulsed, and, hotly pursued by the white people and their black aids, they were driven across the Savannah and sought shelter under the guns of the Spanish fortress at St. Augustine. No longer useful to them, the Spaniards drove their savage allies into the wilderness, and fearing to return to their hunting-grounds north of the Savannah, the Indians set up their wigwams among the everglades of Florida, and became, it is believed, the ancestors of the powerful Seminoles of our day.

When the division of the Carolinas occurred in 1729, and the southern portion became a royal province, the first care of the administration was to secure the friendship of the neighboring tribes. In 1730, an embassy under Sir Alexander Cumming, visited and explored the Cherokee country, three hundred miles from Charleston. They made a favorable impression, secured advantageous treaties, and laid, as they hoped, the foundation of a permanent peace. For twenty years the treaty remained unbroken. In 1755, the Cherokees renewed their treaty with the Carolinians, and at the same time made cessions to them of large tracts of land. Upon this ceded territory, stretching along the Savannah to the Tennessee River, Glenn, then governor of South Carolina, built forts, and named them respectively Prince George, **41** Moore, and Loudon. The first was upon the Savannah, three hundred miles from Charleston; the second was about one hundred and seventy miles below; and the latter was upon the waters of the Tennessee River, five hundred miles from Charleston. These forts were garrisoned by troops from Great Britain, and, promising security, settlements rapidly extended in that direction. They served to awe the Indian nations, and peace might have been always secured, had the white people exercised ordinary prudence. But one rash act scattered the power of treaties to the wind, and lighted the flames of war along the Carolina frontier.

In 1759, during the administration of Governor Lyttleton (afterward Lord Wescott), while a large party of the Cherokees, who had been assisting the English against the French on the Ohio, were returning home, they took possession of some horses from the back settlers of Virginia. The white people pursued them, killed a number of warriors, and took several captive. This violence exasperated the Indians, and they retaliated by scalping every white man whom they met. Parties of young warriors fell upon the border settlements of the Carolinas, and war was kindled along the whole frontier. Lyttleton called the Carolinians to arms. The Cherokee chiefs were alarmed, and sent a deputation to Charleston to appease the wrath of the English. Lasting friendship might have been at once secured had not Lyttleton indiscreetly refused to listen. He collected fourteen hundred men upon the Congaree, conducted the Cherokee delegation thither, under guard, and, extorting a pledge of peace and alliance, he returned to Charleston, after sending to Fort George twenty-two hostages, whom he had demanded for the delivery of the warriors who had desolated the border settlements. The Cherokees were very indignant, and the governor had scarcely reached his capital, when he received intelligence that fourteen white people had been murdered within a mile of Fort George. Soon the Cherokees surrounded that fortress, led on by Occonastota, a chief of great influence, and the implacable enemy of the English. Perceiving the power of his arms to be vain, he had recourse to stratagem. Withdrawing his warriors, he spread them in ambush, and while conferring with the commander of the garrison and two other officers, whom he had decoyed to the margin of a stream by expressions of friendship, he gave a signal, and instantly they were surrounded by armed savages. The commander was slain, and the other two were wounded and made prisoners. The garrison proceeded to put the hostages in irons. They made a deadly resistance, and were all slain. This event maddened the whole Indian nation, and, with gleaming hatchets, they swept along the Carolina frontier like the scythe of Death. Men, women, and children were butchered without mercy; and the war-belt was sent to the Catawbas and other tribes, inviting them to confederate for the extermination of the English.

About this time, Charleston was severely scourged by the small-pox, and was too weak to send efficient succor to the frontiers. Lyttleton had been appointed governor of Jamaica, and, sailing for that island about this time, was succeeded by William Bull, a native Carolinian. Bull sent to Virginia and North Carolina for aid, and those states furnished seven troops of rangers for the service. These, with the British regulars under Colonel Montgomery (afterward Earl of Eglinton), sent from Canada by General Amherst, marched into the Indian country. Before proceeding, Montgomery rendezvoused at Monk's Corner in April 1760, near Charleston, where volunteers flocked to his standard. The Cherokees were advised of these preparations for invading their territory, and were at first uneasy. Their beautiful domain spread out between the Broad and Savannah Rivers, and was fenced in by rugged mountains. They had then sixty-four towns and villages, and upon an emergency could call six thousand warriors to the field. Reflecting upon this force, they felt strong. Montgomery, with only two thousand men, proceeded against the Indians. In several engagements he chastised them severely, and pressed on to the relief of Fort Prince George, then closely invested by the red warriors. The Indians fled at his approach toward the secure fastnesses of the mountains and morasses, and hither Montgomery pursued them. The wilderness was vast and fearful over which he marched, and the streams to be forded were often deep and turbid. The enemy finally made a stand at Etchoee, the nearest town of their middle settlements. Within five miles of this village a severe battle was fought. The Cherokees fell back slowly before the cold bayonet; and when they saw the English pressing toward the town, they fled thither precipitately, to save their women and children. Montgomery, feeling unsafe in that far off and desolate region, returned to Fort Prince George, and from thence toward Charleston. All the way to the populous settlements, he was annoyed by the Indians, who hung upon his rear, and the purpose of the campaign was only half accomplished. Montgomery and his regulars soon afterward returned to New York.

While this retreat was in progress, the distant post of Fort Loudon, on the Tennessee, was invested by the Cherokees. The garrison of two hundred men was daily melting away by famine. The Virginia Rangers attempted its relief, but without success. The garrison finally surrendered. Safe guidance to the frontier settlements, with ammunition and other baggage was promised them; but they had gone only a short distance on their way, when their guides forsook them, and another body of Indians fell upon and massacred twenty-six of them. A few escaped, and Stuart, their commander, and some others, remained captives a long time.

The Cherokees were now willing to treat for peace, but the French had sent emissaries among them, who kept their fears and animosities constantly excited. Soon the war was renewed with all its former violence, while Carolina was left almost wholly to her own resources. She raised a provincial regiment of twelve hundred men, and gave the command to Colonel Middleton, a brave and accomplished officer. Among his subordinates were Henry Laurens, Francis Marion, William Moultrie, Isaac Huger, and Andrew Pickens, all of whom were very distinguished patriots during the Revolution. This was their first military school, and the lessons they were there taught were very useful in a subsequent hour of need. When this little band was ready to march into the Cherokee country, Colonel James Grant, with the regiments formerly commanded by Montgomery, landed at Charleston (April, 1761). The united forces of Grant and Middleton, with some of the Chickasaw and Catawba Indians as allies, in all twenty-six hundred men, reached Fort Prince George on the twenty-ninth of May. Nine days afterward, on June 7, they advanced toward Etchoee, where, upon the ground where Montgomery fought them, a large body of Cherokees were gathered. Well skilled in the use of fire-arms, and now well supplied by the French, they presented a formidable front. They also had the advantage of superior position, and the battle which ensued was severe and bloody. For three hours the conflict raged in that deep wilderness; and it was not until the deadly bayonet, in the hands of desperate men, was brought to bear upon the Indians, that they gave way. Inch by inch they fell back, until finally, completely overpowered, they fled, hotly pursued by their conquerors. How many were slain is not known; the English lost nearly sixty men. Like Sullivan in the Seneca country, Grant followed up his victory with the torch. Etchoee was laid in ashes; the cornfields and granaries were destroyed, and the wretched people were driven to the barren mountains. **42** So terrible was the punishment, that the name of Grant was to them a synonym for devastation.

By this victory, the spirit of the Cherokee Nation was broken, and the French, whose machinations had urged them to continued hostilities, were hated and despised by them. Through the venerable sachem, Attakullakulla, who had remained a friend of the white people, the chiefs of the Nation humbly sued for peace. "The Great Spirit," said the old man, "is the father of the white man and the Indian; as we all live in one land, let us all live as one people." His words of counsel were heeded; a treaty of amity was concluded, and a bloody war was ended. The Treaty of Paris, between the English and French, was concluded in 1763, and, except the feeble Spaniards on the South, the Cherokees had no enemies of the English thereafter to excite them to war.

From 1761, until the war of the Revolution commenced, the Indians upon the Carolina and Georgia frontiers were generally quiet and peaceful. Pursuant to the secret instructions which the royal governors received from the British ministry, to band the Indians against the colonists, Tory emissaries went up from the sea-board and excited the Cherokees and their neighbors to go upon the war-path. Among the most active and influential of these emissaries of the crown was John Stuart, a Scotchman, and at that time his majesty's Indian agent for the Southern colonies. **43** Stuart arranged a plan with Wright, Campbell, Martin, Dunmore, and other royal governors, to land a British army at St. Augustine, in Florida, which, uniting with the Indians and Tories, might invade the state at an interior point, while a fleet should blockade its harbors, and land an invading army on the sea-board. This plan was discovered by the Carolinians, but not in time entirely to defeat it; for, when Parker and Clinton made their attack upon Charleston (June 28, 1776), the Cherokees commenced a series of massacres upon the western frontiers of the province. Already a few stockade forts had been erected in that section, and to these the terrified borderers fled for safety. Colonel Williamson, of the district of Ninety-Six, who was charged with the defense of the upper country, raised about five hundred true men, and in his first skirmish with the Indians, in which he took some prisoners, discovered thirteen white men, Tories, disguised as savages, and wielding the tomahawk and scalping knife. The indignation excited against these men extended to their class, and this discovery was the beginning of those bloody scenes between bands of Whigs and Tories which characterized many districts of South Carolina. The domestic feuds which ensued were pregnant with horrid results; the ferocity of the tiger usurped the blessed image of God in the hearts of men, and made them brutes, with fearful power to be brutal.

When intelligence of the affair at Charleston reached the interior, the patriots were encouraged, and Williamson soon found himself at the head of a force of twelve hundred men, and daily augmenting. With a detachment of three hundred horsemen, he proceeded to attack an Indian and Tory force at Oconoree Creek. He fell into an ambuscade, and himself and companions narrowly escaped destruction. His horse was shot under him; his squadron were thrown into disorder; and but for the skill and coolness of Colonel Hammond in rallying them, they would have been routed, and many slain. They were victorious, and shortly after this event, Williamson marched, with two thousand men, to lay waste the Cherokee country. Again he fell into an ambuscade, in a narrow defile among the rugged mountains, near the present town of Franklin. From the rocky heights, and from behind the huge trees of the forest, twelve hundred warriors, with some Tories, poured a destructive fire upon the Whigs. But again the Indians were repulsed, and Williamson pressed forward cautiously but efficiently in the work of conquest and desolation. The valleys were smiling with crops of corn, and numerous villages dotted the water-courses. Towns were laid in ashes; the standing corn was trampled down and destroyed; and over all the Indian settlements eastward of the Apalachian Mountains, the broom of desolation swept with terrible effect. The destruction of food invited famine to a revel, and, to avoid starvation, five hundred warriors crossed the Savannah and fled to the Loyalists in Florida.

In the mean while, General Rutherford, of North Carolina, with a force fully equal to Williamson's, crossed the Blue Ridge at Swannanoa Gap, and proceeded to the valley of the Tennessee River, laying waste the Indian country on the line of his march. There he joined Williamson on the fourteenth of September. The work of destruction being completed, Rutherford returned to Salisbury in October, where he disbanded his troops. The conquest was consummate. The Cherokees sued for peace, but they had no Attakullakulla to intercede for them, for he had gone down into silence. They were compelled to submit to the most abject humiliation, and to cede to South Carolina all their lands beyond the mountains of Unacaya, now comprised within the fertile districts of Greenville, Anderson, and Pickens, watered by the tributaries of the Savannah, the Saluda, and the Ennoree. **44**

Only once again did the Cherokees lift the hatchet, during the war. In 1781, British emissaries induced them to go upon the war-path. With a large number of disguised white men, they fell upon the inhabitants in Ninety-Six, massacred some families, and burned their houses. General Pickens, with a party of militia, penetrated the Cherokee country, and in the space of fourteen days he burned thirteen of their villages, killed more than forty of the Indians, and took nearly seventy of them prisoners. They sued for peace, promised never to listen to the British again, and from that time they remained quiet. **45**

The spirit of the North Carolina Regulators was infused into the back settlers of South Carolina, beyond the Broad River, and about 1769, the leading men of that region took the law into their own hands. To suppress their rising power and importance, the governor employed a man of low habits, but of haughty demeanor, named Scovill, to go thither and enforce the laws of the province. He gave him the commission of colonel, and, with the mistaken policy of a narrow mind, he used rigorous measures, instead of evincing forbearance and a spirit of conciliation. The sufferings which they endured made them reprobate all government, and when asked to espouse the cause of Congress, they refused, on the ground that all congresses or instruments of government are arbitrary and tyrannical. These formed the basis of the Tory ascendency in that section of the state at the beginning of the war; and before the names of Whig and Tory became distinctive appellations, the name of Scovillites was applied to those who opposed the Republicans. There were also many Dutch settlers between the Broad and Saluda Rivers, who had received bounty lands from the king. Government emissaries persuaded these settlers to believe that an espousal of the rebel cause would be the sure precursor of the loss of their lands. These augmented the loyal population when the inhabitants were called upon to make a political decision. Still another class, the Scotch-Irish Protestants, had experienced the bounty of the king, and these, with a feeling of gratitude, adhered to the royal government. Over all these, Lord William Campbell, the royal governor when the war broke out, had unbounded influence, and probably in not one of the thirteen colonies was loyalty more rampant and uncompromising than in South Carolina. Many, whose feelings were all in harmony with the opposers of royal rule, were urged by self-interest to remain quiet; for they felt secure in person and property under present circumstances, and feared the result of commotion. Thus active and passive loyalty sat like an incubus upon the real patriotism of South Carolina; and yet, in every portion of the state, the Tories were outnumbered by the Whigs, except in the section we are now considering, between the Broad and Saluda Rivers. The inhabitants there could not be persuaded to furnish men and arms for the army of Congress, nor to sign the American Association.

Early in 1776, William Henry Drayton, **46** Colonel William Thomson, Colonel Joseph Kershaw, and Reverend William Tennent were sent by the Council of Safety at Charleston into that district, to explain to the people the nature of the dispute. Emissaries of government counteracted their influence by persuading the people that the inhabitants of the seaboard desired to get their tea free of duty, while those in the interior would be obliged to pay a high rate for salt, osnaburgs, and other imported necessaries. The baneful seeds of suspicion and mutual distrust were sown broad-cast among the settlers. The men of each party banded together in fear of the violence of the other, and soon opposing camps were formed. Moderate men endeavored to prevent bloodshed, and a conference of their respective leaders was finally effected. A treaty of mutual forbearance was agreed to, and for a while agitation almost ceased. But restless spirits were busy. Among these, Robert and Patrick Cunningham, **47** Tory leaders, were the most active, and they soon disturbed the repose of party suspicion and animosity. By their machinations, it was aroused to wakefulness. The Whigs, fearful of Robert Cunningham's influence, seized and conveyed him to Charleston, where he was imprisoned. His brother Patrick raised a force to attempt a rescue.

At about this time, a thousand pounds of powder, on its way as a present to the Cherokees, was seized by these Loyalists. This excited the already vigorous efforts of the Council of Safety to more efficient measures. Colonel Williamson (the same officer who chastised the Cherokees), with a party of patriots, was sent to regain the powder. They seized Patrick Cunningham, the leader, when the Tories gathered in strength, and drove Williamson into a stockade fort at Ninety-Six. After remaining there some days, an agreement for a cessation of hostilities was concluded, and both parties dispersed to their homes.

The treaty at Ninety-Six was soon violated by the Tories, when the Provincial Congress, resolving no longer to rely upon words, sent a large body of militia and newly-raised regulars, under Colonels Richardson **48** and Thomson, **49** to apprehend the leaders of the party which seized the powder, and to do all other things necessary to suppress the present and future insurrections. **50** They were joined by seven hundred militia from North Carolina, under Colonels Thomas Polk and Griffith Rutherford, and two hundred and twenty regulars, commanded by Colonel James Martin. This was a wise step. It gave the Tories an exalted idea of the strength of the friends of government, and entirely destroyed their organization. Colonel Richardson used his discretionary powers with mildness. The most obstinate leaders were seized and carried to Charleston. Quiet was restored, and the Loyalists made no demonstration of moment until after the reduction of Savannah, when a considerable party arose in favor of the royal government, having for their leader Colonel Boyd, who had been secretly employed by the British government to head the Tories. These were routed and dispersed at Kettle Creek, while on their way to the British posts in Georgia. This event will be noticed in detail hereafter. From that time until the British took possession of Charleston, in 1780, the Tories remained rather quiet upon their plantations. On the eighteenth of August, 1780, Colonel Williams (who was killed at King's Mountain a few weeks afterward), with Colonels Shelby and Clarke, attacked quite a large body of British under Colonel Innis and Major Fraser, near Musgrove's Mill, upon the Ennoree River, in the northeast corner of Laurens's District. Many Tories were collected there, and were joined on the seventeenth by Innis and Fraser. The whole force was about three hundred strong, and were encamped upon the south side of the river, where they commanded a bad, rocky ford. The Americans, whose force was much less, took post upon the north side, upon a small creek which empties into the Ennoree just below the Spartanburg line, about two miles above Musgrove's Mill. It was agreed that Williams should have the chief command. He drew up his little army in ambush, in a semicircle within a wood, and then proceeded to entice his enemy across the river. For this purpose he took a few picked men, appeared at the ford, and fired upon the enemy. The stratagem was successful. Innis immediately crossed the ford to dislodge the "rebels." Williams and his party retreated, hotly pursued by Innis until within the area of the patriot ambuscade, when a single shot by Colonel Shelby gave the signal for attack. With a loud shout, the concealed Americans arose, and within two minutes the Tories were completely surrounded. Colonel Innis was slightly wounded, but with the larger part of his regulars he escaped. Major Fraser was killed, with eighty-five others. Colonel Clary, the commander of the militia, escaped, but most of his men were made prisoners. The Americans lost four men killed and eleven wounded. After this victory, Williams, with the prisoners, encamped at the Cedar Spring, in Spartanburg District, and from thence proceeded to Charlotte. Williams and Clarke returned to the western frontier, and the prisoners, under Major Hammond, marched to Hillsborough.

General Sumter, **51** after his defeat at the mouth of the Fishing Creek, on the Catawba, on August 18, 1780, collected a small volunteer force at Sugar Creek. Although, when the defeat of Gates at Camden was effected, there was no regular army in the field in South Carolina for three months, Sumter with his volunteers, maintained a warfare, and kept up the spirit of liberty upon the waters of the Broad River and vicinity for a long time. He crossed that stream, and by rapid marches ranged the country watered by the Ennoree and Tyger Rivers, in the neighborhood of the Broad. His men were all mounted. They would strike a blow in one place to-day; to-morrow, their power would be felt far distant. Marion was engaged, at the same time, in similar service in the lower country; while Clarke and Twiggs of Georgia, and Williams, Pickens, and others of Ninety-Six, were equally active. The utmost vigilance of Cornwallis, then at Winnsborough, was necessary to maintain a communication between his various posts. While Tarleton was engaged in endeavors to find, fight, and subdue Marion, the "Swamp Fox," then making his valor felt on and near the banks of the Santee, Cornwallis perceived the operations of Sumter with alarm. He surmised (what was really the fact) that Sumter designed to attack his fort at Ninety-Six; he accordingly detached Major Wemyss, a bold and active officer, to surprise the partisan, then on the east side of the Broad River, at Fish Dam Ford, in Chester District, fifty-three miles from Camden. Wemyss, with a considerable force of well-mounted men, reached the vicinity on the evening of the 11th of November (1780). Fearing Sumter might be apprised of his proximity before morning, and cross the river, Wemyss resolved to attack him at midnight, and immediately formed his corps for battle. At about one o'clock in the morning, he rushed upon Sumter's camp. That vigilant officer was prepared to receive him. Colonel Taylor, who commanded Sumter's advanced guard, had taken particular precautions. The horses were all saddled and bridled, ready to retreat or pursue, as circumstances might require. This preparation astonished the British, for they believed their approach was unknown. As soon as they were within rifle shot, Sumter gave a signal; a deadly volley ensued, and twenty-three of the enemy were laid dead upon the field. The British recoiled, but rallying in a moment, they renewed the attack. A hot skirmish ensued, when the British gave way and retreated precipitately, leaving their commander (who was wounded at the first attack), with many slain and wounded comrades, upon the field. Major Wemyss was found the next morning, bleeding profusely. The blood was stanched, and, notwithstanding he had been guilty of various cruelties toward the Whigs, and in his pocket was a list of houses he had burned, Sumter treated him kindly, and allowed him to go to Charleston on parole.

Sumter now prepared to cross the Broad River, for the purpose of effecting his design upon Ninety-Six. He had agreed with Colonels Clarke, Twiggs, and others, from Georgia, to join them on the west side of the Broad River, and proceed to invest that post. For the purpose of covering this expedition, and deceiving the British, he first approached and menaced Camden, and then wheeling, by forced marches he crossed the Broad River and joined Clarke and his associates between the Tyger and Ennoree. Sumter took the command of the whole, and had crossed the Ennoree, when he was intercepted by Tarleton. Cornwallis, alarmed for the safety of Ninety-Six, had recalled that officer from the expedition against Marion, and ordered him to proceed immediately in pursuit of Sumter. With his usual celerity, Tarleton soon crossed the Broad River, and, pushing up the southern side of the Ennoree, attempted to gain Sumter's rear. A deserter from the British infantry informed that officer of the approach and design of Tarleton, and he immediately ordered a retreat. Backward they turned, but so near was the enemy, that, while crossing the Ennoree, the rear guard of the Americans were handled roughly by Tarleton's van. They escaped, however, with a trifling loss. Sumter continued his retreat until he reached the plantation of Blackstocks, on the southwest side of the Tyger River (in the extreme western part of Union District), still closely pursued by Tarleton. That place appeared favorable for a small force to do battle, and Sumter resolved there to face his pursuers, maintain his ground during the day, if possible, and, if compelled to retreat, to cross the river at night. Tarleton did not approach as early as was apprehended, and it was near the close of the afternoon on November 20, 1780, when, with about four hundred of his command, he appeared near Blackstocks's. He was in such haste to overtake Sumter before he should cross the Tyger, that he pressed forward without waiting for the remainder of his force. He found the Americans upon a hill near Blackstocks's house, ready for battle and determined to fight. Major Jackson, of Georgia, who acted as Sumter's volunteer aid on that occasion, assisted him essentially in the proper formation of his troops, and in directing their movements.

In Sumter's front was a very steep bank, with a small rivulet at its base, a fence, and some brush wood. His rear, and part of his right flank, was upon Tyger River; his left was covered by a large log-barn. Tarleton took position upon an eminence near by, and, believing the victory for himself quite sure, he leisurely prepared to attack the Americans, as soon as the remainder of his command should arrive. When Sumter perceived that the whole of Tarleton's force was not with him, he determined not to wait to be attacked, but to act on the offensive. He issued his orders hastily, and in a few minutes his troops descended suddenly from the hill, and poured a well-directed fire upon the British. The latter met the unexpected shock with great valor, and then rushed upon the American riflemen with bayonets. These fell back in good order, when a reserve of riflemen, with a second volley, slew many of the British, and repulsed the remainder. Tarleton, now observing the peril of his little army, charged directly up the hill with his cavalry. The Americans stood firm, and, making sure aim with their rifles, drove the cavalry back beyond the rivulet. Tarleton, amazed at the result, drew off his whole force, then, wheeling his cavalry, made a furious charge upon Sumter's left flank, where the hill was less precipitous. Here he was met by a little band of one hundred and fifty Georgia militia, under Twiggs and Jackson, who, like veterans of many wars, stood firm, and made a noble resistance for a long time, **52** until hoof, and saber, and pistol, bore too hard upon them, and they gave way. At that moment, the rifles of a reserve, under Colonel Winn, and a sharp fire from the log-barn, decided the day. Tarleton fled, leaving nearly two hundred upon the field. Of these, more than ninety were killed, and nearly one hundred wounded. The Americans lost only three killed and five wounded. Among the latter was General Sumter, who received a ball in his breast early in the action, and was taken to the rear, when Colonel Twiggs assumed the command. Though Sumter's wound was severe, and kept him from the field for several months afterward, it did not completely disable him at the time. Without waiting for the remainder of Tarleton's force to come up, Sumter, as soon as he had buried the dead, and made the wounded of the enemy as comfortable as possible, forded the swift-flowing Tyger, bearing his wounded on litters, and continued his retreat to the eastern side of the Broad River, where a large portion of his followers separated, some to go home, others to join new commanders. He proceeded into North Carolina, and remained there until his wounds were healed. The Georgians turned westward, and marched along the base of the mountains toward Ninety-Six. The valorous achievements of Sumter (several more of which will be noticed in detail hereafter) during the campaign of 1780 acquired for him the title of the Carolina Gamecock. Cornwallis was obliged to speak of him as the most troublesome of his enemies. On the thirteenth of January, 1781, Congress passed a very complimentary resolution of thanks to him and his men, in the preamble of which, his victory at Hanging Rock, and his defeat of Wemyss and Tarleton, are particularly mentioned. **53** With these latter events ended all the important military operations westward of the Broad River, and north of the Saluda. **54**

The day is waning; let us cross the Eswawpuddenah, and resume our journey.

Chapter XVI
Endnotes

1 The song called "The Battle of King's Mountain," from which these lines are taken, was very popular in the Carolinas until some years after the close of the war. It was sung with applause at political meetings, wedding parties, and other gatherings, where the ballad formed a part of the proceedings. Mr. M'Elwees, an old man of eighty-seven, who fought under Sumter, and with whom I passed an evening, within two miles of King's Mountain, remembered it well, and repeated the portion here given.

2 These are Randolph, Montgomery, Richmond, Davidson, Stanley, Anson, Cabarras, Rowan, Iredell, Mecklenburg, and Lincoln, all east of the Catawba.

3 This view is from the western bank of the Catawba, looking down the stream.

4 See page 391 in original text.

5 The sides of this peak are very precipitous, and its top is accessible to man only upon one side.

6 This view is from the foot of the hill, whereon the hottest of the fight occurred. The north slope of that eminence is seen on the left. In the center, within a sort of basin, into which several ravines converge, is seen the simple monument erected to the memory of Ferguson and others; and in the foreground, on the right, is seen the great tulip-tree, upon which, tradition says, ten Tories were hung.

7 The range known as King's Mountain extends about sixteen miles from north to south, with several spurs spreading laterally in each direction. One of these extends to the Broad River, near the Cherokee Ford, where I crossed that stream on my return from the Cowpens. Many of its spurs abound in marble and iron, and from its bosom a great number of streams, the beginning of rivers, gush out. The battle-ground is about twelve miles northwest of Yorkville, and one hundred and ninety from Charleston.

8 The Wateree River is that portion of the Catawba which flows through South Carolina. It is the Catawba to the dividing-line of the states, and, after its junction with the Congaree, is called the Santee. The Congaree is formed by a union of the Broad and Saluda Rivers at Columbia, the head of steam-boat navigation upon the Santee and Congaree, from the ocean.

9 This was the regiment that behaved so gallantly at the battle of Guilford.

10 The pioneers who had settled in the wilderness beyond the mountains, now Kentucky and Tennessee, were called Mountain Men.

11 While Ferguson was in Spartanburg District, on his way toward Gilbert Town, a detachment of his little army had a severe skirmish with Colonel Clarke and his men at Greene's Spring. Clarke and his company, some two hundred in number, had stopped at the plantation of Captain Dillard, who was one of them, and, after partaking of refreshments, proceeded to Greene's Spring. The same evening Ferguson arrived at Dillard's, whose wife soon learned, from the conversation of some of his men, that they knew where Clarke was encamped, and intended to surprise him that night. She hastily prepared supper for Ferguson and his men, and while they were eating she stole from the room, bridled a young horse, and, without a saddle, rode to the encampment of Clarke, and warned him of impending danger. In an instant every man was at his post, prepared for the enemy. Very soon Colonel Dunlap, with two hundred picked mounted men, sent by Ferguson, fell upon the camp of Clarke. Day had not yet dawned, and the enemy were greatly surprised and disconcerted when they found the Americans fully prepared to meet them. For fifteen minutes the conflict raged desperately in the gloom, when the Tories were repulsed with great slaughter, and the survivors hastened back to Ferguson's camp.

12 Those of his recruits who were without arms Ferguson furnished with rifles. Some of them so fixed the large knives which they usually carried about them, in the muzzle of their rifles, as to be used as bayonets, if occasion should require.

13 General Joseph Graham, who lived in the vicinity of King's Mountain, and knew many of those who were employed in the battle, wrote a graphic account of the events connected with that affair. His account is published in Foote's Sketches of North Carolina, page 264-269, inclusive.

14 The M'Dowells were all brave men. Joseph and William, the brothers of Charles, were with him in the battle on King's Mountain. Their mother, Ellen M'Dowell, was a woman of remarkable energy. Mrs. Ellet relates that on one occasion some marauders carried off some property during the absence of her husband. She assembled some of her neighbors, started in pursuit., and recovered the property. When her husband was secretly making gunpowder in a cave, she burned the charcoal for the purpose upon her own hearth, and carried it to him. Some of the powder thus manufactured was used in the battle on King's Mountain. – Women of the Revolution, iii., 356.

15 General Gates sent a copy of this report to Governor Jefferson for his perusal, and desired him to forward it to Congress. His letter to Jefferson is dated Hillsborough, November 1, 1780.

16 Isaac Shelby was born on the eleventh of December, 1750, near the North Mountain, a few miles from Hagerstown, in Maryland. His ancestors were from Wales. He learned the art of surveying, and at the age of twenty-one years settled in Western Virginia. He was with his father, Evan Shelby, in the battle at Point Pleasant, in 1774. He was afterward employed as a surveyor under Henderson & Co., in Kentucky. In July, 1776, he was appointed captain of a company of minute-men by the Virginia Committee of Safety. Governor Henry appointed him a commissary of supplies in 1777, and in 1778 he was attached to the Continental Commissary Department. In the spring of 1779, he was elected a member of the Virginia Legislature, from Washington county, and in the autumn Governor Jefferson gave him the commission of a major. He was engaged in defining the boundary-line between Virginia and North Carolina, the result of which placed his residence in the latter state. Governor Caswell soon afterward appointed him a colonel of the new county of Sullivan. In the summer of 1780, he was engaged in locating lands for himself in Kentucky, when he heard of the fall of Charleston. He returned home to engage in repelling the invaders. He raised three hundred mounted riflemen, crossed the mountains, and joined Colonel Charles M'Dowell, near the Cherokee Ford, on the Broad River. In that vicinity he was very active, until he joined other officers of like grade in an attack upon Major Ferguson, on King's Mountain. Colonel Shelby soon afterward suggested to Greene the expedition which resulted so brilliantly at the Cowpens. In the campaign of 1781, Shelby served under Marion, and was in the skirmish at Monk's Corner. Colonel Shelby was a member of the North Carolina Legislature in 1782; and ten years afterward, he was among the framers of the Constitution of Kentucky. In May of that year, he was elected the first governor of the new state. He served one term with great distinction; and in 1812, consented again to an election to the chief magistracy of Kentucky. His energy and Revolutionary fame aroused the patriotism of his state when the war with Great Britain broke out. At the head of four thousand volunteers, he marched to the shores of Lake Erie, to assist General Harrison in his warfare with the British and Indians in the Northwest. During the whole war, his services were great and valuable in the highest degree; and for his bravery at the battle of the Thames, Congress honored him with a gold medal. In 1817, President Monroe appointed him his Secretary of War, but on account of his age (being then sixty-seven), he declined the honor. His last public act was that of holding a treaty with the Chickasaw Indians, in 1818, in which General Jackson was his colleague. He was attacked with paralysis, in February, 1820, which somewhat disabled him. He died of apoplexy, on the eighteenth of July, 1826, at the age of seventy-six years. Shelby county, in Kentucky, was named in honor of him in 1792. A college at Shelbyville also hears his name. The Legislature of North Carolina voted him a sword. It was presented by Henry Clay in 1813.

17 Colonel Charles M'Dowell. His brother, Major M'Dowell, commanded his regiment till his return.

18 CAMPBELL was a native of Augusta, Virginia. He was of Scotch descent, and possessed all the fire of his Highland ancestors. He was among the first of the regular troops raised in Virginia in 1775, and was honored with a captain's commission. In 1776, he was made lieutenant colonel of the militia of Washington county, and, on the resignation of Evan Shelby, the father of Governor Shelby, he was promoted to colonel. That rank he retained until after the battle on King's Mountain and at Guilford, in both of which he greatly distinguished himself, when he was promoted by the Virginia Legislature to the rank of brigadier. La Fayette gave him the command of a brigade of riflemen and light infantry. He was taken sick a few weeks before the siege of Yorktown, and soon afterward died at the house of a friend. He was only in the thirty-sixth year of his age when he died. His military career, like those of Warren and Montgomery, was short, but brilliant, and on all occasions bravery marked his movements. Foote relates that in the battle on King's Mountain he rode down two horses, and at one time was seen on foot, with his coat off, and his shirt collar open, fighting at the head of his men. He also says, that on one occasion Senator Preston, of South Carolina, a grandson of Campbell, was breakfasting at a house near King's Mountain, and, while eating, the old landlady frequently turned to look at him. She finally asked him his name, and remarked, apologetically, that he appeared very much like the man she had most dreaded upon earth. "And who is that?" Preston inquired. "Colonel Campbell," replied the old lady, "that hung my husband at King's Mountain." *

19 James Williams was a native of Granville county, in North Carolina. He settled upon Little River, Laurens District, in South Carolina, in 1773, where he engaged in the pursuit of a farmer and merchant. He early espoused the patriot cause. Williams first appears as a colonel in the militia, in April, 1778. In the spring of 1779, he went into actual service, and he was probably at the siege of Savannah. He was with Sumter in 1780, but does not seem to have been permanently attached to the corps of that partisan. In the early part of that year, he was engaged in the battle at Musgrove's mill, on the Ennoree River. After that engagement, he went to Hillsborough, where he raised a corps of cavalry and returned to South Carolina; and during Ferguson's movements, after crossing the Wateree, Williams continually hovered around his camp. In the sanguinary battle upon King's Mountain, he was slain. He was near Major Ferguson and both officers received their death-wound at the same moment. He died on the morning after the battle, and was buried within two miles of the place where he fell. Tradition says that his first words, when reviving a little soon after he was shot, were, "For God's sake, boys, don't give up the hill!"

20 Colonel Williams had just been joined by sixty men from Lincoln, under Colonel Hambrite and Major Chronicle.

21 Joseph Winston was a native of North Carolina, and was the first senator in the Republican Legislature, from Stokes county. He was a member of Congress from 1793 to 1795, and again from 1803 to 1807. He died in 1814.

22 John Sevier was descended from an ancient French family. The original orthography of the name was Xavier. His father settled on the Shenandoah, in Virginia, where this son was born, about 1740. In 1769, he accompanied an exploring party to East Tennessee, where, with his father and brother, he settled on the Holston River. He aided in the construction of Fort Watauga; and while in that fortress as commander, bearing the title of captain, he caught a wife! One day, in June, 1776, he saw a young lady speeding, like a fawn, toward the fort, closely pursued by Cherokees, under "Old Abraham." She leaped the palisades, and fell into the arms of the gallant captain. Her name was Catharine Sherrill; and in 1779 she became the second wife of Sevier, by whom he had ten children. Sevier was with Shelby at the battle of Point Pleasant, in 1774. During the first five years of the war, he was an active Whig partisan, on the mountain frontier of the Carolinas, was raised to the rank of colonel, and greatly distinguished himself at King's Mountain. He was in the battle near Musgrove's Mills, and early in the following year he chastised some of the turbulent Indians among the mountains. At the close of the war, he received the commission of brigadier; and he was so much beloved by the people, that by acclamation he was acknowledged governor of the "State of FRANKLIN" or FRANKLAND." * He was so often engaged in treaties with the Indians, that they called him the treaty-maker. When the State of Tennessee was organized, and admitted into the Union, Sevier was elected its first governor. In 1811, he was elected to a seat in Congress, with Felix Grundy and John Rhea, and in 1813 was re-elected. During the war, Madison appointed him Indian commissioner, and while engaged in his duties, near Fort Decatur, on the east side of the Tallapoosa River, he died, on the twenty-fourth of September, 1815. Under the direction of the late General Gaines, he was buried with the honors of war. No stone marks his grave; but in the Nashville cemetery, a handsome marble monument to his memory has lately been erected. Upon the monument is the following inscription "SEVIER, noble and successful defender of the early settlers of Tennessee; the first, and for twelve years governor; representative in Congress; commissioner in many treaties with the Indians. He served his country faithfully for forty years, and in that service died. An admirer of patriotism and merit unrequited erects this cenotaph."

* At the close of the Revolution, that portion of North Carolina bordering East Tennessee contained quite a large and exceedingly active population. Dissatisfied with the course pursued by North Carolina, they called a convention, adopted a Constitution, and organized a state government, which they called FRANKLAND, in honor of Dr. Franklin. They chose John Sevier for governor, and organized a judiciary, &c. When informed of this movement, Governor Caswell issued a proclamation against "this lawless thirst for power," and denounced it as a revolt. But the mountaineers did not heed official menaces. Violence ensued. The difficulties were finally settled, and the State of Frankland disappeared.

23 Captain Depeyster belonged to a corps of Loyalists, called the King's American Regiment. His signature, here given, I copied from a letter of his to General Gates a few days after the battle, while Depeyster was a prisoner.

24 The following is a copy of the inscriptions: North side. – "Sacred to the memory of Major WILLIAM CHRONICLE, Captain JOHN MATTOCKS, WILLIAM ROBB, and JOHN BOYD, who were killed here fighting in defence of America, on the seventh of October, 1780." South side. - Colonel FERGUSON,* an officer belonging to his Britannic majesty, was here defeated and killed."

* Major Patrick Ferguson was a Scotchman, a son of the eminent jurist, James Ferguson, and nephew of Patrick Murray (Lord Elibank). He entered the army in Flanders at the age of eighteen years. He came to America in the spring of 1777, and was active in the battle on the Brandywine, in September of that year. He was active on the Hudson in 1779, and accompanied Sir Henry Clinton to South Carolina. He so distinguished himself at the siege of Charleston in 1780, that he was particularly mentioned by the commander-in-chief. He was on the high road to military fame, when he was slain on King's Mountain. He was a major in the British army, and lieutenant colonel of the Tory militia.

25 This name is derived from the circumstance that, some years prior to the Revolution, before this section of country was settled, some persons in Camden (then called Pine-tree) employed two men to go up to the Thicketty Mountain, and in the grassy intervales among the hills, raise cattle. As a compensation, they were allowed the entire use of the cows during the summer for making butter and cheese, and the steers for tilling labor. In the fall, large numbers of the fattest cattle would be driven down to Camden to be slaughtered for beef, on account of the owners. This region, so favorable for rearing cows, on account of the grass and fine springs, was consequently called The Cowpens.

26 They have a dangerous practice at the South in clearing their wild lands. The larger trees are girdled and left standing, to decay and fall down, instead of being felled by the ax. Cultivation is carried on among them, and frequently they fall suddenly, and endanger the lives of the laborers in the field. Such was the condition of the field here represented.

27 DANIEL MORGAN was a native of New Jersey, where he was born in 1737, and at an early age went to Virginia. He was a private soldier under Braddock, in 1755, and after the defeat of that officer, returned to his occupation of a farmer and wagoner. When the war of the Revolution broke out, he joined the army under Washington, at Cambridge, and commanded a corps of riflemen. He accompanied Arnold across the wilderness to Quebec, and distinguished himself at the siege of that city. He was made a prisoner there. After his exchange, he was appointed to the command of the 11th Virginia regiment, in which was incorporated his rifle corps. He performed great service at Stillwater, when Burgoyne was defeated. Gates unjustly omitted his name in his report of that affair to Congress. He served under Gates and Greene at the South, where he became distinguished as a partisan officer. His victory at the Cowpens was considered a

most brilliant affair, and Congress voted him a gold medal. (See below). At the close of the war, he returned to his farm. He commanded the militia organized to quell the Whisky Insurrection in Western Virginia, in 1794, and soon afterward was elected a member of Congress. His estate in Clarke county, a few miles from Winchester, Virginia, was called Saratoga. He resided there until 1800, when he removed to Winchester, where he died on the sixth of July, 1802, in the sixty-seventh year of his age. The house in which he died stood in the northwest part of the town, and a few years since was occupied by the Reverend Mr. Boyd. His grave is in the Presbyterian grave-yard at Winchester; and over it is a plain horizontal slab, raised a few feet from the ground, upon which is the following inscription:

Flag of Morgan's Rifle Corp.*

"Major-general DANIEL MORGAN departed this life on July the 6th, 1802, in the sixty-seventh year of his age. Patriotism and valor were the prominent features of his character, and the honorable services he rendered to his country during the Revolutionary war crowned him with glory, and will remain in the hearts of his countrymen, a perpetual monument to his memory."

In early life General Morgan was dissipated, and was a famous pugilist; yet the teachings of a pious mother always made him reverential when his thoughts turned toward the Deity. In his latter years, he professed religion, and became a member of the Presbyterian church in Winchester. "Ah!" he would often exclaim, when talking of the past, "people said old Morgan never feared – they thought old Morgan never prayed – they did not know old Morgan was often miserably afraid." He said he trembled at Quebec, and in the gloom of early morning, when approaching the battery at Cape Diamond, he knelt in the snow and prayed; and before the battle at the Cowpens, he went into the woods, ascended a tree, and there poured out his soul in prayer for protection. In person, Morgan was large and strong. He was six feet in height, and very muscular.

---

* This sketch of the flag of Morgan's rifle corps I made from the original in the Museum at Alexandria, in Virginia.

Gold Medal Awarded to Morgan Ü

Ü The following are the devices and inscriptions upon the medal: An Indian queen with a quiver on her back, in the act of crowning an officer with a laurel wreath; his hand resting upon his sword. A cannon lying upon the ground; various military weapons and implements in the back-ground. Legend: DANIEL MORGAN DUCI EXERCITUS COMITIA AMERICANA – "The American Congress to General Daniel Morgan." Reverse: An officer mounted, at the head of his troops, charging a flying enemy. A battle in the back-ground. In front, a personal combat between a dragoon unhorsed and a foot soldier. Legend: VICTORIA LIBERTATIS VINDEX –"Victory, the assertor of Liberty." Exergue: FUGATIS, CAPTIS AUT C SIS AD COWPENS HOSTIBUS, 17TH JANUARY, 1781 – "The foe put to flight, taken, or slain, at the Cowpens, January 17, 1781."

---

28 John Eager Howard was born in Baltimore county, Maryland, on the fourth of June, 1752. When the war commenced, he entered the service as captain of one of those bodies of militia termed flying camps. He was present at the battle near White Plains, New York. His corps was dismissed in December, 1776, and at the solicitation of his friends, he accepted of the commission of major in one of the Continental battalions of Maryland. In the spring of 1777, he joined the army under Washington, in New Jersey, with which he remained until the close of June, when he returned home, on account of the death of his father. A few days after the battle on the Brandywine, he rejoined the army, and was distinguished for his cool courage in the battle at Germantown, of which he wrote an interesting account. In that engagement, he was major of the 4th regiment, commanded by Colonel Hall, of Maryland. Major Howard was present at the battle of Monmouth, in 1778. On the first of June, 1779, he received a commission as lieutenant colonel of the 5th Maryland regiment, "to take rank from the eleventh day of March, 1778." In 1780, he went with the Maryland and Delaware troops to the South, and served under Gates until the arrival of Greene. Soon after this, we find him with Morgan, winning bright laurels at the Cowpens; and for his bravery there, Congress awarded him the honor of a silver medal. Howard again distinguished himself at the battle of Guilford, where he was wounded. At the conclusion of the war, Colonel Howard married Margaret, the daughter of Chief-justice Chew, around whose house at Germantown he had valiantly battled. In November, 1788, he was chosen governor of Maryland, which office he held for three years. He was commissioned major general of militia in 1794, but declined the honor. Washington invited him to a seat in his cabinet, at the head of the War Department, in 1795. That honor he also declined. He was then a member of the Maryland Senate. In 1796, he was elected to the Senate of the United States, where he served until 1813, when he retired from public life. When, in 1814, Baltimore was threatened with destruction by the enemy, the veteran soldier prepared to take the field. The battle at North Point, however, rendered such a step unnecessary. He lost his wife in 1827; and on the twelfth of October, 1827, he, too, left the scenes of earth, at the age of seventy-five years. Honor, wealth, and the ardent love of friends, were his lot in life, and few men ever went down to the grave more truly lamented than John Eager Howard.

Silver Medal Awarded to Colonel Howard*

* The following are the device and inscriptions: An officer mounted, with uplifted sword, pursuing an officer on foot bearing a stand of colors. Victory is seen descending in front, over the former, holding a wreath in her right hand over his head. In her left band is a palm branch. Legend: JOHN EAGER HOWARD, LEGIONIS PEDITUM PR FECT O COMITIA AMERICANA – "The American Congress to John Eager Howard, commander of a regiment of infantry." Reverse: A laurel wreath, inclosing the inscription, QUOD IN NUTANTEM HOSTIUM ACIEM SUBITO IRRUENS, PR CLARUM BELLIC VIRTUTIS SPECIMEN DEDIT IN PUGNA, AD COWPENS, 17TH JANUARY, 1781 – "Because, rushing suddenly on the wavering line of the foe, he gave a brilliant specimen of martial courage at the battle of the Cowpens, January 17, 1781."

29 No accurate plan of the arrangement of the troops on this occasion has ever been made. Captain Hammond made a sketch many years afterward from memory, which is published in Johnson's Traditions and Reminiscences of the Revolution. As it does not fully agree with official reports, I forbear copying it.

30 Between this eminence and the one on which Howard was stationed, the Mill-gap road passes.

31 WILLIAM WASHINGTON, "the modern Marcellus," "the sword of his country," was the eldest son of Baily Washington, of Stafford county, Virginia, where he was born on the 28th of February, 1752. He was educated for the Church, but the peculiar position of public affairs led him into the political field. He early espoused the patriot cause, and entered the army under Colonel Hugh (afterward General) Mercer as captain. He was in the battle near Brooklyn, Long Island, distinguished himself at Trenton, and was with his beloved general when he fell at Princeton. He was afterward a major in Colonel Baylor's corps of cavalry, and was with that officer when attacked by General Grey, at Tappan, in 1778. The following year, he joined the army under Lincoln in South Carolina, and was very active in command of a light corps in the neighborhood of Charleston. He became attached, with his corps, to the division of General Morgan, and with that officer fought bravely at the Cowpens. For his valor on that occasion, Congress presented him with a silver medal. He was an active officer in Greene's celebrated retreat, and again fought bravely at Guilford Court House. He behaved gallantly at Hobkirk's Hill, near Camden, and at the battle at Eutaw Springs he exhibited signal valor; but his horse being shot under him, he was there made a prisoner. He remained a captive until the close of the war. Having become attached to a South Carolina lady during his captivity, he married her, and settled in Charleston. He represented that district in the State Legislature. His talents as a statesman were so conspicuous, that he was solicited to become a candidate for governor. He declined the honor, chiefly because he could not make a speech. When President Adams appointed General Washington commander-in-chief of the American army, he chose Colonel Washington to be one of his staff, with the

Silver Medal Awarded to Washington*

rank of brigadier. Colonel Washington died on the sixth of March, 1810. He was tall in person, possessed of great strength and activity, and in society was taciturn and modest.

---

* The following are the device and inscriptions: An officer mounted at the head of a body of cavalry, charging flying troops; Victory is flying over the heads of the Americans, holding a laurel crown in her right hand and a palm branch in her left. Legend: GULIELMO WASHINGTON LEGIONIS EQUITUM PR FECT O COMITIA AMERICANA – "The American Congress to William Washington, commander of a regiment of cavalry." Reverse: QUOD PARVA MILITUM MANU STRENUE PROSECUTUS HOSTES VIRTUTIS INGENIT PR CLARUM SPECIMEN DEDIT   IN PUGNA AD COWPENS, 17TH JANUARY, 1781 – "Because, having vigorously pursued the foe with a small band of soldiers, he gave a brilliant specimen of innate valor in the battle at the Cowpens, 17th January, 1781." This inscription is within a laurel wreath.

---

32 It is related that this wound was twice the subject for the sallies of wit of two American ladies, who were sisters, daughters of Colonel Montfort, of Halifax county, North Carolina. When Cornwallis and his army were at Halifax, on their way to Virginia, Tarleton was at the house of an American. In the presence of Mrs. Wilie Jones (one of these sisters), Tarleton spoke of Colonel Washington as an illiterate fellow, hardly able to write his name. "Ah! colonel," said Mrs. Jones, "you ought to know better, for you bear on your person proof that he knows very well how to make his mark!" At another time, Tarleton was speaking sarcastically of Washington, in the presence of her sister, Mrs. Ashe. "I would be happy to see Colonel Washington," he said, with a sneer. Mrs. Ashe instantly replied, "If you had looked behind you, Colonel Tarleton, at the battle of the Cowpens, you would have enjoyed that pleasure." Stung with this keen wit, Tarleton placed his hand on his sword. General Leslie, who was present, remarked, "Say what you please, Mrs. Ashe, Colonel Tarleton knows better than to insult a lady in my presence." – Mrs. Ellet's Women of the Revolution.

33 See Stedman, ii., 324.

34 These two pieces of artillery were first taken from Burgoyne at Saratoga; then retaken by the British at Camden; now were recovered by the Americans, and afterward fell into the hands of Cornwallis at Guilford. They were of the kind of small field-pieces called "grasshoppers."

35 Ramsay, Gordon, Marshall, Lee, Johnson, Tarleton, Moultrie.

36 Journals of Congress, vii., 47.

37 South Carolina was occupied by twenty-eight Indian nations when the Europeans first made a permanent settlement upon the Ashley River. The domain of these tribes extended from the ocean to the mountains. The Westos, Stonos, Coosaws, and Sewees occupied the country between Charleston and the Edisto Rivers. They were conquered by the Savannahs, and expelled from the country. The Yamassees and Tluspahs held the territory in the neighborhood of Port Royal. The Savannahs, Serannahs, Cussobos, and Euchees occupied the middle country, along the Isundigia, or Savannah River. The Apalachians inhabited the head waters of the Savannah and Alatamaha, and gave their name to the mountains of Apalachy, and the bay of Apalachicola. The Muscoghees or Creeks occupied a part of the country between the Savannah and Broad Rivers, being divided by the latter from the country of the Cherokees. The Congarees, Santees, Waterees, Saludas, Catawbas, Peedees, and Winyaws lived along the rivers which bear their respective names. The Muscoghees and Catawbas were the most warlike; the Cherokees were more numerous than either, but more peaceful. These various nations, when Charleston was founded, could muster probably fifty thousand warriors. – See Simms's History of South Carolina, page 67.

38 Bancroft, iii., 246.

39 This massacre was at Pocotaligo, an old village in the parish of Prince William, in Beaufort District. It then contained about three hundred inhabitants. There stood Fort Balfour, which was captured, during the Revolution, by a few Americans under Colonel Harden.

40 This is the name of the south fork of the Combahee River, which empties into St. Helena Sound. The place of the encampment was near Barnwell, the capital of Barnwell District.

41 Fort Prince George was a strong work. It was quadrangular, with an earthen rampart six feet high, upon which stockades were placed. Around it was a ditch, and it had a natural glacis on two sides At each angle was a bastion, on which four small cannons were mounted. It contained barracks for a hundred men.

42 Marion, in a letter quoted by Weems, mentioned the wanton destruction of the corn, then in full ear, and said, "I saw every where around the footsteps of the little Indian children, where they had lately played under the shelter of the rustling corn. No doubt they had often looked up with joy to the swelling shocks, and gladdened when they thought of their abundant cakes for the coming winter. When we are gone, thought I, they will return, and, peeping through the weeds with tearful eyes, will mark the ghastly ruin poured over their homes, and the happy fields where they had so often played. 'Who did this?' they will ask their mothers. 'The white people; the Christians did it!' will be the reply."

43 John Stuart came to America with Oglethorpe, probably with the Highlanders under M'Intosh, the father of General Lachlin M'Intosh, of the Revolution, who settled upon the Alatamahaw, and called the place New Inverness. The Indians were greatly pleased with the dress and character of the Highlanders, and to this circumstance is attributed Stuart's influence among them. Stuart went to Charleston; became Indian agent; married Miss Fenwick, daughter of one of the wealthiest men in the province, and finally became one of the king's council. He lived in the house on the corner of Wadd and Orange Streets, Charleston, now (1851) owned by William Carson, Esq. He had commanded a corps on Cumberland Island, who gallantly repulsed the Spaniards in 1745, and this was the commencement of his popularity which led up to the civil station that he held in council. He chose the royal side when the Revolution broke out, and to him was attributed all of the difficulties with the Indians upon the frontier during the first year of that struggle. Alarmed for his personal safety, he fled to St. Augustine. His estate was confiscated. He died in England. His son, Sir John Stuart, became a distinguished general in the British army. – See Johnsons Traditions of the Revolution, page 107.

44 Moultrie, Ramsey, Simms, Johnson.

45 A greater portion of the Cherokee Nation, now in existence, occupy territory west of the Mississippi. A remnant of them remain in North Carolina, at a place called Qualla Town, in Haywood county. They were allowed to remain when the general emigration of their nation took place. They have a tract of seventy-two thousand acres of land. Almost every adult can read in the Cherokee language, and most of them understand English. They manufacture all their necessaries; have courts, lawyers, and judges of their own, and have all the political rights of free citizens of the state. They are sober, industrious, and religious. Their present business chief (1851) is William H. Thomas, Esq., senator from that district (50th). The Qualla Town Cherokees exhibit some remarkable cases of longevity. In 1850, Messrs. Mitchell and Smoot, while on an official visit there, saw Kalosteh, who was then one hundred and twenty years old. His wife "went out like a candle," as Kalosteh said, the year before, at the age of one hundred and twenty-five years. It is said that people one hundred years old are not uncommon there.

46 Mr. Drayton was, at this time, quite a young man, a descendant of one of the leading families of South Carolina. He was a nephew of Governor Bull. When Republican principles began to work up to the surface, and become visible at the South, in 1771, his pen was employed on the side of government, in opposition to Christopher Gadsden and others. These essays brought him into notice. He was introduced at court, and was appointed one of Governor Bull's council. As the Revolution advanced to a crisis, Drayton saw the injustice of Great Britain, and espoused the Republican cause. He became a favorite of the people, and, while a delegate in the Continental Congress, he died in their service in 1779.

47 Robert Cunningham was an Irish settler in the District of Ninety-Six, now Abbeville, where he was commissioned a judge in 1770. After his release, in 1776, he removed to Charleston. In 1780, he was appointed a brigadier general to command the Loyalists of that province. His estate was confiscated in 1782, and not being allowed to remain in the province at the close of the war, he went to Nassau, New Providence, where he died in 1813, at the age of seventy-four years. The British government indemnified him for his losses, and gave him a pension. His brother Patrick was deputy surveyor of the colony in 1769. He received the commission of colonel, under Robert, in 1780. His property, also, was confiscated in 1782, and at the close of the war he went to Florida. The South Carolina Legislature afterward treated him leniently, and restored a part of his property. He was elected a member of the Legislature by his Tory friends. He died in 1794.

48 Richard Richardson was a native of Virginia, where he was employed as a land-surveyor at the time when Washington was engaged in the same pursuit. He afterward settled in old Craven county, in South Carolina; and during the Indian border wars, he commanded a regiment. As a representative in the Provincial Congress of South Carolina, Colonel Richardson assisted in forming the first Republican Constitution for that state. He was with General Lincoln in his Southern campaigns, and with that officer became a prisoner at Charleston, at which time he was a brigadier. With others, he was sent to St. Augustine, from whence he returned in September with a broken constitution, and soon died at his residence, near Salisbury, in Sumter District, at the age of about seventy-six years. Soon after his death, Tarleton occupied his house, and, believing the family plate was buried with him, had his body disinterred. When he was about leaving, that cruel man applied the torch to the house with his own hand, avowing his determination to make it the "funeral pile of the widow and her three young rebels." His son, James B., was afterward governor of South Carolina. – See Johnson's Traditions, &c., page 158.

49 William Thomson was a native of Pennsylvania, and a relative of Charles Thomson, the secretary of the Continental Congress. He was born about the year 1727, and, while a child, was taken to Orangeburg District, in South Carolina. He was a patriot, and was placed in command of the 3d regiment, called the Rangers. With his regiment, he fought in the battle on Sullivan's Island in 1776. He was with General Howe in Georgia. and served under the command of D'Estaing at Savannah. He behaved gallantly, and suffered much during the greater part of the war. At its close, he returned to his estate at Belleville, near Fort Motte, with shattered health and fortune. There he continued in the pursuit of an indigo planter, which he began before the war, until 1796, when declining health induced him to go to medicinal springs in Virginia. He died there on the twenty-second of November of that year, at the age of sixty-nine years.

50 Instructions of the Provincial Congress to Colonel Richardson.

51 Thomas Sumter was one of the South Carolina patriots earliest in the field. Of his early life and habits very little is known. In March, 1776, he was a lieutenant colonel of a regiment of riflemen. After the fall of Charleston, in 1780, when a partisan warfare was carried on in the Carolinas, Sumter began to display those powers which made him so renowned. Governor Rutledge, perceiving his merits, promoted him to brigadier of militia. His battles at Rocky Mount and Hanging Rock gave him great eclat. He was defeated by Tarleton at Fishing Creek, on the Catawba, just after the unfortunate battle near Camden. With a few survivors, and other volunteers, he crossed the Broad River, ranged the districts upon its western banks, and on the eighth of November, 1780, defeated Colonel Wemyss, who had attacked his camp. He afterward defeated Tarleton at Blackstocks. Sumter was wounded, but was able to take the field early in February, 1781. While Greene was retreating before Cornwallis, Sumter, with Marion, was humbling British garrisons in the lower country. He continued in active service during the whole campaign of 1781. Ill health caused him to leave the army before the close of the war. He served a long time in the Congress of the United States. He died at his residence at Statesburg, near Bradford Springs, in Sumter District, on the first of June, 1832, at the remarkable age of ninety-eight years.

52 Colonel (afterward General) James Jackson, in a letter to the late Mathew Carey, of Philadelphia, written many years subsequent to the war (the original of which is in possession of H. C. Baird, Esq., of Philadelphia), says, "General Sumter was wounded early in the action, and retired. Colonel (now General) Twiggs and myself fought the enemy three hours after this, and defeated them totally, bringing off upward of thirty dragoon horses."

53 Journals of Congress, vii., 14.

54 Tradition has preserved many thrilling accounts of the sufferings, self-sacrifice, and great courage of the women westward of the Broad River. The gentle maiden and the rough woodsman were taught in the same school of rude experience, and imbibed from the events of daily life a spirit of self-reliance seldom seen in more refined society. Among the heroines of this region, Sarah Dillard, of Spartanburg District, mentioned on page 424, and Dicey Langston, of Laurens District, were among the most conspicuous. Of the latter, Mrs. Ellet, in her admirable sketches of Women of the Revolution, has recorded many interesting anecdotes. One of these will suffice to illustrate the courage of this young girl – a noble type of her class. Her father was infirm; her brothers were abroad; and Dicey, then only sixteen, was her father's chief companion and solace. A Tory band, called the Bloody Scout, under the notorious Bill Cunningham, spread terror over that lonely region; and the known patriotism of Dicey often jeoparded the life and property of her father. On one occasion, she learned that the Scout were about to fall upon a settlement beyond the Tyger, where her brothers dwelt. She resolved to save them. At night and alone, she crossed the Ennoree and hastened to the banks of the Tyger. It was swollen, yet she did not recoil from the danger. The blackness of midnight was upon the land, yet she went boldly into the stream; Neck deep in the channel, she became confused, and did not know which way to go. God led her to the northern bank; and, like an angel of mercy, she sped to the settlement. When the Bloody Scout reached there the next day, no man was to be found.

Miss Langston married Thomas Springfield, of Greenville, South Carolina, where many of her descendants are still living. She died only a few years ago. Mrs. Thomas, Mrs. Simms, Mrs. Otterson, Miss Jackson, Mrs. Potter, and other less conspicuous of the women west of the Broad River, were copatriots with Dicey Langston. Of these, Mrs. Ellet has made many interesting records.

Chapter XVII

"Ours are no hirelings train'd to the fight,
With cymbal and clarion, all glittering and bright;
No prancing of chargers, no martial display;
No war-trump is heard from our silent array.
O'er the proud heads of freemen our star-banner waves;
Men, firm as their mountains, and still as their graves,
To-morrow shall pour out their life-blood like rain:
We come back in triumph, or come not again!"
                                        – T. GRAY.

At noon I crossed the Broad River at the Cherokee Ford, and turning to the southeast, pressed on toward Yorkville and the interesting fields of conflict beyond, near the waters of the Catawba and its surname, the Wateree, where the chivalrous partisans of the South, scorning the Delilah lap of ease, retained their strength and battled manfully with the Philistines of the crown. The river at the ford is about eight hundred yards wide, and upon the firm pathway, which has been constructed at considerable expense, the average depth of water did not exceed one foot. Unless the river is much swollen, the ford is perfectly safe. A strong dam, owned by the proprietors of the iron-works, crosses the river an eighth of a mile above; and so shallow and rapid is the current, and so rocky the bed of the river, for many miles in this vicinity, that it is quite unnavigable, except in a few places.

Soon after leaving the ford, I passed through a gorge of a spur of King's Mountain, which here comes down in a precipitous ridge to the Broad River. The scenery within this gorge was the most romantic I had observed in the Southern country. From a ravine, just wide enough for the passage of a small stream and the high-way, the hills rise almost perpendicularly to a considerable altitude. They were covered with the various evergreens which give beauty to Southern forests in winter;

View at the Cherokee Ford. 1

and from the fissures of the rocks, where the water-fountains were bursting forth, hundreds of icicles were glittering in prismatic beauty wherever the sun shed its rays upon them. It was truly a gorgeous scene. Along

Mountain Gorge near the Cherokee Ford.

this sinuous mountain stream, rock-bound on either side, the road continued to an iron establishment, where it ascends the steep margins of the hills, presenting a surface of deep adhesive red earth. Descending the eastern side of the eminence, I crossed King's Creek, a dozen miles below the place where I passed it two days before when on my way to the Cowpens. Soon again I was among the rough hills, and so bad was the road, that at sunset I had traveled only ten miles from the Cherokee Ford. I discovered that the temporary repairs of my wagon had not been sufficient to withstand the rough usage of the way, and that more thorough work was necessary before I could pursue my journey with safety. Yorkville, the nearest place in advance where a smith could be found, was fourteen miles distant, so I was compelled to halt for the night at a small log-house, of forbidding aspect, among the mountains. The food and shelter was of the plainest kind imaginable. There was no "light in the dwelling," except the blaze of pine wood upon the hearth, and I wrote a letter by the glare of a resinous knot, brought from the "wood pile" for the

purpose. Lying in bed, I could count the stars at the zenith while the open floor below afforded such ample ventilation, that my buffalo robe, wrapped around me, was not uncomfortable on that keen frosty night. But generous, open-handed hospitality was in that humble cabin, which made amends for trifling discomforts, and I felt satisfied.

> "Out upon the calf, I say,
>   Who turns his grumbling head away,
>   And quarrels with his feed of hay,
>   Because it is not clover.
>   Give to me the happy mind,
>   That will ever seek and find
>   Something fair and something kind,
>   All the wide world over."

> "Our hungry eyes may fondly wish
>   To revel amid flesh and fish,
>   And gloat upon the silver dish
>   That holds a golden plover
>   Yet if our table be but spread
>   With bacon and with hot corn-bread,
>   Be thankful if we're always fed
>   As well, the wide world over."

Unwilling to risk a journey to Yorkville in my broken buggy, I hired a team of mules and a lumber-wagon from my host, to convey myself and baggage thither; and placing Charley and the vehicle in charge of his son, a lad of fourteen years, we started for the distant village at daybreak the next morning. All the way over that rough road I had practical evidence that mules are, like facts, "stubborn things." I was furnished with a hickory goad as long as an angler's rod, and with this I labored faithfully, full half of the way, to whip the animals into a trot where a level space occurred. But I made no visible impression; walk they would, until they reached the brow of a hill, when they would descend with the vehemence of the swine of old, who, filled with devils, ran down into the sea. Down three long hills, rocky and gullied, they ran, while my energies were fully occupied in pulling at the reins with one hand, and securing my seat upon a loose board, covered with a sheepskin, with the other. I reached Yorkville in safety at a little past meridian, resolved never again to play postillion with mules or donkeys, whether biped or quadruped.

Yorkville, the capital of York District, in South Carolina, almost two hundred miles from Charleston, is a very pleasant village of about eight hundred inhabitants, situated in the midst of a high plain, on the dividing-ridge between the waters of the Broad and Catawba Rivers. Sheltered from the northwest winds by the mountains, the climate is mild in winter; elevated far above the low country of the Carolinas, it is salubrious in summer. The streets of the village are regularly laid out, and adorned with beautiful Pride of India trees, filled, when I was there, with clusters of fruit. I saw some elegant mansions; and in the gardens, fine palmettoes, the first I had seen, were growing. I passed the Sabbath pleasantly in Yorkville, and left it early on Monday morning, with the impression that not a lovelier village flourishes in the "upper country" of the South. Leaving the great highway to Columbia on the right, I traversed the more private roads in the direction of the Catawba, to visit the scenes of valor and suffering in the vicinity of that stream. The weather was fine, and the roads generally good. Soon after leaving Yorkville, I passed through a part of the Catawba reservation, a narrow tract of land on the Catawba River, near the southeast corner of Yorkville District. The Catawba tribe, once so powerful, have dwindled down to the merest remnant. For their general adherence to the patriots during the Revolution, they have always received the fostering care of the state. Their number now does not exceed one hundred, and in a few years that once great rival tribe of the Five Nations will be extinct. **2** So the aborigines pass away, and the few survivors in our land may chant in sorrow,

> "We, the rightful lords of yore,
> Are the rightful lords no more;
> Like the silver mist, we fail,
> Like the red leaves in the gale –
> Fail, like shadows, when the dawning
> Waves the bright flag of the morning."
> - J. M'LELLAN, Junior.

> "I will go to my tent and lie down in despair;
> I will paint me with black, and will sever my hair;
> I will sit on the shore when the hurricane blows,
> And reveal to the God of the tempest my woes;
> I will weep for a season, on bitterness fed,
> For my kindred are gone to the hills of the dead;
> But they died not of hunger, or lingering decay –
> The hand of the white man hath swept them away!"
> - HENRY ROWE SCHOOLCRAFT.

I crossed the Fishing Creek at sunset; and at the house of a young planter, a mile beyond, passed the night. There I experienced hospitality in its fullest degree. The young husbandman had just begun business life for himself, and, with his wife and "wee bairn," occupied a modest house, with only one room. I was not aware of the extent of their accommodations when I asked for a night's entertainment, and the request was promptly complied with. It made no difference to them, for they had two beds in the room, and needed but one for themselves; the other was at my service. The young man was very intelligent and inquiring, and midnight found us in pleasant conversation. He would accept no compensation in the morning; and I left his humble dwelling full of reverence for that generous and unsuspecting hospitality of Carolina, where the people will give a stranger lodgings even in their own bedrooms, rather than turn him from their doors.

> "Plain and artless her sons; but whose doors open faster
> At the knock of the stranger or the tale of disaster?
> How like to the rudeness of their dear native mountains,

With rich ore in their bosoms, and life in their fountains."
                                                    - GASTON.

My journey of a day from Fishing Creek to Rocky Mount, on the Catawba, was delightful. The winter air on January 15, 1849, was like a breath of late April in New England; and the roads, passing through a picturesque country, were generally good. Almost every plantation, too, is clustered with Revolutionary associations; for this region, like Westchester county, in New York, was the scene of

View of the Great Falls of the Catawba.

continual partisan movements, skirmishes, and cruelties, during the last three years of the war. Near the mouth of the Fishing Creek (which empties into the Catawba two miles above the Great Falls), Sumter suffered defeat, after partial success at Rocky Mount below; and down through Chester, Fairfield, and Richland, too, Whigs and Tories battled fearfully for territorial possession, plunder, and personal revenge. Some of these scenes will be noticed presently. Turning to the left at Beckhamville, 3 I traversed a rough and sinuous road down to the banks of the Catawba, just below the Great Falls. Here yet remain the foundations of a projected United States military establishment, to be called Mount Dearborn, which was abandoned; and upon the brink of the foaming waters stands a cotton-mill, the property of Daniel M'Cullock, operated by white hands, and devoted chiefly to the production of cotton-yarns. At this place, in the midst of a fine cotton-growing country, almost inexhaustible water-power invites capital and enterprise to seek good investment, and confer substantial benefit upon the state. The place is wild and romantic. Almost the whole volume of the river is here compressed by a rugged island into a narrow channel, between steep, rocky shores, fissured and fragmented, as if by some powerful convulsion. There are no perpendicular falls; but down a rocky bed the river tumbles in mingled rapids and cascades, roaring and foaming, and then subsides into comparative calmness in a basin below.

It was late in the afternoon when I finished my sketch of the Falls, and leaving Mount Dearborn, crossed Rock Creek and reined up in front of the elegant mansion of Mrs. Barkley, at Rocky Mount. Her dwelling, where refined hospitality bore rule, is beautifully situated upon an eminence overlooking the Catawba and the surrounding country, and within a few rods of the remains of the old village and the battle-ground. Surrounded by gardens and ornamental trees, it must be a delightful summer residence. Yet there was grief in that dwelling and the habiliments of mourning indicated the ravages of death. The husband and father had been an honored member of the Legislature of South Carolina, and in the midst of his useful public life he was thrown from his gig and killed. Yet the light of hospitality was not extinguished there, and I shall long remember, with pleasure, the night I passed at Rocky Mount. Accompanied by Mrs. Barkley's three daughters, and a young planter from "over the river," I visited the battleground before sunset, examined the particular localities indicated by the finger of tradition. and sketched the accompanying view

View at Rocky Mount.

of the principal place of conflict. Here, in the porch, sitting with this interesting household in the golden gleams of the declining sun, let us open the clasped volume of history, and read a brief but brilliant page.

Almost simultaneously, three distinguished partisans of the South appeared conspicuous, after the fall of Charleston (May 12, 1780); Marion, between the Pedee and Santee; Sumter, upon the Catawba and Broad Rivers; and Pickens, in the vicinity of the Saluda and Savannah Rivers. With the surrender of Charleston, the hopes of the South Carolina patriots withered; and so complete was the subjugation of the state by the royal arms, that on the fourth of June, Sir Henry Clinton wrote to the ministry, "I may venture to assert that there are few men in South Carolina who are not either our prisoners or in arms with us." Many unsubdued patriots sought shelter in North Carolina, and others went up toward the mountains and gathered the cowed Whigs into bands to avenge the insults of their Tory oppressors. Early in July, Sumter (who had taken refuge in Mecklenburg), with a few chosen patriots who gathered around him, returned to South Carolina.

> "Catawba's waters smiled again
> To see her Sumter's soul in arms;
> And issuing from each glade and glen,
> Rekindled by war's fierce alarms,
> Thronged hundreds through the solitude
> Of the wild forest, to the call
> Of him whose spirit, unsubdued,
> Fresh impulse gave to each, to all."
> - J. W. SIMMONS.

Already Whigs between the Catawba and Broad Rivers, led by Bratton, M'Clure, Moffit, Winn, **6** and others, had smitten the enemy at different points. The first blow, struck at Beckhamville, is noticed on the preceding page. To crush these patriots and to band the Loyalists, marauding parties, chiefly Tories, were sent out. At Mobley's meeting-house, on the banks of Little River, in Fairfield District, a party of these men were collected just after the affair at Beckhamville in June, 1780. Around them were gathering the Tories of the district, when Captains Bratton and M'Clure fell upon and dispersed them. This disaster, following closely upon the other, alarmed the commander at Rocky Mount, and he sent out Captain Christian Huck, a profane, unprincipled man,**7** with four hundred cavalry, and a body of well-mounted Tories, to "push the rebels as far as he might deem convenient." He executed his orders with alacrity. At one time he destroyed Colonel Hill's iron-works; at another he burned the dwelling of the Reverend William Simpson, of the Fishing Creek church, and murdered an unoffending young man on Sunday morning, while on his way to the meeting-house, with his Bible in his hand. He hated Presbyterians bitterly, and made them suffer when he could. Loaded with the spoils of plunder, Huck fell back to Rocky Mount, and prepared for other depredations.

About this time, Bill Cunningham and his "Bloody Scout" were spreading terror in Union and Spartanburg Districts, and also south of the Ennoree. Against this monster, John M'Clure was dispatched. He chased him across Union District, and almost thirty miles further toward Ninety-Six. Four of the scout were captured, and carried in triumph into Sumter's camp, on the Waxhaw; their leader barely escaped.

Sumter was now gathering his little army, and Huck proceeded to execute his commission as speedily as possible, before the newly-made brigadier should approach. He encamped upon the plantation of James Williamson **8** (now Brattonville), and there passed the night of the eleventh of July (1780). At a little past midnight, Colonel Neil and the companies of Captains Bratton and M'Clure came down from Sumter's camp, in Mecklenburg, and cautiously approached the sleeping enemy in his encampment, which was in the middle of a lane. At dawn on July 12, they entered each end of the lane, and fell upon Huck's party with fury. The surprise was complete, and for an hour a fierce battle ensued, when Huck, with Colonel Ferguson of the Tory militia, was killed, and his party dispersed. The whole patriot force was only one hundred and thirty-three men. M'Clure and his party, well mounted, pursued the fugitives almost to Rocky Mount, and within four hours the army of Huck was as completely dissolved as if they had never seen each other. Colonel Neil lost only one of his command.

The defeat of Huck had an important bearing upon the future condition of the state. It encouraged the Whigs, and many joined the standard of Sumter; while the Tories, abashed, were fearful and silent. Strengthened by daily recruits, until he had more than six hundred men under his command, Sumter determined to attack the royal post at Rocky Mount. The massacre of Buford's command on the Waxhaw, on May 29, had fired the Whigs with a desire for revenge; and Sumter felt strong enough to attack a force known to be a third larger than his own. The post at Rocky Mount was now commanded by Lieutenant Colonel Turnbull, with a small garrison, consisting of one hundred and fifty New York volunteers, and some South Carolina militia. These were stationed principally in three buildings, upon a slope surrounded by a ditch and abatis, and encircled by an open wood.

On the thirtieth of July (1780), Sumter left Major Davie's camp, at the parting of the roads for Rocky Mount and Landsford, and crossing the Catawba at Blair's Ford, proceeded cautiously, but swiftly, toward Rocky Mount. Davie, in the mean while, was to attack the outposts of the British camp at Hanging Rock, east of the Catawba, twelve miles distant. Sumter was accompanied by Colonels Neil, Irvine, and Lacy, **9** and Captain M'Clure and some of the Gastons. At an early hour of the day, he appeared with his whole force upon the crown of the hill now occupied by the servants' houses of Mrs. Barkley. The British commander, warned of his approach by a Tory, was prepared to receive him, and though the Americans poured severe volleys upon the fortification (if it might be called one), they produced but little effect. Having no artillery, they resorted to means for dislodging the enemy, seldom used in war. Leaping the abatis after three assaults, they drove the garrison into the houses. These, according to Mr. M'Elwees, who was in the engagement, were situated near the bottom of the slope, and were composed of logs. They first attempted to set them on fire by casting burning fagots upon them. Not succeeding in this, an old wagon was procured, and upon it was placed a quantity of dry brush and straw taken from the abatis. These were ignited, and then rolled down against the houses. The British, perceiving their danger, hoisted a flag. Supposing they intended to surrender, Sumter ordered the firing to cease. At that moment a shower of rain extinguished the flames, and the enemy defied him. Having no other means at hand to dislodge or seriously injure the garrison. Sumter withdrew, first to the north side of Fishing Creek, near the Catawba (where he was surprised eighteen days afterward), and then to Landsford, where he crossed the river. Seven days afterward, in August 1780, he was battling with the enemy at Hanging Rock. Early in the action, in front of the abatis, the gallant Colonel Neil was slain, with two other white men and a Catawba Indian. Sumter had ten wounded, also. The British lost ten killed, and an equal number wounded.

Appearance of the Road.

On the seventh of August Sumter attacked a British post on Hanging Creek, an event which we shall consider presently. Immediately after that engagement, he recrossed the Catawba. In the mean while, General Gates, with his army, had arrived in the neighborhood. Advised by Sumter that a British detachment, with stores for the main army at Camden, was on its way from Ninety-Six, Gates ordered that officer to intercept it (Aug. 15.), and detached to his aid one hundred infantry and a company of artillery of the Maryland line, and three hundred North Carolina militia, all under the command of Lieutenant-colonel Woodford, of Virginia. They captured a redoubt at the Wateree Ford, in Fairfield District, and, intercepting the escort from Ninety-Six, they secured forty-four wagon loads of stores and clothing, with a number of prisoners. On the seventeenth, Sumter was informed of the defeat of Gates, near Camden. Continuing up the Catawba (here called Wateree), he managed to elude the pursuit of Colonel Turnbull, whom Cornwallis had sent after him, and, on the eighteenth, encamped at the Fishing Creek, near the Catawba, a little above the Great Falls. Here he determined to allow his wearied troops to repose. But a more vigilant and active foe than Turnbull was upon his trail. Cornwallis, anxious to capture Sumter, dispatched Tarleton to overtake and smite him. With one hundred dragoons and sixty mounted light infantry, that officer pressed forward, without halting, in pursuit of his prey. Crossing the Catawba at Rocky Ford, he got into the rear of Sumter, and fell upon his camp while resting, the patriot leader having had no intimation of his approach. The Americans were routed, with great slaughter. More than fifty were killed, and three hundred were made prisoners. All the stores, clothing, and prisoners, captured by Sumter on the fifteenth, fell into Tarleton's hands. This blow laid South Carolina in submission at the feet of the royal troops, none but Marion, the wily " Swamp Fox," and a few followers, remaining in arms against the king. The subsequent organization of a force under Sumter, his exploits west of the Broad River, and also the important events which followed the assumption, by Greene, of the command of the Southern army, have been detailed in former chapters.

I left the family of Mrs. Barkley with real regret, on the morning after my arrival, and, pursuing a crooked, steep, and rough road down to the brink of the river, crossed the Catawba

Anvil Rock

upon a bateau, at Rocky Mount Ferry, just below the Falls at the mouth of Rocky Mount Creek. The scenery here, and for some miles on my road toward Hanging Rock, my next point of destination, was highly picturesque. I was approaching the verge of the Lowlands, the apparent shore of the ancient ocean, along which are strewn huge bowlders – chiefly conglomerates – the mighty pebbles cast upon the beach, when, perhaps, the mammoth and the mastadon slaked their thirst in the waters of the Catawba and the Eswawpuddenah. For several miles the road passed among the erratic rocks and curiously-shaped conglomerates. When within three miles of Hanging Rock, I passed the celebrated Anvil Rock, one of the remarkable curiosities of the South. It stands alone, on the north side of the road, and is, indeed, a curiosity. It appears to be a concretion of the soil around, being composed of precisely similar material; or the soil may be disintegrated rocks of a similar character. In its sides are cavities from which large pebbles have apparently fallen, and also furrows as if made by rains. Its height above the ground is about twelve feet; its form suggested its name.

Hanging Rock.

I reached the Lancaster and Camden high-way at noon, and, on inquiry, ascertained that the celebrated Hanging Rock, near which Sumter and his companions fought a desperate battle, was about a mile and a half eastward. Thither I went immediately, notwithstanding the temptation of a good dinner, freely offered, was before me, for I desired to get as far on toward Camden, that night, as possible. The roads were now generally sandy, and in many places soft and difficult to travel, making progress slow. Along a by-road, across the high rolling plain upon which (at Coles's Old Field) tradition avers the hottest of the battle was fought, I rode to the brow of a deep narrow valley, through which courses Hanging Rock Creek, one of the head waters of Lynch's Creek, the western branch of the Great Pedee. The mingled sound of falling waters and grinding mill-stones came up from the deep furrow, while from a small cabin by the road side, upon the verge of the steep bank, I heard a broken melody. Alighting, I entered the cabin, and there sat an aged negro dining upon hoe-cake and bacon, and humming a refrain. He was the miller. His hair was as white with the frost of years, as his coarse garb was with flour. To my question respecting his family, he said, shaking his bowed head, "Ah, massa! I lives all alone now; tree years ago dey sole my wife, and she's gone to Mississippi. Hab to bake my own hoe-cake now. But neber mind; needn't work 'less I'm a mind too; 'nough to eat, and pretty soon I die?" He told me that he was more than eighty years old, and remembered seeing "de red coats scamper when Massa Sumter and Jacky M'Clure pitched into 'em." Pointing to the celebrated Hanging Rock upon the opposite side of the stream, "Dar," he said, "a heap o' red coats sleep de night afore de battle, and dar I hid de night arter." From the venerable slave, whose memory appeared unclouded, I learned the location of several points mentioned in the accounts of the engagement.

Leaving Charley to dine upon the verge of the stream, I proceeded to Hanging Rock, of whose immensity I had heard frequent mention. It is a huge conglomerate bowlder, twenty or thirty feet in diameter, lying upon the verge of the high east bank of the creek, nearly a hundred feet above the stream. Around it are several smaller bowlders of the same materials. It is shelving toward the bank, its concavity being in the form of the quarter of an orange paring, and capacious enough to shelter fifty men from rain. Beneath its canopy, let us turn to the record of history.

Near the Hanging Rock, on the western bank of the creek, Lord Rawdon, the British commander in that section, had established a post, which was garrisoned by the infantry of Tarleton's legion, part of

Brown's corps of South Carolina and Georgia Provincials, and Colonel Bryan's North Carolina Loyalists; the whole were under the command of Major Camden, with the Prince of Wales's American regiment, in number about five hundred. The greater portion were Loyalists, the remainder were regulars. In the formation of the camp, the regulars were on the right; a part of the British legion and Hamilton's regiment in the center; and Bryan's corps and other Loyalists some distance on the left, Hanging Rock Creek being in the rear. Major Davie proceeded to an attack upon this post, simultaneously with Sumter's assault on Rocky Mount. Davie, with his cavalry, and some Mecklenburg militia, under Colonel Higgins, marched toward Hanging Rock. As he approached, he was informed that three companies of Bryan's Loyalists, returning from a foraging excursion, were encamped at a farm-house. He fell upon them with vigor, in front and rear, and all but a few of them were either killed or wounded. The spoils of this victory were sixty horses with their trappings, and one hundred muskets and rifles. This disaster made the garrison exceedingly vigilant.

We have observed that after the assault on Rocky Mount, Sumter crossed the Catawba, and proceeded toward Hanging Rock on August 6, 1780. He marched early in the morning cautiously, and approached the British camp in three divisions, with the intention of falling upon the main body, stationed upon the plain at Coles's Old Field. The right was composed of Davie's corps and some volunteers, under Major Bryan; the center, of Colonel Irwin's Mecklenburg militia; and the left, of South Carolina regulars, under Colonel Hill. Through the error of his guides, Sumter came first upon Bryan's corps, on the verge of the western bank of the creek, near the Great Rock, half a mile from the British camp. Irwin made the first attack. The Tories soon yielded and fled toward the main body, many of them throwing away their arms without discharging them. These the Americans seized; and, pursuing this advantage, Sumter next fell upon Brown's corps, which, being on the alert, poured a heavy fire upon him from a wood. They also received him with the bayonet. A fierce conflict ensued, and for a while the issue was doubtful. The riflemen, with sure aim, soon cut off almost all of Brown's officers and many of his soldiers; and at length his corps yielded and dispersed in confusion. The arms and ammunition procured from the vanquished were of great service, for when the action commenced, Sumter's men had not two rounds each. **10**

Now was the moment to strike for decisive victory; it was lost by the criminal indulgence of Sumter's men in plundering the portion of the British camp already secured, and drinking freely of the liquor found there. A similar cause plucked the palm of victory from the hands of Greene at Eutaw Springs. Sumter's ranks became disordered; and while endeavoring to bring order out of confusion, the enemy rallied. Of his six hundred men, only about two hundred, with Davie's cavalry, could be brought to bear upon the remaining portion of the British, who were yet in some confusion, but defended by two cannons. Sumter was not to be foiled. With a shout, he and his handful of brave men rushed forward to the attack. The enemy had formed a hollow square, with the field-pieces in front, and in this position received the charge. The Americans attacked them on three sides, and the contest was severe for a while. At length, just as the British line was yielding, a re-enforcement, under Captains Stewart and M'Donald, of Tarleton's legion, returning from an excursion toward Rocky Mount, appeared, and their number being magnified, Sumter deemed a retreat a prudent measure. This was done at meridian, but the enemy had been so severely handled, that they did not attempt a pursuit. A small party appeared upon the Camden road, but was soon dispersed by Davie. Could Sumter have brought all of his forces into action in this last attack, the rout of the British would have been complete.

> "He beat them back! beneath the flame
> Of valor quailing, or the shock!
> He carved, at last, a hero's name,
> Upon the glorious Hanging Rock!"

With his few prisoners and booty, Sumter retreated toward the Waxhaw, bearing away many of his wounded. The engagement lasted about four hours, and was one of the best-fought battles, between militia and British regulars, during the war. Sumter's loss was twelve killed and forty-one wounded. Among the former were the brave Captain M'Clure, **11** of South Carolina, and Captain Read, of North Carolina; Colonel Hill, Captain Craighead, Major Winn, Lieutenants Crawford and Fletcher, and Ensign M'Clure, were wounded. The British loss exceeded that of the Americans. Captain M'Cullock, commander of the legion infantry, and two officers and twenty privates of the same corps, were killed, and forty were wounded. **12** Brown's regiment also suffered much. Bryan's Tories did not stop to fight,

> "——————————— but ran away,
>   And lived to fight another day."

About nine miles north of the present Lancaster Court House, and between twenty and twenty-three miles above Hanging Rock, upon the Waxhaw Creek, **13** the regiment of Colonel Abraham Buford was massacred by Tarleton on the twenty-ninth of May, 1780. Sir Henry Clinton took possession of Charleston on the twelfth, and immediately commenced measures for securing the homage of the whole state. He sent out three large detachments of his army. The first and largest, under Cornwallis, was ordered toward the frontiers of North Carolina; the second, under Lieutenant-colonel Cruger, was directed to pass the Saluda, to Ninety-Six; and the third, under Lieutenant-colonel Brown, was ordered up the Savannah, to Augusta. Soon after he had passed the Santee, Cornwallis was informed that parties of Americans who had come into South Carolina, and had hurried toward Charleston to assist Lincoln, were as hastily retreating. Among these was Colonel Buford. His force consisted of nearly four hundred Continental infantry, a small detachment of Washington's cavalry, and two field-pieces. He had evacuated Camden, and, in fancied security, was retreating leisurely toward Charlotte, in North Carolina. Cornwallis resolved to strike Buford, if possible, and, for that purpose, he dispatched Tarleton, with seven hundred men, consisting of his cavalry and mounted infantry. That officer marched one hundred and five miles in fifty-four hours, and came up with Buford upon the Waxhaw. Impatient of delay, he had left his mounted infantry behind, and with only his

View at Rugeley's. 18

cavalry, he almost surrounded Buford before that officer was aware of danger. Tarleton demanded an immediate surrender upon the terms granted to the Americans at Charleston. Those terms were humiliating, and Buford refused compliance. **14** While the flags for conference were passing and repassing, Tarleton, contrary to military rules, was making preparations for an assault, and the instant he received Buford's reply, his cavalry made a furious charge upon the American ranks. Having received no orders to defend themselves, and supposing the negotiations were yet pending, the Continentals were utterly dismayed by this charge. All was confusion, and while some fired upon their assailants, others threw down their arms and begged for quarter. None was given and men without arms were hewn in pieces by Tarleton's cavalry. One hundred and thirteen were slain; one hundred and fifty were so maimed as to be unable to travel; and fifty-three were made prisoners, to grace the triumphal entry of the conqueror into Camden. Only five of the British were killed, and fifteen wounded. The whole of Buford's artillery, ammunition, and baggage, fell into the hands of the enemy. For this savage feat, Cornwallis eulogized Tarleton, and commended him to the ministry as worthy of special favor. It was nothing less than a cold-blooded massacre; and Tarleton's quarter became proverbial as a synonym to cruelty. **15** The liberal press, and all right-minded men in England, cried shame.

After the battle, a large number of the wounded were taken to the log meeting-house of the Waxhaw Presbyterian congregation, where they were tenderly nursed by a few who had the boldness to remain, With the defeat of Buford, every semblance of a Continental army in South Carolina was effaced. This terrible blow spread consternation over that region, and women and children were seen flying from their homes to seek refuge from British cruelty in more distant settlements. Among the fugitives was the widowed mother of Andrew Jackson (the seventh President of the United States), who, with her two sons, Robert and Andrew, took refuge in the Sugar Creek congregation, at the house of the widow of the Reverend J. M. Wilson, near Charlotte. This was the first practical lesson of hatred to tyranny which young Jackson learned, and it doubtless had an abiding influence upon his future life. **16**

View at the site of Rugeley's Mill. 20

Returning to the Lancaster road at two o'clock, I rode on toward Camden, about thirty-five miles distant, passing on the way the celebrated Flat Rock, a mass of concrete, like that of Anvil Rock, five hundred yards across. It lies even with the surface of the ground, and presents numerous pits or cisterns, supposed to have been hollowed out by the Indians for the purpose of holding water. The road passed over this mass with a gentle descent. Near its southern side, the place was pointed out to me where a severe skirmish occurred in August, 1788, between some militia and Tories, but the result was not very sanguinary. At sunset I arrived at the house of Mrs. Fletcher, within nine miles of Rugeley's Mill, where I was well entertained for the night. **17** I departed at sunrise the following morning. Being now fairly within the sandy region upon the slopes between the upper and the lower country, the traveling was very heavy. At the first house after leaving Mrs. Fletcher's, I saw Mr. Paine, the brother of Mrs. Lee, an intelligent old man of eighty-four years. During half an hour's conversation with him, I obtained some valuable information respecting the various historical localities between there and Camden. The first of these is Clermont, sometimes called Rugeley's, about thirteen miles north of Camden, where I arrived at an early hour in the forenoon. This is the place where General Gates concentrated his army for an attack upon the British at Camden. The place is also memorable on account of a military event which occurred near Rugeley's Mill, on the fourth of December, 1780. This mill was about one hundred yards east of the road where it crosses Rugeley's Creek. No traces of the mill remain; but an embankment, several rods in extent, partly demolished, and overgrown with pines and shrubbery interlaced with the vines of the muscadine, mark the place of the dam, a part of which, where the creek passes through, is seen in the engraving. Let us consider the event which immortalizes this spot.

When Cornwallis retreated from Charlotte, Gates advanced to that place, and General Smallwood was directed to encamp lower down the Catawba, on the road to Camden. Morgan, with his light corps, composed partly of Lieutenant-colonel Washington's cavalry, was ordered to push further in advance, for the purpose of foraging, and to watch the movements of Cornwallis. Smallwood having received information that a body of Tories under Colonel Rugeley, were on the alert to intercept his wagons, ordered Morgan and Washington to march against them. They retreated, and took post at Rugeley's house, on the Camden road, which he had stockaded, together with his log-barn. Washington, with his cavalry, pursued, and at about ten o'clock on the fourth of December (1780), appeared at Rugeley's Mill, on the south side of the creek. The Loyalists were strongly posted in the log-barn, in front of which was a ditch and abatis. Having no artillery, Washington could make but little impression upon the garrison, so he resorted to stratagem. Fashioning a pine-log so as to resemble a cannon, he placed it in such a position near the bridge as, apparently, to command both the house and barn of Colonel Rugeley. He then made a formal demand for a surrender, menacing the garrison with the instant demolition of their fortress. Alarmed at the apparition of a cannon, Rugeley sent out a flag, and, with his whole force of one hundred and twelve men, immediately surrendered. Poor Rugeley never appeared in arms afterward. Cornwallis, in a December 4 letter to Tarleton, said, "Rugeley will not be made a brigadier." **19**

View at Gum Swamp. 21

Soon after leaving Rugeley's, I came to a shallow stream which flows out of Gum Swamp, and known in the Revolution as Graney's Quarter Creek. It was thickly studded with gum shrubs and canes, the latter appearing as green and fresh as in summer. It was now about noon, and while I made the accompanying sketch, Charley dined upon corn, which the generous driver of a team "hauling cotton," gave me from his store. Between this stream and Sander's Creek, within seven miles of Camden, is the place of Gates's defeat on August 16, 1780. The hottest of the engagement occurred upon the hill, just before descending to Sander's Creek from the north, now, as then, covered with an open forest of pine-trees. When I passed through it, the undergrowth had just been burned, and the blackened trunks of the venerable pines, standing like the columns of a vast temple, gave the whole scene a dreary, yet grand appearance. Many of the old trees yet bear marks of the battle, the scars of the bullets being made very distinct by large protuberances. I was informed that many musket-balls have been cut out of the trees; and I saw quite a number of trunks which had been recently hewn with axes for the purpose. Some pines had been thus cut by searchers for bullets which must have been in the seed when the battle occurred. Within half a mile of Sander's Creek, on the north side, are some old fields, dotted with shrub pines, where the hottest of the battle was fought. A large concavity near the road, filled with hawthorns, was pointed out to me as the spot where many of the dead were buried.

Sander's Creek is a considerable stream, about two hundred feet wide, and quite shallow at the ford. Though flowing through a swamp like Graney's Quarter, its waters were very limpid. Numerous teams drawing heavy loads of cotton, on their way to Camden, were passing at the time, and the songs and loud laughter of the happy teamsters enlivened the dreary aspect of nature. **22**

Let us consider the important events which occurred here.

Misfortune is too often mistaken for a fault, and censoriousness seldom makes candid distinctions. When General Lincoln was finally obliged to surrender Charleston and his army to Sir Henry Clinton on May 1, 1780, calumny, with its busy tongue, decried his fair fame, and whispered doubts respecting his skill and courage. That blow, struck by a skillful hand, almost demolished the Southern army, and for a moment the patriots were dismayed. But the elasticity of hope was found in the national councils, and preparations were soon made to concentrate the various detachments of the regular army then in the South, and the volunteers whom Sumter and others were collecting, to turn back toward the sea-board the flood of invasion.

View at Sander's Creek.

A month before the fall of Charleston, when it was perceived that the chief theater of the campaign of 1780 was to be in the Southern States, Maryland and Delaware troops were sent thither, under the Baron De Kalb, **23** a German officer, who had distinguished himself in the French service. He left Morristown on April 14, 1780, with fourteen hundred effective men; reached the head of Elk in May; left Petersburg early in June, passed through Hillsborough, and halted on Deep River, in North Carolina, on the sixth of July.

In the mean while, Charleston had been captured, General Lincoln was a prisoner on parole, and De Kalb became the commander-in-chief at the South. Although Congress reposed confidence in the skill of De Kalb, it was thought proper to send an officer better known to the people for past services, and on the thirteenth of June (1780), General Gates **24** was appointed to the command. **25** He was then at his estate in Virginia, a few miles from Shepherdstown, and the glory of Saratoga was not yet dimmed. He immediately departed on June 26 for the camp of De Kalb, taking with him, as secretary, his friend William Clajon, and reached his destination on the twenty-fifth of July. The prospect before him was far from flattering. An army without strength; a military chest without money; but little public spirit in the Commissary Department; a climate unfavorable to health; the spirits of the Republicans pressed down; Loyalists swarming in every direction, and a victorious enemy pressing to spread his legions over the territory he had come to defend, were obstacles in the way of success. Yet he did not despond, and, retaining De Kalb in command of his division, prepared to march into South Carolina. His whole force consisted of the Maryland and Delaware troops, a legionary corps of sixty horse and as many foot soldiers, under Colonel Armand, and three companies of artillery. There was elsewhere a considerable force of North Carolina militia in the field, under General Caswell; and on the morning of the twenty-seventh of July, 1780, Gates marched at the head of his little army to effect a junction with those troops. He passed the Deep River at the Buffalo Ford, and in the

The Baron de Kalb

afternoon encamped upon Spinks's farm, on the road to Camden. There the plan of immediate operations was decided upon. De Kalb and Colonel Otho H. Williams (the deputy adjutant general) thought it expedient to march to Charlotte, establish a hospital and magazine at Salisbury, leave the women and all the heavy baggage there, and from thence proceed toward Camden, without impediment, through a well-cultivated and friendly country, by the way of the Waxhaw. These opinions had no weight with Gates, whose vanity overruled his judgment, and on the twenty-eighth, having been joined that morning by Lieutenant-colonel Porterfield with about one hundred Virginians, he marched directly for Camden.

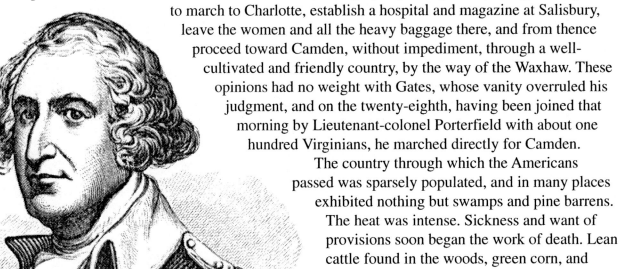

The country through which the Americans passed was sparsely populated, and in many places exhibited nothing but swamps and pine barrens. The heat was intense. Sickness and want of provisions soon began the work of death. Lean cattle found in the woods, green corn, and peaches, constituted the principal portion of their food. Dysentery ensued, and at one time the total destruction of the army seemed inevitable. Yet Gates pressed slowly forward, and on the day when Sumter achieved his partial victory at Hanging Rock, he reached the banks of Little Lynch's Creek, a few miles distant, where he was joined by General Caswell. **26**

General Horatio Gates.

Let us glance a moment at the movements of the British troops We have noted how the grand army was divided and spread over South Carolina soon after the fall of Charleston, the northern portion of which was placed under the command of Cornwallis. This disposition of the forces of the enemy had hardly taken place, when intelligence of the approach of De Kalb was received; also of the gathering of Virginians under Porterfield; of North Carolinians, under Rutherford, in the west; and of a large body of North Carolina militia, under Caswell, in the east. Then came the intelligence that Gates, the conqueror of Burgoyne, was on his way, with a large force, to recover all that Lincoln had lost, and more, if possible. Rumor magnified their numbers. The Loyalists became alarmed; the patriots took courage; and, as we have seen, Marion and Sumter had raised their standards. The British officers were perplexed; and Lord Rawdon, who was second in command to Cornwallis, and had his post at Camden, called in some of his more distant outposts. Major M'Arthur, who was at Cheraw to encourage the Loyalists, was ordered to fall back toward Camden; and the most distant outposts were upon Lynch's Creek, at Hanging Rock, and at Rocky Mount. These, as we have seen, were attacked by Sumter, Davie, and other active officers, with their men.

Cornwallis, perceiving the gathering storm on the borders of South Carolina, hastened from Charleston to join Rawdon at Camden. He arrived there on the thirteenth of August, and learned, with much concern, the successes of Sumter, and the disaffection of the people, especially in the county between the Black River and the Pedee. Nearly eight hundred of his troops were sick at Camden, and his effective force amounted to only a little more than two thousand men, fifteen hundred of whom were regulars. The remainder were militia and North Carolina refugees. Cornwallis would gladly have retreated to Charleston, but the consideration that he must leave his sick behind, abandon or destroy his magazines, and relinquish all the territory they had gained, except Charleston, prevented that step. He therefore resolved to move forward and attack Gates before the Virginia troops, known to be approaching, could join him.

On the day when Cornwallis reached Camden, Gates advanced to Clermont, and encamped near Rugeley's Mill. Those who had opposed Sumter at Hanging Rock had fled to Camden on the approach of Gates, and Lord Rawdon had also called in the garrison which he had stationed at Rugeley's. The day after his arrival there (August 14, 1780), Gates was joined by General Stevens, with seven hundred militia; and, at about noon, a message from Sumter announced the approach of stores and clothing on the west side of the Wateree, for the enemy at Camden. The capture of these stores, and the dispersion of the escort, we have considered earlier.

Notwithstanding Gates had weakened his army by sending a strong re-enforcement to Sumter, he prepared to march upon Camden, to divert attention from Sumter's enterprise, and to fight, if necessary. On the evening of the fifteenth, he sent his sick, extra stores, and heavy baggage, under guard, to the Waxhaw, and at ten o'clock at night commenced his march. Colonel Armand's legion composed the van, flanked upon the right by Porterfield's infantry, in Indian file, two hundred yards from the road; and upon the left by Armstrong's infantry, in the same order. Next followed the first and second Maryland brigades, under Brigadiers Smallwood and Gist, 27 and the Delaware troops, all commanded by De Kalb: then the North Carolina division, under Caswell; the Virginia division, under Stevens; with a rear-guard of volunteer cavalry upon the flanks of the baggage. Confident in his strength by such a disposition of his troops, he ordered Colonel Armand to withstand the attack of the enemy's cavalry, whatever its number. The most profound silence was commanded, and instant death was threatened to the soldier who should fire a gun until ordered. 28

Cornwallis, notwithstanding his inferior force, marched to attack Gates at Rugeley's, being informed that his position was a weak one. At the same hour when Gates marched toward Camden, Cornwallis struck his tents at that place, and proceeded cautiously toward Rugeley's. His troops consisted of the 23d and 33d regiments, under Lieutenant-colonel Webster (who was afterward mortally wounded at Guilford); Tarleton's legion; Irish Volunteers; a part of Lieutenant-colonel Hamilton's North Carolina regiment; and Bryan's corps of Loyalists, under Lord Rawdon, with two six and two three pounders commanded by Lieutenant M'Leod; and the 71st regiment. Camden was left in the care of Major M'Arthur, with the sick and convalescents. Silently both armies marched in the gloom of night. The air was sultry; no moon was in the heavens, but the stars looked down in serene radiance upon the earth. Not a footfall was heard in the deep sand, and neither party was aware that the other had struck his tents, until the advanced guards of each met at about two o'clock in the morning on August 16, upon the gentle slope about half a mile north of Sander's Creek. Both parties were surprised, and each fired almost at the same moment. Some of Armand's troops were killed at the first fire, and so sudden and unexpected was the attack that the remainder fell back in disorder upon the first Maryland brigade. That column was broken by the shock, and the whole line was filled with consternation. Porterfield, with his usual gallantry, rushed forward and attacked the left of the enemy's van, while Armstrong, with equal gallantry and decision, attacked them on the right, and they were brought to a pause. Porterfield was severely wounded, carried to the rear of the army, and died a few days afterward. Both armies halted, and some prisoners having been taken by both parties, the position of the respective forces became known to each other. The situation of the British was far more advantageous than that of the Americans. They had crossed Sander's Creek, and they were completely guarded in the rear by an impenetrable swamp. The Americans were upon rising ground in an open wood, and were obliged to be watchful of their flanks.

When the first excitement of the encounter had subsided, Gates called a council of officers. A retreat was practicable, and would doubtless have been prudent. No one seemed willing to propose it; and when, to Gates's remark, "Gentlemen, you know our situation, what are your opinions?" General Stevens replied, "It is now too late to retreat;" the silence that ensued was interpreted as favorable to an attack, and the commander-in-chief remarked, "Then we must fight; gentlemen, please take your posts."

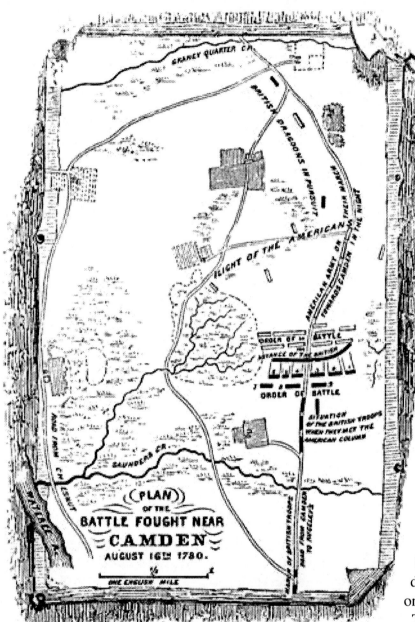

The British army formed in line for battle, the right under the command of Webster, and the left under Rawdon, and anxiously awaited the dawn. The Americans, also, soon recovered from the panic produced by the attack, and formed in battle order. The second Maryland brigade, and the Delaware troops, under General Gist, took the right; the North Carolina militia, under Caswell, the center; and the Virginians, under Stevens, the left. The first Maryland brigade, under Smallwood, was formed in reserve. De Kalb, charged with the line of battle, took post on the right. The artillery of both armies was planted directly in front of the center. All these preparations were made in darkness, and the belligerents were ignorant of each others' movements. In the plan here given, copied from Stedman, the black parallelograms denote the British troops, and the open ones the Americans.

The first beam of morning was the signal for attack. While the British were maneuvering to gain a better position, the American artillery opened its volleys upon them. At the same moment, Colonel Williams, with a band of volunteers, pressed forward upon the enemy's right, followed by Stevens, with his Virginians, who were urged to rely upon the bayonets with which they had been furnished the day before. Webster immediately brought the British right to bear upon Williams and Stevens, with such force, as to break the Virginia column and scatter it to the winds. They delivered only a single fire, and then, panic-stricken, threw away their arms, and fled in great confusion. The North Carolina militia (except Dixon's regiment, which was next to the Continentals) followed the shameful example, and the exertions of Stevens, Caswell, and even of Gates himself, to stop or rally the fugitives, were unavailing. Only the Continental troops, with Dixon's regiment, were now left to oppose the enemy. Upon the Maryland and Delaware troops fell the weight of battle, and for a while they nobly sustained it. On the right, De Kalb and Gist maintained their ground, though sorely pressed by Rawdon and his regulars. Lieutenant-colonel Howard (the subsequent "hero of the Cowpens"), with Williams's regiment, charged the enemy with great vigor, and disconcerted them. Inch by inch the Marylanders gained ground, and, had the militia stood firm, and kept Webster employed, the British must have been routed and driven in confusion across Sander's Creek. That skillful officer had detached Tarleton in pursuit of the fugitives, and when Smallwood **29** came forward with his reserve to fill the place of the scattered militia, Webster brought his regiments to bear upon him. Finally, the battle raged along the whole line, and victory was uncertain. Firm as a rock the phalanx of De Kalb and Gist remained. At length, perceiving an advantage, De Kalb ordered a bayonet charge. The slaughter was great; the enemy recoiled, and fifty men became the prisoners of the Americans.

Smallwood, in the mean time, sustained himself gallantly; but at length Webster gained his flank, and his brigade receded. It soon regained its position; was again driven back, and speedily it rallied to the combat. Cornwallis perceived the point of strength to be with De Kalb and Gist, and, concentrating his whole force, he made a terrible charge there. It was the decisive stroke which smote down the American strength and won the victory. Another charge was made; the brave Marylanders gave way, and, with the Delaware regiment, broken and maimed, fled to the swamps. They were hotly pursued, and many were killed in the flight. The militia fell in great numbers under the sabers of Tarleton's cavalry, and for more than two miles the open wood was strewn with the dead and dying. Arms, artillery, horses, and baggage were scattered in every direction. More than a third of the Continental troops were killed; and of the wounded, one hundred and seventy men were made prisoners. The Delaware regiment was nearly annihilated, and Colonel Vaughn and Major Patten being taken prisoners, the remnant, less than two companies, were placed under the command of the brave Kirkwood, the senior captain, who had been with Washington at Trenton and Princeton. De Kalb, while trying to keep his troops firm when the last charge was made, fell, pierced with eleven wounds. His lieutenant, Du Buysson, threw his arms around him, gave his name and rank, and while saving him from instant death, was terribly wounded himself by British bayonets. In the mean while Gates had fled, "borne off the field by a current of dismayed militia," who "constituted so great a part of his army, that when he saw them break and flee, he lost all hope of victory." **30** With Caswell, he hastened to Clermont, hoping to check and rally the militia at their old encampment, near Rugeley's Mill. This hope was vain, for the further the dismayed troops fled, the more they became dispersed, and the generals giving up all as lost, proceeded, with a few attendants, to Charlotte, where they arrived in the evening of the same day, though about eighty miles distant. On his way, Gates heard of the success of Sumter at the Wateree Ford, but that triumph came too late to afford him aid, and, as we have seen, two days afterward (Aug. 18, 1780), Sumter and his band were surprised and dispersed at Fishing Creek. General Rutherford surrendered to a party of the British legion. The other generals escaped, but were separated from their respective commands. The rout was complete, and only Major Andrus, of the third Maryland regiment, succeeded in rallying any part of the fugitives. Most of the Virginia militia retired to Hillsborough by the road they came to camp, and there General Stevens gathered many of them together. Their time of service soon expiring, they were discharged. **31**

The victory of Cornwallis was complete, and for a moment the hopes of the patriots, particularly at the South, were crushed; their only chance of success seemed to be the intervention of European nations. **32** Within the space of three months, two armies had been almost annihilated by capture and dispersion, and the most active partisan corps scattered to the winds. **33** Cornwallis considered the subjugation of South Carolina accomplished, and, confident of future success, moved toward the North State to establish royal rule there. His march to, and retreat from Charlotte; the defeat of his detachments at King's Mountain and the Cowpens; the pursuit of Greene; the battle at Guilford; the retreat of the British to Wilmington; their march into Virginia; and the final capture of Cornwallis's army at Yorktown, have been considered in preceding chapters.

General Gates was much censured on account of the defeat of the Americans on Sander's Creek, because he provided for no place of rendezvous in the event of being obliged to retreat; for not having his baggage and stores at a proper distance from the scene of action, and because of an improper arrangement of his army for attack, placing his unskilled militia on the right, opposite the British veterans of Webster. Armand spoke harshly of Gates, and even intimated that he was a coward or a traitor. Gates's great fault appears to have been a too sanguine belief that he could easily crush the inferior force of his enemy. His vanity was always the source of his greatest trouble. In this instance he was too confident of success, and made no provision for the contingencies of adversity; and hence his utter weakness when the victorious blow was struck by the British, and he was obliged to flee.

View at the Spring; Hobkirk's Hill. **36**

On the seventeenth and eighteenth of August, 1780, Smallwood and Gist arrived at Charlotte, with several other officers, and there they found more than one hundred regular infantry, Armand's cavalry, Major Davie's partisan corps from the Waxhaw settlement, and a few militia. Gates began to hope that another army might be speedily reorganized, when intelligence of the disaster of Sumter at Fishing Creek reached him. He retreated to Hillsborough, where the Provincial Congress was in session, with Governor Abner Nash **34** at its head. That officer exerted all the power and influence of his station to aid the discomfited general. The Legislature provided for procuring arms, ammunition, and stores; ordered militia drafts, and took other vigorous measures for the defense of the state. Salisbury, toward which it was believed Cornwallis would march, was made the place of rendezvous. The fragments of the army broken at Sander's Creek were collected together at Hillsborough early in September, and on the sixteenth of that month, Colonel Buford, having recruited his corps so cruelly handled by Tarleton, reached head-quarters, from Virginia. There he was joined by sixty Virginia militia, and about fifty of Porter-field's light infantry. All of these, with the Maryland and Delaware regiments, were formed into a brigade, under Smallwood. The intervening events, from this time until Greene succeeded Gates in the command of the Southern army on December 3., 1780, have already been considered. **35**

An hour's ride from Sander's Creek, over a very sandy and gently rolling country, brought me to the summit of Hobkirk's Hill, a high ridge overlooking the plains of Camden. Upon the table-land of its summit is a beautiful village, composed of many fine houses, the residences of wealthy inhabitants of that region, who have chosen this spot for its salubrity in summer. It was just at sunset when I first looked from this eminence upon the town below and the broad plain around it. Although it was midwinter, the profusion of evergreens gave the landscape the appearance of early autumn. Here was fought one of the memorable battles of our War for Independence; and yonder, stretching away toward the high hills of Santee, is the plain once red with British legions, and glittering with British bayonets. Before descending to Camden, a mile distant, let us open the old chronicle, and peruse an interesting page. It is a balmy evening on January 17, 1849; birds are chirping their vespers among the dark-green foliage of the wild olives in the gardens, and buds are almost bursting into blossoms upon every tree. Here, upon a bench by the bubbling spring, where General Greene was at breakfast when surprised by Lord Rawdon, we will read and ponder in the evening twilight.

We left General Greene and his broken army on their march from Cornwallis's camp, on the Deep River on April 6, 1781, toward Camden. Greene had determined to strike a blow for the recovery of South Carolina. To secure the provisions which grow upon the borders of the Santee and Congaree Rivers, and to keep a communication with the Indians on the frontier, the British had established military posts at several points, the most important of which was Fort Watson, upon Wright's Bluff, in the present Sumter District. These, with the more remote post of Ninety-Six, Greene resolved to attack almost simultaneously with his movement against Lord Rawdon, then at Camden. He dispatched Lieutenant-colonel Lee with his legion, to join Marion, then encamped in the swamps on Black River, in Williamsburg District. **37** These brave partisans met on April 14, 1781, and immediately prepared to march against Fort Watson. Brigadiers Sumter and Pickens were informed of the intended movements, and refused to co-operate. Greene desired Sumter to join him at Camden, while Pickens was directed to assemble the western militia and invest Ninety-Six, or, at least, to prevent a re-enforcement marching from that post to the relief of Rawdon. With only about fifteen

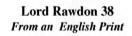

Lord Rawdon 38
From an English Print

hundred men (after detaching Lee's force), Greene descended the Southern slope of Hobkirk's Hill on April 19, and encamped at Log Town, within half a mile of the enemy's works, at Camden.

Lord Rawdon, who had been left in command of the Southern division of the royal army when Cornwallis marched into North Carolina, was now at Camden. He was apprised of Greene's approach, and notwithstanding his force was inferior (about nine hundred men), he was too strongly intrenched to fear an attack. Greene perceived that his little army was unequal to the task of carrying the place by storm, or even of completely investing it. **39** Hoping to be joined by a re-enforcement of militia, he withdrew to Hobkirk's Hill, and encamped. On the twenty-first, he received the startling information that Colonel Watson, with between four and five hundred men, was marching up the Santee to join Rawdon. To prevent this junction, it was necessary to intercept Watson some distance from Camden. To this task Greene immediately applied himself. He crossed Sand Hill Creek, and encamped on the east of Camden on April 22, upon the Charleston road. It being impossible to transport the artillery across the marshes on the borders of that creek, Lieutenant-colonel Carrington was directed to return with it toward Lynch's Creek, where it would be safe from the patrolling parties of the enemy. Finally, convinced that the intelligence of the approach of Watson was false, **40** Greene hastened back to Hobkirk's Hill on April 24, and ordered Carrington to join him, with the artillery, immediately. The hill was then completely covered with a forest, and the Americans were so strongly posted, with the swamp on Pine Tree Creek in their rear, that they felt no fear of an attack from the enemy. Yet the ever-cautious Greene had the army encamped in battle order, ready to repel a sortie of Rawdon, should he have the temerity to attempt one. During the day, he had received information of the capture of Fort Watson by Marion and Lee, and just at evening the prisoners were brought into camp, among whom were several American soldiers, previously captured, and who, as they said, had enlisted in the British service as the best means of escaping to their friends.

During the night of the twenty-fourth, a drummer, named Jones, one of the Americans taken at Fort Watson, deserted, and made his way to the British camp. He informed Rawdon of the detachment of the artillery from the main army, the lack of provisions in the American camp, and the fact that Sumter had not arrived. Rawdon resolved to strike a blow at this favorable moment, for his own provisions were almost exhausted; and before daylight his garrison was in marching order. The country between Hobkirk's Hill and Camden was so thickly wooded that the movements of the enemy were not discerned until his van-guard approached the American pickets. The patriots were unsuspicious of danger. Greene and his officers were leisurely taking breakfast under the shade of the trees at the spring (for it was a clear, warm morning); some of the soldiers were washing their clothes, and the horses of Washington's cavalry were unsaddled. Rawdon did not march directly for the American camp, on the Waxhaw road, but took a circuitous route, toward the Pine Tree Creek. At about ten o'clock, the American advanced guard discerned the approach of the enemy. Their pickets were commanded by Captain Benson, of Maryland, and Captain Morgan, of Virginia, supported by Captain Kirkwood, **41** with the remains of the Delaware regiment. These, at a distance of about a quarter of a mile from the camp, gallantly received and returned the fire of the British van, and kept them at bay while Greene formed his army in more complete battle order.

Fortunately for Greene, Carrington, with the artillery, had joined him early in the morning, and brought to camp a competent supply of provisions. The line was soon formed, and so confident was Greene of success, that he unhesitatingly ordered Lieutenant-colonel Washington, with his cavalry, to turn the right flank of the British, and to charge in their rear. The American line was composed of the Virginia brigade on the right, under Brigadier Huger, with Lieutenant-colonels Campbell and Hawes; the Maryland brigade, led by Colonel Williams, seconded by Colonel Gunby, and Lieutenant-colonels Ford and Howard, occupied the left; and in the center was Colonel Harrison, with the artillery. The reserve consisted of Washington's cavalry, and a corps of two hundred and fifty North Carolina militia, under Colonel Reade. (See the map on next page.)

The skirmish of the van-guards was severe for some time, when Rawdon, with his whole force, pressed forward, and drove Kirkwood and his Delawares back upon the main line. The King's American regiment was on his right; the New York Volunteers in the centre; and the 63d regiment composed the left. His right was supported by Robertson's corps, and his left by the Irish Volunteers. (See map on next page.) The British presented a narrow front, which was an advantage to Greene. As they moved slowly up the slope, Campbell and Ford were ordered to turn the flanks of the British, while the first Maryland regiment, under Gunby, was ordered to make an attack in front. Rawdon perceived this movement, and, ordering the Irish corps into line, strengthened his position by extending his front. The battle opened from right to left with great vigor. The two Virginia regiments, led by Greene in person, aided by Huger, Campbell, and Hawes, maintained their ground firmly, and even gained upon the enemy. At the same time, Washington, with his cavalry, was sweeping every thing before him upon the right flank of the British. The artillery was playing upon the center with great execution, and Gunby's veteran regiment rushed forward in a deadly charge with bayonets. Notwithstanding their inferiority of numbers and disadvantage of position, the British maintained their ground most gallantly until Gunby's charge, when they faltered. Hawes was then descending the hill to charge the New York Volunteers, and the falchion that should strike the decisive blow of victory for the Americans was uplifted. At that moment, some of Gunby's veterans gave way: their commander was killed. Colonel Williams, who was near the center, endeavored to rally them, and Gunby and other officers used every exertion to close their line. In this attempt, Colonel Ford was mortally wounded and carried to the rear. Gunby, finding it impossible to bring them into order, directed them to rally by retiring partially in the rear. This order was fatal. Perceiving this retrograde movement, the British advanced with a shout, when a general retreat of the Americans took place. Greene, with his usual skill and energy, conducted the retreat in such order that few men were lost after this first action. Washington had been eminently successful; and at the moment when the retreat began, he had two hundred prisoners. He hastily paroled the officers, and then, wheeling, made a secure retreat, with the loss of three men, and took with him fifty of his prisoners. The action continued at intervals until about four o'clock in the afternoon, when the Americans had retreated four or five miles, closely pursued by parties of the enemy. Washington, with cavalry and infantry, then turned upon the pursuers, and charging the mounted New York Volunteers with great intrepidity, killed nine and

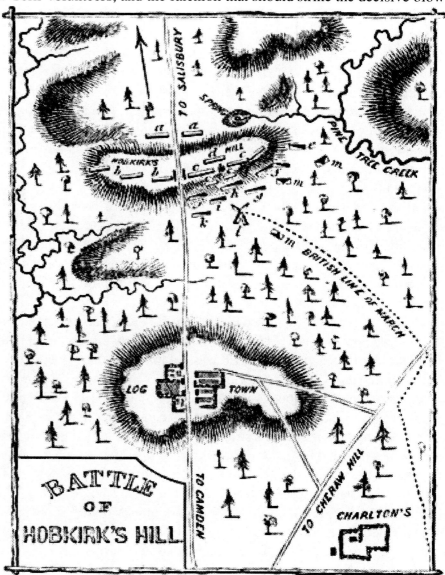

NOTE. – Explanation of the Plan. – This plan of the battle on Hobkirk's Hill is copied from Stedman. a a, are the American militia, on the Waxhaw road, leading from Camden to Salisbury; b b, the Virginia line; c c, the Maryland line; d, the reserve, with General Greene; e, British light infantry, approaching the American camp from Pine Tree Creek; f, volunteers from Ireland; g, South Carolina Loyalists; h, 63d regiment; i, New York Loyalists; j, King's American regiment; k, convalescents; l, with swords crossed, the place where the first attack was made; m m, British dragoons. The spring was known as Martin's.

dispersed the rest. This terminated the battle. The British returned to their works at Camden, and Greene, with his little army, encamped for the night on the north side of Sander's Creek. The dead, alone, occupied the battle-field. So well was the retreat conducted, that most of the American wounded (including six commissioned officers), and all of their artillery and baggage, with Washington's fifty prisoners, were carried off. The loss of the Americans in killed, wounded, and missing, according to Greene's return to the Board of War, was two hundred and sixty-six; that of the enemy, according to Rawdon's statement, two hundred and fifty-eight. The killed were not very numerous. Greene estimates his number at eighteen, among whom were Ford and Beatty, **42** of the Maryland line. **43** Rawdon's loss in killed was thirty-eight, including one officer. **44**

This defeat was very unexpected to General Greene, and for a moment disconcerted him, for, with the exception of the success of Marion and Lee, in capturing Fort Watson, he did not know how the Southern partisans were proceeding. **45** The Maryland troops, so gallant and firm on all former occasions, had now failed; his provisions were short; Sumter, the speedy partisan, had not joined him; and supplies came in tardily and meager. Yet Greene was not the man to be crushed by adversity. On the contrary, he seemed to rise with renewed strength, after every fall. Accordingly, on the morning succeeding the battle (April 26, 1781), he retired as far as Rugeley's, and after detaching a small force with a six pounder under Captain Finley, to Nelson's Ferry, to join Marion and Lee, and prevent Watson from re-enforcing Rawdon, he crossed the Wateree, and took a strong position, where he could not only cut off supplies for the garrison at Camden from that quarter, but prevent the approach of Watson in that direction. In the mean while, Marion and Lee were closely watching Colonel Watson. That officer had now approached near to the confluence of the Congaree and Wateree, in Orangeburg District; where he would cross it was difficult to tell and the vigilant partisans, fearing he might elude them if they took post on the north side of the Congaree, crossed over, and endeavored to overtake him. But Watson, who was equally vigilant and active, crossed the Congaree on May 6, 1781, near its junction with the Wateree, and on the seventh of May passed the latter stream and joined Rawdon at Camden.

Greene was early apprised of this junction, and, persuaded that Rawdon would resume offensive operations at once, withdrew from the vicinity of Camden Ferry to the high ground beyond Sawney Creek, on the border of Fairfield District. He was not mistaken. On the eighth of May, Rawdon crossed the Wateree, at the ferry below Camden, **46** and proceeded toward Greene's encampment. The two armies were now equal in numbers; about twelve hundred each. On the approach of the British, Greene retired to Colonel's Creek; at the same time, Rawdon became alarmed at the intelligence of the increase of the American army and of Greene's strong position, and returned to Camden. Believing it impossible to drive Greene from his neighborhood, and anxious for the safety of his menaced posts between him and Charleston, Rawdon resolved to evacuate Camden, and with it all the country north of the Congaree. He sent orders to Lieutenant-colonel Cruger to abandon Ninety-Six, and join Lieutenant-colonel Brown at Augusta, and also directed Major Maxwell to leave Fort Granby (near the present city of Columbia), and fall back upon Orangeburg, on the bank of the North Edisto. He then burned the jail, mills, and several private houses at Camden; destroyed all the stores which he could not carry with him, and on the tenth left that place for Nelson's Ferry, hoping to cross there in time to drive off Marion and Lee, then besieging Fort Motte. He took with him almost five hundred negroes and the most violent Loyalists, fearing the vengeance of the patriots, followed him in great numbers. **47** Within six days afterward, Orangeburg (May 11), Fort Motte (May 12), the post at Nelson's Ferry (May 14), and Fort Granby (May 15), fell into the hands of the Americans. Greene, in the mean while, had marched toward Ninety-Six, where he arrived on the twenty-second of May. The military events at these several places will be noticed presently, in the order in which I visited them.

It was almost dark when I rode into Camden and alighted at Boyd's Hotel. Here was the end of my tedious but interesting journey of almost fourteen hundred miles with my own conveyance; for, learning that I could reach other chief points of interest at the South easier and speedier by public conveyance, I resolved to sell my traveling establishment. Accordingly, after passing the forenoon of the next day (Jan. 18, 1849) in visiting the battle-ground on Hobkirk's Hill, sketching the scenery at the Spring, and the monument erected to the memory of De Kalb, on the green in front of the Presbyterian church in Camden, **48** I went into the market as a trafficker. A stranger both to the people and to the business, I was not successful. I confess there was a wide difference between my "asking" and my "taking" price. My wagon was again broken, and, anxious to get home, I did not "dicker" long when I got an offer, and Charley and I parted, I presume, with mutual regrets. He was a docile, faithful animal, and I had become much attached to him. A roll of Camden bank-notes soothed my feelings, and I left the place of separation at dawn the next morning in the cars for Fort Motte and Columbia, quite light-hearted.

Chapter XVII
Endnotes

1 This view is from the east bank of the river. Toward the extreme right is seen the dam, made to supply water-power for the iron-works delineated toward the left of the picture. The fording-place, which crosses a small island in the middle of the stream, is indicated by the slight fall toward the left.

2 The Catawbas spoke a language different from any of the surrounding tribes. They inhabited the country south of the Tuscaroras, and adjoining the Cherokees. In 1672, the Shawnees made settlements in their country, but were speedily driven away. In 1712, they were the allies of the white people against the Corees and Tuscaroras; but in 1715, they joined the other tribes in a confederacy against the Southern colonies. In 1760, they were auxiliaries of the Carolinians against the Cherokees, and ever afterward were the friends of the white people. Their chief village was on the Catawba, twenty-four miles from Yorkville. The following eloquent petition of Peter Harris, a Catawba warrior during the Revolution, is preserved among the colonial records at Columbia, in South Carolina. The petition is dated 1822:

"I am one of the lingering survivors of an almost extinguished race. Our graves will soon be our only habitations. I am one of the few stalks that still remain in the field where the tempest of the Revolution has passed. I fought against the British for your sake. The British have disappeared, and you are free; yet from me have the British took nothing; nor have I gained any thing by their defeat. I pursued the deer for subsistence; the deer are disappearing, and I must starve. God ordained me for the forest, and my ambition is the shade. But the strength of my arm decays, and my feet fail me in the chase. The hand which fought for your liberties is now open for your relief. In my youth I bled in battle, that you might be independent; let not my heart in my old age bleed for the want of your commiseration."

This petition was not unheeded; the Legislature of South Carolina granted the old warrior an annuity of sixty dollars.

3 Here was the scene of exciting events during the early part of the summer of 1780. Rocky Mount was made a royal post. Captain Houseman, the commander, sent forth hand-bills, calling the inhabitants together in an "old field," where Beckhamville post-office now stands, to receive protection and acknowledge allegiance to the crown. One aged patriot, like another Tell, refused to bow to the cap of this tiny Gesler. That patriot was Joseph Gaston, who lived upon the Fishing Creek, near the Catawba. In vain Houseman, who went to his residence with an armed escort, pleaded with and menaced the patriot. His reply was, "Never!" and as soon as the British captain had turned his back, he sent his sons out to ask the brave among his neighbors to meet at his house that night. Under Captain John M'Clure, thirty-three determined men were at Judge Gaston's at midnight. They were clad in hunting-shirts and moccasins, wool hats and deer-skin caps, each armed with a butcher-knife and a rifle. Early in the morning, they prepared for the business of the day. Silently they crept along the old Indian trail by the margin of the creek, and suddenly, with a fearful shout, surrounded and discomfited the assembled Tories upon the "old field," at Beckhamville. The thenceforth never to submit to oppression, and from that time they all bore arms in defense of liberty. – See Mrs. Ellett's Domestic History of the Revolution, pages 169-174, inclusive.

4 This view is from the west side of the Catawba, looking northeast, toward Lancaster District.

5 This view is from the garden-gate at Mrs. Barkley's, looking northeast. On the left is seen part of a store-house, and on the right, just beyond the post with a pigeon-house, is a hollow, within which are the remains of houses. At the foot of the hill may still be seen the foundations of the house mentioned in the text as having been occupied by the British when attacked by Sumter. The small log buildings across the center, occupying the slope where the conflict occurred, are servants' houses.

6 Richard Winn was a native of Virginia. He entered the service early, and in 1775 was commissioned the first lieutenant of the South Carolina rangers. He served under Colonel William Thomson, in General Richardson's expedition against the Tories, in the winter of that year. He had been with Thomson in the battle on Sullivan's Island. He afterward served in Georgia, and was in command of Fort M'Intosh, on the north side of the Santilla River. He was subsequently promoted to colonel, and commanded the militia of Fairfield District. He was with Sumter at Hanging Rock, where he was wounded. He was active during the remainder of the war, and at the conclusion, was appointed a brigadier, and finally a major general of militia. He represented his district in Congress from 1793 to 1802. He removed to Tennessee in 1812, and died soon afterward. Winnsborough, the present seat of justice of Fairfield District, was so named in his honor, when he was colonel of that district in 1779.

7 Huck had often been heard to say, says Ramsay (ii., 136), that "God Almighty was turned rebel; but that if there were twenty Gods on their side, they should all be conquered."

8 The house of Colonel Bratton was only half a mile distant from Williamson's. There Huck had first halted, and rudely demanded of Colonel Bratton's wife where her husband was. "In Sumter's army," was her prompt reply. Huck tried to win her to the royal cause, or force her, by menaces, to disclose the place of her husband's retreat. She firmly refused all compliance, even when a sharp reaping-hook was at her throat, in the hands of a brutal soldier. This courageous act of Mrs. Bratton is still remembered with reverence in that section; and as late as 1839, a toast, complimentary of the "fortitude of Martha Bratton," was given at the anniversary of Huck's* defeat. – See Mrs. Ellet's Women of the Revolution, i., 237.

---

* This name is spelled by different authors, Huyck, Huck, and Hucke.

---

9 Colonel Lacy was one of the most resolute and sturdy patriots of South Carolina. It is related that when the Americans were pursuing Huck, Lacy sent a small party to secure his own father, who was a Tory, and prevent his giving information to that marauder. Lacy was a man of great personal strength, and was a general favorite with the people. He was one of the most active participators in the action on King's Mountain.

10 Mrs. Ellet relates a circumstance which has some interest in this connection. Colonel Thomas, of Spartanburg District, was intrusted by Governor Rutledge with a quantity of arms and ammunition. A party, under Colonel Moore (who was defeated at Ramsour's Mill), attacked the house of the colonel, during his absence, for the purpose of seizing the powder. His heroic wife, Jane Thomas, with a son-in-law, her daughter, and a lad, formed the garrison in the house. Mrs. Thomas and her daughter loaded guns as fast as the son-in-law could fire; and the Tories, believing that the house was filled with men, decamped, and the ammunition was saved. This powder constituted a part of Sumter's supply at Rocky Mount and Hanging Rock.

11 John M'Clure was one of the master spirits of South Carolina. He was a nephew of the venerable Judge Gaston, and partook of that patriot's purity and zeal in the cause of Republicanism. Of him General Davie said, "Of the many brave men with whom it was my fortune to become acquainted in the army, he was one of the bravest; and when he fell, we looked upon his loss as incalculable." He fell at the first fire of Bryan's Loyalists, pierced by two bullets, and at the same time, four of his cousins, sons of Judge Gaston, lay bleeding near him. When his friends came to his aid, be urged them to leave him and pursue the enemy. After the battle, he was taken, with other wounded soldiers, to Waxhaw church, where his mother went to nurse him. From thence he was taken to Charlotte, and on the eighteenth, the very day when his commander was surprised at Fishing Creek (see page 454 in original text), he expired in Liberty Hall, where the celebrated Mecklenburg resolutions were drawn up. M'Clure was a native of Chester District, and his men were known as the Chester Rocky Creek Irish. The first wound which he received in the engagement was in the thigh. He stanched it with wadding, when another bullet passed through him at the breast. Two of the Gastons fell dead across each other; a third was mortally wounded; and a fourth had a cheek shot away. Doctor Richard E. Wylie, of Lancaster, wrote a ballad of twenty stanzas commemorative of this event.

12 Gordon, Ramsay, Moultrie, Lee.

13 This name is derived from the Waxhaw Indians, a tribe now extinct, who inhabited this region.

14 Buford's answer, as given by Tarleton in his Memoirs, was brief and positive, as follows:

"Waxhaws, May 29th, 1780.

"Sir, – I reject your proposal, and shall defend myself to the last extremity.

"Lieutenant-Colonel Tarleton, commander of British Legion.

15 Justice demands an audience for Tarleton. In his account of the affair, he alleges that a demand for a surrender was made before his main body had overtaken Buford, and that after that officer's defiant letter was received, both parties prepared for action. He excuses the refusal to grant quarter by the plea that some of the Continentals continued to fire. As Marshall suggests, the fact that Buford's field-pieces were not discharged and so few of the British were wounded, is evidence enough that the attack was unexpected. Tarleton was taunted with his cruelty on this occasion, on his return to England. Stedman, the British historian of the war says, "On this occasion, the virtue of humanity was totally forgot." – See Marshall, i., 338; Gordon, iii., 53; Lee, 78; Stedman, ii., 193.

16 I am informed by the Honorable David L. Swain, that the birth-place of General Jackson is in Mecklenburg county, North Carolina, just above the state line. It is about half a mile west of the Waxhaw Creek, upon the estate of W. J. Cureton, Esq.. twenty-eight miles south of Charlotte. A month or two after his birth, his mother removed to the southward of the state line, to a plantation about twelve miles north of Lancaster Court House. That plantation is also the property of Mr. Cureton. The house in which she resided when Tarleton penetrated the settlement is now demolished. So the honor of possessing the birthplace of that illustrious man belongs to North, and not to South Carolina, as has been supposed. The massacre of Buford's regiment fired the patriotism of young Andrew Jackson; and at the age of thirteen he entered the army, with his brother Robert, under Sumter. They were both made prisoners; but even while in the power of the British, the indomitable courage of the after man appeared in the boy. When ordered to clean the muddy boots of a British officer, he proudly refused, and for his temerity received a sword-cut. After their release, Andrew and his brother returned to the Waxhaw settlement with their mother. That patriotic mother and two sons perished during the war. Her son Hugh was slain in battle, and Robert died of a wound which he received from a British officer while he was prisoner, because, like Andrew, he refused to do menial service. The heroic mother, while on her way home from Charleston, whither she went to carry some necessaries to her friends and relations on board a prison-ship, was seized with prison-fever, and died. Her unknown grave is somewhere between what was then called the Quarter House and Charleston. Andrew was left the sole survivor of the family. – See Foote's Sketches of North Carolina, p. 199.

17 There I saw Mrs. Lee, the step-mother of Mrs. Fletcher, who was then ninety-two years of age. She lived near Camden during the war, but was so afflicted with palsy when I saw her, that she could talk only with great difficulty, and I could not procure from her any tradition of interest. Mrs. Lee had buried five husbands.

18 This view is from the south side of the bridge. The counterfeit cannon was placed in the road where the first wagon is seen. The house and barn of Rugeley were in the cleared field seen beyond the wagons.

19 Tarleton's Memoirs, &c., 205.

20 This view is from the south side of the stream.

21 This view is from the north side of the Creek. Like the other stream, it is filled with canes, shrubs, and many blasted pines.

22 All the way from Yorkville I passed caravans of wagons with cotton, on their way to Camden or Columbia. The teams are driven by negroes, sometimes accompanied by an overseer. They carry corn and fodder (corn-stalks) with them, and camp out at night, in the woods, where they build fires, cook their bacon, bake their hoe-cake, and sleep under the canvas covering of their wagons. It is a season of great delight to those who are privileged to "haul cotton" to market.

23 The Baron De Kalb, knight of the royal military order of merit, was a native of Alsace (a German province ceded to France), and was educated in the art of war in the French army. He was connected with the quarter-master general's department, and his experience in the duties of that station rendered his services very valuable to the American army. Toward the close of the Seven Years' War, he was dispatched to the British colonies in America, as a secret agent of the French government. He traveled in disguise; yet on one occasion, he was so strongly suspected, that he was arrested as a suspicious person. Nothing being found to confirm the suspicion, he was released, and soon afterward returned to Europe. De Kalb came to America again, in the spring of 1777, with La Fayette and other foreign officers, and was one of the party who accompanied the marquis in his overland journey, from South Carolina to Philadelphia. Holding the office of brigadier in the French service, and coming highly recommended, Congress commissioned him a major general on the fifteenth of September, 1777. He immediately joined the main army under Washington, and was active in the events which preceded the encampment of the troops at Valley Forge. He was afterward in command at Elizabethtown and Amboy, in New Jersey; and while at Morristown in the spring of 1780, was placed at the head of the Maryland division. With these, and the Continental troops of Delaware, he marched southward in April, to re-enforce General Lincoln, but was too late to afford him aid at Charleston. Gates succeeded Lincoln in the command of the Southern army, and reached De Kalb's camp, on the Deep River, on the twenty-eighth of July, 1780. In the battle near Camden, which soon followed, De Kalb, while trying to rally the scattered Americans, fell, pierced with eleven wounds. He died at Camden three days afterward, and was buried there. An ornamental tree was placed at the head of his grave,* and that was the only token of its place until a few years since, when the citizens of Camden erected over it the elegant marble monument depicted in the engraving. The corner stone was laid by La Fayette in 1825. It is upon the green, in front of the Presbyterian church, on De Kalb Street. The large base, forming two steps, is of granite; the whole monument is about fifteen feet in height. Upon the four sides of the monument are the following inscriptions:

South side, fronting the street. – "Here lie the remains of BARON DE KALB, a German by birth, but in principle a citizen of the world." North side. – "In gratitude for his zeal and services, the citizens of Camden have erected this monument." East side. – "His love of Liberty induced him to leave the Old World to aid the citizens of the New in their struggle for INDEPENDENCE. His distinguished talents and many virtues weighed with Congress to appoint him MAJOR GENERAL, in their Revolutionary army." West side. – "He was second in command in the battle fought near CAMDEN, on the sixteenth of August, 1780, between the British and Americans; and there nobly fell, covered with wounds, while gallantly performing deeds of valor in rallying the friends and opposing the enemies of his adopted country."

DeKalb's Monument.

The death of De Kalb was a great public loss. Congress, on the fourteenth of October, 1780, ordered a monument to be erected to his memory in the city of Annapolis, in Maryland, Ü with an appropriate inscription, but, like kindred resolves, the order was never obeyed.

---

* Alluding to this fact, an anonymous poet wrote:

> "But where, O where's the hallowed sod
> Beneath whose verd the hero's ashes sleep?
> Is this the cold, neglected, moldering clod?
> Or that the grave at which I ought to weep?
>
> Why rises not some massy pillar high,
> To grace a name that fought for Freedom's prize?
> Or why, at least, some rudely-etch'd stone nigh,
> To show the spot where matchless valor lies?

Yet, soldier, thy illustrious name is known,
Thy fame supported, and thy worth confess'd,
That peerless virtue which in danger shone,
Is shining still, where thou art laid in rest.

And though no monumental script is seen.
Thy worth to publish, and thy deeds proclaim,
Each son of Freedom, passing near this green,
Shall hail DE KALB, and venerate his name."

Ü In the inscription ordered by Congress (Journal, vi., 147) to be placed upon De Kalb's monument, it is said that he was "in the forty-eighth year of his age." General Henry Lee, who knew him well, says in his Memoirs, page 425, "Although nearer seventy than sixty years of age, such had been the temperance of his life, that he not only enjoyed to the last day the finest health, but his countenance still retained the bloom of youth; which circumstance very probably led to the error committed by those who drew up the inscription on the monument to be erected by Congress." Lee speaks of him as "possessing a stout frame, moderate mental powers;" "sober, drinking water only; abstemious to excess, and exceedingly industrious." The pay of De Kalb was considerably in arrears at the time of his death. Within a few years, some of his immediate descendants have petitioned the American Congress for the payment of these arrearages, principal and interest. Reports upon the subject were made, but the matter was not definitely settled until January, 1855, when both Houses of Congress agreed to give the surviving heirs the sum of $66,000. Among the petitioners are five of De Kalb's great grandchildren, who, by the loss of both parents, are cast upon the support and protection of an aunt, a grand-daughter of the baron. They were residing in 1854 about thirty miles from Paris.

---

24 Horatio Gates was a native of England, and was educated to the military profession. He was an officer under Braddock when that general was defeated, but does not seem to have acquired particular distinction. When the Continental army was organized in 1775, he was appointed adjutant general, with the rank of brigadier. He was then residing in Virginia. He accompanied Washington to Cambridge, in July, 1775; and in June, 1776, the chief command of the Northern army was conferred upon him, and he was promoted to major general. In the autumn of that year, he joined the main army in the Jerseys, with a detachment of his command, but his career was not marked by any brilliant action. In the summer of 1777, he was unjustly placed in command of the Northern army, in place of General Schuyler, who had succeeded him in the spring of that year; and the victory over Burgoyne, at Saratoga, by the army under his command, gave him great eclat. The glory of that achievement was not due to him, but to the previous operations of Schuyler, and the bravery and skill of Arnold and Morgan. In the winter of 1778, he was involved in attempts to wrest the supreme command from Washington. His position as President of the Board of War enabled him to throw obstacles in the way of the chief, nor were they withheld. From that period until appointed to the command of the Southern army, his military operations were of little account, and were chiefly in Rhode Island. When Congress gave him the command of the Southern forces, General Charles Lee said to Gates, "Take care that you do not exchange Northern laurels for Southern willows." This caution was prophetic. The disastrous battle near Camden scattered his troops, and, apparently panic-stricken himself, he fled toward Charlotte. He was superseded in his command by General Greene in the autumn of that year, and his conduct was scrutinized by a committee of Congress. Upon their report he was acquitted of blame. He was reinstated in his military command in the main army in 1782, but active service was no longer required. At the close of the war, he retired to his estate in Virginia, and in 1790 took up his permanent abode upon Manhattan Island, almost three miles from the then city of New York. His mansion, which was an elegant country residence, near Rose Hill, was standing as late as 1845, near the corner of Twenty-third Street and Second Avenue. In 1800, he was elected a member of the Legislature of New York, where he served but one term. He died at his residence, on the tenth of April, 1806, at the age of seventy-eight years.

General Gates was an accomplished gentleman in his manners, but did not possess a brilliant or highly-cultivated intellect. He possessed many excellent social qualities, but was entirely deficient in the qualifications necessary for a great military commander. His vanity misled his judgment, and often perverted the finer feelings of his nature. He was always a generous friend, and not an implacable enemy. Humanity marked his treatment of prisoners, and benevolence was a ruling principle of his heart. A few years before his death, he manumitted all his slaves, but so great was the attachment of many, that they preferred to remain in his family. He died without surviving issue, his only son having been taken from him by death, at the moment when he was informed that General Greene had superseded him. On that occasion, Washington wrote him a most touching letter, consoling him for his domestic affliction, and sympathizing with him on account of the troubles of his public life. His patriotism is undoubted, and the faults of his military career may be charged to errors of judgment.

25 This appointment was made without consulting the commander-in-chief. He intended to recommend General Greene.

26 Richard Dobbs Spaight, afterward (1792) governor of North Carolina, was General Caswell's aid on this occasion.

27 Mordecai Gist was born in Baltimore, Maryland, in 1743. His ancestors, early emigrants to Maryland, were English. He was educated for commercial pursuits, and was engaged in the vocation of a merchant when the storm of the Revolution began to lower. The young men of Baltimore associated under the title of the "Baltimore Independent Company," and elected Gist captain. This was the first company raised in Maryland for the defense of popular liberty. Gist was appointed major of a battalion of Maryland regulars in 1776, and was with them in the battle near Brooklyn, at the close of the summer of that year. He was promoted to colonel in 1777, and was in the battle at Germantown in October of that year. In January, 1779, Congress appointed him a brigadier in the Continental army, and he was honored with the command of the 2d Maryland brigade. He fought bravely, and suffered defeat in the battle near Camden, in 1780. Gist was present at the surrender of Cornwallis, and afterward joined the Southern army, under Greene. When that commander remodeled the army, in 1782, while lying near Charleston, he gave General Gist the command of the "light corps." It was a part of his command, under Colonel Laurens, that dealt one of the last blows upon the enemy, in an engagement upon the banks of the Combahee. At the close of the war, he retired to a plantation which he bought near Charleston, where he resided until his death, which occurred in Charleston, in 1792. General Gist had but two children, sons; one he named Independent, and the other States.

28 When Deputy-adjutant-general Williams received these orders from Gates, with the estimates of the forces, he perceived that the commander was much deceived in his idea of the number of the troops. Instead of there being almost seven thousand men, he showed, by his returns, that there were only three thousand six hundred and sixty-three, exclusive of those detached in aid of Sumter. Gates did not alter his plan on account of this discovery.

29 William Smallwood was a native of Maryland, and was among the patriots of that colony who earliest expressed their attachment to Republican principles. He was appointed a brigadier by the Continental Congress, in October, 1776, and major general in September, 1780. He was in the battle near Brooklyn, in August, 1776, where his command suffered severely. It was chiefly composed of young men from Maryland, many of them members of the most respectable families of that state. He was in the Brandywine and Germantown battles in

1777. He accompanied Gates to the South, and shared in the mortifications of defeat near Camden. It was a month after that event that Congress promoted him to major general. He was elected a delegate in Congress, for Maryland, in 1785, and the same year was chosen to succeed William Paca as governor of the state. He was succeeded in office by John Eager Howard, in 1788 General Smallwood died in February, 1792.

30 Gordon, iii., 104.

31 Ramsay, ii., 145-152. Gordon, iii., 98-107. Marshall, i., 344-348. Lee, 92-100.

32 It was during the summer of 1780, that Rochambeau and his army arrived at Newport; an auspicious event for the Americans. A movement in Europe, known in history as the Armed Neutrality, at about the same time threatened to cripple the power of England, and promised indirect aid to the Americans. The Empress Catharine, of Russia, with the duplicity which has ever marked the diplomacy of that government, professed great friendship toward England, and abhorrence of the rebellion in America. She even entered into negotiations for sending Russian troops to America to assist the British. All this while she was building a navy, and the English were made to believe it was to aid them. As soon as she felt strong enough to set England at defiance, her tone and policy were changed, and on the twenty-sixth of February, 1780, she issued a manifesto, in which she declared the international doctrine (with a qualification) so eloquently promulged and advocated by Kossuth in America, in 1851-2, namely, that neutral states have a right to carry on their commerce with belligerent powers unmolested, and even to convey from one port to another of a belligerent power, all goods whatsoever, except what could be deemed contraband in consequence of previous treaties.* Hitherto ports were blockaded, not always by squadrons of ships, but by a simple proclamation. Catharine declared that no port should be considered blockaded, unless there was a sufficient force present to maintain a blockade, and this was the qualification of the doctrine concerning the rights of neutral nations; a qualification which contains the essential maxim of despotism, "Might makes right." This doctrine was contrary to the maritime policy of England, and inimical to her interests. In the course of the summer, Prussia, Denmark, and Sweden became parties to the policy declared by the Czarina, and entered into a league with her; and in November the States General of Holland acceded to the measure. Spain and France acquiesced in the new maritime code, and at one time a general Continental war against England appeared inevitable. But the personal caprices of Catharine, and her known faithlessness, made the other powers hesitate, and the next year the alliance resulted in inaction.

---

* See Florida Bianca's Representation, as cited by Arch-deacon Coxe in his Memoirs of the Kings of Spain, of the Throne of Bourbon.

---

33 The exact loss sustained by the Americans in the engagement on the sixteenth, and Sumter's surprise on the eighteenth, was never ascertained. The estimated loss was as follows: exclusive of De Kalb and General Rutherford, four lieutenant colonels, three majors, fourteen captains, four captain lieutenants, sixteen lieutenants, three ensigns, four staff, seventy-eight subalterns, and six hundred and four rank and file. They also lost eight field-pieces, and other artillery, more than two hundred baggage wagons, and the greater part of their baggage. That of Gates and De Kalb, with all their papers, was saved. The loss of the British was severe. Gates estimated that more than five hundred of the enemy were killed and wounded; Stedman (ii., 210) says the British loss was three hundred less than the Americans. A great many of the fugitive militia were murdered in their flight. Armed parties of Tories, alarmed at the presence of the Americans, were marching to join Gates. When they heard of his defeat, they inhumanly pursued the flying Americans, and butchered a large number in the swamps and pine barrens.

34 Abner Nash was a member of the Provincial Council of North Carolina, and an active politician. When the war of the Revolution broke out, he and his brother Francis* were found in the ranks of the patriots; Abner in the council, Francis in the field. Their father emigrated from Wales, and settled in Prince Edward county, Virginia, where Abner was born. At an early age he went to North Carolina, where he was educated for the bar. He was the first speaker of the North Carolina Legislature under its Republican Constitution; and in 1779, succeeded Caswell, the first governor, in the office of chief magistrate of the state. He represented a constituency in the Assembly, from 1782 to 1785, and was a member of the Continental Congress from 1782 to 1785. He resided for many years at Newbern, where he died, greatly respected for his public and private virtues. His memory is perpetuated in the state by a county called by his name. Governor Nash's first wife was the young widow of the venerable Governor Dobbs.

---

* I have noticed the death of General Francis Nash at Germantown, elsewhere. Since writing that account, I have been informed that his wound consisted of a laceration of the flesh and the fracture of the bone of his thigh by a cannon-ball, which killed his horse, and also his aid, Major Witherspoon, son of Dr. Witherspoon, of Princeton College. His remains lie in the Mennonist Burying-ground, at Kulpsville, twenty-six miles from Philadelphia. Through the patriotic endeavors of John F. Watson. Esq., the annalist, the citizens of Germantown and Norristown have erected a neat marble monument to the memory of General Nash, upon which is the following inscription: "VOTA VIA MEA JUS PATRI . In memory of General Nash of North Carolina, mortally wounded at the battle of Germantown, here interred, October 17, 1777, in presence of the army here encamped. J. F. W."

Nash's Monument.

Among the gallant officers who accompanied General Nash to the North, and fought at Brandywine and Germantown, was Colonel Edward Buncombe. He was wounded and made a prisoner at Germantown, and died soon afterward at Philadelphia. His character for generous hospitality may be inferred from the following distich, which he affixed over the door of his mansion, in Washington county, North Carolina:

> "Welcome, all,
> To Buncombe Hall."

In 1791, his name was given to a county in North Carolina. From 1817 to 1823, the district which includes Buncombe was represented in congress by one, not an orator. On one occasion, he attempted to address the House in favor of a bill providing pensions for militiamen; but a determination not to hear him was manifested. He appealed to the late Mr. Lowndes to interpose in his behalf, intimating that he would be satisfied with the allowance of five minutes for a speech that might be published in the newspapers, and assuring him that his remarks were not intended for the House, but for Buncombe. He was gratified, and spoke under the five minutes' rule. To the astonishment of the good people of Buncombe the speech of their representative (a curious specimen of logic and oratory) appeared in the Washington City Gazette, covering nearly a broadside of that paper. "Speaking for Buncombe" (not Bunkum) is a term often applied since to men who waste the time of legislative bodies in making speeches for the sole purpose of receiving popular applause.

35 The irritation which Gates exhibited when he was succeeded by General Schuyler in the command of the Northern army, in 1777, was not visible when Greene reached Charlotte, and gave him the first notification of his having been superseded. On the contrary, he received Greene with the utmost courtesy, and expressed his warmest thanks for the tender manner in which that officer announced the action of Congress and the commander-in-chief. On the morning after Greene's arrival, Gates issued the following order:

"Head-quarters, Charlotte, 3d December, 1780.

Parole, Springfield; countersign, Greene. The Honorable Major-general Greene, who arrived yesterday afternoon in Charlotte, being appointed by his excellency, General Washington, with the approbation of the Honorable Congress,

Form of Parole and Countersign*

to the command of the Southern army, all orders will, for the future, issue from him, and all reports are to be made to him. General Gates returns his sincere thanks to the Southern army for their perseverance, fortitude, and patient endurance of all the hardships and sufferings they have undergone while under his command. He anxiously hopes their misfortunes will cease therewith, and that victory and the glorious advantages attending it may be the future portion of the Southern army."

---

* This parole (Alexandria) and countersign (Bedford, Colchester), upon a small slip of paper, is in the handwriting of Washington. The original is in the possession of J. Wingate Thornton. Esq., of Boston. It is the practice in camps for the commander-in-chief to issue a parole and countersign every morning. It is given in writing to his subordinates, and by them communicated to those who wish to leave the camp and return during the day and evening, &c. The object is to guard against the admission of spies into the camp.

---

36 The site of this spring, the source of one of the tributaries of Pine Tree Creek, is at the head of a ravine, scooped out of the northeastern slope of Hobkirk's Hill. The noble trees which shadow it are tulips, poplars, and pines. The house seen on the top of the hill, toward the left, is the residence of William E. Johnson, Esq., president of the Camden Bank. A few yards below the spring a dike has been cast up, across the ravine, by which a fine duck pond is formed, and adds beauty to the scene, in summer.

37 Lee, in his Memoirs (page 215), relates an amusing circumstance which occurred while he was on his way to join Marion among the swamps on Black River, in Williamsburg District. Lee's detachment had reached Drowning Creek, a branch of the Pedee, and were encamped for the night. Toward morning, the officer of the day was informed that noises, like the stealthy movements of a body of men, were heard in front of the pickets, toward the creek. Presently a sentinel fired, the bugles sounded for the horse patroles to come in, and soon the whole detachment were on the alert for the approaching enemy. Soon another sentinel fired in a different direction, and intelligence came that an invisible enemy were in the swamp. The troops were formed in accordance with the latest information of the whereabouts of the secret foe. With great anxiety they awaited the approach of dawn, not doubting that its first gleam would be the signal for a general assault by the enemy. Suddenly the line of sentinels in their rear, upon the great road they had traversed, fired in quick succession, and the fact that the enemy had gained their rear in Force could not be doubted. Lee went cautiously along his line; informed his troops that there was no alternative but to fight; reminded them of their high reputation, and enjoined them to be firm throughout the approaching contest. He conjured the cavalry to be cautious, and not allow any partial success to tempt them to pursue, for no doubt the enemy would ambuscade. At break of day, the whole column advanced cautiously to the great road, infantry in front, baggage in the center, and cavalry in the rear. No enemy appeared, and the van officer cautiously examined the road to find the trail of the foe. He soon discovered the tracks of a large pack of wolves! These animals had attempted to pass along their accustomed path. but finding it obstructed, had turned from point to point when met by the fire of the sentinels. The circumstance occasioned great merriment among the troops. Each considered himself a dupe. The poor pickets, patroles, and officer of the day were made the butt of severest ridicule.

38 Francis Rawdon, son of the Earl of Moira, was born in 1754, and entered the army in 1771. He was distinguished for his bravery during his first campaign in America, and in 1778 was appointed adjutant general of the British forces. He was at the storming of Forts Clinton and Montgomery in 1777, and was with Sir Henry Clinton at the battle of Monmouth. He was promoted to brigadier, and was succeeded in his office of adjutant general by Major Andre. Rawdon afterward received the commission of a major general. In 1812, he was appointed Governor General of British India, which office he held until 1822. During his administration, the Nepaulese, Pindarees, and other native powers, were subjugated, and the British authority made supreme in India. During his absence in the East, he was created Marquis of Hastings. He died in 1825.

39 Camden, the capital of Kershaw District, stands upon a gentle elevation, covered on the southwest by the Wateree at a mile distant, and on the east by Pine Tree Creek, a considerable stream. The country around it was heavily wooded at the time in question, and the town itself (formerly called Pine Tree, but then named in honor of Lord Camden) was but a small village of a few houses.

40 Colonel Watson had really commenced his march up the Santee, but was obliged to turn back because Marion and Lee, after capturing Fort Watson, had got in front of him, and effectually guarded all the passes and ferries.

41 That portion of Hobkirk's Hill, on its southeastern slope, where the first of the battle commenced, is now called Kirkwood. It is covered with fine residences and beautiful gardens, and is valued as a healthful summer resort by the people of Camden.

42 See note on next page.

43 Marshall (ii., 6) says that the fall of Captain Beatty, of Gunby's regiment, was the cause of its defection. His company and the one adjoining it were thrown into confusion, and dropped out of the line, and then the fatal disorder ensued.

44 Marshall, ii., 1-8. Ramsay, ii., 230-31. Gordon, iii., 189-91. Lee, 220-24. Stedman, ii., 356-58.

45 The momentary despondency of Greene is expressed in the following extract from a letter which he wrote to the Chevalier Luzerne, three days after the battle: "This distressed country, I am sure, can not struggle much longer without more effectual support. They may struggle a little while longer, but they must fall; and I fear their fall will lay a train to sap the independence of the rest of America. . . . . . We fight, get beaten, rise and fight again. The whole country is one continued scene of blood and slaughter." To La Fayette he wrote, on the first of May: "You may depend upon it, that nothing can equal the sufferings of our little army but their merit." To others he wrote in a similar strain, imploring prompt and decisive action for supplying his handful of troops with sustenance for the summer campaign, and with re-enforcements. It must be remembered, that at this time the French army, under Rochambeau, was lying idle in New England; and through Luzerne (the French minister) and La Fayette, Greene hoped to hasten their advent in the field of active operations. To Governor Read, of Pennsylvania, he wrote, on the fourth of May: "If our good friends, the French, can not lend a helping hand to save these sinking states, they must and will fall."

46 There is now a fine bridge across the Wateree at this place, which cost twenty thousand dollars.

47 Many of these, who had occupied their farms near Camden, were reduced to the most abject poverty. Outside of the lines at Charleston, men, women, and children were crowded into a collection of miserable huts, which received the name of Rawdontown. – Simms's History of South Carolina, 223.

48 I was informed, after I left Camden, that the house in which Cornwallis was quartered, while there, was yet standing, and very little altered since the Revolution. It was one of the few saved when Rawdon left the place. I was not aware of this fact while I was in Camden.

NOTE. – Since the publication of the first edition of this work, I have obtained some information concerning the brave Captain Beatty, and here make brief mention of the chief events in his public career. Captain William Beatty was born in Frederick county, Maryland, on the 19th of June, 1758. His father, Colonel William Beatty, commanded a regiment in General Mercer's Flying Camp during a part of the summer and autumn of 1776. He had with him his two sons, William and Henry. The latter was distinguished as a commander at the repulse of the British at Craney Island, near Norfolk, in 1813. William was made an ensign in 1776, at the age of 18 years, and was in active service, under the immediate command of Washington, until Greene took command of the Southern army in the autumn of 1780, when he went South, and was under that general until his death. He had risen to the rank of captain, and greatly distinguished himself in leading his men to a successful bayonet charge at the battle of Guilford Court House. He was leading a battalion of Gunby's command to a bayonet charge in the battle of Hobkirk's Hill, when a musket-ball entered his forehead, and he fell dead. To save him from the British bayonets, then close at hand, the officers, not knowing that he was killed, rushed forward to pick him up. This produced a halt, and some confusion. The British perceived it, pushed forward, broke the line of the battalion, and caused a general retreat. To the fall of the brave Beatty must be attributed the loss of victory to the Americans.

Chapter XVIII

Marion. Friends! fellow-soldiers! we again have heard
The threats of our proud enemies; they come,
Boasting to sweep us, like the chaff, away.
Shall we yield? shall we lie down like dogs beneath
The keeper's lash? Then shall we well deserve
The ruin, the disgrace that must ensue.
Ne'er dream submission will appease our foes;
We shall be conquered rebels, and they'll fear
The spirit of liberty may rouse again;
And therefore will they bind us with strong chains,
New cords, green withes, like those which Samson bound,
And we, alas! shall have been shorn and weak,
On Folly's lap, if we yield up our freedom.

-Mrs. S.J. Hale's Tragedy,
"ORMOND GROSVENOR." Act IV.

It was a brilliant, frosty morning when I left Camden to visit the scenes of some of the exploits of Marion and his partisan compatriots. Soon after crossing the Big Swift and Rafting Creeks, we reached the high hills of Santee, whereon General Greene encamped before and after the battle at the Eutaw Springs. They extend southward, in Sumter District, from the Kershaw line, twenty-two miles, parallel with the Wateree. They are immense sand hills, varying in width on the summit from one to five miles, and are remarkable for the salubrity of the atmosphere and for medicinal springs. Just at sunrise, while swiftly skirting the base of these hills, with the Wateree Swamp between us and the river on the west, we saw the sharp pencilings of the few scattered houses of Statesburg against the glowing eastern sky. There was the residence of General Sumter after the war, and in his honor the surrounding district was named. **1** After skirting the Wateree Swamp some distance, the road passes through a high sand bluff, and then crosses the great morass to the river, a distance of four miles. Beyond that stream, it joins the rail-way from Columbia. Through the swamp, the iron rails are laid upon a strong wooden frame-work, high enough to overtop a cane-brake. The passage is made at a slow rate to avoid accidents. The scenery was really grand, for below were the green canes waving like billows in the wind, while upon either side of the avenue cut for the road, towered mighty cypresses and gum-trees, almost every branch draped with long moss. Clustered around their stately trunks were the holly, water-oak, laurel, and gall-bush, with their varied tints of green;

and among these, flitting in silence, were seen the gray mocking-bird and the brilliant scarlet tanniger. Here, I was told opossums and wild cats abound, and upon the large dry tracts of the swamp wild deers are often seen.

We arrived at the junction station at a little past eight o'clock, and, crossing a narrow part of the Congaree Swamp and River, reached Fort Motte Station, on the southern side of that stream, before nine, a distance of forty-four miles from Camden

The plantation of Mrs. Rebecca Motte, whose house, occupied and stockaded by the British, was called Fort Motte, lies chiefly upon a high rolling plain, near the Buck's Head Neck, on the Congaree, a little above the junction of that river with the Wateree, **3** thirty-three miles below Columbia, the capital of the state. This plain slopes in every direction, and is a commanding point of view, overlooking the vast swamps on the borders of the Congaree. It is now owned by William H. Love, Esq., with

Scene in a Southern Swamp. 2

whom I passed several hours very agreeably. His house (seen in the engraving) is built nearly upon the site of Mrs. Motte's mansion, desolated by fire at her own suggestion, while occupied by the British. The well used by that patriotic lady is still there, close by the oak-tree seen on the right; and from it to the house there is a slight hollow, which indicates the place of a covered way, dug for the protection of the soldiers when procuring water. The other large tree seen in the picture is a blasted sweet-gum, and in the extreme distance is seen the Congaree Swamp. This house was built by Mrs. Motte immediately after the close of the war. The Americans, whose exploits we shall consider presently, were stationed upon an eminence about a quarter of a mile northeast of the house, toward the Congaree, in the direction of M'Cord's

Fort Motte.

Ferry. A little eastward of the house there was an oval mound, when I was there in 1849, about twelve feet in height, and dotted with the stumps of trees recently cut down. This is the vestige of a battery, upon which the assailants planted a field-piece to dislodge the British. We shall better understand these localities after consulting the oracle of history.

Among the bold, energetic, and faithful patriots of the South, none holds a firmer place in the affections of the American people than General Francis Marion. **4** His

Vestige of a Battery.

adventures were full of the spirit of romance, and his whole military life was an epic poem. The followers of Robin Hood were never more devoted to their chief than were the men of Marion's brigade to their beloved leader. Bryant has sketched a graphic picture of that noble band, in his

SONG OF MARION'S MEN.

Our band is few, but true and tried,
  Our leader frank and bold;
The British soldier trembles
  When MARION'S name is told.
Our fortress is the good green wood,
  Our tent the cypress-tree;
We know the forest round us,
  As seamen know the sea.
We know its walls of thorny vines,
  Its glades of reedy grass;
Its safe and silent islands
  Within the dark morass.

Woe to the English soldiery,
  That little dread us near!
On them shall light at midnight,
  A strange and sudden fear;
When, waking to their tents on fire,
  They grasp their arms in vain,
And they who stand to face us
  Are beat to earth again;
And they who fly in terror deem
  A mighty host behind,
And hear the tramp of thousands
  Upon the hollow wind.

Then sweet the hour that brings release
  From danger and from toil;
We talk the battle over,
  And share the battle's spoil.
The woodland rings with laugh and shout,
  As if a hunt were up,
And woodland flowers are gather'd
  To crown the soldier's cup.
With merry songs we mock the wind
  That in the pine-top grieves,
And slumber long and sweetly
  On beds of oaken leaves.

Well knows the fair and friendly moon
  The hand that MARION leads –
The glitter of their rifles,
  The scampering of their steeds.
'Tis life to guide the fiery barb
  Across the moonlight plain;

'Tis life to feel the night wind
  That lifts his tossing mane.
A moment in the British camp –
  A moment – and away
Back to the pathless forest.
  Before the peep of day.

Grave men there are by broad Santee;
  Grave men with hoary hairs,
Their hearts are all with MARION,
  For MARION are their prayers.
And lovely ladies greet our band
  With kindliest welcoming,
With smiles like those of summer,
  And tears like those of spring.
For them we wear these trusty arms,
  And lay them down no more,
Till we have driven the Briton
  Forever from our shore.

When Gates was pressing forward toward Camden, Marion, with about twenty men and boys, was annoying the Tories in the neighborhood of the Pedee. With his ragged command, worse than Falstaff ever saw, he appeared at the camp of Gates, and excited the ridicule of the well-clad Continentals. **5** Gates, too, would doubtless have thought lightly of him, if Governor Rutledge, who was in the American camp, and knew the partisan's worth, had not recommended him to the notice of that general. Gates listened to his modestly-expressed opinions respecting the campaign, but was too conceited to regard them seriously, or to offer to Marion a place in his army. While he was in Gates's camp, the Whigs of Williamsburg District, who had arisen in arms, sent for him to be their commander. Governor Rutledge gave him the commission of a brigadier on the spot, and he hastened to organize that brigade, which we shall hereafter meet frequently among the swamps, the broad Savannahs, and by the water-courses of the South. **6**

Fort Motte, where the brave Marion exhibited his skill and courage, was the principal depot of the convoys between Charleston and Camden, and also for those destined for Granby and Ninety-Six. The British had taken possession of the fine large mansion of Mrs. Rebecca Motte, **7** a widow of fortune, which occupied a commanding position. They surrounded it with a deep trench (a part of which is yet visible), and along the interior margin of it erected a high parapet. Mrs. Motte and her family, known to be inimical to the British, were driven to her farm-house, upon a hill north of the mansion, and their place was supplied by a garrison of one hundred and fifty men, under Captain M'Pherson, a brave British officer. After Colonel Watson eluded the pursuit of Marion and Lee, and crossed the Congaree, those indefatigable partisans moved upon Fort Motte. A few hours before their arrival at that place, M'Pherson was re-enforced by a small detachment of dragoons sent from Charleston with dispatches for Lord Rawdon. They were on the point of leaving, when Marion and Lee appeared upon the height at the farm-house where Mrs. Motte was residing.

After cautiously reconnoitering, Lee took position at the farm-house, and his men, with the field-piece sent to them by Greene, occupied the eastern declivity of the high plain on which Fort Motte stood. This gentle declivity is a little southwest of the rail-way station, in full view of passengers upon the road. Marion immediately cast up a mound (see page 147 in original text), upon which he planted the six-pounder, in a position to rake the northern face of the parapet of the fort, against which Lee prepared to approach. M'Pherson had no artillery, and his safety depended upon timely extraneous aid, either from Camden or Ninety-Six.

Between the height on which Lee was posted and Fort Motte is a narrow vale, which allowed the assailants to approach within four hundred yards of the fort. From that vale they began to advance by a parallel, which, by the assistance of some negroes from neighboring plantations, was sufficiently advanced by the tenth of May, 1781 to warrant the Americans in demanding a surrender. A flag was accordingly dispatched, with a formal summons, but M'Pherson gallantly refused compliance. That evening, intelligence of Rawdon's retreat from Camden toward Nelson's Ferry was communicated to the Americans, and in the course of the night a courier from Greene confirmed the report. Delay would be dangerous, for Rawdon, with his superior force, could easily repulse them. Early on the morning of the eleventh, the light of his beacon-fires were seen on the high hills of Santee, and that night their gleamings upon the highest ground of the country, opposite Fort Motte, gave great joy to the beleagured garrison. To batter down the enemy's works with the field-piece, or to approach by a trench, was too slow for the exigency of the case. The fertile mind of Lee, full of expedients, suggested a quicker plan for dislodging the garrison. The mansion of Mrs. Motte, in the center of the enemy's works, was covered with shingles, now very dry, for no rain had fallen for several days, and the rays of the sun were powerful. To communicate fire to this mansion was Lee's expedient. That officer had enjoyed the hospitality of Mrs. Motte during the siege, and her only marriageable daughter was then the wife of his friend, Major Thomas Pinckney. These circumstances made it a painful duty for him to propose the destruction of her property. Her cheerful acquiescence, and even patriotic desire to be able to serve her country by such a sacrifice, gave him joy and, communicating his plan to Marion, they hastened to execute it. It was proposed to hurl ignited combustibles upon the roof of the house, by arrows. These were prepared, when Mrs. Motte, observing their inferiority, brought out a fine bow and a bundle of arrows which had been brought from the East Indies, and presented them to Lee. On the morning of May 12, 1781, Lee sent Dr. Irvine, of his cavalry, with a flag, to state truly the relative position of the belligerents; that Rawdon had not yet crossed the Santee, and that immediate surrender would save many lives. M'Pherson still refused compliance and at meridian, when the ditch was advanced within bow-shot of the fort, several arrows from the hand of Nathan Savage, a private in Marion's brigade, winged their way, with lighted torches, toward the house. Two struck the dry shingles, and instantly a bright flame crept along the roof. Soldiers were ordered up to knock off the shingles and put out the fire, when one or two shots from Marion's battery, raking the loft, drove them below. M'Pherson hung out a white flag, the firing ceased, the flames were extinguished, and at one o'clock the garrison surrendered themselves prisoners of war. By invitation of Mrs. Motte, both the victorious and the captive officers partook of a sumptuous dinner from her table, while she presided with all the coolness and easy politeness for which she was remarkable when surrounded by friends in the enjoyment of peace. **8**

The prisoners were treated with great humanity, notwithstanding some of them were Tories of a most obnoxious stamp. As soon as paroled, they were sent off to Lord Rawdon, then crossing the Santee at Nelson's Ferry, near Eutaw Springs. The fall of Fort Motte greatly alarmed that officer, and two days afterward (May 14), he blew up the fortifications at Nelson's Ferry, and hastened toward Charleston. During the day of the capitulation, Greene arrived with a small troop of cavalry, being anxious to know the result of the siege, for he was aware Rawdon was hastening to the relief of the garrison. **9** Finding every thing secure, he returned to his camp, then on the north side of the Congaree, after ordering Marion to proceed against Georgetown, toward the head of Winyaw Bay, near the coast, and directing Lee with his legion, and Captain Finley with his six pounder, to attack Fort Granby, thirty-two miles above Fort Motte, near the present city of Columbia. Thither we will presently proceed.

About a mile eastward of Fort Motte is the residence of Charles Thomson, Esq., known as Belleville. It was taken possession of, stockaded, and garrisoned by the Loyalists for a while. The fine old mansion, which I am told exhibits many bullet-marks made by some Whigs, who attacked a party of Tories stationed in the house, was owned by William Thomson, who, next to Moultrie, was most conspicuous in the battle on Sullivan's Island, at the entrance to Charleston harbor, in 1776. I intended to visit Belleville, but it was so late when I had finished dinner with Mr. Love, that I was obliged to mount one of his horses and hasten to the station to take passage for Columbia. While waiting for the cars, the overseer of a plantation near requested me to write a pass for a sick female slave, whom he was about to send to her master at Columbia for medical aid. Regardless of the penalty, **10** I wrote upon a card from my port-folio, "PASS DIDO TO COLUMBIA, January 19, 1849. J. SMOKE." Two hours afterward I was there also, but did not again see the namesake of the Queen of Carthage.

Columbia, the capital of South Carolina, is a fine town, handsomely located upon a high plain three or four miles in extent, a little below the junction of the Broad and Saluda Rivers, where they form the Congaree. It was laid out in 1787, when the region around it was very sparsely populated. The Legislature first met there in 1790. There was a settlement on each side of the river, about two miles below, called Granby, which was a point of departure for the wilderness of the Cherokee country. The climate is mild and salubrious; and Columbia promises to be, from its geographical and political situation, a large inland city. It is the favored seat of learning in the state, the South Carolina College and Theological Seminary of South Carolina and Georgia being located there.

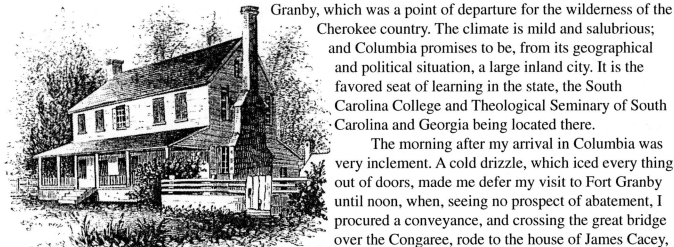

Fort Granby. 11

The morning after my arrival in Columbia was very inclement. A cold drizzle, which iced every thing out of doors, made me defer my visit to Fort Granby until noon, when, seeing no prospect of abatement, I procured a conveyance, and crossing the great bridge over the Congaree, rode to the house of James Cacey, Esq., the "Fort Granby" of the Revolution, two miles below. It is a strong frame building, two stories in height, and stands upon an eminence near the Charleston road, within three fourths of a mile of Friday's Ferry, upon the Congaree. It overlooks ancient Granby and the country around. Several houses of the old village are there, but the solitude of desolation prevails, for not a family remains. Mr. Cacey was a hopeless invalid, yet he was able to give me many interesting reminiscences connected with that locality, and I passed an hour very pleasantly with him and his family.

The dwelling of Mr. Cacey was originally built by some gentlemen of Pine Tree (Camden) as a store-house for cotton and other products of the country, whence they were sent upon flat-boats down the river to the sea-board. When the chain of military posts from Camden to Charleston was established, this building, eligibly located, was fortified, and called Fort Granby. A ditch was digged around it; a strong parapet was raised; bastions were formed; batteries were arranged; and an abatis was constructed. The garrison consisted of three hundred and fifty men, chiefly Loyalists, with a few mounted Hessians, under the command of Major Maxwell (a refugee from the eastern shore of Maryland), of the Prince of Wales's regiment. He was neither brave nor experienced, and the want of these qualities of the commandant being known to Lee, he felt no hesitation in attacking him in his strong position. Detaching a small troop of cavalry, under Captain Armstrong, to watch the movements of Rawdon, Lee pushed forward with his usual celerity, to the investment of Fort Granby. Sumter, instead of joining Greene before Camden, had made a demonstration against Fort Granby, a few days before, but finding it too strong for his small arms, had retired, and marched to attack the British post at Orangeburg, fifty miles below. Lee arrived in the vicinity of the fort on the evening of May 14, 1781, the day on which Sumter took possession of Orangeburg; and in the edge of a wood, within six hundred yards of the fort, he began the erection of a battery. A dense fog the next morning enabled him to complete it, and mount the six pounder brought by Captain Finley from Fort Motte, before they were discovered by the garrison. When the fog rolled away, Captain Finley discharged his cannon, and, at the same moment, the legion infantry advanced, took an advantageous position, and opened a fire upon the enemy's pickets. This sudden annunciation of the presence of an enemy, and his imposing display, alarmed Maxwell excessively, and he received Captain Eggleston, who was sent with a flag to demand a surrender, with great respect. After a brief consultation with his officers, the major agreed to surrender the fort, on condition that private property of every, sort, without an investigation of title, should be left in the hands of its possessors; **12** that the garrison should be permitted to retire to Charleston as prisoners of war, until exchanged; that the militia should be held in the same manner as the regulars; and that an escort, charged with the protection of persons and property, should attend the prisoners to Rawdon's camp. Lieutenant-colonel Lee's practice was always to restore plundered property, when captured, to the rightful owners; yet, knowing the danger of delay, with Rawdon so near, he acquiesced, on the condition that all the horses fit for public service should be left. To this the mounted Hessians objected, and the negotiations were suspended. During this suspense, Captain Armstrong arrived with the intelligence that Rawdon had crossed the Santee, and was moving upon Fort Motte. Lee waved the exception; the capitulation was signed, and before noon Captain Rudulph raised the American flag on one of the bastions, and the captive garrison marched, with its escort, for Rawdon's camp. **13** Among the spoils of victory were two pieces of cannon, and a considerable quantity of ammunition, salt, and liquor. It was a glorious, because almost a bloodless victory, for no life was lost.

On the surrender of the fort, Lee dispatched a messenger to Greene, who with great expedition had pressed forward, and was within a few miles of Friday's Ferry. He crossed that ferry, and on the evening of the fifteenth of May, 1781, encamped upon Ancram's plantation, near the river, where the victors and the main army had a joyous meeting. During the night a courier from Fort Motte announced the fact that Rawdon had retreated, after a day's march, toward that post, destroyed the works at Nelson's Ferry, and was pushing on toward Charleston. Early in the morning another courier came with the cheering intelligence of Sumter's success at Orangeburg on May 14, and the seventeenth of May was a day of rejoicing by the little American army at Fort Granby.

Resting one day, General Greene moved toward Ninety-Six, which place he reached on the twenty-second of May. In the mean while, he strengthened Lee's legion by the addition of some North Carolina levies under Major Eaton, and then directed him to hasten toward Augusta, on the Savannah River, to join Pickens, who, with a body of militia, was in the vicinity of that post. We will follow them presently.

The house of Mr. Cacey yet bears many "honorable scars" made by the bullets of Lee's infantry; and in the gable toward the river, between the chimney and a window (indicated by a black spot in the engraving), is an orifice, formed by the passage of a six-pound ball from Finley's field-piece. In one of the rooms are numerous marks made by an ax when cutting up meat for the use of the garrison; and an old log barn near, which stood within the intrenchments, has also many bullet scars.

I returned to Columbia at four o'clock, where I remained until Monday morning.

While at Columbia, I met a gentleman from Abbeville District, in the vicinity of old Fort Ninety-Six. He informed me that the traveling was wretched, and quite dangerous in that direction, and that nothing of Revolutionary interest worth visiting yet remained at that military post, now the pleasant village of Cambridge, seventy-nine miles westward of Columbia. He also informed me that a gentleman of Cambridge, who was familiar with every historical event in his neighborhood, would cheerfully communicate all I could possibly learn by a personal visit. Willing to avoid a long and tedious journey unless it was necessary, I wrote to that gentleman, and by his kind and prompt compliance I am furnished with all necessary details respecting the locality, together with the plan of the fortification, printed on page 154. We will here consider the events which render Ninety-Six historically famous.

Old Ninety-Six was so called because it was within ninety-six miles of the frontier fort, Prince George, which was upon the Keowee River, in the present Pickens District. Its locality is in the eastern part of Abbeville District, near the borders of Edgefield, and within six miles of the Saluda River. No portion of the state suffered more during the war than the district around Ninety-Six. Like the neutral ground in West Chester, New York, Whig nor Tory could dwell there in peace, for armed bands of each were continually disturbing the inhabitants, and in close proximity were the hostile Cherokees, ready, when they dared, to scourge the settlers.

The little village of Ninety-Six was stockaded to defend it from the incursions of the Indians; and when, after the fall of Charleston, the British established several posts in the interior, its location and salubrity indicated it as an important point for a fortification. It was in a position to maintain a communication with the Indians, keep in check the Whig settlements west of it, and cover those of the

Loyalists in other directions; and it afforded an excellent recruiting-station for the concentration of Tory material in that quarter.

Ninety-Six was garrisoned by about five hundred and fifty Loyalists, three hundred and fifty of whom were from New York and New Jersey, **14** and the remainder were South Carolina Tories, under Colonel King, the whole commanded by Lieutenant-colonel John Cruger, a native of the city of New York. Cruger was an energetic officer, and possessed the entire confidence of his superiors in the royal army. He did not receive instructions from Rawdon when that officer abandoned Camden, for Sumter cut off all communications; therefore, he had not prepared to evacuate Ninety-Six and join Colonel Browne at Augusta, as Rawdon desired him to do. When he learned that Greene was approaching Camden, he began to strengthen his works; and when informed that Lee, with his legion, had got between him and the post at Augusta, and that Greene was approaching to besiege him, his garrison labored night and day still further to strengthen the defenses. Already he had built a stockade fort on the borders of the village, in addition to a star redoubt. This was strengthened; a parapet was raised; a ditch was dug around it, and a covered way, communicating with the palisaded village, was prepared. Block-houses, formed of notched logs, were erected on the northeastern side of the village, near where a star redoubt was constructed. Before Greene reached there, Cruger's energy and skill had so directed the efforts of the garrison, under the superintendence of Lieutenant Haldane, one of Cornwallis's aids, that the place presented an apparently insurmountable strength against the attacks of Greene's little army of a thousand men.

Plan of the Seige of Ninety-Six.
This plan is from a sketch sent to me by James M. M'Cracken, Esq., of Cambridge, South Carolina. a indicates the spring, with a rivulet running from it; b, a stockade fort; c, the old jail, which was also fortified; d, the court-house; e, star redoubt; f, first mine, traces of which are yet visible; g g g g, the besieging encampments; h h h, stockades inclosing the village; i, the covered way from the stockade fort to the lines around the village.

In the mean while, Marion and Sumter were directed to keep watch between the Santee and Edisto Rivers, and hold Rawdon in check, if he should attempt to march to the relief of either Ninety-Six or Augusta, now menaced by the Americans; while Lee, who left Fort Granby, with his legion, in the evening after its capture, was scouring the country between those two posts, and proceeding to form a junction with Pickens. Informed that quite a large quantity of powder, balls, small arms, liquor, salt, blankets, and other articles, intended for the Indians, and much wanted by the Americans, were deposited at Fort Galphin (sometimes called Fort Dreadnought), a small stockade at Silver Bluff, upon the Carolina side of the Savannah, twelve miles below Augusta,15 he hastened thither to capture them. On the morning of the twenty-first of May (1781), he reached the vicinity, and Captain Rudulph, with some of the legion infantry, gallantly rushed upon the fort, while a small body of militia attacked the garrison from another quarter. With the loss of only one man, the fort, with all its contents, was captured by the Americans. After resting a few hours, Lee ordered Major Eggleston, who was a Continental officer, to cross the Savannah, join bodies of militia in that neighborhood, proceed to Augusta with a flag, inform Colonel Browne of the approach of Greene, and demand an instant surrender of Forts Cornwallis and Grierson, at that place. The events which followed will be detailed in another chapter.

Greene arrived before Ninety-Six on the twenty-second of May (1781), with less than one thousand regulars 17 and a few undisciplined militia. He found quite a strong fort, well situated. On the left of the village, in a valley, was a spring and rivulet, which furnished water to the garrison. On the western side of this rivulet, upon an eminence, was a stockade fort, and upon the other side, near the village, was a fortified jail. These were to defend the water of the rivulet, for none could be had within the town. Eastward of the village stood the principal work, a star redoubt, consisting of sixteen angles, salient and re-entering, with a ditch and abatis, and furnished with three pieces of cannon. Every thing was judiciously arranged for defense, and Lieutenant-colonel Cruger defied Greene when he appeared.

Colonel Kosciuszko was with Greene, and under his direction the besiegers began approaches by parallels. They broke ground near the star redoubt on the evening of the twenty-second. Perceiving this, Cruger placed his three cannons upon a platform, in that direction, before noon the next day, and manned the parapet with infantry. Under cover of these, a sally party, under Lieutenant Roney, rushed out upon the besiegers, drove the guards back toward the lines, bayoneted all who fell in the way, destroyed the American works as far as they had progressed, and carried off all of the intrenching tools. Lieutenant Roney was mortally wounded, and that was all the loss the enemy sustained. All this was accomplished with great gallantry, before a detachment sent by Greene to re-enforce Kosciuszko, arrived upon the ground. Kosciuszko now commenced another approach to the star redoubt. He broke ground on the night of the twenty-third, under cover of a ravine, and day by day slowly approached the fortress. In the mean while, Pickens and Lee besieged and captured Forts Cornwallis and Grierson at Augusta, and hastened to the assistance of Greene. Lee arrived on the eighth of June (1781), and Pickens soon afterward joined him. These active partisans were directed to attack the enemy's works on the west. They immediately commenced regular approaches to the stockade to cut off the enemy's supply of water; and at a proper distance from it erected a battery to cover further approaches, and planted a six pounder upon it, under the direction of Lieutenant Finn. Cruger saw the inevitable destruction of the garrison when these parallels, made slowly, day by day, should be completed. He had found means to inform Lord Rawdon of his critical situation, and hourly he expected aid from him. To gain time for this succor to arrive, he made nightly sallies, and bloody encounters frequently occurred, while almost daily the American foraging parties were attacked by bands of Tories. 18 Yet slowly and surely the Americans approached; and when the second parallel was completed, Greene sent Colonel Williams to demand a surrender, with promises of kind treatment. Cruger promptly replied that he should defend the fort till the last extremity, and regarded neither the threats nor the promises of the American general. A battery, constructed in the second parallel, now opened upon the redoubt, and under its cover Kosciuszko pressed forward his approach with vigor. On June 11, 1781, Greene received a dispatch from Sumter, announcing the startling intelligence that on the third, a fleet arrived from Ireland with re-enforcements for Rawdon, consisting of three regiments, a detachment from the Guards, and a considerable body of volunteers, under the command of Lieutenant-colonel Gould. Rawdon had been anxiously awaiting at Monk's Corner, near Charleston, this propitious event. He had heard of the fall of Fort Cornwallis at Augusta and the investment of Ninety-Six, but with his small force, and Marion and Sumter before him, he dared not march to the aid of Cruger. On the arrival of these troops, he repaired to Charleston, and on June 7, marched to the relief of Ninety-Six, with seventeen hundred foot and one hundred and fifty horse. A few other troops from his camp at Monk's Corner joined him, and with more than two thousand men he proceeded toward Orangeburg. Greene dispatched Pickens to the aid of Sumter, and ordered Marion from the lower country to joint them in retarding the advance of the royal army. They could do little to oppose him, and Greene began to despair of reducing the garrison to submission before Rawdon's arrival.

The besiegers now deplored the fact that earlier attention had not been bestowed upon attempts on the western side to deprive the garrison of water, and thus force a capitulation. To this object the chief efforts were now directed, and the most effectual step to accomplish it was to destroy the stockade. The method of approaches was too slow, and it was resolved to endeavor to burn it. A dark storm was gathering, and toward evening, covered by its impending blackness, a sergeant and nine privates, with combustibles, cautiously approached, and four of them gained the ditch. While in the act of applying the fire, they were discovered. A volley of musketry was immediately opened upon them, and the sergeant and five of his party were killed; the other four escaped. The attempt was unsuccessful.

On the evening of the nineteenth, a countryman was seen riding along the American lines south of the town, talking familiarly with officers and soldiers. It was a circumstance too common to excite special notice. At length, reaching the great road leading directly into the town, he put spurs to his horse, and, amid a storm of bullets, rode safely to the gate, holding a letter in his raised hand. He was received with the greatest joy, for he was the bearer of a dispatch from Lord Rawdon, announcing his approach with a large force. The beleaguered garrison, almost on the point of surrendering (for this was the first intelligence Cruger had received from Rawdon since his evacuation of Camden), were animated with fresh hope, while the besiegers, aware of the approach of succor for the besieged, were nerved to greater exertions. They completed their parallels, and commenced the erection of a Mayham Tower, **19** from which to fire into the star redoubt. To guard against this advantage of height, Major Greene, the commander of the redoubt, piled bags of sand upon the parapets. On the morning of the seventeenth, a general fire was opened upon the works, and so effectual was it upon the stockade and its vicinity, that the garrison was deprived of water from the rivulet. Had this advantage been maintained, and Rawdon been delayed thirty hours longer, Cruger must have surrendered.

Rawdon managed to elude the vigilance of Sumter, after passing Orangeburg, and now approached Ninety-Six. Greene perceived that he must either storm the works at once, fight Rawdon, or retire. He determined upon the former; and at noon onJune 18, 1781, the Mayham Tower being completed, and two trenches and a mine nearly let into the enemy's ditch, the center battery opened upon the star, as a signal for a general attack. Lieutenant-colonel Campbell, of the first Virginia regiment, with a detachment from the Maryland and Virginia brigades, led the attack on the left; Lieutenant-colonel Lee, with Kirkwood's Delawares, advanced on the right; Lieutenants Duval, of Maryland, and Selden, of Virginia, commanded the forlorn hope of Campbell; and Captain Rudulph that of Lee. Riflemen were stationed in the tower, fascines were constructed to fill the ditch, and long poles, with iron hooks, were prepared to pull down the sand-bags from the parapets. Campbell and Lee rushed to the assault simultaneously. Cruger received the attack with firmness, and, from apertures between the sand-bags, Colonel Greene's riflemen did great execution. Duval and Selden boldly entered the ditch, and commenced pulling down the sand-bags. The parapet bristled with pikes and bayonets, yet they could not reach the assailants. Rapidly the bags were disappearing in the ditch below, and Campbell was pressing to ascend the parapet and fight hand to hand with the garrison, when Captain French, of Delancey's corps, and Captain Campbell, of New Jersey, issued from a sally-port of the star redoubt with a few men, and taking opposite directions in the ditch, fiercely assailed Duval and Selden, at the same time, with bayonets. Terrible was the conflict which followed. The brave patriots were assailed both in front and overhead, yet they maintained their ground for some minutes. At length both leaders of the forlorn hope were wounded, and the whole party retreated to the trenches.

While this bloody scene was transpiring at the star redoubt, one more successful effort for the besiegers occurred at the stockade. Rudulph made his way into the fort, and the enemy, with some prisoners,**20** hastily retreated to the main works. This advantage Lee intended to follow up, by entering the town, assailing the fortified jail, and then to assist in reducing the star redoubt; but General Greene, perceiving the slaughter in the ditch, and desirous of saving his troops, ordered Lee to do nothing more than to hold the stockade he had gained. Greene then sent a flag to Cruger, proposing a cessation of hostilities for the purpose of burying the dead. Cruger refused, claiming that service for the victor, whoever he might be. Believing the reduction of the post to be doubtful before the arrival of Rawdon, and unwilling to encounter that general's superior force, Greene withdrew the detachment from the stockade, and prepared for a general retreat. Thus ended the siege of Ninety-Six, which continued twenty-seven days. During this siege, the Americans lost about one hundred and fifty men in killed, wounded, and missing. Captain Armstrong, of the

Arrest of Emily Geiger.

Maryland line, a most valuable officer, was shot through the head, during the assault on the eighteenth, and fell dead. He was the only American officer who was killed. Captain Benson, also of the Maryland line, was severely wounded in the neck and shoulder. The exact loss of the besieged was not reported.

On the evening of the nineteenth, Greene raised the siege, crossed the Saluda on June 20, 1781, and rapidly retreated toward the Ennoree. **21** He had communicated to Sumter notice of the events of the eighteenth, advised him of the route of his retreat, and ordered the corps in his front, with the cavalry of Washington, to join him as speedily as possible.

On the morning of the twenty-first, Rawdon and his army reached Ninety-Six, and were welcomed with every expression of joy. Cruger was greatly and justly applauded for his gallant defense. On the same evening, when their mutual congratulations had ceased, and his army, after forced marches for fourteen days, were rested, Rawdon started in pursuit of Greene. He was eager to strike and utterly destroy or disperse his little army; regain the various posts he had lost; scatter the partisan forces of Marion and Sumter; revive the hopes and energies of the Loyalists, and thus strengthen the power of Cornwallis, who at this time was devastating Lower Virginia. Rawdon crossed the Saluda in quest of Greene (who had now got beyond the Tyger, in Union District), and gained the banks of the Ennoree, where he acquired information which convinced him that further pursuit would be useless, and with his wearied troops he returned to Ninety-Six.

When Greene heard of the retrograde movement of Rawdon, he halted, and ordered Lieutenant-colonel Lee to follow the enemy with his corps, for the purpose of obtaining intelligence. Greene had intended to retreat to Charlotte, but now his future movements depended upon those of his adversary. Lee soon ascertained that Rawdon had determined to abandon Ninety-Six, and to join a force under Colonel Stewart, whom he had ordered to advance from Charleston to Friday's Ferry at Granby; while Colonel Cruger, with his garrison and those Loyalists, with their property, who might choose to follow, were to march directly to Orangeburg. While Rawdon was thus preparing to abandon the upper country, Sumter intercepted a letter to that officer from Colonel Balfour at Charleston, informing him that he had recalled Stewart after he had commenced his march for Friday's Ferry. This letter was sent to Greene, who immediately directed his hospital and heavy baggage, then at Winnsborough, to be forwarded to Camden, while he prepared to pursue Rawdon with all his force. He sent Lee to gain the front of the British army before it should reach Friday's Ferry, and dispatched messages to Marion and Sumter, ordering them to take a similar position. **22** Lee accomplished his purpose, and in a skirmish with a part of his corps, under Captain Eggleston, a foraging party of fifty or sixty dragoons, with some wagons, were captured and sent to Greene's camp, then on the banks of the Saluda, near its junction with the Broad River at Columbia. Rawdon, not meeting with Stuart, and ignorant of the cause of his delay, was baffled, and turning southward, pushed on toward Orangeburg, unwilling now to encounter the Americans, for he had only a thousand men with him. In the mean while, Stuart had again marched from Charleston; and Marion and Lieutenant-colonel Washington being engaged in retarding his progress, did not join Lee until the morning of the tenth of July, when that officer and his corps were upon Beaver Creek, in the present Lexington District.

Rawdon halted at Orangeburg, with the intention of establishing a post there, and awaiting the arrival of Cruger and his Loyalists. Greene, advancing rapidly, approached that place with a force now augmented to almost two thousand men, before the British general had time properly to arrange his camp and cast up defenses. Rawdon's force, though inferior to Greene's, was so

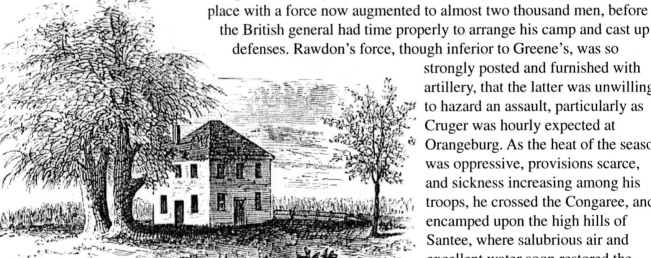

The Old Court-House.

strongly posted and furnished with artillery, that the latter was unwilling to hazard an assault, particularly as Cruger was hourly expected at Orangeburg. As the heat of the season was oppressive, provisions scarce, and sickness increasing among his troops, he crossed the Congaree, and encamped upon the high hills of Santee, where salubrious air and excellent water soon restored the vigor of his army. Sumter, Marion, and Lee were ordered to make rapid marches toward Charleston, beat up the British quarters at Dorchester and Monk's Corner, cut off convoys between Rawdon and the capital, and then join the main army upon the Santee Hills. Here we will leave the belligerents for a moment.

I left Columbia at seven o'clock on Monday morning, January 23, 1849, and was at Orangeburg, fifty-one miles distant, at half past nine. The weather was delightful. A dreamy haziness was in the atmosphere, and the air was as mild as early June. Leaving my baggage at the rail-way station, I strolled over that village and vicinity, for an hour, with a gentleman from Columbia, who was familiar with its historical localities. The village (which was settled as early as 1735) is beautifully situated upon a gently-rolling plain, near the banks of the Edisto (which is here skirted with swamps), and contains about four hundred inhabitants. There are several elegant dwellings standing upon each side of the broad street extending from the rail-way to the heart of the village, all shaded by lofty trees. It is about eighty miles west of Charleston, and being the seat of justice, is the largest town in Orange District. It has a handsome court-house and jail, and is regularly laid out. The old jail, which the British fortified while they occupied the place, was built of brick, in 1770, and stood upon the crown of the gentle hill, a few yards northwest of the old court-house (represented in the picture), which is yet standing. The court-house is a frame building, and was used for a blacksmith's shop when I was there. The two trees seen on the left are venerable Pride-of-Indias, choice shade-trees of the South. This edifice exhibited several bullet-marks, the effect of Sumter's assault in 1781. After sketching this – the only remaining relic of the Revolution at Orangeburg, except some vestiges of the works cast up by Rawdon, half a mile westward, near the Edisto – I hired a horse and gig to visit Eutaw Springs, about forty miles distant, near the south bank of the Santee. It was with great difficulty that I could ascertain their probable distance from Orangeburg; and the person from whom I procured a conveyance supposed it to be twenty-five or thirty miles. His price was determined by the distance, and he was agreeably surprised, on my return, to learn that I had traveled eighty miles. Before departing on this journey, let us consider for a moment the Revolutionary events which distinguish Orangeburg.

Orangeburg was one of the chain of military posts established by the British after the fall of Charleston (May, 1780). The jail was fortified and garrisoned by about seventy militia and a dozen regulars. Sumter, when marching to join Greene at Camden, according to orders, conceived a plan for capturing Fort Granby, and therefore did not re-enforce his general. He began the siege successfully, when, learning the fact that Rawdon had ordered the evacuation of Orangeburg, he left Colonel Taylor, with a strong party, to maintain the siege of Fort Granby, while he should strike the garrison at the former place, before it should retire. By a rapid march he reached Orangeburg on the morning of the eleventh of May (1781), and, after one or two volleys, the garrison surrendered themselves unconditional prisoners of war. Paroling his prisoners, Sumter hastened toward Fort Granby; but before his arrival, Lee had invested and reduced it, allowing, as we have seen, the most favorable terms. Sumter was incensed at the conduct of Lee, for he felt that he had not only snatched from him the laurels he had almost won, but that he had hastened the capitulation, and allowed favorable terms, in order to accomplish the surrender before Sumter could arrive. No doubt the garrison would have surrendered unconditionally, if besieged a day or two longer. Sumter sent an indignant letter of complaint to Greene, inclosing his commission. Greene, knowing his worth, returned it to him with many expressions of regard, and Sumter, sacrificing private resentment for the good of the cause, remained in the army.

On the day after Rawdon's arrival at Orangeburg, he was joined by Lieutenant-colonel Stewart, with the third regiment from Ireland, called the Buffs, whom Rawdon had ordered from Charleston. The retirement of Greene to the high hills of Santee, and the rendezvous there of the several corps of Marion, Sumter, and Lee, indicating a present cessation of hostilities, Lord Rawdon proceeded to Charleston, and embarked for Europe, for the purpose of recruiting his health. **23** The command of all the troops in the field now devolved upon Colonel Stuart. That officer soon left Orangeburg, and, moving forward, encamped upon the Congaree, near its junction with the Wateree. The two armies were only sixteen miles apart by air line, but two rivers rolled between, and they could not meet without making a circuit of seventy miles. Stuart's foraging parties soon spread over the country. Marion was detached toward the Combahee Ferry, and Washington went across the Wateree to disperse them. Many brisk skirmishes ensued. In the mean time, Greene was re-enforced by a brigade of Continental troops from North Carolina, under General Sumner. **24** Intent upon the recovery of South Carolina, he determined, with his augmented strength, to attack the enemy. He left the Santee Hills on the twenty-second of August (1781), with about twenty-six hundred men (only sixteen hundred of whom were fit for active service), crossed the Wateree at the Camden Ferry, and made rapid marches to Friday's Ferry, on the Congaree. There he was joined by General Pickens, with the militia of Ninety-Six, and a body of South Carolina state troops recently organized, under Colonel Henderson. On hearing of Greene's approach, Stuart decamped from Orangeburg, and pitched his tents at Eutaw Springs, forty miles below, vigorously pursued by the Americans. Thither let us proceed, where we shall meet the two armies in terrible conflict.

I left Orangeburg for Eutaw Springs at eleven o'clock on January 26, 1849. The day was so warm that the shade of the pine forests was very refreshing. My horse was fleet, the gig light, the road level and generally fine, and at sunset I arrived at the house of Mr. Avinger (Vances's Ferry post-office), thirty miles distant. About fourteen miles from Orangeburg I crossed the Four-hole Swamp, **25** upon a narrow causeway of logs and three bridges. The distance is about a mile, and a gloomier place can not well be imagined. On either side was a dense undergrowth of shrubs, closely interlaced with vines; and above, draped with moss, towered

A Southern School-House.

lofty cypresses and gums. At two o'clock I passed one of those primitive school-houses, built of logs, which the traveler meets occasionally in the South. It stood in the edge of a wood, and in front was a fine Pride-of-India Tree, under which the teacher sat listening to the efforts of half a dozen children in the science of orthography. The country is very sparsely populated, and many of the children, living four or five miles away from the school-house, are conveyed on horseback by the negro servants. I stopped a moment in conversation with the pedagogue, who was a Vermonter, one of those New England people described by Halleck as

"Wandering through the Southern countries, teaching
The A B C from Webster's Spelling-book;
Gallant and godly, making love and preaching."

He appeared satisfied with his success in each vocation, and hinted that the daughter of a neighboring planter had promised him her heart and hand. When obtained, he intended to cultivate cotton and maize, instead of the dull intellects of other people's children.

I passed the night at Mr. Avinger's, and very early in the morning departed for Eutaw, ten miles distant. I was now upon the Congaree road, and found the traveling somewhat heavier than upon ways less used. About three miles from Avinger's, I passed Burdell's plantation, where the American army encamped the night before the battle of Eutaw. It was another glorious morning, and at sunrise I was greeted with the whistle of the quail, the drum of the partridge, the sweet notes of the robin and blue-bird, and the querulous cadences of the cat-bird, all summer tenants of our Northern forests. They appeared each to carol a brief matin hymn at sunrise, and were silent the remainder of the day. I saw several mocking-birds, but they flitted about in silence, taking lessons, I suppose, from their Northern friends, to be sung during their absence.

> "Winged mimic of the woods! thou motley fool!
>   Who shall thy gay buffoonery describe?
>   Thine ever ready notes of ridicule
>   Pursue thy fellows still with jest and gibe:
>   Wit, sophist, songster, YORICK of thy tribe,
>   Thou sportive satirist of Nature's school!"
>   - RICHARD HENRY WILDE

Occasionally a wild turkey would start from a branch, or a filthy buzzard alight by the wayside, until, as I came suddenly upon a water-course, a wild fawn that stood lapping from the clear stream wheeled and bounded away among the evergreens of the wood.

At about eight o'clock, I arrived at the elegant mansion of William Sinkler, Esq., upon whose plantation are the celebrated Eutaw Springs. It stands in the midst of noble shade-trees, half a mile from the high-way, and is approached by a lane fringed with every variety of evergreen tree and shrub which beautify Southern scenery in winter. I was courteously received by the proprietor; and when the object of my visit was made known, he ordered his horse and accompanied me to the springs and the field of battle, which are about half a mile eastward of his mansion. The springs present a curious spectacle, being really but the first and second apparition of the same subterranean stream. They are a few rods north of the forks of the Canal and the Monk's Corner roads, at the head of a shallow ravine. The first spring is at the foot of a hill, twenty or thirty feet in height. The water bubbles up, cold, limpid, and sparkling, in large volumes, from two or three orifices, into a basin of rock-marl, and, flowing fifty or sixty yards, descends, rushing and foaming, into a cavern beneath a high ridge of marl **26** covered with alluvium and forest-trees. After traversing its subterraneous way some thirty rods, it reappears upon the other side, where it is a broader stream, and flows gently over a smooth rocky bed toward the Santee, its course marked by tall cypresses, draped with moss. The whole length of the Eutaw Creek, in all its

Eutaw Springs. 27

windings, is only about two miles. Where it first bubbles from the earth there is sufficient volume to turn a large mill-wheel, but the fountain is so near the level of the Santee at Nelson's Ferry, where the Eutaw enters, that no fall can be obtained; on the contrary, when the Santee is filled to the brim, the waters flow back to the springs.

Just at the forks of the road, on the side toward the springs, was a clump of trees and shrubbery, which marked the spot where stood a strong brick house, famous as the citadel of the British camp, and a retreat for some of the warriors in the conflict at Eutaw. Nothing of it now remains but the foundation, and a few broken bricks scattered among some plum-trees. Let us sit down here, in the shadow of a cypress, by the bubbling spring, and consider the event when human blood tinged the clear waters of the Eutaw, where patriots fought and died for a holy principle.

> "They saw their injured country's woe,
> The flaming town, the wasted field;
> Then marched to meet the insulting foe;
> They took the spear, but left the shield!
> Led by thy conquering standards, GREENE,
> The Britons they compelled to fly:
> None distant viewed the fatal plain,
> None grieved in such a cause to die;
> But, like the Parthians, famed of old,
> Who, flying, still their arrows threw;
> These routed Britons, full as bold,
> Retreated, and retreating, slew. – PHILIP FRENEAU.

At Orangeburg, General Greene was informed that Stuart had been re-enforced by a corps of cavalry, under Brevet-major John Coffin 28 (whose real rank was captain), which Rawdon had formed on his arrival at Charleston. He immediately issued an order on September 4, 1781 for Marion (who was then, with his command, scouring the country toward the Edisto, in rescuing Colonel Harden from the toils of Major Fraser) to join him, and then pressed forward toward Eutaw. Marion, by a forced night march, reached Laurens's plantation, 29 a few miles from Eutaw, in advance of the American army, on the fifth. In the mean while, Greene's army slowly approached the British camp, preceded by Lee's legion and Henderson's South Carolina corps. The main army reached Burdell's plantation, on the Congaree road, within seven miles of Eutaw, on the afternoon of September 7, 1781, and there it encamped for the night.

While the Americans were reposing, two men of Sumner's North Carolina conscripts deserted to the British lines, and gave Colonel Stuart the first intimation of the close proximity of the Republican army. Stuart regarded them as spies, and would not listen to their information, for his scouts, who were out upon the Congaree road the day before, brought him no intelligence of the approach of Greene. His feelings of security were not disturbed by the deserters, and he sent out his foraging parties in the morning (Sept. 8), as usual, to collect vegetables. Prudence, however, dictated caution, and he detached Captain Coffin, with his cavalry, as a corps of observation, and, if necessary, to call in the foraging parties.

At dawn on the morning of the eighth, the Americans moved from Burdell's in two columns, each composed of the troops intended to form the respective lines of battle. Greene's whole force, according to Lee, 30 amounted to twenty-three hundred men, of whom the Continentals, horse, foot, and artillery, numbered about sixteen hundred. The front or first line was composed of four small battalions of militia – two of North, and two of South Carolinians. One of the South Carolinians was under the immediate command of Brigadier Marion, who commanded the whole front line. The two North Carolina battalions, under the command of Colonel Malmedy, were posted in the center; and the other South Carolina battalion, under the command of General Pickens, was placed on the left. The second line consisted of three small brigades of Continental troops, one each from North Carolina, Virginia, and Maryland. The North Carolinians were formed into three battalions, under the command of Lieutenant-colonel Ashe, and Majors

Armstrong and Blount; the whole commanded by General Sumner, and posted on the right. The Virginians consisted of two battalions, commanded by Major Snead and Captain Edmonds, and the whole by Lieutenant-colonel Campbell, and were posted in the center. The Marylanders also consisted of two battalions, commanded by Lieutenant-colonel Howard and Major Hardman, the whole brigade by Colonel Otho H. Williams, the deputy adjutant general, and were posted on the left. Lieutenant-colonel Lee, with his legion, covered the right flank; and Lieutenant-colonel Henderson, with the State troops, commanded by Lieutenant-colonels Polk, **31** Wade Hampton, and Middleton, the left. Lieutenant-colonel Washington, with his horse, and the Delaware troops, under Captain Kirkwood, formed a reserve corps. Two three pounders, under Captain-lieutenant Gaines, advanced with the front line, and two sixes, under Captain Brown, with the second. The legion and the State troops formed the advance.

The British army, under Stuart, at Eutaw, was drawn up in a line extending from the Eutaw Creek, north of the Congaree or Charleston road, near Mr. Sinkler's mansion, across that high-way and the road leading to Roche's plantation, an eighth of a mile southward. The Irish Buffs (third regiment) formed the right; Lieutenant-colonel Cruger's Loyalists the center; and the 63d and 64th veteran regiments the left. Near the creek was a flank battalion of grenadiers and infantry, under Major Majoribanks. These were partially covered and concealed by a thicket on the bank of the stream. To the cavalry of Coffin, and a detachment of infantry held in reserve in the rear, were assigned the support of the left. The artillery was distributed along the front of the line. About fifty yards in the rear of the British line, at the forks of the present Canal and Monk's Corner roads, was a cleared field. There was their camp, and so certain was Stuart of victory, that he left his tents all standing. Close by the road was a two-story brick house with servant's huts around it. This was palisaded, and so likewise was the garden, extending to the Eutaw Creek. **32** This house was intended as a citadel if their line should be forced back. Such was the situation of the two armies at sunrise on the morning of the eighth of September, 1781.

At about eight o'clock, when the Americans were within four miles of Eutaw, Lee fell in with Captain Coffin, who was acting as an escort for a foraging party of about four hundred men. Ignorant of the proximity of the main army of Greene, Coffin attacked Armstrong, who led Lee's advance. Armstrong fell back to the van, and Lee and Henderson received the assault with spirit. A severe skirmish ensued, when Lee's cavalry, under Major Eggleston, gained Coffin's flank, and attacked him in the rear. The firing drew out the foraging party into the road, when the whole fled precipitately, pursued by Lee's dragoons. Many of Coffin's infantry were killed, and the captain and forty men were made prisoners. Some of the cavalry were also slain, and many of the foraging party were captured.

This little success inspirited the Americans, and they pushed forward with vigor. Within a mile of the British camp they encountered another detachment of the enemy, whom Stuart had sent out to aid Coffin and the foragers. It was a surprise for both. While the British fell back a little, Greene quickly prepared for battle, and, pressing forward, the action commenced with spirit in the road and fields, very near the present entrance gate to the seat of Mr. Sinkler. The enemy's cannon swept the road with a destructive fire until

Colonel Williams brought up the artillery of Gaines, in full gallop, and returned their fire with severe effect. The British detachments soon yielded and fell back to their lines, dividing right and left, and taking position on the flanks. The Americans, with their line extended on either side of the road, continued to advance, and at a little past nine opened a sharp fire with musketry and artillery upon the British line. The latter received the attack with great gallantry, and a bloody conflict ensued. The artillery of both parties played incessantly, and a continual fire ran from flank to flank, along the whole line of the militia, while it continued to advance. Stuart was now fully convinced that Greene and his whole army were upon him, and every portion of his line was brought into action. In the mean while, Lee's legion infantry were warmly engaged with the veteran 63d of the enemy, when the 64th advanced with a part of the center and fell furiously upon Malmedy and his corps. They soon yielded to the pressure, and the enemy's left pushed forward. Now the corps, under Henderson, sustained not only the fire of the British right, but also of the flank battalion, under Majoribanks. At this moment one of the British field pieces was disabled, and both of Gaines's three pounders were dismounted. Yet the militia, even when unsupported by artillery, fought with all the skill and bravery of veterans. They faced the storm of grape-shot and bullets until they had fired seventeen rounds, when the 64th and center, who had borne down Malmedy, pressed so powerfully upon inferior numbers, that the militia gave way, while Lee and Henderson continued fighting manfully upon the wings of the retiring patriots.

    Greene now ordered up the second line, under General Sumner, to fill the space occupied by the militia. At the same time, the British reserved infantry were brought into action, and these fresh troops fought each other desperately. Colonel Henderson received a wound that disabled him, and temporary confusion ensued. Order was soon restored by Hampton, Polk, and Middleton; but Sumner's brigade, which was composed chiefly of recruits from the militia, gave way before the fire of superior numbers, and retreated in much confusion. The British pursued so eagerly that their ranks became disordered. The vigilant eye of Greene perceived this, and he instantly issued the order, "Let Williams advance and sweep the field with bayonets." Like a full-winged storm, pregnant with destruction, the Virginians and Marylanders advanced, the former led by Colonel Campbell, the latter by Colonel Williams. When within forty yards of the British, these Continentals delivered their fire, and the whole second line of the Americans rushed forward, with trailed arms and loud shouts, to a bayonet charge. The confusion of the British was increased by this blow; and as the smoke rolled away and exposed their broken lines, Captain Rudulph, of Lee's legion, wheeled upon its flank, and swept down many with an enfilading fire. In so close that some of the combatants were mutually transfixed with bayonets. The Marylanders, under Williams, with the Virginians, now pressed upon the British right and center so furiously that the line gave way, and they retreated in confusion. Loud arose a shout of victory from the Americans; but there was, at the same time, occasion for a voice of wail. In the shock which scattered the British line, Colonel Campbell fell, mortally wounded. Informed of the rout of the enemy, he exclaimed, with a faltering voice, like Wolfe at Quebec. "I die contented!" and expired.

    When the second line advanced, Majoribanks was ordered to the conflict, and terribly annoyed the American flank. Colonel Washington, with the reserve, and Colonel Wade Hampton, with his corps, were directed to dislodge him. The thicket behind which Majoribanks was covered was impervious to cavalry. Washington perceived a small space between him and Eutaw Creek, and determined, by a quick movement, to gain his rear at that point. Without waiting for Hampton, he divided his cavalry into sections, and, ordering them to wheel to the left, attempted this bold enterprise. It was a fatal step to many of his brave horsemen, for they were brought within range of the enemy's fire. A terrible volley from behind the thicket rolled many horses and their riders in the dust. They laid strewn upon the ground in every direction. Lieutenant Stuart, of Maryland, who commanded the first section, was badly wounded, and many of his corps were killed or maimed. Lieutenants Simmons and King were also wounded. Washington's horse was shot dead under him, and as he fell himself, he was cruelly bayoneted. A moment more, and he would have been sacrificed. A British officer kindly interposed, saved his life, and made him prisoner. Of his whole cavalry corps, one half were killed or wounded, with all the officers except two.

Hampton, in the mean time, covered and collected the scattered cavalry; and Kirkwood, with his Delawares, fell upon Majoribanks. The whole British line were now retreating, and Majoribanks fell back to cover the movement. They abandoned their camp, destroyed their stores, and many fled precipitately along the Charleston road; while some rushed for immediate safety into the brick house near the great springs. Majoribanks halted behind the palisades of the garden, with his right upon Eutaw Creek; and Captain Coffin, with his cavalry, took post in the road below, to cover the British left. During the retreat, the Americans captured more than three hundred prisoners and two pieces of cannon. Upon one of these field pieces, Lieutenant Duval, who fought so bravely in the fosse of the star redoubt at Ninety-Six, leaped, and, taking off his hat, gave three hearty cheers. A bullet from a retreating soldier brought him to the ground, and, he expired within half an hour afterward.

Although a large portion of the British had retreated, yet the victory was far from complete. Majoribanks was at the garden; a large number of Cruger's New York Volunteers, under Major Sheridan, were in the brick house; and Stuart was rallying the fugitives in considerable force a little below, on the Charleston road. The American soldiers, considering the conflict over, could not be made to think otherwise by their officers; and instead of dislodging Majoribanks, and pursuing the enemy far away from his camp, they stopped to plunder the stores, drink the liquors, and eat the provisions found in the tents. Many became intoxicated; and others, by over-indulgence in eating, and drinking cold water (for the day was very warm), were disabled. Irretrievable confusion followed; and before order could be restored, the British were forming to regain their lost advantage. A heavy fire was poured from the house upon the Americans in the British camp, and at the same time Majoribanks moved from his covert upon the right, and Coffin upon the left of the disordered Americans.

Fortunately, Lee and his legion had not been tempted to indulge in the sensualities of the camp; and so closely had they followed upon those who fled to the house, that the fugitives prevented the entrance of the Americans only by shutting the doors upon them. By so doing, several of their own number were shut out, among whom were two or three officers. Those of the legion who had followed to the door seized each a prisoner, and interposing him as a shield, retreated back beyond the fire from the windows. 33 The two six pounders belonging to the second line were now brought to bear upon the house, but, being in range of a swivel in the second story, and of the muskets, a large portion of the artillerymen were soon killed or wounded, and they were obliged to withdraw the cannons. At the same time, Coffin was advancing on the

Gold Medal awarded to Greene. 36

left. He had fallen upon Captain Eggleston, and drove him back, and was about to attack those who yet lingered among the British tents, when Colonel Hampton, who had been ordered up to the support of Eggleston, charged upon him so vigorously that he was compelled to retreat. The legion cavalry pursued with so much eagerness that they were in front of Majoribanks, and received a murderous volley from his ranks before they were aware of danger. A great number fell, and the remainder were thrown into confusion. Majoribanks perceived this, sallied out, seized the two field-pieces, and ran them under the windows of the house. One of these was soon rescued by Lieutenant Gaines, and remained with the Americans, a trophy of victory.

At every point success now seemed to be turning against the Americans. Colonel Howard, who had just commenced an attack upon Majoribanks with Oldham's company, was wounded near the Great Spring, and his troops fell back. At the same time, the broken ranks of Stuart had been united, and were marching up the Charleston road to renew the battle. Despairing of success in the present crippled condition of his army, his battalions all broken, his artillery gone, his cavalry shattered, and many of his best officers wounded, **34** Greene deemed it prudent to retreat. Leaving Colonel Hampton near the British camp with a strong picket, he withdrew, with the remainder of the army, to Burdell's plantation, seven miles in the rear. The British were contented to repossess themselves of their camp, and did not attempt a pursuit. Both parties claimed the honor of victory; it belonged to neither, but the advantage was with the Americans. The conflict lasted four hours, and was one of the most severely contested battles of the Revolution. Congress and the whole country gave warm expressions of their appreciation of the valor of the patriots. **35** The skill, bravery, caution, and acuteness of Greene was highly applauded; and Congress ordered a gold medal, emblematical of the battle, to be struck in honor of the event, and presented to him, together with a British standard. **37** The loss of both parties, considering the number engaged, was very heavy. The Americans had one hundred and thirty rank and file killed, three hundred and eighty-five wounded, and forty missing; in all, five hundred and fifty-five. There were twenty-two officers killed, and thirty-nine wounded. The loss of the British, according to their own statement, was six hundred and ninety-three men, of whom eighty-five were killed on the field. Including seventy-two wounded, whom they left in their camp when they abandoned it the day after the battle, Greene took five hundred prisoners.

On the day succeeding the battle, Lieutenant-colonel Stuart, confident that he could not maintain his position, decamped for Charleston, after destroying a great quantity of his stores. So precipitate was his retreat, that he left seventy-two of his wounded to be taken care of by the Americans. He also left behind him one thousand stand of arms. He was pursued for some distance, when intelligence being received that Major M'Arthur was advancing with re-enforcements for Stuart, the Americans returned to their camp. It was fortunate for M'Arthur that he met Stuart on September 10, 1781, as soon as he did, for Marion and Lee had been dispatched to fall upon any detachment coming up from Charleston, and were then only a few miles off. Even with this re-enforcement Stuart did not feel strong enough to meet Greene in battle, and he continued his retreat to Monk's Corner,

View at Nelson's Ferry.

twenty-five miles from Charleston, leaving the Americans the acknowledged victors at Eutaw.

When Greene was apprised of the positive retreat of Stuart, he followed and pursued him almost to Monk's Corner. Perceiving the strength of the enemy there, he returned to Eutaw, and having a vast number of his troops sick, he proceeded from thence, by easy marches, to his favorite retreat upon the high hills of Santee on September 18, 1781. **38** There he remained until the eighteenth of November, when the health of his army being recruited, he marched into the low country, where he might obtain an abundance of food. In the mean while, the army of Cornwallis had been captured at Yorktown (Oct. 19); St. Clair had driven the British from Wilmington; and the whole upper country of the Carolinas and Georgia were in possession of the patriots. Nothing now remained but to drive in the British outposts, and hem them within the narrow precincts of their lines at Charleston and Savannah. With this view, Greene, at the head of his cavalry, and about two hundred infantry, proceeded toward Dorchester, a British post in the neighborhood of Charleston, while the main army, under Colonel Williams, crossed the Santee, and marched to the fertile plains upon the Four-hole Creek, a tributary of the Edisto. Here we will leave the two armies for the present, to meet many of the troops again upon other fields of conflict.

As there were no works of consequence thrown up at Eutaw, not a vestige of the camp or of the battle remained when I visited the spot in 1849, except the few scattered bricks of the "citadel" already referred to. On returning to his house, Mr. Sinkler showed me a gold watch which one of his negroes found ten years before, while making holes with a stick in planting cotton seed, in the field where Washington was defeated. The negro hit a hard substance, and as there are no stones in the field, he had the curiosity to search for the obstruction, when he drew forth the watch. The hands were almost destroyed by rust; otherwise the watch is well preserved.

Guided by one of Mr. Sinkler's servants, I crossed the Eutaw Creek, near his house, and rode down to Nelson's Ferry, at the mouth of the stream, about a mile and a half distant. At its entrance into the Santee, the bateau of the ferryman was moored, and almost filled its narrow channel. Beneath the moss-draped trees upon the bank of the river, some negro women were washing clothes, and when they found themselves portrayed in my drawing, in all the dishabille of a washing-day, they wanted to arrange their dresses and caps, and be sketched in better plight. Time was too precious to allow compliance, for I wished to get as far toward Orangeburg that evening as possible. Promising to improve their toilet when I got home, I closed my port-folio, and, taking the reins, hastened toward Vance's Ferry.

Nelson's Ferry, the spot here portrayed, was an important locality during the Revolution. It was the principal crossing-place of the Santee for travelers or troops passing between Camden and Charleston, and as such, commanded the attention of the British after they captured the latter city. A redoubt was cast up there upon the north side of the Santee, and garrisoned by a small detachment; and to that point, as we have seen, Lord Rawdon retreated from Camden.

We have noticed that Marion, while in the camp of Gates, was called to the command of the patriots of Williamsburg District, and went to duty in the lower country. Ignorant of the operations of the Americans under Gates, that brave partisan was striking successful blows against the enemy here and

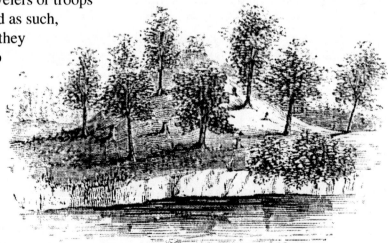

Site of Fort Watson.

there, while his commander-in-chief was becoming ensnared in the net of disaster which gathered around him near Camden. On August 17, 1780, the day after Gates's defeat, Marion had placed Colonel Peter Horry in command of four companies of cavalry, which he had just formed and sent to operate against the British in the vicinity of Georgetown, while he, with a small band of followers, marched rapidly toward the Upper Santee. On his way, he was informed of the defeat of Gates, but withheld the sad intelligence from his men, fearing its effects upon their spirits. That night his scouts advised him of the approach to Nelson's Ferry of a strong British guard, with a large body of prisoners from Gates's army. Though much inferior in numbers, he resolved to attack them. Just before daylight, he detached Colonel Hugh Horry, with sixteen resolute men, to occupy the road at the Horse Creek Pass, in a broad swamp, while with the remainder he should fall upon the enemy's rear. The maneuver was successfully performed at dawn on August 20, 1780, and on that day the brave partisan wrote the following dispatch to Colonel Peter Horry: "On the 20th instant, I attacked a guard of the 63d and Prince of Wales's regiment, with a number of Tories, at the Great Savannah, near Nelson's Ferry; killed and took twenty-two regulars and two Tories prisoners, and retook one hundred and fifty Continentals of the Maryland line; **39** one wagon and a drum; one captain and a subaltern were also captured. Our loss is one killed; and Captain Benson is slightly wounded on the head."

It was past meridian when I reached Vance's Ferry, about ten miles above Eutaw, and one from Mr. Avinger's, where I lodged the night before. I crossed the Santee into Sumter District in a bateau; and driving about five miles up the river, reached Scott's Lake, an expansion of the Santee, a few miles below the junction of the Congaree and Wateree. Upon the north side of the lake, upon the land of Mr. Rufus Felder, at Wright's Bluff Post-office, is an ancient tumulus, almost fifty feet in height, and now covered with trees. Upon the top of this mound the British erected a stockade; and in honor of Colonel Watson, under whose direction it was built, it was called Fort Watson. Its elevated position, and its close proximity to the water, made it a strong post, yet not sufficiently impregnable to resist the successful assault of Marion and Lee in April, 1781. Let us consider that event.

We have noticed the junction of the forces of Marion and Lee, in the swamps of the Black River, in Williamsburg District (April 14, 1781). Lee immediately laid the plans of General Greene before Marion; and a scheme of operations was decided upon within a few hours. Colonel Watson, with about five hundred infantry, was near the site of the present town of Marion, on Cat-fish Creek, in Marion District. He had received orders to re-enforce Lord Rawdon at Camden. For some time he had been greatly annoyed by Marion, who would appear on his flank or rear, strike a severe blow, and then as suddenly disappear among the interminable swamps of the low country. Marion was preparing to smite Watson once more, when he was informed of the approach of Lee. He sent a guide to conduct that partisan over the Pedee, in boats which he kept concealed; and on the day after their forces were united, they started toward Fort Watson on April 15, **40** leaving Captain Gavin Witherspoon on the trail of Watson, then fleeing toward Georgetown. They sat down before Fort Watson on the evening of the same day.

Fort Watson was garrisoned by eighty regulars and forty Loyalists, under the command of Lieutenant M'Kay, a brave and active young officer of the British army. Marion immediately sent a flag demanding the unconditional surrender of the fort and the garrison. M'Kay promptly refused, for he doubtless hourly expected the approach of Watson with his large force, who, he knew, was on his march thither from Georgetown. Perceiving the garrison to be well supplied with water from Scott's Lake, that resource was cut off by the besiegers; but M'Kay and his men opened another communication with the lake three days afterward. They sunk a well within the stockade to a depth below the level of the lake, and dug a trench at the base of the mound from the well to the water, and secured it by an abatis. This circumstance perplexed the assailants, for they had no cannons, and the stockade was too high to be seriously affected by small arms. To the fertile genius of Lieutenant-colonel Maham, **41** of Marion's brigade, this disadvantage was overcome. Near the fort was a small wood. The trees were cut down, carried upon the shoulders of the men within rifle shot of the fort, and piled up so as to form a quadrangular tower of sufficient height to overlook the stockades. Upon the top of this, a parapet was made of smaller trees, for the defense of those upon the top of the tower. All of this work was accomplished during the darkness of the night, which was intensified by a cloudy sky; and at dawn the garrison were awakened by a deadly shower of balls from a company of sure marksmen upon the top of the tower. At the same moment, a party of volunteers of Marion's militia, under Ensign Johnson, and another from the Continentals, of Lee's legion, ascended the mound and attacked the abatis with vigor. Resistance was vain; and the fort thus assailed was untenable. M'Kay had anxiously awaited the approach of Watson, but that officer, unwilling to allow any thing to impede his progress toward

Camden, left this post to its fate. The garrison, no longer able to hold the fort, surrendered by capitulation on April 23, 1781, and Marion with his prisoners and booty, pushed forward and encamped upon the high hills of Santee, to await further orders from Greene, while Lee turned his attention to the movements of Watson. The loss of the Americans was only two killed, and three Continentals and three militia-men wounded. The subsequent movements of Marion and Lee, in efforts to prevent Watson's junction with Rawdon, have been noticed in the preceding chapter.

I tarried at the site of Fort Watson only long enough to make the sketch on page 167, when I hastened back to Vance's Ferry, and pushed on toward Orangeburg. Late in the evening I reached the house of Mr. M'Ance, within fifteen miles of Orangeburg, where I was hospitably entertained. There I met an elderly lady who had been very intimate with the wife of Marion for several years previous to her death. She informed me that Mrs. Marion (whose maiden name was Videau, one of the Huguenot families) was much younger than the general. She was a large woman, weighing, a year or two before her death, two hundred and thirty pounds. My informant had often visited her at her residence, built by the general at Pond Bluff, on the Santee (near the Nelson's Ferry road to Charleston), about three miles below Eutaw Springs. Miss Videau brought wealth to her husband, and their dwelling was always the abode of liberal hospitality.

I left M'Ance's before daylight on the following morning, traversed the narrow causeway across the Four-hole Swamp by the feeble light of the stars, and arrived at Orangeburg in time to enter the cars for Augusta, on the Savannah River, eighty-five miles distant.

Marion's Residence.

Chapter XVIII
Endnotes

1 I was informed that the house of General Sumter and several others, with a large tract of land, was owned by a mulatto named Ellison, who, with his wife and children, were once slaves. He was a mechanic, and with the proceeds of his labor he purchased the freedom of himself and family. He is now (1850) about sixty years of age, and owns a large number of slaves. His sons and daughters are educated, and the former occupy the position of overseers on his plantation. Mr. Ellison is regarded as one of the most honorable business men in that region.

2 This little sketch is from the pencil of J. Addison Richards, one of our most accomplished landscape painters. The cypress "knees," as they are called, are here truthfully shown. They extend from the roots of the trees, sometimes as much as two feet above the earth or the water, but never exhibit branches or leaves. They appear like smooth-pointed stumps.

3 The Congaree is formed by the junction of the Broad and Saluda Rivers at Columbia. Its junction with the Wateree (the Catawba of North Carolina), at the lower end of Richland District, forms the Santee, which name is borne by the whole volume of united waters from that point to the ocean. Buck's Head Neck is formed by a sweep of the Congaree, of nearly eight miles, when it approaches itself within a quarter of a mile. The swamp land of this neck has been reclaimed in many places, and now bears good cotton. At the rundle of this bow of the river is the ancient M'Cord's Ferry, yet in use.

4 Francis Marion was born at Winyaw, near Georgetown, South Carolina, in 1732. He was so small at his birth, that, according to Weems, "he was not larger than a New England lobster, and might easily enough have been put into a quart pot." Marion received a very limited share of education, and until his twenty-seventh year (1759), he followed agricultural pursuits. He then became a soldier, by joining an expedition against the Cherokees and other hostile tribes (see page 440 in original text) on the Western frontier of the Carolinas. When the Revolution broke out, he was found on the side of liberty, and was made captain in the second South Carolina regiment. He fought bravely in the battle at Fort Sullivan, on Sullivan's Island. He was afterward engaged in the contest at Savannah, and from that period until the defeat of Gates, near Camden, in the summer of 1780, he was an active soldier. Soon after that affair, he organized a brigade, having passed through the several grades to that of brigadier of the militia of his state. While Sumter was striking heavy blows, here and there, in the northwestern part of North Carolina, Marion was performing like service in the northeastern part, along the Pedee and its tributaries. In 1781, he was engaged with Lee and others in reducing several British posts. After the Battle at Eutaw, Marion did not long remain in the field, but took his seat as senator in the Legislature. He was soon again called to the field, and did not relinquish his sword until the close of the war. When peace came, Marion retired to his plantation, a little below Eutaw, where he died on the twenty-ninth of February, 1795, in the sixty-third year of his age. His last words were, "Thank God, since I came to man's estate I have never intentionally done wrong to any man." Marion's remains are in the church-yard at Belle Isle, in the parish of St. John's, Berkeley. Over them is a marble slab, upon which is the following inscription: "Sacred to the memory of Brigadier-general FRANCIS MARION, who departed this life on the twenty-ninth of February, 1795, in the sixty-third year of his age, deeply regretted by all of his fellow-citizens. History will record his worth, and rising generations embalm his memory, as one of the most distinguished patriots and heroes of the American Revolution; which elevated his native country to Honor and Independence, and secured to her the blessings of liberty and peace. This tribute of veneration and gratitude is erected in commemoration of the noble and disinterested virtues of the citizen, and the gallant exploits of the soldier, who lived without fear and died with out reproach."

5 Colonel Otho H. Williams, in his Narrative of the Campaigns of 1780, thus speaks of Marion and his men, at that time: "Colonel Marion, a gentleman of South Carolina, had been with the army a few days, attended by a very few followers, distinguished by small leather caps and the wretchedness of their attire; their numbers did not exceed twenty men and boys, some white, some black, and all mounted, but most of them miserably equipped; their appearance was, in fact, so burlesque, that it was with much difficulty the diversion of the regular soldiery was restrained by the officers; and the general himself was glad of an opportunity of detaching Colonel Marion, at his own instance, toward the interior of South Carolina, with orders to watch the motions of the enemy, and furnish intelligence."

6 So certain was Gates of defeating Cornwallis, that when Marion departed, he instructed him to destroy all the boats, flats, and scows, which might be used by the British in their flight.

7 Rebecca Brewton was the daughter of an English gentleman. She married Jacob Motte, a planter, in 1758, and was the mother of six children. General Thomas Pinckney, of South Carolina, married in succession her two eldest daughters; the third married Colonel William Alston, of Charleston. Her other three children did not live to reach maturity. Mrs. Motte died in 1815, at her plantation on the Santee. The portrait here given is copied, by permission of the author, from Mrs. Ellet's Women of the Revolution. The original is in the possession of Mrs. Motte's descendants.

8 Lee's Memoirs, 229-32. Simm's Life of Marion, page 236, 239. In this siege Marion lost two of his brave men, Sergeant M'Donald and Lieutenant Cruger. The British did not lose a man killed, and the prisoners were all paroled. Colonel Horry, in his narrative, mentions some pleasing incidents which occurred at the table of Mrs. Motte on this occasion. Among the prisoners was Captain Ferguson, an officer of considerable reputation. Finding himself near Horry, Ferguson said, "You are Colonel Horry, I presume, sir." Horry replied in the affirmative, when Ferguson continued, "Well, I was with Colonel Watson when he fought your General Marion on Sampit. I think I saw you there with a party of horse, and also at Nelson's Ferry, when Marion surprised our party at the house. But," he continued, "I was hid in high grass, and escaped. You were fortunate in your escape at Sampit, for Watson and Small had twelve hundred men." "If so," replied Horry, "I certainly was fortunate, for I did not suppose they had more than half that number." "I consider myself," added the captain, "equally fortunate in escaping at Nelson's Old Field." "Truly you were," answered Horry drily, "for Marion had but thirty militia on that occasion." The officers present could not suppress laughter. When Greene inquired of Horry how he came to affront Captain Ferguson; he answered, "He affronted himself by telling his own story." – Horry's MS. Narrative, quoted by Simms, Life of Marion, p. 239.

9 Some writers attribute Greene's presence at Fort Motte on this occasion to other motives than here represented. An unsatisfactory correspondence had recently taken place between Greene and Marion, the former having blamed the latter for not furnishing cavalry horses when in his power to do so. Marion, conscious of having been eminently faithful, felt deeply wronged, and tendered the resignation of his commission to Greene. The latter soon perceived the injustice of his suspicions, and took this, the first opportunity, for a personal interview to heal the wound.

10 A slave found in the streets of a town after dark, without a pass, is liable to be locked in prison until morning, and this was written to prevent such an occurrence. The laws of South Carolina inflict the penalty of fine and imprisonment upon a person found guilty of writing a pass for a slave without authority. I was informed of a curious circumstance connected with this fact, which occurred near Fort Motte, a few days previous to my visit there. Two slaves, carpenters, had escaped from their home, and were found near Camden with well-written passes or permits to find work, signed by the name of their master. Who wrote the forged passes, was a question which puzzled the neighborhood. A mulatto on the plantation was suspected, and, on being accused, confessed that he wrote them, having been secretly taught to write by an overseer. A jury was called to try him for the offense, but as the law did not contemplate the ability of a slave to write, and as the term person did not apply to a negro, no punishment could be legally awarded. The jury simply recommended his master to flog him.

11 Mr. Friday, the father-in-law of Mr. Cacey, and his brother, were the only Whigs of that name in the state, and often suffered insults from their Tory kinsman. Mr. Friday owned mills at Granby, and also a ferry called by his name; and when the British fortified that post, the garrison supplied themselves with flour from his establishment. He gave the British the credit of dealing honorably, paying him liberally for every thing they took from him – flour, poultry, cattle, &c. On one occasion, when called to the fort to receive his pay, Major Maxwell, the commandant of the garrison, said to him, "Mr. Friday, I hope you are as clever a fellow as those of your name who are with us." "No!" shouted his Tory uncle, who was standing near, "he's a damned rebel, and I'll split him down!" at the same time rushing forward to execute his brutal purpose. Colonel Maxwell protected the patriot, but dared not rebuke the savage, for fear of offending his Tory comrades. After the battle at Eutaw, Colonel Maxwell, and two or three other officers, passing through Granby, stopped one night at Mr. Friday's. Early in the morning, Maxwell said to Mr. Friday, "You Dutchmen are celebrated for fine gardens; let us go and look at yours." When a little distance from the other officers, the colonel remarked, "Mr. Friday, you are a friend to your country. Remain so. We have not conquered it yet, and never will, and your name will yet be honored, while those of your countrymen who are with us will be despised." I gladly record the patriotism of Mr. Friday, in fulfillment of this prediction.

12 Lee says, in his Memoirs (page 234), that Maxwell, "zealous to fill his purse, rather than to gather military laurels, had, during his command, pursued his favorite object with considerable success, and held with him in the fort his gathered spoil." This fact accounts for the major's desire to have all private property confirmed to its possessors "without investigation of title."

13 The garrison had only sixty regulars (the Hessians); the remainder were Tory militia.

14 According to M'Kenzie, in his Strictures on Tarleton's History, there were one hundred and fifty men of Delancey's battalion (Loyalists of New York), and two hundred Jersey volunteers. Lieutenant-colonel Cruger was Colonel Delancey's son-in-law. Colonel Cruger died in London in 1807, aged sixty-nine. His widow died at Chelsea, England, in 1822, at the age of seventy-eight years.

15 The house of George Galphin, deputy superintendent of Indian affairs, inclosed within stockades, was used for barracks, and as a store-house for various Indian supplies. The land is now owned by Ex-governor Hammond, of South Carolina. Previous to 1773, Galphin, by his dealings with the Creek Indians, had made them indebted to him in the sum of $49,000. To secure the payment of this and other debts, the Creeks conveyed to the British government, in 1773, a large tract of land lying within the present limits of Georgia. At the close of the Revolution, this land belonged to that state, and to the local Legislature Galphin applied for the payment of his claim. It was refused. In 1847, Milledge Galphin, surviving heir and executor of the Indian agent, petitioned Congress for a payment of the claim, principal and interest; and in 1850, the general government allowed what the local government had pronounced illegal. The "Galphin claim" took a large sum from our National Treasury, for interest had been accumulating for about seventy years.

16 Mr. M'Cracken observes, "The trees and shrubbery on the battle-ground are considered by the inhabitants too sacred to be molested. The land is now (1849) owned by John C. M'Gehee, of Madison

county, Florida. The present village of Cambridge is within a few hundred yards of the battle-ground, and the road leading through it, north and south, is the great thoroughfare from Hamburg (opposite Augusta) to Greenville. I have three small cannons in my possession, one six and two four pounders, taken from the enemy at the siege of Ninety-Six."

17 Colonel Williams, deputy adjutant general, in his returns stated them thus: Fit for duty, rank and file, Maryland brigade, 427; Virginia ditto, 431; North Carolina battalion, 66; Delaware ditto (under Captain Kirkwood), 60; in all, 984. The number of the militia is not mentioned.

18 Among the most active of these parties was the "Bloody Scout," under the notorious Bill Cunningham. They hovered around the American camp like vultures, and picked off the patriots in detail. The most active opponent of this scoundrel was William Beale, of Ninety-Six. He formed a scouting party of Whigs, and soon they became a terror to the Tories. On one occasion, Cunningham and his party plundered the house of Beale's mother, during his absence. On his return, Beale went in pursuit, and approaching Cunningham, that marauder wheeled and fled. The race continued for almost three miles, when Cunningham turned, and with a pistol, shot Beale's horse dead. Beale retreated backward, daring the Tory to follow. The latter, fearing a Whig ambush, rode off. On another occasion, Cunningham and his party surrounded a house where Beale and a Whig were stopping. They heard the approach of the Tories, when, rushing to their horses and rattling their swords, Beale gave command as if to a troop. It was dark, and Cunningham, who had thirteen men with him, fled in great haste. Cunningham was so mortified, when he learned that they had been frightened away by a couple of Whigs, that he swore vengeance against Beale. – Letter of James M. M'Cracken, Esq., to the Author.

19 For description of the Mayham Tower, and the origin of its name, see an account of the attack upon Fort Watson.

20 Mr. M'Cracken relates, that among the prisoners in one of the redoubts was one named Benjamin Eddins. Lieutenant-colonel Cruger frequently visited him, and often importuned him to eschew Republicanism and join the British army. Eddins at length became tired of these importunities, and one day said to Cruger, "Sir, I am a prisoner in your power; you may cut out my heart (baring his bosom), or you may drag my limbs and body asunder with ropes and horses; all this will I endure rather than desert my country's flag." Charmed by his boldness and patriotism, Colonel Cruger replied, "Sir, you are too true a rebel to remain here; you are liberated from this moment."

21 The wives of Lieutenant-colonel Cruger and Major Greene were at a farm-house in the neighborhood of Ninety-Six when the American army arrived. General Greene soon quieted their fears, and as they preferred to remain where they were, to joining their husbands in the beleaguered town, he placed a guard there to protect them. This kindness Mrs. Cruger reciprocated on the day when the Americans left, by informing some light troops who had been out scouting, and were passing by the farm-house toward the post, of the termination of the siege and the direction taken by General Greene in his retreat. Without this timely information, they would have been captured.

22 It is related that the message to Sumter from Greene was conveyed by Emily Geiger, the daughter of a German planter in Fairfield District. He prepared a letter to Sumter, but none of his men appeared willing to attempt the hazardous service, for the Tories were on the alert, as Rawdon was approaching the Congaree. Greene was delighted by the boldness of a young girl, not more than eighteen years of age, who came forward and volunteered to carry the letter to Sumter. With his usual caution, he communicated the contents of the letter to Emily, fearing she might lose it on the way. The maiden mounted a fleet horse, and crossing the Wateree at the Camden Ferry, pressed on toward Sumter's camp. Passing through a dry swamp on the second day of her journey, she was intercepted by some Tory scouts. Coming from the direction of Greene's army, she was an object of suspicion, and was taken to a house on the edge of the swamp, and confined in a room. With proper delicacy, they sent for a woman to search her person. No sooner was she left alone, than she ate up Greene's letter piece by piece. After a while, the matron arrived, made a careful search, but discovered nothing. With many apologies, Emily was allowed to pursue her journey. She reached Sumter's camp, communicated Greene's message, and soon Rawdon was flying before the Americans toward Orangeburg. Emily Geiger afterward married Mr. Thurwits, a rich planter on the Congaree. The picture of her capture, here given, I copied from the original painting by Flagg, in possession of Stacy G. Potts, Esq., of Trenton, New Jersey.

23 While Rawdon was in Charleston preparing to sail for Europe, the execution of Colonel Hayne occurred. This foul stain upon the character of Rawdon and Colonel Balfour, the commandant at Charleston, we shall consider hereafter.

24 Although the name of General Jethro Sumner does not appear very conspicuous in the general histories of the War for Independence, his services in the Southern campaigns were well appreciated by his peers and compatriots in the field. He was a native of Virginia, and as early as 1760 his merits caused him to be appointed a paymaster in the provincial army of that state, and commander of Fort Cumberland. In 1776, he lived in North Carolina, was appointed colonel of a regiment of Continental troops, and joined the army at the North, under Washington. He went South with General Gates, and was in the battle at Sander's Creek (Camden) when the Americans were defeated. He was actively engaged when Greene took command of the army, and continued in North Carolina until he marched to re-enforce Greene upon the High Hills of Santee. When Greene heard of the abduction of Governor Burke, after the battle at Eutaw, in which Sumner was engaged, he sent that officer into North Carolina to awe the Tories and encourage the Whigs. After the war, General Sumner married a wealthy widow at Newbern. He died in Warren county, North Carolina, and was buried near old Shocco Chapel, and Bute old Court House. The following inscription is upon his tomb-stone: "To the memory of GENERAL JETHRO SUMNER, one of the heroes of '76." – See Wheeler's History of North Carolina, page 425.

25 This swamp derives its name from the fact that the deep and sluggish stream, a branch of the South Edisto, which it skirts, disappears from the surface four times within this morass. Plunging into one pit, the water boils up from the next; disappearing again in the third, it reappears in the fourth, and then courses its way to the Edisto. These pits are about half a mile apart, and are filled with remarkably fine fish which may be taken with a hook and line at the depth of thirty feet.

26 This marl appears to be a concretion of oyster-shells, and is said to be an excellent fertilizer when crushed into powder. In this vicinity, many bones of monsters, like the mastodon, have been found.

27 This is a view of the reappearance of the stream (or lower spring) from the marl ridge thirty feet in height. These springs are in Charleston District, near the Orangeburg line, about sixty miles northwest of Charleston. It is probable that a subterranean stream here first finds its way to the surface of the earth.

28 John Coffin was a native of Boston, and brother of Admiral Sir Isaac Coffin, of the Royal Navy. He accompanied the British army in the action on Breed's Hill. He soon obtained a commission, rose to the rank of captain in the Orange Rangers, and finally, effecting an exchange into the New York Volunteers, went with that corps to Georgia in 1778. In the campaigns of 1779 and 1780, his conduct won the admiration of his superiors. His behavior in the battle of Eutaw attracted the attention of Greene and his officers. He retired to New Brunswick at the close of the contest. In the war of 1812, he commanded a regiment. He filled several civil offices in the province until 1828, when he retired from public life. He had been a member of the Assembly, chief magistrate of King's county, and a member of the council. He died at his seat in King's county in 1838, at the age of eighty-seven years. He held the rank of lieutenant general at the time of his death. – Sabine's Lives of the Loyalists.

29 This plantation belonged to Henry Laurens, who was one of the presidents of the Continental Congress.

30 Memoirs, 331. See, also, Greene's Dispatch to the President of Congress, September 11, 1781.

31 William Polk, son of Colonel Thomas Polk, of Mecklenburg, North Carolina, was born in that county in 1759. He was present at the celebrated Mecklenburg convention, in May, 1775. He joined the army early in 1777, and went to the North with General Nash, who was killed at Germantown. He was in the battles on the Brandywine and at Germantown, and was wounded at the latter place. He went South with General Gates, and was with him in the battle at Sander's Creek, near Camden. He was with Greene at Guilford and Eutaw. In the latter battle he received a wound, the effects of which he felt until his death. At the close of the war, he returned to Charlotte, his native place, and in 1787 represented his county in the North Carolina Legislature. He subsequently removed to Raleigh, where he resided until his death. In 1812, President Madison offered him the commission of a brigadier, but, being opposed to the war, he declined the honor. He died on the fourteenth of January, 1835, in the seventy-sixth year of his age. Colonel Polk was the last surviving field officer of the North Carolina line. Bishop Leonidas Polk, of the Protestant Episcopal Church of Louisiana, and General Thomas G. Polk, of Mississippi, are his sons.

32 Stuart's dispatch to Lord Cornwallis, September 9th, 1781; Stedman, ii., 378; Lee, 333.

33 Major Garden relates an amusing anecdote in connection with this affair. Among the prisoners captured outside the house was Captain Barre, a brother of the celebrated Colonel Barre, of the British Parliament. He was taken by Captain Manning, who led the legion infantry. In the terror of the moment, Barre began solemnly to recite his titles: "I am Sir Henry Barre," he said, "deputy adjutant general of the British army, captain of the 52d regiment, secretary of the commandant at Charleston – " "Are you, indeed?" interrupted Manning; "you are my prisoner now, and the very man I was looking for; come along with me." He then placed his titled prisoner between himself and the fire of the enemy, and retreated.

34 Colonel Otho H. Williams and Lieutenant-colonel Lee were the only officers, of six Continental commanders of regiments, who were not wounded. Washington, Howard, and Henderson were wounded, and Campbell was killed.

35 On the twenty-ninth of October, Congress adopted a series of resolutions, expressive of its high appreciation of the services of Greene and his officers and soldiers. In these resolutions, the various corps engaged in the battle were named; also Captains Pierce and Pendleton, Major Hyrne, and Captain Shubrick, his aids-de-camps. Marion was also thanked for the part he had taken in this battle, and also for his gallant conduct on the thirtieth of August, in attacking the British at Parker's Ferry. Congress ordered the Board of War to present a sword to Captain Pierce, who bore Greene's dispatches to that body – See Journals of Congress, vii., 166. On the same day, Congress adopted the complimentary resolutions in honor of the defeat of Cornwallis at Yorktown.

36 This is a representation of each side of the medal, the full size of the original. On one side is a profile of Greene, with the words, NATHANIELI GREENE EGREGIO DUCI COMITIA AMERICANA; "The American Congress to Nathaniel Greene, the distinguished leader." Upon the other side is a figure of Victory, lighting upon the Earth, and stepping upon a broken shield. Under her feet are broken weapons, colors, and a shield. The legend is, SALUS REGIONUM AUSTRALIUM; "The Safety of the Southern Department." Exergue – HOSTIBUS AD EUTAW DEBELLATIS VIII SEPT. MDCCLXXXI; "The Foe conquered at Eutaw, 8th of September, 1781."

37 Journals of Congress, vii., 167.

38 A mutinous spirit was soon manifested in the camp upon the hills, chiefly among the Marylanders. They wished to go home, complained of want of pay and clothing, and in petitions to Greene set forth their various grievances. Finally, some stole away from the camp with their arms, when stringent measures were deemed necessary to prevent open disorder. Things were brought to a crisis by a South Carolina soldier, named Timothy Griffin. He had heard whispers of disaffection, and one day, while drunk, went up to a group of soldiers who were talking to an officer, and said, "Stand to it boys – damn my blood if I'd give an inch!" He supposed they were altercating with the officer, which was not the fact. Griffin was instantly knocked down by Captain M'Pherson, of the Maryland line, and then sent to the provost. The next day he was tried for mutinous conduct, found guilty, and at five o'clock in the evening was shot in the presence of the whole army. This terrible example suppressed all mutinous proceedings – Gordon, iii., 246

39 "It will scarcely be believed," says Simms (Life of Marion, page 126), "that, of this hundred and fifty Continentals, but three men consented to join the ranks of the liberator. It may be that they were somewhat loth to be led, even though it were to victory, by the man whose ludicrous equipments and followers, but a few weeks before, had only provoked their amusement." The reason they gave was, that they considered the cause of the country to be hopeless, and that they were risking life without an adequate object.

40 Marion was very anxious to pursue Watson, who, to facilitate his march toward Camden, had sunk his two field-pieces in Cat-fish Creek, burned his baggage, and was making forced marches toward Georgetown. It was evident, from the circuitous direction of his march, that Watson feared Marion excessively; for, instead of making a direct line westward toward Camden, across the Great Pedee, he crossed the Little Pedee eastward; marched southward through the present Horry District; crossed the Waccamaw at Greene's Ferry, and Winyaw Bay where it was three miles wide; traversed its western border to Georgetown, and from thence crossed the country toward the Santee, following that stream up as far as the junction of the Congaree and Wateree. Greene's instructions to operate against the British posts below Camden prevented a pursuit.

41 Hezekiah Maham was born on the twenty-sixth of June, 1739. We have no record of his early life. He was a member of the first Provincial Congress of South Carolina; and in the spring of 1776 was elected a captain in Colonel Isaac Huger's regiment. He was with that officer at the siege of Savannah, and at the battle of Stono. As lieutenant colonel of an independent corps of cavalry, he performed many daring exploits in the low country of the Carolinas. At the close of the campaign of 1781, he was obliged to leave active service on account of sickness. While at home, he was made a prisoner and paroled, by which he was not allowed to enter the army again during the war. He died in 1789, at the age of fifty years. His descendant, J. J. Ward, Esq., living near Georgetown, erected a handsome monument to his memory in 1845, upon which are the following inscriptions:

FRONT SIDE. – "Within this Cemetery, and in the bosom of the homestead which he cultivated and embellished while on earth, lie the mortal remains of COLONEL HEZEKIAH MAHAM. He was born in the parish of St. Stephen's, and died A. D. 1789, at fifty years; leaving a name unsullied in social and domestic life, and eminent for devotion to the liberties of his country, and for achievements in arms, in the Revolution which established her independence."

RIGHT SIDE. – "Impelled by the spirit of freedom which animated his countrymen, he devoted himself to its support, and promoted the cause of American Independence, by his service in the state committees, instituted by recommendation of the General Congress, in the Jacksonborough Assembly, and in various other civil capacities."

LEFT SIDE. – "Successively a captain in the first rifle regiment, a commander of horse in Marion's brigade, and lieutenant colonel of an independent corps of cavalry, raised by authority of General Greene, he bore an efficient and conspicuous part in the capture of the British posts, and in the series of skillful maneuvers and gallant actions, which resulted in the final extinction of the British dominion in South Carolina, and secured to her and to the confederacy the blessings of Peace, Liberty, and Independence."

ON THE BACK. – "His relative, Joshua John Ward, of Waccamaw, unwilling that the last abode of an honest man, a faithful patriot, and a brave and successful soldier, should be forgotten and unknown, has erected this memorial, A. D. 1845."

42 This mansion was demolished a few years before my visit to Eutaw and vicinity (1849), and this drawing was made from a minute description given me by a gentleman with whom I rode in the mail-coach from Augusta to the Ninety-mile station, on the great central rail-way, in Georgia. His brother had resided there for many years and he was perfectly familiar with its appearance. At the station I made this sketch, and my informant pronounced it an excellent representation of the residence of General Marion.

Chapter XIX

The rail-way journey from Orangeburg to Augusta was extremely monotonous in scenery and incident. At Branchville, on the banks of the Edisto, where the rail-way from Charleston connects, the immobility into which the passengers were subsiding was disturbed by the advent among us of a "turban'd Turk," in full Oriental costume. His swarthy complexion, keen eye, flowing black beard, broad turban, tunic, and trowsers, made him the "observed of all observers," and kept the passengers awake for an hour, for "Yankee curiosity" was too busy to allow drowsiness. "Whence I came, and whither I go, ye know not," were as plain as a written phylactery upon his imperturbable features, and I presume the crowd who gathered around him in the street at Augusta knew as little of his history and destiny as we. It is pleasant sometimes to see curiosity foiled, even though

> "It came from heaven – it reigned in Eden's shades –
> It roves on earth, and every walk invades:
> Childhood and age alike its influence own;
> It haunts the beggar's nook, the monarchs throne;
> Hangs o'er the cradle, leans above the bier,
> Gazed on old Babel's tower – and lingers here."
> – CHARLES SPRAGUE.

The scenery by the way-side alternated between oozy swamps embellished with cypresses, cultivated fields, and extensive forests of oak and pine, garnished occasionally by a tall broad-leaved magnolia. The country was perfectly level through Barnwell District, until we passed Aiken into Edgefield, and turned toward Silver Bluff, on the Savannah River, **1** when we encountered the sand hills of that region. These continued until we reached the termination of the road at Hamburg, on the northern bank of the Savannah, opposite Augusta. **2** There we were packed into huge omnibuses, and conveyed to the city across Schultz's bridge on January 24, 1849. It was sunset – a glorious sunset, like those at the north in September – when we reined up at the United States. A stroll about the city by moon-light that evening, with a Northern friend residing there, was really delightful; for the air was balmy and dry, and the moon and stars had nothing of the crisp, piercing, and glittering aspect which they assume in a clear January night in New England.

Early on the following morning we rode over to Hamburg, and ascended to the summit of Liberty Hill, a lofty sand bluff three fourths of a mile from the river. Flowers were blooming in the gardens on its brow; and over its broad acres green grass and innumerable cacti were spread. The view from this eminence was charming. At our feet lay the little village of Hamburg, and across the shining Savannah was spread out in panoramic beauty the city of Augusta – the queen of the inland towns of the South. Like a sea in repose, the level country extended in all directions; and city, river, forest, and plain were bathed in the golden haziness which characterizes our Indian summer at the North. From that point the eye could survey the whole historic arena around Augusta, where Royalists and Republicans battled, failed, and triumphed during our war for independence. While the spirit is charmed with associations awakened by the gleanings of sensuous vision, let us for a moment open the tome of history, and give inquiring thought free wing.

Augusta has a history anterior to the Revolution. Her local historians have preserved but little of it which is of general interest, and its records do not bear date back to that period. It was founded in 1735, under the auspices of Oglethorpe; and in 1736, a small garrison was stationed there, in a stockade fort, as a protection for the settlers against any enemy that might appear. Warehouses were built, and quite an extensive trade was opened with the friendly Indians upon the Savannah and its tributaries. Fort Augusta became a general resort for the Indian traders; and there, and at Fort Moore, on the bluff near Sand-bar Ferry, all the Indian treaties were held, down to the year 1750. In 1751, several Quaker families settled there and at a place called Quaker Springs. When French emissaries, about 1754, stirred up the Indian tribes against the English, the fort was strengthened, its magazine was well supplied, and the men were "mustered and drilled for service." Nothing of importance occurred to disturb the quiet of the people, and the settlement flourished. Living in almost unrestrained freedom, far away from the sea-board and its varieties, the agitations wrought throughout the colonies by the Stamp Act and kindred measures, scarcely elicited a thought from the quiet people of this region; but when, month after month, intelligence arrived that chains were forging to fetter their free spirits, they were aroused, and all through the region between the Alatamaha and Savannah Rivers, and especially in the vicinity of Augusta, the Tree of Liberty budded and blossomed, green, vigorous, and beautiful as the native magnolia. Although Georgia was not represented in the first Continental Congress, yet her children were not less alive to the teachings of the spirit of liberty; and the *American Association* was early approved, and its operations efficiently established. The lines between Whigs and Tories were distinctly drawn, and the requirements of the association were promptly enforced. **3**

When the British attacked Savannah, in March, 1776, the Legislature, a majority of which was inimical to the royal government, adjourned to Augusta, where the people were generally friendly. On the fall of Savannah, in 1779, the Legislature was dispersed. John Wereat, then president of the executive council, issued a proclamation, ordering an election of legislators, who were to assemble at Augusta. That town now became the center of Republican power in Georgia, and thither the most active friends of the patriot cause at Savannah fled. George Walton, one of the signers of the Declaration of Independence, was chosen governor under the Constitution (adopted in 1777), **4** notwithstanding Sir James Wright had now (in 1779) re-established royal rule in the province. William Glascock was chosen speaker, and the Legislature transacted business without reference to the existence of any other power in the state. **5**

For the encouragement and support of the Loyalists in the interior, and to awe the Republicans in that quarter after the fall of Savannah, Colonel Campbell, who commanded at the siege of that city, was ordered by General Prevost to advance with about two thousand regulars and Loyalists in January 1779, upon Augusta. **6** Already he had sent emissaries among the South Carolina Tories to encourage them to make a general insurrection; and he assured them that, if they would cross the Savannah and join him at Augusta, the Republicans might be easily crushed, and the whole South freed from their pestilential influence. Thus encouraged, about eight hundred Loyalists of North and South Carolina assembled westward of the Broad River, under Colonel Boyd, and marched along the frontier of South Carolina, toward the Savannah. Like a plundering banditti, they appropriated every species of property to their own use, abused the inhabitants, and wantonly butchered several who opposed their rapacious demands. While these depredators were organizing, and Campbell was proceeding toward Augusta, General Elbert **7** crossed the Savannah, joined Colonels Twiggs and Few, and skirmished with the British van-guard at Brier Creek and other places, to impede their progress. They effected but little, and on the twenty-ninth of January (1779) Campbell took possession of Augusta, and placed the garrison under Lieutenant-colonel Brown, the Loyalist just mentioned, who, with Lieutenant-colonel M'Girth, had preceded him thither. Campbell then proceeded to establish military posts in other parts of Western Georgia. The Whigs who could leave with their families crossed the Savannah into Carolina. The oath of allegiance was every where administered; the habitations of those who had fled into Carolina were consumed; and Georgia seemed, for the moment, permanently prostrate at the feet of the invaders. The quiet that ensued was only the calm before a gathering storm. Colonel John Dooly collected a body of active militia on the Carolina shore, thirty miles above Augusta, while Colonel M'Girth, with three hundred Loyalists, was watching him on the other side. Dooly crossed over into Georgia, and these partisans had several skirmishes. Finally, Major Hamilton, an active officer under M'Girth, drove Dooly across the Savannah, a short distance below the mouth of Broad River, and encamped at Waters's plantation, about three miles below the present town of Petersburg, in Elbert county. Dooly took post opposite to Hamilton, where he was joined by Colonel Pickens. Their united forces amounted to about three hundred and fifty men.

Colonel Pickens, who was the senior officer, assumed the command of the whole, and with Dooly crossed the river at Cowen's Ferry, to attack Hamilton on February 10, 1779. That officer had broken up his encampment and marched to Carr's Fort, not far distant, to examine its condition and administer the oath of allegiance to the surrounding inhabitants. The Americans besieged the fort, and were confident of capturing it, having cut off the supply of water for the garrison, when, at ten o'clock at night, a message came to Colonel Pickens, from his brother, informing him of the march of Boyd and his banditti through the district of Ninety-Six. Unwilling to distress the families who had taken shelter within the fort, Pickens declined a proposition to burn it, and raising the siege, he hastened to confront Boyd, the more important foe. He crossed the Savannah near Fort Charlotte, when Boyd, hearing of his approach, hastened toward the Cherokee Ford. At that ford was a redoubt, garrisoned by eight men, with two swivels. They successfully disputed the passage of Boyd, and he marched five miles up the river, crossed on rafts, and pushed on toward Augusta. He was pursued by a detachment of Americans, under Captain Anderson, who attacked him in a cane-brake. A severe skirmish ensued. Boyd lost one hundred men in killed, wounded, and missing; the Americans lost sixteen killed, and the same number taken prisoners. Boyd hastened forward, and on the morning of the thirteenth of February 1779, crossed the Broad River, near the fork, in Oglethorpe county, closely pursued by Pickens, with about three hundred militia. The latter marched in battle order. Colonel Dooly **8** commanded the right wing; Lieutenant-colonel Clark the left; and Colonel Pickens the center. Boyd, ignorant of the proximity of his pursuers, halted on the north side of Kettle Creek, turned his horses out to forage upon the reeds of a neighboring swamp, and proceeded to slaughter cattle for his army. In this condition he was attacked on February 14 by the Americans. The Tory pickets fired, and fled to the camp. The utmost confusion prevailed, and Boyd and his followers began to retreat in great disorder, while skirmishing with the assailants. The contest lasted almost two hours. About seventy of the Tories were killed, and seventy-five were made prisoners. The Americans lost nine killed and twenty-three mortally wounded. Colonel Boyd was severely wounded, and expired that night. His whole force was scattered to the winds. The seventy prisoners were taken to South Carolina, tried for high treason, and condemned to death. Five of the most active ones were hanged, the remainder were pardoned. **9** This was one of the severest blows which Toryism in the South had yet received.

Encouraged by this success, General Lincoln, then in command of the Southern army, determined to drive the British from their posts in the interior, back to Savannah. He formed encampments at Black Swamp, and nearly opposite Augusta, while small detachments of militia took post at various points on the Savannah, above Augusta. Lincoln ordered General John Ashe, then in the neighborhood of Purysburg, to march up the easterly side of the Savannah with about fifteen hundred North Carolina militia, and the remains of the Georgia Continentals, to re-enforce General Williamson opposite Augusta. Ashe arrived at Williamson's camp on the evening before the defeat of Boyd on February 13, 1779. This imposing display opposite Augusta, and intelligence of the close pursuit of Boyd, alarmed Campbell, and he speedily decamped that same night with all his force, and hastened toward the sea-coast. He left behind him a considerable quantity of provisions, ammunition, and some arms. At Hudson's Ferry, fifty miles below Augusta, Lieutenant-colonel Prevost had constructed a fortified camp and mounted some light artillery. There Campbell halted, with the determination to attempt to regain the advantage he had just lost, but finally continued his retreat to Savannah.

General Lincoln, who was then encamped at Purysburg, in Beaufort District, about twenty-five miles above Savannah, with three thousand men, sent orders to Colonel Ashe on February 16 to cross the Savannah, and proceed as far as Brier Creek in pursuit of Campbell. At this time, General Rutherford, of North Carolina, was encamped at Black Swamp, on the Carolina side of the Savannah, a few miles above the mouth of Ebenezer Creek, with seven hundred men; and General Williamson, **10** with twelve hundred men, was opposite Augusta. General Ashe crossed the river on the twenty-fifth, and proceeded toward Brier Creek, a considerable stream, which flows into the Savannah in Severn county, about forty-five miles below Augusta. He reached Brier Creek on Saturday morning, the twenty-seventh (Feb. 1779), and discovered that the bridge across the stream (which is there skirted with a deep swamp three miles wide) was completely destroyed by the enemy. General Rutherford, with part of his brigade, was at Mathew's Bluff, five miles above, on the opposite side of the Savannah; and Colonel Marbury, of the Georgia horse, lay a few miles up Brier Creek. Ashe's force consisted of General Bryan's brigade, Lieutenant-colonel Lyttle's light infantry, and some Georgia Continentals; in all about twelve hundred men. His artillery consisted of one four pound brass field-piece, and two iron two pound swivels, mounted as field-pieces. Bryant and Elbert were instructed to form the camp, while Ashe crossed the river to confer with General Lincoln. A guard was dispatched to conduct the baggage across to Mathew's Bluff, in case it was found necessary to retreat; and other guards were stationed at the fords of the creek above, while fatigue-parties were detailed to construct bridges, and to make a road to the river for the passage of Rutherford's troops with two brass field-pieces.

Ashe returned on the evening of the third (March 1779), and was chagrined at not finding the bridge which Campbell had destroyed, repaired. Early the following morning workmen were employed in that duty, but it was too late, and the Americans were quite unprepared for offensive or defensive operations. While in this exposed situation, intelligence came from General Williamson, then on his march from Augusta, that the enemy, under the general command of Prevost, was within eight miles of the American camp above, approaching in full force. Already Marbury, with his dragoons, had encountered the British van, but his express to Ashe had been intercepted. Reconnoitering parties had approached the American pickets, yet they produced neither apprehension nor vigilance. That indifference proved fatal. Prevost, with about eighteen hundred men, had crossed Brier Creek, fifteen miles above Ashe's camp, made a wide circuit, and, unperceived, had gained his rear. To retreat was now impossible. The drums immediately beat to arms; the troops were formed for action, and cartridges were distributed among them. **11** They then advanced about a quarter of a mile; General Elbert and his command, with Colonel Perkins's regiment, forming the advance. The British formed their line when within one hundred and fifty yards of the Americans, and at the moment of their advance, Elbert and Perkins opened a severe fire upon them, The Georgians, after delivering two or three rounds, unfortunately inclined to the left, by which the fire of the advancing Newbern regiment was impeded. At the same moment, the Edenton regiment, moving to the right, left a vacancy in the line. This the enemy perceived, and pushed forward on a run, with a loud shout. The Halifax regiment on the left, panic-stricken, broke and fled, without firing a gun. The Wilmington regiment, except a small part under Lieutenant-colonel Young, advanced and delivered two or three volleys, wheeled, and retreated. The Newbern and Edenton regiments followed their example, and in a few minutes the whole of the North Carolina troops were flying to the coverts of the swamps. The Georgia Continentals maintained their ground gallantly for some time; but they, too, were finally repulsed, and General Elbert and a large number of his men were made prisoners. General Ashe tried in vain to reach the front of the fugitives and rally them. They had scattered in all directions; took shelter in the swamps; and, on reaching the Savannah, escaped across it, some by swimming, and others upon rafts. In this retreat many were drowned, and others were lost in the swamps. General Ashe reached Mathew's Bluff in safety, and afterward collected the remnants of his little army at Zubley's Ferry on March 16, 1779, two miles above Purysburg. The loss of the Americans in this action was estimated at one hundred and fifty killed and drowned; twenty-seven officers, and one hundred and sixty-two non-commissioned officers and privates, were taken prisoners; and seven pieces of artillery, a quantity of ammunition, provisions, and baggage, with five hundred stand of arms, were either lost or fell into the hands of Prevost. The British lost only one commissioned officer, and fifteen privates killed and wounded. **12**

General Ashe **13** was much censured by contemporary opinion and early historians; and modern compilers have repeated those censures, because he allowed himself to be surprised. Viewing the whole affair from this remote point, and in the light of calm judgment, he appears no more censurable than most other men who were losers instead of winners. Had he succeeded in becoming a victor, his alleged remissness would never have been mentioned; the unfortunate are always blamed. Conscious of having exercised both courage and vigilance, General Ashe appealed from the voice of public opinion to a court-martial, of which General Moultrie **14** was president on March 9, 1779. The court acquitted him of every charge of cowardice and deficiency of military skill, but gave their opinion that he did not take all necessary precautions to secure his camp and watch the movements of the enemy. It was an unfortunate affair, for it deprived Lincoln of about one third of his available force, and opened a free communication between the

View from the site of Fort Cornwallis. 16

British, Indians, and Tories, in Florida, Western Georgia, and the Carolinas.

We have observed that after the fall of Charleston on May 12, 1780, and the dispersion of Lincoln's army, royal power in South Carolina and Georgia was fully established. The Republican governor of Georgia and part of his council fled into North Carolina, and narrowly escaped being captured on the way. Lieutenant-colonel Thomas Brown, whom Campbell placed in command of Augusta early in 1779, now proceeded to that place and garrisoned the fort with a strong force. Brown, as we have seen, was an early victim of Whig indignation at Augusta, his native place, and he used his power, while in command there, with a fierceness commensurate with his wrath. He sent out detachments to burn the dwellings of patriots in his vicinity, and dispatched emissaries among the Indians to incite them to murder the inhabitants on the frontier. **15** His command at Augusta consisted of two hundred and fifty men, of several corps, principally of Florida rangers; two hundred and fifty Creek and fifty Cherokee Indians; in all, five hundred and fifty. The defenses consisted of a strong fort, situated on the northwest side of the town, upon a bank about one hundred yards from the river. This was the main work, and was called Fort Cornwallis. A little less than half a mile westward of Fort Cornwallis, was a swampy ravine extending up from the river, with a stream running through it. On the western margin of this lagoon, between the present Upper Market and the river, was a smaller work called Fort Grierson, so named in honor of the militia colonel who commanded its garrison.

About the first of September (1780), Colonel Elijah Clark, a brave partisan of Wilkes county, Georgia, and Lieutenant-colonel M'Call, made efforts to raise a sufficient force to capture the fort at Augusta, and drive the British from the interior of the state to the sea-coast. These were the brave partisans who fought at the Cowpens a few months later. Clark recruited in his own county, and M'Call went to the district of Ninety-Six and applied to Colonel Pickens for aid. He wanted five hundred men, but procured only eighty. With these he marched to Soap Creek, forty miles northwest of Augusta, where he was joined by Clark, with three hundred and fifty men. With this inadequate force they marched toward Augusta. So secret and rapid were their movements, that they reached the outposts before the garrison was apprised of their approach on September 14, 1780. The right was commanded by M'Call, the left by Major Samuel Taylor, and the center by Clark. The divisions approached the town separately. Near Hawk's Creek, on the west, Taylor fell in with an Indian camp, and a skirmish ensued. The Indians retreated toward the town, and Taylor pressed forward to get possession of a strong trading station called the *White House*, a mile and a half west of the town. The Indians reached it first, and were joined by a company of King's Rangers, under Captain Johnson. Ignorant of the approach of other parties, Brown and Grierson went to the aid of Johnson and the Indians. While absent, the few men left in garrison were surprised by Clark and M'Call, and Forts Cornwallis and Grierson fell into their hands. A guard was left to take charge of the prisoners and effects in the fort, and Clark, with the remainder, hastened to the assistance of Taylor. Brown and Grierson, perceiving their peril, took shelter in the *White House*. The Americans tried in vain to dislodge them. A desultory fire was kept up from eleven o'clock in the morning until dark, when hostilities ceased. During the night the besieged cast up a slight breast-work around the house, made loop-holes in the building for musketry, and thus materially strengthened their position. Early in the morning of September 15, Clark ordered two field-pieces to be brought from Grierson's redoubt, to be placed in a position to cannonade the White House. They were of little service, for Captain Martin, of South Carolina, the only artillerist among the besiegers, was killed soon after the pieces were brought to bear upon the building.

No impression was made upon the enemy during the fifteenth. On that morning, before daylight, the Americans drove a body of Indians from the river bank, and thus cut off the supply of water for those in the house. Colonel Brown and others had been severely wounded, and now suffered great agony from thirst. On the night of the fifteenth, fifty Cherokee Indians, well armed, crossed the river to re-enforce Brown, but were soon repulsed. Little was done on the sixteenth, and on the seventeenth Clark summoned Brown to surrender. He promptly refused; for, having sent a messenger to Colonel Cruger at Ninety-Six, on the morning when the Americans appeared before Augusta, Brown confidently expected relief from that quarter. Nor was he disappointed. On the night of the seventeenth, Clark's scouts informed him of the approach of Colonel Cruger with five hundred British regulars and Loyalists, and on the morning of the eighteenth this force appeared upon the opposite side of the river. Clark's little army was greatly diminished by the loss of men who had been killed and wounded, and the desertion of many with plunder found in the forts. At ten o'clock he raised the siege, and departed toward the mountains. The American loss on this occasion was about sixty killed and wounded; that of the British is not known. Twenty of the Indians were killed. Captain Ashby and twenty-eight others were made prisoners. Upon these Brown and his Indian allies glutted their thirst for revenge. Captain Ashby and twelve of the wounded were hanged upon the stair-way of the *White House*, so that the commandant might have the satisfaction of seeing their sufferings. Others were given up to the Indians to torture, scalp, and slay. Terrible were the demoniac acts at Augusta on that beautiful autumnal day, when the white and the red savage contended for the meed of cruelty!

The British remained in possession of Augusta until the spring and summer of 1781, when their repose was disturbed. After the battle at Guilford Court House, and when the determination of Greene to march into South Carolina was made known, Clark and M'Call proceeded to co-operate with him by annoying the British posts in Georgia. M'Call soon afterward died of the small-pox, and Clark suffered from the same disease. After his recovery, he, with several other partisans, was actively engaged at various points between Savannah and Augusta, and had frequent skirmishes with the British and Tory scouts. In an engagement near Coosawhatchie, in Beaufort District, South Carolina, where Colonel Brown then commanded, the Americans were defeated; and several who were taken prisoners were hanged, and their bodies given to the Indians to scalp and otherwise mutilate. **17** This was Brown's common practice, and made his name as hateful at the South as that of "Bloody Bill Cunningham."

On the sixteenth of April (1781), the Georgia militia, under Colonels Williams, Baker, and Hammond, Major James Jackson (afterward governor of the state), and other officers, assembled near Augusta, and placed the garrison in a state of siege. Williams, who had the general command during Clark's sickness, encamped within twelve hundred yards of Forts Cornwallis and Grierson, and fortified his camp. Colonel Brown, who was again in command at Augusta, deceived respecting the numbers of the Americans, dared not attack them; and in this position the respective forces remained until the middle of May, when Clark came with one hundred new recruits and resumed the command. About that time, Major Dill approached Augusta with a party of Loyalists to force the Americans to raise the siege. A detachment of Carolina mountaineers and Georgians, under Shelby and Carr, sent by Clark, met them at Walker's bridge, on Brier Creek, killed and wounded several, and dispersed the rest. Other little successes made the Americans at Augusta feel so strong that Clark determined to attempt an assault. An old iron five pounder, which he had picked up, was mounted within four hundred yards of Fort Grierson, and other dispositions for an attack were made. Powder was scarce, and he sent a message to Colonel Pickens, **18** who was maneuvering between Augusta and Fort Ninety-Six, asking for a supply, and also a re-enforcement of men.

Pickens could not immediately comply, for the Indians having recommenced hostilities on the frontiers of Georgia and Carolina, he had sent part of his force in that direction. Perceiving the importance of seizing Augusta, Pickens informed Greene of the situation of affairs there. That general, then advancing upon Ninety-Six, immediately ordered Lieutenant-colonel Lee, with his legion, to join Pickens and Clark in besieging Augusta.

The capture of Fort Galphin on May 21, 1781 was an important prelude to the siege of Augusta, for it deprived Colonel Brown of a considerable body of reserved troops and of valuable stores. The latter were of great importance to Greene, then approaching Ninety-Six. After the capture of this redoubt, Lee allowed his troops to repose a few hours, and then ordered Major Eggleston, with Captains O'Neal and Armstrong, to cross the Savannah with the cavalry, a little below Augusta, and join Pickens and Clark. On the same evening, Lee, with the field-piece of Captain Finley, crossed the river, and on the morning of the twenty-third joined the besiegers.

Eggleston, on his arrival, summoned Brown to surrender, at the same time informing him of the approach of a strong force from General Greene's army. Brown did not credit the information, treated the flag with contempt, and declined giving a written answer. Lee had now arrived, and an immediate assault on Fort Grierson was determined upon. The first measure attempted was to cut off his retreat to Fort Cornwallis. Pickens and Clark were to attack Fort Grierson on the northwest, with the militia; Major Eaton's battalions and some Georgia militia, under Major Jackson, were to pass down the river and attack it on the northeast; while Lee, with his infantry, took a position south of the fort, so as to support Eaton, or check Brown if he should make a sortie in favor of Grierson. In the skirt of the woods south of Lee, Eggleston, with the cavalry, was stationed. When Brown discovered the peril of Grierson, he made a sortie with two field-pieces, but was soon checked by Lee. Grierson, at the same time, endeavored to evacuate his redoubt, and attempt to throw his command into Fort Cornwallis. Passing down the ravine on the margin of the lagoon, some of the garrison effected their purpose; but thirty of them were slain, and forty five were wounded and taken prisoners. Grierson was captured, but was instantly killed by a Georgia rifleman, who, on account of cruelties inflicted upon his family by his victim, could not be restrained from dealing a blow of vengeance. **19** In this assault Major Eaton was slain.

The Americans now turned their attention to Fort Cornwallis. They were without artillery except the old iron piece in possession of Clark, and Finley's grasshopper; and their rifles had but little effect upon the fort. Lee suggested the erection of a Mayham tower, which was used so efficiently at Fort Watson and Ninety-Six. This was done, under cover of an old frame house which stood directly in front of the present Episcopal church. This procedure made Brown uneasy, and on the night of the twenty-eighth he sent out a detachment to drive the Americans from their labor. After a severe skirmish, the enemy were driven into the fort at the point of the bayonet. On the succeeding night, a similar attempt was made, with the same result. The tower was completed on the first of June, and for its destruction Brown used every effort in his power. Sallies were made under cover of night, and some severe conflicts ensued. He tried stratagem, **20** and failed in that.

On the thirty-first of May, Brown was summoned to surrender. He refused, and that night a six pounder, brought from Fort Grierson, was placed in battery on the tower. Toward noon, riflemen stationed upon it opened a galling fire upon the garrison, which was continued throughout the day. The guns were soon unmanned by the rifle balls, and the six pounder dismounted them. The garrison dug vaults within the fort to save themselves from the murderous fire of the assailants, and thus the siege went on until the morning of the fourth (June 1781), when a general assault was agreed upon. While the Americans were forming for attack, Brown, perceiving the maintenance of his post to be impossible, sent out a flag and offered to make a conditional surrender to Pickens and Lee. The day was spent in negotiations, and early the next morning the fort was surrendered to Captain Rudulph, who was appointed to take possession. The garrison marched out and laid down their arms, and Brown and his fellow-prisoners were paroled to Savannah under a sufficient guard, who marched down the river on the Carolina side. **21** Pickins and Lee soon hastened to the aid of Greene, then investing Ninety-Six. In this siege of Augusta, the Americans had sixteen killed and thirty-five wounded; seven of them mortally. The loss of the British was fifty-two killed; and three hundred and thirty-four, including the wounded, were made prisoners of war. **22** The British never had possession of Augusta after this event.

Let us close the chronicle for a while.

It was toward noon when we descended Liberty Hill, looked in upon the slave-market at Hamburg (the first and last I ever saw), and crossed Shultz's bridge to Augusta. After dinner I visited the site of Fort Cornwallis, and made the sketch on page 176; also the site of Fort Grierson, of which no vestiges remain. The rivulet is still there, and the marshy lagoon on the brink of the river; but the "gulley" mentioned in the local histories was filled, and houses and gardens covered the site of the redoubt and its ravelins. At the office of the mayor, I saw (and was permitted to copy) a sketch of the proposed monument to be erected in the middle of the broad and beautifully shaded Greene Street, directly in front of the City Hall, in honor of the Georgia Signers of the Declaration of Independence. It is to be a granite obelisk, forty-five feet in height, composed of square blocks of stone. The base of the obelisk will be six feet eight inches square at the bottom, and gradually tapered to the top. It will rest upon a base twelve feet eight inches square, elevated two feet above the ground. The corner-stone is already laid, and it is to be hoped that another will soon be added to the few monuments already erected to the memory of Revolutionary patriots.

I left Augusta on the evening of the twenty-fifth (Jan. 1849) with real regret, for the beauty of the city, ornamented with water-oaks, wild olives, holly, palmettoes, magnolias, and other evergreens; the gardens blooming; the orange-trees budding in the bland air, and the courtesy of the citizens whom I met, wooed me to a longer tarry. But "home, sweet home," beckoned me away, and at eight o'clock I entered a mail-coach,

with a single fellow-passenger, for a ride of fifty-two miles to the "Ninety-mile Station," on the Great Central Railway. I had a pleasant companion while he kept awake, and we whiled away the tedious night hours by agreeable conversation until we reached Waynesborough, **23** where we exchanged horses and the mails. After leaving the village, I endeavored to sleep. My companion complained that he never could slumber in a coach; and I presume his loud snoring always keeps him awake, for in ten minutes after leaving the post-office his nasal pipes were chanting bass to the alto of the coach-wheels.

We breakfasted at sunrise at a log-house in the forest, and arrived at the rail-way, on the upper border of Severn county, near the banks of the Great Ogeeche, at eleven o'clock, where we dined, and at one departed for Savannah. Swamps, plantations, and forests, with scarcely a hill, or even an undulation, compose the monotonous scenery. While enjoying the pleasing anticipation of an early arrival in Savannah, our locomotive became disabled by the breaking of a piston-rod. We were yet forty miles from our goal, in the midst of a vast swamp, ten miles from any habitation, near the road. The sun went down; the twilight faded away, and yet we were immovable. At

Greene and Pulaski Monument.

intervals the engineer managed to start his steed and travel a short distance, and then stop. Thus we crawled along, and at eleven o'clock at night we reached the thirty mile station, where we supped at the expense of the railway company. At our haltings we started light-wood fires, whose blaze amid the tall trees draped with moss, the green cane-brakes, and the dry oases, garnished with dwarf palmettoes, produced the most picturesque effects. A hand-car was sent down to Savannah for another engine, and at six o'clock in the morning we entered that city. I breakfasted at the Pulaski House, a large building fronting upon Johnson Square, amid whose noble trees stands a monument erected by the citizens of Savannah to the memory of General Greene and the Count Pulaski. **24**

Savannah is pleasantly situated upon a sand- bluff, some forty feet above low-water-mark, sloping toward swamps and savannahs, at a lower altitude in the interior. It is upon the south side of the river, about eighteen miles from the ocean. The city is laid out in rectangles, and has ten public squares. The streets are generally broad and well shaded, some of them with four rows of Pride-of-India trees, which, in summer, add greatly to the beauty of the city and comfort of the inhabitants. Before noting the localities of interest in Savannah and suburbs, let us open the interesting pages of its history, and note their teachings respecting Georgia in general, and of the capital in particular, whose foundations were laid by General Oglethorpe.

We have already considered the events which led to the settlement of the Carolinas, within whose charter limits Georgia was originally included, and we will here refer only to the single circumstance connected with the earlier efforts at settlement, which some believe to be well authenticated, namely, that Sir Walter Raleigh, when on his way to the Orinoco, in South America, entered the Savannah River. and upon the bluff where the city now stands stood and talked with the Indian king. **25** There are reasonable doubts of the truth of this statement.

As late as 1730, the territory lying between the Savannah and Alatamaha Rivers was entirely uninhabited by white people. On the south the Spaniards held possession, and on the west the French had Louisiana, while the region under consideration, partially filled with powerful Indian tribes, was claimed by Great Britain. To prevent France and Spain from occupying it (for the latter already began to claim territory even north of the Savannah), and as a protection to the Carolina planters against the encroachments of their hostile neighbors, various schemes of emigration thither were proposed, but without being effected. Finally, in 1729, General James Oglethorpe, a valorous soldier and humane Christian, then a member of Parliament, made a proposition in that body for the founding of a colony to be composed of poor persons who were confined for debt and minor offenses in the prisons of England, **26** He instituted an inquiry into

General Oglethorpe. 29   their condition, which resulted in the conviction that their situation would be more tolerable in the position of a military colony, acting as a barrier between the Carolinians and their troublesome neighbors, than in the moral contamination and physical miseries of prison life. The class of persons whom he designed to transplant to America were not wicked criminals, but chiefly insolvent debtors. Oglethorpe also proposed to make the new colony an asylum for the persecuted Protestants of Germany and other Continental states, and in this religious idea he included the pious thought of spiritual benefit to the Indian tribes. The Earl of Shaftesbury (the fourth bearing that title) and other influential men warmly espoused the scheme, and a general enthusiasm upon the subject soon pervaded the nation. A royal charter was obtained in 1732 for twenty-one years, **27** large sums were subscribed by individuals; and in the course of two years, Parliament voted one hundred and eighty thousand dollars in support of the scheme. **28**

Oglethorpe volunteered to act as governor of the new colony, and to accompany the settlers to their destination. Accordingly, in November, 1732, he embarked with one hundred and twenty emigrants, and in fifty-seven days arrived off the bar of Charleston. He was warmly welcomed by the Carolinians, and on the thirteenth of January he sailed for Port Royal. While the colonists were landing, Oglethorpe, with a few followers, proceeded southward, ascended the Savannah River to the high bluff, and there selected a spot for a city, the capital of the future state. With the Yamacraw Indians, half a mile from this bluff, dwelt Tomo Chichi, the grand sachem of the Indian confederacy of that region. Oglethorpe and the chief both desired friendly relations; and when the former invited the latter to his tent, Tomo Chichi came, bearing in his hand a small buffalo skin, appropriately ornamented, and addressed Oglethorpe in eloquent and conciliatory terms. **30** Friendly relations were established, and on the twelfth of February (1732) the little band of settlers came from Port Royal and landed at the site of the future city of Savannah.

For almost a year the governor lived under a tent stretched upon pine boughs, while the streets of the town were laid out, and the people built their houses of timber, each twenty-four by sixteen feet in size. In May following, a treaty with the Indian chiefs of the country was held; and on the first of June, it was signed, by which the English obtained sovereignty over the lands of the Creek nation, as far south as the St. John's, in Florida. Such was the beginning of one of the original thirteen states of our confederacy.

Within eight years after the founding of Savannah, twenty-five hundred emigrants had been sent out to Georgia, at an expense of four hundred thousand dollars. **31** Among these were one hundred and fifty Highlanders, well disciplined in military tactics, who were of essential service to Oglethorpe. Very strict moral regulations were adopted; **32** lots of land, twenty-five acres each, were granted to men for military services, and every care was exercised to make the settlers comfortable. Yet discontent soon prevailed, for they saw the Carolinians growing rich by traffic in negroes; they also saw them prosper commercially by trade with the West Indies. They complained of the Wesleyans as too rigid, and these pious Methodists left the colony and returned home. Still, prosperity did not smile upon the settlers, and a failure of the scheme was anticipated.

Oglethorpe, who went to England in 1734, returned in 1736, with three hundred emigrants. A storm was gathering upon the southern frontier of his domain. The Spaniards at St. Augustine regarded the rising state with jealousy, and as a war between England and Spain was anticipated, vigilance was necessary. Oglethorpe resolved to maintain the claim of Great Britain south to the banks of the St. John's, and the

Ruins of Oglethorpe's Barracks at Frederica

Highlanders, settled at Darien, volunteered to aid him. With a few followers, he hastened in a scout-boat to St. Simon's Island, where he laid the foundations of Frederica, and upon the bluff near by he constructed a fort of *tabby*, **33** the ruins of which may still be seen there. He also caused forts to be erected at Augusta, Darien, on Cumberland Island, and near the mouth of the St. Mary's and St. John's. Perceiving these hostile preparations, the Spanish authorities at St. Augustine sent commissioners to confer with Oglethorpe. They demanded the evacuation of the whole of Georgia, and even of the region north of the Savannah to St. Helena Sound. This demand was accompanied by a menace of war in the event of non-compliance. Thus matters stood for several months.

In the winter of 1736-7, Oglethorpe again went to England, where he received the commission of brigadier general, with a command extending over South Carolina as well as Georgia. There he remained a year and a half, when he returned to his colony with a regiment of six hundred men to act against the Spaniards. England declared war against Spain in the latter part of 1739, and Oglethorpe immediately planned an expedition against St. Augustine. The St. Mary's was then considered (as it remains) the boundary between Georgia and Florida. Over that line Oglethorpe marched in May, 1740, with four hundred of his regiment, some Carolinians, and a large body of friendly Indians. He captured a Spanish fort within twenty-five miles of St. Augustine. A small fortress, within two miles of that place, was surrendered on his approach, but a summons to give up the town was answered by defiant words. The invaders maintained a siege for some time, when the arrival of re-enforcements for the garrison, and the prevalence of sickness in the camp, obliged them to withdraw and return to Savannah in July 1740.

In 1742, the Spaniards invaded Georgia. A fleet of thirty-six sail, with more than three thousand troops from Havana and St. Augustine, entered the harbor of St. Simons on July 16, 1742, and a little above the town of the same name, erected a battery of twenty guns. Oglethorpe, with eight hundred men, exclusive of Indians, was then on the island. He withdrew to his fort at Frederica, and anxiously awaited re-enforcements from Carolina. He skirmished successfully with attacking parties, and arranged for a night assault upon the enemy's battery. A deserter (a French soldier) defeated his plan; but the sagacity of Oglethorpe used the miscreant's agency to his subsequent advantage, by bribing a Spanish prisoner to carry a letter to the deserter, containing information that a British fleet was about to attack St. Augustine. Of course the letter was handed to the Spanish commander, who arrested the Frenchman as a spy. The intelligence contained in Oglethorpe's letter alarmed the garrison, and the Spaniards determined to assail the English immediately, and then return to St. Augustine as speedily as possible. On their march to the attack of Frederica, they fell into an ambuscade. Great slaughter ensued, and they retreated precipitately. The place of conflict is called Bloody Marsh to this day. On their retreat, by water, they attacked Fort William, at the southern extremity of Cumberland Island, but were repulsed with loss. The expedition was disastrous to the Spaniards in every particular, and the commander was tried by a court-martial at Havana, and dismissed from the service in disgrace.

After ten years of service in and for the colony of Georgia, Oglethorpe returned to England, and his feet never again pressed the soil of America. His rule had been chiefly military. A civil government was now established (1743), under the control of a president and council, who were instructed to administer it as the trustees should dictate. Prosperity did not yet gladden the settlers, and the colony had a sickly existence. At length the moral and commercial restrictions began to be evaded; slaves were brought from Carolina, and hired first for a few years, and then for a hundred years, or during life. This was equivalent to a purchase, and was so considered by the parties; for a sum, equal to the value of the slave, was paid in advance. Finally, slave ships came directly to Savannah from Africa; slave labor was generally introduced, and Georgia, like Carolina, became a planting state. In 1752, the trustees, wearied with the complaints of the colonists, resigned the charter into the hands of the king, and from that period until the war of the Revolution, Georgia was a royal province.35 When the treaty of Paris in 1763 guarantied, as far as possible, general peace in America, the province, for the first time, began to flourish and take an important place among the Anglo-American colonies; and in the hostilities against the Indians on the frontiers, its people performed their part well in furnishing provisions and men for the armies.

The inhabitants of Georgia first began to feel the hand of British taxation, when, in 1767, Governor Wright communicated his instructions from the king to require implicit obedience to the Mutiny Act. **36** They were compelled to acquiesce, but it was with reluctance. They had not realized the practical iniquity of the Stamp Act; and when, in 1768, the Assembly at Savannah appointed Dr. Franklin an agent to attend to the interests of the colony in Great Britain, they had no formal special complaint to make, nor difficulties with government for him to adjust. They generally instructed him to use efforts to have the acts of Parliament repealed, which were offensive to all the colonies. To a circular letter from the speaker of the Massachusetts Assembly (1768), proposing a union of the colonies, an answer of approval was returned. In February 1770, the Legislature spoke out boldly against the oppressive acts of the mother country, by publishing a Declaration of Rights, similar in sentiment to that of the "Stamp Act congress" at New York. Governor Wright was displeased, and viewing the progress of revolutionary principles within his province with concern, he went to England (1771) to confer with ministers. He remained there about a year and a half. During his absence, James Habersham, president of the council, exercised executive functions.

The Republicans of Georgia had become numerous in 1773, and committees of correspondence were early formed, and acted efficiently. A meeting of the friends of liberty was called in Savannah in the autumn of that year, but Sir James Wright, supported by a train of civil officers, prevented the proposed public expression of opinion. The wealthy feared loss of property by Revolutionary movements, while the timid trembled at the thought of resistance to royal government. Selfishness and fear kept the people comparatively quiet for a while. In the mean time, a powerful Tory party was organizing in South Carolina and in Georgia, and emissaries were sent by the governors of these provinces among the Indians on the frontiers, to prepare them to lift the hatchet and go out upon the war-path against the white people, if rebellion should ensue. Such was the condition of Georgia when called upon to appoint representatives in the Continental Congress, to be held at Philadelphia in 1774. Half encircled by fierce savages, and pressed down by the heel of strongly-supported royal power in their midst, the Republicans needed stout hearts and unbending resolution. These they possessed; and in the midst of difficulties they were bold, and adopted measures of co-operation with the other colonies in resistance to tyranny.

On the fourteenth of July (1774), the Sons of Liberty were requested to assemble at the "liberty pole at Tondee's tavern, **37** in Savannah, on Wednesday, the twenty-seventh instant, in order that public matters may be taken under consideration, and such other *constitutional measures* pursued as may then appear most eligible."**38** The call was signed by Noble W. Jones (who in 1780 was a prisoner in Charleston), Archibald Bullock, John Houstoun, and George Walton. A meeting was accordingly held at the watch-house in Savannah on July 27, 1774, where letters from Northern committees were read, and a committee to draft resolutions was appointed.**39** These proceedings were published, and the governor, alarmed at the progress of rebellion around him, issued a countervailing proclamation in August. He called upon the people to discountenance these seditious men and measures, and menaced the disobedient with the penalties of stern British law.

On the tenth of August another meeting was held, when it was resolved to concur with their sister colonies in acts of resistance to oppression. After strongly condemning the Boston Port Bill, they appointed a committee to receive subscriptions for the suffering people of that city, and within a few hours after the adjournment of the meeting, five hundred and seventy-five barrels of rice were contributed and shipped for Massachusetts. The governor assembled his friends at the court-house a few days afterward, and their disapprobation of the conduct of the Republicans was expressed in strong terms. Agents were sent throughout the province to obtain the signatures of the people to a printed denunciation of the Whigs; and, by means of menaces and promises, an apparent majority of the inhabitants declared in favor of royal rule. **40** So powerfully did the tide of opposition against the Whigs flow for a while, that they did not appoint delegates to the Continental Congress, which convened in Philadelphia in September, and Georgia was not represented in that first Federal Republican council, **41** yet they heartily approved of the measure, and by words and actions nobly responded to that first great resolution, adopted by the Continental Congress on the eighth of October, 1774, **42** which approved of the resistance of Massachusetts.

The Republicans continued to assemble during the winter of 1774-5, and in May following they determined to anticipate an act on the part of Governor Wright similar to that of Gage at Boston.

Accordingly, on the night of the eleventh of May (1775), six of the members of the Council of Safety, **43** and others, broke open the magazine, **44** took out the powder, sent a portion of it to Beaufort, South Carolina, and concealed the remainder in their garrets and cellars. The governor offered a reward of one hundred and fifty pounds sterling for the apprehension of the offenders, but the secret was never revealed till the patriots used the powder in defense of their liberties.

Savannah and Vicinity

On the first of June, Governor Wright and the Loyalists of Savannah prepared to celebrate the king's birth-day. On the night of the second, some of the leading Whigs spiked the cannon on the battery, and hurled them to the bottom of the bluff. Nineteen days afterward, a meeting was called for the purpose of choosing a committee to enforce the requirements of the *American Association*, put forth by the Congress of 1774. **45** The first victim to his temerity in opposing the operations of the committee was a man named Hopkins. He ridiculed the Whigs, and they, in turn, gave him a coat of tar and feathers, and paraded him in a cart through the town for four or five hours.

About this time, a letter from Governor Wright to General Gage was intercepted by the vigilant Whigs of Charleston. It contained a request for Gage to send some British troops to suppress the rebellious spirit of the Georgians. **46** The Republicans were exceedingly indignant; and when, a day or two afterward, it was known that Captain Maitland had arrived at Tybee Island, at the mouth of the Savannah, with thirteen thousand pounds of powder and other articles for the British and Indians, it was determined to seize the vessel. The Georgia Assembly was then in session. **47** The leading Whigs approved of the enterprise, and on the night of the tenth of July, thirty volunteers, under commodore Bowen and Colonel Joseph Habersham, embarked in two boats, took possession of the ship, discharged the crew, and placed the powder in the magazine in Savannah, except five thousand pounds, which they sent to the army then investing Boston, under General Washington. **48** The Indian hostilities, which occurred at this time on the western frontiers, we have considered in preceding chapters.

The spirit of resistance waxed stronger and stronger during the autumn of 1775. In January, 1776, it assumed a form of strength and determination hitherto unknown in Georgia. On the eighteenth of that month, Colonel Joseph Habersham, **49** who was a member of the Assembly, raised a party of volunteers, took Governor Wright a prisoner, and paroled him to his own house, **50** before which a sentinel was placed, and forbid all intercourse between him and persons inimical to the Republican cause. On the night of the eleventh of February 1776, during a storm, the governor escaped from a back window of his house, with John Muloyne, and went down the river five miles, to Bonaventure, the residence of that gentleman. There a boat and crew were waiting for him, and he was conveyed to Tybee Sound, and took shelter on board the armed ship Scarborough.

Royal rule had now actually ceased in Georgia, and the Assembly assumed governmental powers. They elected new delegates to the Continental Congress (1776); **51** passed a resolution to raise a battalion of Continental troops (February 4); **52** and issued bills of credit in the form of certificates, and ordered them to be received at par in payment of debts and for merchandise.

Governor Wright wrote a letter to the Assembly (February 13) very conciliatory in its tone, but receiving no answer, he resolved to allow the armed vessels at the mouth of the river to force their way to the town, and procure such supplies as they needed. Eleven merchant vessels, laden with rice, were then at Savannah ready to sail. These were seized by the war ships, and Majors Maitland and Grant landed, with a considerable force, upon Hutchinson's Island, opposite Savannah, preparatory to an attack upon the town on March 6, 1776. The patriots were on the alert, and sent a flag to Maitland, warning him to desist. This flag was detained, and another was fired upon. Further parley was deemed unnecessary, and the next day two merchant vessels, lying in the stream, were set on fire by the patriots. Floating down to the one containing Maitland and Grant, with their men, great consternation was produced. Some of the soldiers jumped overboard and swam ashore; some stuck in the mud, and many lost their fire-arms; while the officers escaped in boats to Hutchinson's Island. At this critical moment, four hundred Carolinians, under Colonel Bull, arrived, and aided the Georgians in repulsing the assailants. Three of the merchant vessels were burned, six were dismantled, and two escaped to sea.

Thebreach between the Whigs and Tories was now too wide to be closed, and the line was very distinctly drawn by stringent measures on the part of the former. **53** These tended to winnow the chaff from the wheat, and many Tories, possessed of no property, left Georgia and took refuge in East Florida, where Governor Tonyn was actively engaged in fitting out privateers to prey upon the infant commerce of the Southern colonists, and to ravage their coasts. The Tories there organized under the title of the *Florida Rangers*, and were led by Thomas Brown, the Augusta Loyalist, who afterward commanded the garrison at that place. A fort built by Governor Wright's brother, on the St. Mary's, was their place of rendezvous, whence they went out and levied terrible contributions, in the way of plunder, upon the people of Southern Georgia, who were thinly scattered over the country.

The war had now fairly commenced, and the flame of patriotism which burned so brightly at the North was not less intense in Georgia. The Declaration of Independence was received in Savannah on August 10, 1776 with great joy. **54** Pursuant to the recommendation of the Continental Congress, the people turned their attention to the organization of civil government, upon the basis of independence, and in strengthening their military power. To weaken the British and Tories in the South, an expedition against St. Augustine (then in possession of the English) was planned, and General Charles Lee, then at Charleston, was invited to take the command of troops that might be sent. Lee perceived the advantages to be derived from such a measure, and acquiescing, he immediately ordered Brigadier Robert Howe to proceed to Savannah with troops. Howe had marched as far as Sunbury, at the mouth of the Midway River (August 1776), when sickness, want of artillery and other necessaries for the campaign, caused Lee to abandon the enterprise. The effect of this movement was disastrous to the Whigs. The Tories gained confidence; and on the seventh day of February, 1777, they attacked Fort M'Intosh. **55** The garrison was commanded by Captain Richard Winn, of South Carolina. After holding out for two days, he was obliged to surrender. The officers and privates of the garrison were all paroled except two young officers, who were taken to St. Augustine and kept as hostages.

During the autumn of 1776, a convention was held in Savannah to form a state Constitution. It was adopted on the 5th of February following (1777), and Button Gwinnett, one of the signers of the Declaration of Independence, was chosen president of the council, an office equivalent in its functions to that of governor. In consequence of military rivalry, a serious difficulty arose between Gwinnett and Colonel M'Intosh, **56** who had just been elected brigadier general of the Georgia Continental troops. A duel ensued, when both were wounded, each with a bullet in the thigh. M'Intosh recovered; Gwinnett died. M'Intosh was tried for murder, at the instance of Gwinnett's friends, and was acquitted. This quarrel produced a serious local agitation, which at one time menaced the Republican stability of Georgia, and the true friends of the cause were alarmed. To allay party feeling, General M'Intosh consented to accept of a station at the North; and Washington appointed him commander-in-chief of the Western Department, with his head-quarters at Pittsburg, where we have already met him.

During the summer and autumn of 1777, Colonels Elbert, Scriven, Baker, and others, attempted to dislodge the Tories from East Florida, and several skirmishes occurred. These expeditions were fruitless of advantage to the patriots, and much suffering ensued. Frederica was attacked by the enemy; some Americans and negroes were captured, and considerable property was carried off. Often, during the autumn, predatory excursions were made upon the southern frontiers of Georgia, the marauders frequently penetrating as far as the Alatamaha and even beyond, and the settlements suffered terribly.

During the winter and spring of 1778, the opponents of the new government became formidable, and indications of an invasion of Georgia, from Florida and from the Indian territory in the West, was perceived. Tories gathered at Ninety-Six, and crossed the Savannah, while those of Florida, joined by the Indians, continued to scatter desolation along the southern frontier. Robert Howe, **57** of North Carolina, now promoted to the rank of major general, was in the chief command of the Southern army, and favored the yet cherished design to march into Florida and disperse the Loyalists. In fact, this measure had become a chief desideratum, for the gathering storm on the frontier of that state was pregnant with evil omens for the whole South. The Loyalists were gaining strength on the St. Mary's, St. John's, and at Pensacola, and re-enforcements of British troops were expected at St. Augustine (April 1778). Howe moved his head-quarters from Charleston to Savannah. His regulars, who were in a condition to take the field, did not exceed five hundred and fifty men. These were joined by the commands of Colonels C. C. Pinckney, Bull, and Williamson. Governor Houstoun, of Georgia, who was requested to furnish three hundred and fifty militia, cheerfully complied. Thus prepared, Howe marched toward the Alatamaha, when he was informed that a body of British regulars, under General Augustine Prevost, a large force of Loyalists, under Colonel Brown, and numerous Indians, were moving toward the St. Mary's for the purpose of invading Georgia. Already Colonel Elbert had been victorious at Frederica, **58** and Howe felt certain of success, when, on the twentieth of May (1778), he reached the Alatamaha, and learned how rumors of his expedition had alarmed the Tories of East Florida. His enterprise was exceedingly popular, and the sympathy of the whole Southern people, who were favorable to Republicanism, was with him. With scanty supplies, he pushed forward in the midst of many difficulties, to Fort Tonyn, on the St. Mary's by June 1778, which the enemy abandoned and partly demolished on his approach. Here he ordered a general rendezvous of all the troops, and of the galleys, under Commodore Bowen, preparatory to making an assault upon St. Augustine.

On the day of his arrival at Fort Tonyn, Howe was informed that twelve hundred men had marched from St. Augustine for the St. John's, and that two galleys, laden with twenty-four pounders, had been sent to the mouth of that river, to co-operate with the land force in opposing the Americans. He was also informed by a deserter that the whole force of the enemy was about fifteen hundred men fit for duty. Sudden, united, and energetic action was now necessary, but Howe experienced the contrary on the part of his compatriots. The governor of Georgia was at the head of his own militia, and refused to be commanded by Howe; Colonel Williamson (the imputed traitor) took the same course with his volunteers; and Commodore Bowen would not be governed by any land officer. The necessary consequence was tardy, divided, and inefficient operations.

Sickness soon prostrated almost one half of the troops, for, unprovided with sufficient tents, they slept exposed to the deadly malaria of the night air among the swamps; and Howe clearly perceived that in future movements failure must result, unless the forces could be united under one commander. He called a council of war, and ascertained that Houstoun would not be governed by another, and that the army was rapidly melting away. A retreat was unanimously agreed upon. Pinckney and the remains of his command returned by water to Charleston, while Howe, with the remnants of his force, reduced by sickness and death from eleven hundred to three hundred and fifty, returned to Savannah by land. Thus ended an expedition upon which the South had placed great reliance. Howe was much censured, but the blame should properly rest upon those who, by proud assumption of separate commands, retarded his movements and weakened his power. No expedition was ever successful with several commanders.

The British, emboldened by this second failure of the Americans to invade Florida, and counting largely upon the depressing influence it would have upon the patriots, hastened to invade Georgia in turn. Savannah was the chief point of attack. It was arranged that a naval force, with land troops from the North, should enter the river and invest the city; while General Prevost, who commanded in East Florida, should march toward the same point from St. Augustine, with his whole motley band of regulars, Tories, and Indians, to awe the people in that direction, and by preliminary expeditions weaken the Americans. **59** Hitherto the British arms had been chiefly directed against the Northern and Middle States, but with little effect. The patriots had steadily maintained their ground, and the area actually out of possession of the Americans was very small. Sir Henry Clinton was master of New York city, but almost every where else the Americans held possession. To the South he looked for easier and more extensive conquests; and against Savannah, the apparently weakest point, he directed his first operations. Lieutenant-colonel Campbell, an efficient and reliable officer, sailed from Sandy Hook on the twenty-seventh of November (1778), with more than two thousand land troops, **60** covered by a small squadron, under Commodore Parker. The fleet arrived at Tybee Island (see map page 192), near the mouth of the Savannah, on the twenty-third of December. Six days afterward, the vessels and transports had crossed the bar, and the troops were landed at daybreak on

December 29, without much opposition, three miles below the town, above Five-fathom Hole, opposite Brewton's Hill. **61**

General Howe, whose army was now augmented to a little less than seven hundred men, was at Sunbury when intelligence was received at Savannah of the approach of the British fleet. Governor Houstoun immediately sent an express to Howe with the information. At the same time, another messenger arrived at Sunbury from the South, informing Howe that General Prevost, with all his force, was on his way from St. Augustine to invade Georgia. All was alarm and confusion when the latter intelligence reached Savannah. The governor sent the public records to Purysburg for safety, from whence they were afterward carried to Charleston. The small battery on the eastern extremity of the city was strengthened, and the people aided the soldiers in casting up intrenchments. **62**

Howe hastened to his camp at Savannah to prepare for the invasion. His little army was encamped southeast of the town, near the eastern extremity of the present remains of the French works. There he anxiously awaited promised re-enforcements from South Carolina, under General Lincoln. The militia from the surrounding country came in very slowly, day after day; and on the morning of the battle which ensued, his whole force was about nine hundred men. Believing the British army to be really weaker than it appeared, he resolved to defend the town; and when, on the morning of the twenty-eighth, the fleet appeared at Five-fathom Hole, where Fort Jackson now is, he prepared for battle. On that morning, Colonel Elbert, perceiving the necessity of keeping the enemy from the advantageous position of Brewton's Hill, offered to defend it with his regiment; but Howe, believing they would march immediately toward the town, rejected the proposition. He placed his center at the head of the causeway; his left, under Colonel Elbert, fronted the rice-fields, and was flanked by the river; and his right, commanded by Colonel Isaac Huger, covered the morass in front, and was flanked by the wooded swamp and one hundred Georgia militia, under Colonel George Walton. Having made this disposition, he detached Captain J. C. Smith, of South Carolina, to occupy and defend Brewton's Hill. His little force proved inadequate; and soon after landing, the British took possession of that eminence. Howe now perceived the superiority of the British force, and at ten o'clock in the morning called a council of war to consider the expediency of abandoning the town. It was then too late to deliberate, for the enemy were forming for attack. It was resolved first to fight, and then to retreat, if necessary.

After Campbell had formed his army on Brewton's Hill, he moved forward, and took a position within eight hundred yards of the American front, where he maneuvered in a manner to excite the belief that he intended to attack the center and left. This was at three o'clock in the afternoon. This movement was only a diversion in favor of a body of infantry and New York volunteers, commanded by Sir James Baird, who, under the guidance of an old negro named Quamino Dolly, withdrew unperceived, and by a by-path through the swamp at the South, were gaining the American rear. To this by-path Walton had called Howe's attention in the morning, but knowing its obscurity, the general did not think it worthy of regard. Sir James and his party reached the White Bluff road unperceived. and, pressing forward, attacked Walton's Georgia brigade on flank and rear. Walton was wounded and taken prisoner, and such was the fate of a large portion of his command. At the same moment Campbell moved forward and attacked the Americans in front. The patriot line was soon broken, and, perceiving the growing panic and confusion, Howe ordered a retreat over the causeway across Musgrove's Swamp, west of the town. To that point Colonel Roberts, in obedience to early orders, if the contingency should occur, hastened with the artillery, to cover the retreat. Already the enemy was there in force to dispute the passage. By great exertions, the American center gained the causeway and escaped without loss. The right flank also retreated across, but suffered from an oblique enfilading fire; while to Colonel Elbert, with the left, the passage was closed after a severe conflict. He and his troops attempted to escape by the rice-fields, but it being high water in the creek, none but those who could swim succeeded, and these lost their guns and accoutrements. Many were drowned, and the remainder were taken prisoners. While the British were pursuing the Americans through the town toward Musgrove's Creek, many citizens, some of whom had not been in the battle, were bayoneted in the streets; but when the action was over, life and property were spared. Campbell's humanity and generosity as a man were equal to his skill and bravery as a soldier, and the active terrors of war in the city ceased with the battle. **63** Yet deep sadness brooded over Savannah that night, for many bereaved ones wept in bitter anguish over relatives, slain or mortally wounded. **64** Those few who escaped across Musgrove's Swamp, retreated up the Savannah and joined Howe, who, with the center, fled as far as Cherokee Hill, eight miles distant, and halted. The whole fugitive force then pushed up the Savannah to Zubley's Ferry, where they crossed into South Carolina. Howe saved three field-pieces in his flight. **65**

When Lieutenant-colonel Campbell had secured his prize by garrisoning the fort at Savannah, and by other measures for defense, he prepared to march against Sunbury, the only post of any consequence now left to the Americans, near the Georgia sea-board. He issued orders to the commanders of detachments in the lower part of the state to treat the people leniently, and by proclamation he invited them to join the British standard. These measures had their desired effect, and timid hundreds, seeing the state under the heel of British power, proclaimed their loyalty, and rallied beneath the banner of St. George.

While arranging for his departure southward, Campbell received intelligence that the garrison at Sunbury had surrendered to General Prevost. That officer had left St. Augustine with about two thousand men (including Indians) and several pieces of artillery, on the day when Campbell reached Tybee Island. One division took a land route, the other proceeded in armed boats. They reached the vicinity of Sunbury on the sixth of January, and proceeded to attack the fort. The garrison consisted of about two hundred Continental troops and militia, under Major Lane, who, when Prevost demanded an unconditional surrender on the morning of the ninth, promptly refused compliance. Prevost then placed his cannon in battery and opened upon the fort. Lane soon perceived the folly of resistance, and after considerable parleying he surrendered. The spoils of victory were twenty-four pieces of artillery, with ammunition and provisions; and the men of the garrison were made prisoners of war. The Americans lost one captain and three privates killed, and seven wounded. The British loss was one private killed and three wounded. Two American galleys in the river were taken by their crews to Assabaw Island, stranded, and burned. The crews escaped in a sloop, but, while on their way to Charleston, were captured and carried prisoners to Savannah.

The fall of Sunbury was the death-blow to Republican power in East Georgia, and the conquest of the whole state now appeared an easy thing. The march of Campbell to Augusta, under the direction of Prevost, who proceeded from Sunbury to Savannah; the establishment of military posts in the interior, and the subsequent battle at Brier Creek, we have already considered. Previous to these events, and soon after the failure of Howe's summer campaign against East Florida, General Lincoln **66** had been appointed to the command in the Southern department on September 26, 1778, and Howe was ordered to the North, where we find him in the summer of 1779, at Verplanck's Point. **67**

Several minor expeditions were planned and executed both by Prevost and Lincoln, but they had little effect. The latter arrived at Purysburg, upon the Savannah, on the third of January, 1779, and established his head-quarters there. His force consisted of about twenty-five hundred effective men, and it continually augmented by recruits from the militia. The marches and counter marches of these generals in attempts to foil each other will be noticed while considering the attack upon Charleston in May following, and its immediate antecedent events. **68**

On the twentieth of July (1779), Sir James Wright returned from England and resumed the government of Georgia. It had been under military rule since the fall of Savannah. Governor Wright did not long remain in quiet, for the strong arm of our French ally held the falchion over the head of British power in the South. Early in September, the Count D'Estaing, with twenty ships of the line and eleven frigates, having on board six thousand soldiers, suddenly appeared off the Southern coasts. He had battled successfully with Admiral Byron in the West Indies, and now he came to assist in driving the British out of the Southern States. So sudden was his appearance off Tybee Island on September 3, 1779 that four British vessels fell into his hands without a contest. A plan was soon arranged between Lincoln and D'Estaing to besiege Savannah. The latter urged the necessity of early departure from our coast as a reason for prompt action, and he entreated Lincoln to press forward with his army as rapidly as possible.

From the moment when the French fleet appeared off Tybee, Prevost felt uneasy. He recalled his detachments from the advanced posts, and directed Colonel Maitland, who, with eight hundred men, was stationed at Beaufort, to be in readiness to leave that post. He began in earnest to strengthen the fortifications of the city; and Colonel Moncrief, the talented chief of the engineers, pressed into his service every hand not otherwise employed, including three hundred negroes collected from the neighboring plantations. Thirteen redoubts and fifteen batteries, with lines of communication, were speedily completed, with strong *abatis* in front. Upon these batteries seventy-six pieces of cannon were placed, of six, nine, and eighteen pounds caliber. These were manned by seamen from the vessels of war in the harbor. Several field-pieces were placed in reserve, to be used at any required point at a moment's warning, and intrenchments were opened to cover the reserved troops and artillery.

Pulaski's Seal.

On the evening of the fourth of September the French fleet disappeared, and Prevost rejoiced in the belief that Savannah was not its destination. Still, he continued his preparations for attack. The works on Tybee Island were strengthened, and the garrison there was increased by one hundred infantry under Captain Moncrief. On the sixth the fleet reappeared with increased force; and on the ninth it anchored off Tybee Island, and landed some troops on the south side of it. Moncrief, perceiving resistance to be useless, spiked the guns, embarked the troops, and fled to Savannah. The English shipping near Tybee sailed up to Five Fathom Hole, and the whole British land force in Georgia was now concentrated at Savannah. The next day all the cannons of the armed vessels, except a few which were left to defend the channel, were brought on shore and placed in battery. Every thing was now ready for an attack.

Lincoln marched from Charleston to Zubley's Ferry, where he concentrated his troops on the twelfth of September. Count Pulaski, **69** with his legion, and General M'Intosh, with his command, were dispatched toward Savannah, a little in advance of the main army, to attack the British outposts. Both parties had several skirmishes with the enemy before they reached the French army, already landed at Beaulieu, or Beuley. This junction effected, M'Intosh returned to Miller's plantation, three miles from Savannah, where Lincoln, with the main army, arrived on the sixteenth, and made his head-quarters.

While Lincoln and his force were approaching, the French effected a landing at Beuley and Thunderbolt, without opposition. M'Intosh urged D'Estaing to make an immediate attack upon the British

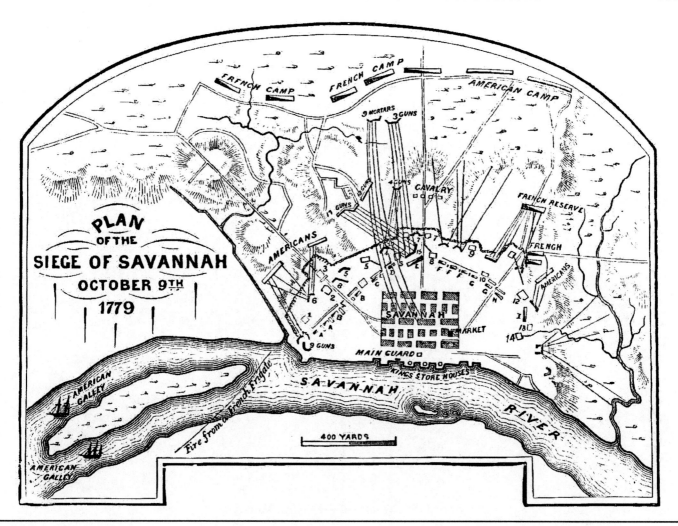

Explanation of the Plan. – 1, Georgia volunteers, under Major Wright. 2, Picket of the 71st. 3, First battalion of Delancey's corps, under Lieutenant-colonel Cruger. 4, Georgia militia. 5, Third battalion Jersey volunteers, under Lieutenant-colonel Allen. 6, Georgia militia. 7, Picket of the line and armed negroes. 8, General's quarters; convalescents of the line. 9, South Carolina Royalists. 10, Georgia militia and detachment of the fourth battalion of the 60th, Lieutenant-governor Graham. 11, Fourth battalion 60th dismounted dragoons and South Carolina Royalists, Captain Taws. 12, North Carolina Loyalists, Lieutenant-colonel Hamilton, Governor Sir James Wright. 13, 14, King's rangers, Lieutenant-colonel Brown. A, First battalion of the 71st, Major M'Arthur. B, Regiment of Trombach. C, Second battalion Delancey's corps, Lieutenant-colonel Delancey. D, New York volunteers, Major Sheridan. E, Light infantry, Major Graham. F, Weisenbach's regiment. G, Second battalion 71st, Major M'Donald. H, 60th Grenadiers, three companies and one of marines, Lieutenant-colonel Glazier, I, North Carolina Loyalists, under Colonel Maitland. The working of the artillery during the siege was under the direction of Captain Charlton.

This map is copied from one in Stedman's History, drawn under the direction of Colonel Moncrief. Neither the French nor Americans made any drawings, and hence we are unable to give the positions of the various parts of the combined armies, in detail.

The city extended, at the time of the siege, on the west to the present Jefferson Street, on the east to Lincoln Street, on the South to South Broad Street, and contained six squares and twelve streets. There were about four hundred and thirty houses in the city.

works. D'Estaing would not listen, but advanced within three miles of Savannah on September 16, 1779, and demanded an unconditional surrender to the King of France. Prevost refused to listen to any summons which did not contain definite provisions, and asked for a truce until the next day to consider the subject. This was granted by D'Estaing, and, in the mean while twelve hundred white men and negroes were employed in strengthening the fortifications, and mounting additional ordnance. This truce Lincoln at once perceived was fatal to the success of the besiegers, for he had ascertained that Maitland, with eight hundred men, was on his way from Beaufort, to re-enforce Prevost, and that his arrival within twenty-four hours was the object hoped to be gained by a truce for that length of time. Such proved to be the fact; Maitland, under cover of a fog, eluded the vigilance of the French cruisers, and entered the town on the afternoon of the seventeenth. **70** His arrival gave Prevost courage, and toward evening he sent a note to D'Estaing bearing a positive refusal to capitulate. The golden opportunity was now lost to the combined armies. **71**

It was now perceived that the town must be taken by regular approaches, and not by assault. To that

View of the Remains of the French Works. 72

end all energy was directed. The heavy ordnance and stores were brought up from the landing-place of the French, and on the morning of September 23, 1779, the combined armies broke ground. The French frigates, at the same time, moved up to the sunken vessels within gunshot of the town, and compelled the British ships to take shelter under the guns of the battery. Night and day the besiegers applied the spade, and so vigorously was the work prosecuted, that in the course of twelve days fifty-three pieces of battery cannon and fourteen mortars were mounted. Prevost, cautious and skillful, did not waste his strength in opposing the progress of the besiegers by sorties, but reserved all for the decisive moment. During the twelve days, only two sorties were made; one under Major Graham (Sept. 24), and the other under Major M'Arthur (Sept. 27). Several were killed on each occasion, but the general operations were not affected.

On the morning of the fourth of October, the batteries being all completed and manned, a terrible cannonade and bombardment was opened upon the British works and the town. The French frigate Truite also opened a cannonade from the water. Houses were shattered, some women and children were killed or maimed, and terror reigned supreme. Families took refuge in the cellars, and in many a frame the seeds of mortal disease were planted while in those damp abodes during the siege. There was no safety in the streets, for a moment. Day and night an incessant cannonade was kept up from the fourth until the ninth; but, while many houses were injured, not much impression was made upon the British works. Slowly but surely the sappers and miners approached the batteries and redoubts. The beleaguered began to be alarmed, for their guns made very little impression upon the works or camp of the combined armies, and the hope that Admiral Byron would follow and attack D'Estaing's vessels, lying off Tybee, faded away.

Another promised victory was now before the besiegers, and almost within their grasp, when D'Estaing became impatient. He feared the autumn storms, and the British fleet which rumor said was approaching. A council was held, and when his engineers informed him that it would require ten days more to reach the British lines by trenches, he informed Lincoln that the siege must be raised forthwith, or an attempt be made to carry the place by storm. The latter alternative was chosen, and the work began on the morning of the following day (Oct. 9). To facilitate it, the *abatis* were set on fire that afternoon by the brave Major L'Enfant and five men, while exposed to heavy volleys of musketry from the garrison, but the dampness of the air checked the flames and prevented the green wood from burning.

Just before dawn on the morning of the ninth, about four thousand five hundred men of the combined armies moved to the assault in the midst of a dense fog, and under cover of a heavy fire from all the batteries.73 They advanced in three columns, the principal one commanded by D'Estaing in person, assisted by General Lincoln; another main column by Count Dillon. The first was directed against the Spring Hill redoubt **74** (between 11 and 12 on the right side of the map); the second was to move silently along the edge of a swamp, pass the redoubts and batteries, and assail the rear and weakest point of the British lines, toward the river on the east; the third column, under General Isaac Huger, was to make a feigned attack in front, to attract attention from the other two. Fog and darkness allowed D'Estaing and Lincoln to approach very near the Spring Hill redoubt before they were discovered. Terrible was the conflict at this point just as the day dawned. The French column led to the assault, and were confronted by a blaze of musketry from the redoubt and by a cross-fire from the adjoining batteries. Whole ranks were mowed down like grass before the scythe. D'Estaing was wounded in the arm and thigh early in the action, and was carried to his camp. The Americans pressed forward: Lieutenant-colonel Laurens led the light troops on the left of the French, while General M'Intosh, with another column, passed the *abatis*, and entered the ditch north of the Spring Hill redoubt. Regardless of the destructive storm, the gallant troops leaped the ditch, and planted the crescent **75** and the *lily* upon the parapet. The gallant and accomplished Maitland commanded this right wing of the besieged, and was prepared for a vigorous assault. **76** His practiced eye at once perceived the peril of the garrison, if this lodgment should be sustained. He united the grenadiers and marines nearest the point of attack, and ordered Lieutenant-colonel Glazier to lead them to a recovery of the lost ground. Within five minutes after receiving this order, Glazier, at the head of his men, rushed to the parapet, and made a furious charge with the bayonet upon the worried ranks of the assailants. This blow by fresh and vigorous men, could not be withstood. The standards of France and of our Carolina were torn down, and the gallant men who had assisted in planting them there were pressed from the parapet into the ditch, and driven through the *abatis*.

While the carnage was occurring at the Spring Hill redoubt, Huger and Pulaski were endeavoring to force the enemy's works on different sides of the town; Huger, with his party, waded almost half a mile through rice-fields, and assailed the works on the east. They were received with a sharp fire of cannon and musketry, and, after losing twenty-eight men, retreated. Pulaski, at the same time, with about two hundred horsemen, endeavored to force his way into the town a little eastward of the Spring Hill redoubt. At the head of his troops he had passed the *abatis*, banner in hand, and was pressing forward, when a small cannon shot struck him in the groin, and he fell to the ground. His first lieutenant seized the banner, and for a few minutes kept the troops in action; but the iron hail from the seamen's batteries and the field artillery, traversing the columns of the assailants in all directions, compelled the whole force of the combined armies to yield, and they retreated to the camp. Back through the smoke, and over the bodies of the dead and dying, some of Pulaski's soldiers returned, found the expiring hero, and bore him from the field. Already the French had withdrawn, and the Continentals, under Lincoln, were retreating. At ten o'clock, after about five hours' hard fighting, the combined armies displayed a white flag, and asked a truce in order to bury the dead. Prevost granted four hours, and during that interval D'Estaing and Lincoln consulted in relation to further operations. The latter, although his force was greatly diminished by the action just closed, wished to continue the siege; but D'Estaing, whose loss had been heavy, resolved on immediate departure. **77** The siege was raised, and on the evening of the eighteent of October 1779 the combined armies withdrew; the Americans to Zubley's Ferry, and the French to Caustin's Bluff, whence they repaired to their ships at Tybee on October 20. Lincoln and his little army hastened to Charleston, wherw we shall meet them again, besieged and made prisoners of war. These events closed the campaigns in the South for that year. **78**

The result of the siege was a death-blow to the hopes of the South, and never since the beginning of hostilities had such gloom gathered over the prospects of the future, or so much real distress prevailed in Georgia. **79** Toward the sea-board every semblance of opposition to royal power was crushed, and only in the interior did the spirit of armed resistance appear. This increased during the following winter and spring, and at last disturbed the quiet of the royal forces in Savannah. These events, sometimes trivial in themselves, but important in the great chain of circumstances, are related in detail by M'Call, Stevens, White, and other chroniclers of the state. The most important we have already considered; let us now glance at the closing events of the war in Georgia.

When General Greene raised the siege of Ninety-Six, Major James Jackson **80** was appointed to the command of the garrison at Augusta. Greene also ordered a legionary corps (composed of part cavalry and part infantry) to be raised in Georgia, and appointed Major Jackson its colonel. As soon as it was organized, Jackson went out with it upon active service.

During the spring of 1781, Captain Howell, the Hyler of the Georgia Inlets, captured several British vessels lying in the bays and the mouths of the rivers on the coast, and finally compelled all that escaped to take refuge in the Savannah. Military matters in Georgia were very quiet during that summer; but in the autumn, the volunteers collected by Colonel Twiggs and his associates became so numerous, that he determined to attempt the capture of British outposts, and confine them within their lines at Savannah, until the arrival of Wayne, then marching from the North. Twiggs marched toward the sea-board, preceded by Jackson and his legion, who skirmished with patroles all the way to Ebenezer. Jackson attempted the surprise and capture of the garrison at Sunbury, but was unsuccessful, and returned, when he found Twiggs ready to march westward to quell the Indians and Tories then assembling on the frontier. Twiggs halted at Augusta on learning that Pickens had marched on the same errand (Jan. 1782). That brave partisan chastised the Indians severely. Every village and settlement eastward of the mountains was laid in ashes, and nothing but a heavy fall of snow prevented his crossing the great hills and spreading desolation over a wide extent of country.

General Wayne arrived early in February (1782), and established his head-quarters at Ebenezer. His force was inferior to that of the British in Savannah, then commanded by Brigadier-general Alured Clarke, **81** and he was obliged to content himself with petty warfare upon outposts and foraging parties, while watching an opportunity to attack Savannah at night. Fearing this, Clarke summoned his detachments to the city, to man the extensive fortifications. They came with provisions plundered from the inhabitants, and applying the torch on the way, left a broad track of desolation behind them.

General Clarke, perceiving the gathering strength of the Republicans, and that he was likely to be shut up within the narrow limits of his lines, sent for the Creeks and Cherokees to come in a body to his relief. They were yet smarting under the chastisement of Pickens, and hesitated. A party sent out to keep a way open to the city were attacked by Major Jackson. Colonel Brown was sent to their aid. He was attacked and defeated by Wayne, after a severe skirmish, but he retreated by by-paths in safety to Savannah.

On the night of the twenty-second of June (1782), three hundred Creek Indians, led by Guristersigo, a powerful warrior, approached Wayne's encampment. He intended to fall upon the American pickets, but ignorantly attacked the main body at three o'clock in the morning of June 23. The infantry seized their arms; the artillery hastened to their guns. Wayne was at a house a short distance from camp, when intelligence came that the whole British force from Savannah was upon him. He leaped into his saddle, rode to the aroused camp, and shouting, "Death or Victory!" ordered a bayonet charge. At that moment his horse was shot dead under him, and he saw his cannons seized by the savages. With sword in hand, at the head of Parker's infantry, he led to the recapture of his field-pieces. A terrible struggle ensued. Tomahawk and rifle were powerless against bayonets, and Guristersigo and seventeen of his chief warriors and white guides were slain. The Indians fled when they saw their leader fall, leaving behind them one hundred and seventeen pack-horses loaded with peltry. Wayne pursued the fugitives far into the forest, captured twelve of them, and at sunrise they were shot. The Americans lost only four killed and eight wounded.

In September (1782), Pickens and Clarke again chastised the Indians, and completely subdued them. Tired of the conflict, and fearful of the scourge which Pickens still held in his hand, they gladly made a treaty by which all the lands claimed by the Indians south of the Savannah River and east of the Chattahoochie were surrendered to the State of Georgia, as the price of peace. This established the boundary line between the State of Georgia and the Indian domain.

Early in 1782, the British Parliament, perceiving the futility of attempts hitherto to subdue the Americans, now began to listen to the voice of reason and of humanity, and steps were taken toward the establishment of peace, between the United States and Great Britain, upon the basis of the independence of the former. On the fourth of March (1782), the House of Commons passed a resolution in favor of peace, and active hostilities ceased. Preparations were now made for the evacuation of Savannah, and on the eleventh of July the British army evacuated it, after an occupation of three years and a half. Wayne, in consideration of the services of Colonel James Jackson, appointed him to "receive the keys of Savannah from a committee of British officers." He performed the service with dignity, and on the same day the American army entered Savannah, when royal power ceased in Georgia forever. **82** A few days afterward, Colonel Posey, with the main body of the Americans, marched to join Greene in South Carolina. Wayne soon followed with the remainder; hostilities ceased, **83** and the beams of peace shed their mild radiance over the desolated state, and gave promise of that glorious day of prosperity and repose which speedily followed.

Governor Martin called a special meeting of the

Dwelling of General McIntosh. 84

Legislature in Savannah in August 1782, about three weeks after the evacuation. They assembled in the house of General M'Intosh, which is yet (1852) standing on South Broad Street, between Drayton and Abercorn Streets. The session was short, but marked by decision and energy. On the first Monday in January following, the constitutional session commenced at the same place. Every branch of the new government was speedily organized, and the free and independent State of Georgia began its career. **85**

Chapter XIX
Endnotes

1 For an account of the capture of Fort Galphin or Dreadnought, at Silver Bluff.

2 This village was projected by a German named Schultz, who called it Hamburg, in honor of the "free city" of that name in his native land. He also built the noble bridge across the Savannah at that place.

3 At about mid-summer in 1775, Thomas Brown and William Thompson having openly reviled the cause of the Whigs, and at a dinner-party gave toasts in which the friends of that cause were ridiculed, the Parish Committee of Safety ordered their arrest. Thompson escaped into South Carolina, but Brown, who attempted to flee with him, was captured and brought back. He was tried, and sentenced to be tarred and feathered, and publicly exposed in a cart, to be drawn three miles, or until he was willing to confess his error, and take his oath that he would espouse the cause of the Republicans. He chose the latter course; but he was not a very warm Republican long. His course illustrated the fact that

> "He who's convinced against his will,
> Remains to be convinced still;"

for he joined the British army, was made lieutenant colonel, and afterward, while commandant of Augusta, fiercely retaliated upon the Whigs.

4 John Adam Trueitlen was chosen the first governor under the new Constitution. He was succeeded in 1778, by John Houstoun; and after the fall of Savannah, Sir James Wright, the last of the royal governors, re-established British rule in the state.

5 A curious legislative act occurred during this session. A resolution was passed censuring Governor Walton for having transmitted a letter to the President of Congress, "containing unjust and illiberal representations respecting General M'Intosh." The attorney general was ordered to prosecute the governor. On the day preceding the passage of these resolutions, the same Legislature had elected Governor Walton chief justice of Georgia. He was thereby made president of the only tribunal competent to try him! To have condemned himself would have been an exercise of "Roman virtue" hardly to be expected.

6 General Prevost had come from St. Augustine, captured the fort at Sunbury on the way, and, with Campbell's troops, had a force of about three thousand regulars and one thousand militia.

7 Samuel Elbert was born in South Carolina in 1740. He became an orphan at an early age, went to Savannah, and there subsequently engaged in commercial pursuits. He joined the Continental army in

Georgia early in 1776, as lieutenant colonel, having been a few months previously a member of the Savannah Committee of Safety. He was promoted to colonel in the autumn of 1776, and in May, 1777, commanded an expedition against the British in East Florida. In the following year he was actively engaged in the neighborhood of Savannah, and behaved bravely when it was attacked by Campbell at the close of December. He was promoted to brigadier, and was with Colonel Ashe at Brier Creek, where he was made prisoner. After his exchange, he went to the North, joined the army under Washington, and was at the capture of Cornwallis at Yorktown. At the close of the war, he was commissioned a major general. He was elected governor of the state in 1785. General Elbert died at Savannah, on the second of November, 1788, at the age of forty-five years. His remains were buried in the family cemetery on the mount, at Rae's Hall, five miles above Savannah. Elbert county, in Georgia, was named in honor of the general.

8 Colonel John Dooly entered the Continental army in Georgia, as captain, in 1776, and, rising to the rank of colonel, was very active in the neighborhood of the Savannah, until 1780, when a party of Tories, sent out from Augusta by Colonel Brown, entered his house, in Wilkes county, at midnight, and barbarously murdered him in the presence of his wife and children. – M'Call, ii., 306.

9 See M'Call's *History of Georgia*, i., 190-203.

10 We have already noticed the services of this gentleman while colonel of militia in the District of Ninety-Six, against the Indians. Andrew Williamson was born in Scotland, and when young was taken by his parents to Ninety-Six, in South Carolina. He was a very active lad, and it is believed that he attended Montgomery in his expedition against the Indians in 1760. He was with Colonel Grant in a similar expedition in 1761. He early espoused the Whig cause, and, as we have seen, was active in opposition to the Cunninghams and other Tories. He was promoted to brigadier, and in that capacity was employed in opposing the inroads of Prevost from Florida into Georgia. After the fall of Savannah, he was engaged in watching the movements of the enemy upon the Savannah River. He took possession of Augusta when Campbell retreated from it, and was for some time engaged against the Tories in that vicinity, in co-operation with General Elbert. He was afterward engaged in the battle at Stono Ferry, below Charleston, and was at the siege of Savannah when D'Estaing aided the Americans. After that, his conduct awakened suspicions that he was becoming unfriendly to the American cause. When Lincoln was besieged in Charleston, he withheld efficient aid; and when that city surrendered, he accepted a British protection. Williamson was called the "Arnold of the South," in miniature. It is generally conceded that he was a double traitor; for while he was with the British in Charleston, he communicated valuable information to General Greene. The time and place of his death is not certainly known. He lived in obscurity and poverty after the war – See Johnson's *Traditions and Reminiscences of the Revolution*, 144: Charleston, 1851.

11 M'Call and others censure General Ashe for not having the soldiers served with cartridges much sooner. Ashe in his letter to Governor Caswell on the seventeenth of March, says, that "prudence forbade a distribution of cartridges until they were wanted; for, lacking cartouch-boxes, the men had already lost a great many." He says that when they marched to meet the enemy, some carried their cartridges under their arms; others in the bosoms of their shirts; and some tied up in the corner of their hunting-shirts." – *MS. Letter of General Ashe to Governor Caswell.*

12 *MS. Letter of General Ashe to Governor Caswell*; Ramsay, ii., 16; Gordon, ii., 415; M'Call, ii., 206.

13 John Ashe was born in England in 1721. He came to America with his father in 1727, who settled on the Cape Fear River, in North Carolina. He served his district in the Colonial Legislature for several years, and was speaker of the Assembly from 1762 to 1765. He warmly opposed the Stamp Act in 1765, and, with others, announced to Governor Tryon his determination to resist its operations. Assisted by General Hugh Waddell, Ashe, then colonel of the militia of New Hanover, headed an armed force, and compelled the stamp-master to resign. He accompanied Tryon against the Regulators in 1771; but when royal rule became odious, and he saw the liberties of his country in peril, he was one of the most zealous advocates, in the North Carolina Assembly, of Republican principles. As a member of the Legislature, and of the Committee of Correspondence and of Safety at Wilmington, he was exceedingly active and vigilant. He was one of the first projectors of a Provincial Congress, and became the most active opponent of Governor Martin, for he was exceedingly popular as a man. With five hundred men, he destroyed Fort Johnston in 1775, and was denounced as a rebel against the crown. He was a member of the first Provincial Congress, convened that year. When he returned home, he raised and equipped a regiment at his own expense; and throughout the whole region around Wilmington, his eloquent words and energetic acts inspired the people with burning patriotism. In 1776, the Provincial Congress appointed him a brigadier of Wilmington District. He was actively engaged in military and civil duties in his district, until the close of 1778, when he joined Lincoln in South Carolina, with regiments from Halifax, Wilmington, Newbern, and Edenton. After his surprise and defeat at Brier Creek, he returned home. Wilmington became a British post in 1781, and Colonel Ashe and his family suffered much at their hands. He was made a prisoner, and suffered a long confinement, during which time he contracted the small-pox. He was released on parole while sick, and died of that disease in October, 1781, at the age of sixty years, while accompanying his family to a place of quiet, in Duplin county.

14 The other members of the court were General Rutherford, Colonels Armstrong, Pinckney, and Locke, and Edmond Hyrne, deputy adjutant general.. —See Moultrie's
Memoirs, i., 338.

15 Brown's authority was a letter which Cornwallis had sent to the commanders of all the British out-posts, ordering that all those who had "taken part in the revolt should be punished with the utmost rigor; and also that those who would not turn out should be imprisoned, and their whole property taken from them or destroyed." Every militia-man who had borne arms in the king's service, and afterward joined the Whigs, was to be "immediately hanged." This letter was a foul stain upon the character of Cornwallis. It was a "lash of scorpions" in the hands of cruel men like Brown. "Officers, soldiers, and citizens," says M'Call (ii., 319), were brought up to the place of execution, without being informed why they had been taken out of prison. The next morning after this sanguinary order reached Augusta, five victims were taken from the jail by order of Colonel Brown, who all expired on the gibbet.

16 Fort Cornwallis occupied the ground in the rear of the Episcopal church, now a grave-yard. This view is from within the inclosure, looking northeast, and includes a portion of Schultz's bridge, the Savannah River, and Hamburg upon the opposite bank. In the foreground is seen portions of the church-yard wall, and upon the brink of the river below are negroes employed in placing bales of cotton upon the wharves for transportation to the sea-coast. The wharves are two stories in height, one to be used at low water, the other when the river is "up." There were remains of the ditch and embankments of the fort within the grave-yard when I was there; and the trench leading to the water-gate, where the "Pride-of-India" tree is seen, was very visible.

17 Among the prisoners taken on this occasion was a young man named M'Koy, the son of a widow, who, with her family, had fled from Darien, in Georgia, into South Carolina. She went to Brown and implored the life of her son, who was only seventeen years of age. The miscreant's heart was unmoved, and the lad was not only hanged, but his body was delivered to the Indians to mutilate by scalping and otherwise. All this occurred in the presence of the mother. Afterward, when Brown, as a prisoner, passed where Mrs. M'Koy resided, she called to his remembrance his cruelty, and said, "As you are now a prisoner to the leaders of my country, for the present I lay aside all thoughts of revenge, but if you resume your sword, I will go five hundred miles to demand satisfaction at the point of it for the murder of my son. – See M'Call's *Georgia*, ii., 365; Garden's *Anecdotes*.

18 Andrew Pickens was born in Paxton township, Pennsylvania, on the nineteenth of September, 1739. His parents were from Ireland. In 1752, he removed, with his father, to the Waxhaw settlement, in South Carolina. He served as a volunteer in Grant's expedition against the Cherokees, in which he took his first lessons in the art of war. He became a warm Republican when the Revolution broke out, and, as we have seen in preceding pages of this work, he was one of the most active of the military partisans of the South. From the close of the war until 1794, he was a member of the South Carolina Legislature, when he was elected to a seat in Congress. He was commissioned major general of the South Carolina militia in 1795, and was often a commissioner to treat with the Indians. President Washington offered him a brigade of light troops under General Wayne, to serve against the Indians in the northwest, but he declined the honor. He died at his seat in Pendleton District, South Carolina – the scene of his earliest battles – on the seventeenth of August, 1817, at the age of seventy-eight years. His remains lie by the side of his wife (who died two years before), in the grave-yard of the "Old Stone Meeting-house" in Pendleton. In 1765, he married Rebecca Calhoun, aunt of the late John C. Calhoun, one of the most beautiful young ladies of the South. Mrs. Ellet, in her *Women of the Revolution* (iii., 302), gives some interesting sketches of this lady and her life during the Revolution. Her relatives and friends were very numerous, and her marriage was attended by a great number. "Rebecca Calhoun's wedding" was an epoch in the social history of the district in which she resided and old people used it as a point to reckon from.

19 This rifleman was Captain Samuel Alexander, whose aged father had been a prisoner in Fort Cornwallis for some time, and was cruelly treated by both Brown and Grierson. The son was the deliverer of his father soon after he dispatched Grierson.

20 Brown opened a communication with a house in front of the tower, and placed a quantity of powder in it. He then sent a Scotchman, under the cloak of a deserter, who advised the Americans to burn that old house, as it stood in their way. Had they done so, the explosion of the powder might have destroyed the tower. Lee suspected the man, and had him confined. Brown finally applied a slow match and blew up the house, but the tower was unharmed.

21 The brother of young M'Koy, who was hanged and scalped by Brown's orders, and who, thirsting for revenge, had joined Clark before Augusta, endeavored to kill Brown, but was prevented by the guard. It was during this march to Savannah, when at Silver Bluff, that Brown encountered Mrs. M'Koy.

22 M'Call, ii., 370; Lee, 238; Ramsay, ii., 238.

23 Waynesborough is the capital of Burke county. It is upon a branch of Brier Creek, about thirty-five miles above the place of General Ashe's defeat.

24 In March, 1825, at a meeting of the citizens of Savannah, it was determined to take the occasion of the expected visit of General La Fayette to that city to lay the corner-stones of two monuments, one to the memory of Greene, in Johnson Square; the other in memory of Pulaski, in Chippewa Square. These corner-stones were accordingly laid by La Fayette on the twenty-first of March, 1825. Some donations were made; and in November, 1826, the State Legislature authorized a lottery, for the purpose of raising $35,000 to complete the monuments. The funds were accumulated very slowly, and it was finally resolved to erect one monument, to be called the "Greene and Pulaski Monument," The structure here delineated is of Georgia marble upon a granite base, and was completed in 1829. The lottery is still in operation, and since this monument was completed has realized a little more than $12,000. – Bancroft's *Census and Statistics of Savannah*, 1848. The second monument, a beautiful work of art, will soon be erected in Chippewa Square. Launitz, the sculptor, of New York, is intrusted with its construction.

25 See M'Call's *History of Georgia*, note, i., 34.

26 In 1728, Oglethorpe's attention was drawn to the condition of debtors in prison by visiting a gentleman confined in the Fleet Jail, who was heavily ironed and harshly treated. He obtained a parliamentary commission to inquire into the state of debtor-prisoners throughout England, of which he was made chairman. They reported in 1729, and efforts at reform were immediately made. The most popular proposition was that of Oglethorpe, to use the prison materials for founding a new state in America.

27 This charter was unlike all that had preceded it. Instead of being given for purposes of private advantage, as a money speculation, it was so arranged that the administrators of the affairs of the new colony could derive no profit from it whatever; they acted solely "in trust for the poor." It was purely a benevolent scheme. They were to manage the affairs of the colony for twenty-one years, after which it was to revert to the crown. In honor of the king, who gave the scheme his hearty approval, the territory included within the charter was called Georgia. The seal of the new province bore a representation of a group of silk-worms at work, with the motto *Non sibi, sed aliis* – "Not for themselves, but for others."

28 Graham, iii., 180-184.

29 James Edward Oglethorpe was born in Surrey, England, on the twenty-first of December, 1698. He entered the army at an early age, and served under Prince Eugene as his aid-de-camp. He was for many years a member of Parliament, and while in that position successfully advocated a scheme for colonizing Georgia. He founded Savannah in 1733. In prosecution of his benevolent enterprise, he crossed the ocean several times. He performed a good deal of military service in Georgia and Florida. He returned to England in 1743, and was married in 1744. In 1745, he was promoted to the rank of brigadier in the British army, and in 1747 to major general. He was employed, under the Duke of Cumberland, against the Pretender, during 1745. When General Gage went to England in 1775, the supreme command of the British army in North America was offered to Oglethorpe. His merciful conditions did not please ministers, and General Howe received the appointment. He died at Grantham Hall, on the thirtieth of June, 1785, at the age of eighty-seven years, and was buried in Grantham Church, Essex, where his tomb bears a poetic epitaph.

30 "Here," said the chief, "is a little present; I give you a Buffalo's skin, adorned on the inside with the head and feathers of an Eagle, which I desire you to accept, because the Eagle is an emblem of speed, and the Buffalo of strength. The English are swift as the bird, and strong as the beast, since, like the former, they flew over vast seas to the uttermost parts of the earth; and like the latter, they are so strong that nothing can withstand them. The feathers of an Eagle are soft, and signify love; the Buffalo's skin is warm, and signifies protection; therefore. I hope the English will love and protect our little families."

31 Among those who went to Georgia during this period were John and Charles Wesley, the founders of the Methodist sect. Also in 1733, quite a large body of Moravians, on the invitation of the Society for the Propagation of the Gospel, left the Old Continent for the New, and pitched their tents near Savannah, after a long voyage. They soon made their way up the Savannah to a beautiful stream, where they settled down permanently, and called the creek and their settlement, Ebenezer, a name which they still bear. Whitfield came in 1740, and established an orphan-house at Savannah. He sustained it for a while, by contributions drawn from the people of the several provinces by his eloquence; but when he was asleep in the soil of New England, it failed. All Christians were admitted to equal citizenship, except Roman Catholics; they were not allowed a residence there.

32 The importation of rum was prohibited, and, to prevent a contraband trade in the article, commercial intercourse with the West Indies was forbidden. The importation of negroes was also forbidden.

33 Tabby is a mixture of lime with oyster-shells and gravel, which, when dry, form a hard rocky mass.

34 This is from a sketch made by W. W. Hazzard, Esq., in 1851. Mr. Hazzard writes: "These ruins stand on the left bank or bluff of the south branch of the Alatamaha River, on the west side of St. Simon's Island, where the steamers pass from Savannah to Florida." This fort was a scene of hostilities during the war of the Revolution, and also that of 1812; and is one of the most interesting military relics of our country. Mr. Hazzard states that, in his field in the rear of it, his men always turn up "bomb-shells and hollow shot whenever they plow there." The whole remains are upon his plantation at West Point.

35 John Reynolds was the first royal governor. He was appointed in 1754, and was succeeded in 1757 by Henry Ellis. Sir James Wright, who was the last royal governor of Georgia, succeeded Ellis in 1760, and held the office until 1776.

36 A proviso of this act required the colonists to provide various necessaries for soldiers that might be quartered among them.

37 The first liberty-pole was erected in Savannah, on the fifth of June, 1775, in front of Peter Tondee's tavern. His house stood upon the spot now (1849) occupied by Smet's new stores.

38 M'Call, ii., 16.

39 John Glenn was chosen chairman of the meeting. The following-named gentlemen were appointed the committee to prepare the resolutions: John Glenn, John Smith, Joseph Clay, John Houstoun, Noble W. Jones, Lyman Hall, William Young, Edward Telfair, Samuel Farley, George Walton, Joseph Habersham, Jonathan Bryan, Jonathan Cochran, George M'Intosh, Sutton Banks, William Gibbons, Benjamin Andrew, John Winn. John Stirk, Archibald Bullock, James Scriven, David Zubley, Henry Davis Bourguin, Elisha Butler, William Baker, Parminus Way, John Baker, John Mann, John Benefield, John Stacey, and John Morel. These were the leading Sons of Liberty at Savannah in 1774.

40 The only newspaper in the province (the *Georgia Gazette*, established in 1762) was under the control of Governor Wright, and through it he disseminated much sophistry, and sometimes falsehoods among the people.

41 The committees of St. John's parish convened on the ninth of February, 1775, and addressed a circular letter to the committees of other colonies, asking their consent to the reception of a representative in Congress from that particular parish. Encouraged by the answer they received, they met again on the twenty-first of March, and appointed Dr. Lyman Hall to represent them. When he went to Philadelphia, he took with him, from Sunbury, one hundred and sixty barrels of rice, and two hundred and fifty dollars, as a present to the people of Boston.

42 The whole record of the proceedings of Congress on that day is as follows:

"*Saturday, October* 8, 1774. – The Congress resumed the consideration of the letter from Boston, and, upon motion,

Resolved, That this Congress approve the opposition of the inhabitants of Massachusetts Bay to the execution of the late Acts of Parliament; and if the same shall be attempted to be carried into execution by force, in such case, all America ought to support them in their opposition."

The proceedings of that one day should be written in brass and marble; for the resolution then adopted was the first Federal gauntlet of defiance cast at the feet of the British monarch. The eighth of October, 1774, should be placed by the side of the fourth of July, 1776, as one of the most sacred days in the calendar of Freedom.

43 These were Noble Wimberly Jones, Joseph Habersham, Edward Telfair, William Gibbons, Joseph Clay, and John Milledge.

44 The magazine was at the eastern extremity of the town. It was sunk about twelve feet under the ground, inclosed with brick, and secured by a door in such a way that the governor did not consider a guard necessary.

45 This committee consisted of sixteen leading men of Savannah, among whom was Samuel (afterward General) Elbert, and George Walton, one of the signers of the Declaration of Independence. M'Call (ii., 45) says that, after the meeting adjourned, "a number of gentlemen dined at Tondee's tavern, where the *Union flag* was hoisted upon the liberty-pole, and two pieces of artillery were placed under it." The Union flag, of thirteen red and white stripes, was not adopted until the first of January, 1776, when it was first unfurled in the American camp, near Boston.

46 The Secret Committee at Charleston, who intercepted this letter, placed another in the cover, with Governor Wright's name counterfeited, and sent it on to Gage. In that letter they said (as if Governor Wright Was penning it), "I have wrote for troops to awe the people, but now there is no occasion for sending them, for the people are again come to some order." Gage was thus misled.

47 They met on the fourth of July. On the fifteenth, they elected Archibald Bullock, John Houstoun, John Joachim Zubley, Noble Wimberly Jones, and Lyman Hall, to represent that province in the Continental Congress. These were the first delegates elected by the representatives of the whole people, for Hall represented only the parish of St. John's. Fifty-three members signed their credentials. Zubley afterward became a traitor. While the subject of independence was being debated in 1776, Samuel Chase, of Maryland, accused Zubley of communicating with Governor Wright. Zubley denied the charge, but while Chase was collecting proof, the recusant fled.

48 One of the men engaged in this adventure was Ebenezer Smith Platt. He was afterward made a prisoner, and being recognized as one of this daring party, was sent to England, where he lay in jail many months, under a charge of high treason. He was eventually considered a prisoner of war, and was exchanged.

49 Joseph Habersham was the son of a merchant of Savannah, who died at New Brunswick, in New Jersey, in August, 1775. Joseph Habersham held the rank of lieutenant colonel in the Continental army. In 1785, he was a member of Congress from Savannah; and in 1795, Washington appointed him postmaster general of the United States. He held that office until 1800, when he resigned. He was made president of the Branch Bank of the United States, at Savannah, in 1802, which position he held until his death, in November, 1815, at the age of sixty-five years. The name of his brother James, late President of the Council, appears upon the first bill of credit issued by the Provincial Congress of Georgia in 1776.

50 Governor Wright's house was on the lot in Heathcote Ward; where the Telfair House now stands. The Council House was on the lot where George Schley, Esq., resided in 1849.

51 Archibald Bullock, John Houstoun, Lyman Hall, Button Gwinnett, and George Walton.

52 Lachlin M'Intosh was appointed colonel; Samuel Elbert, lieutenant colonel; and Joseph Habersham, major.

53 When the British first appeared in the attitude of assailants, the Committee of Safety appraised such houses in Savannah as were owned by Republicans, with the determination of applying the torch if they could not repulse the enemy. The houses of the Tories were not noticed; and therefore, in the event of a general conflagration, *their* property would not be accounted for.

54 Archibald Bullock, president of the council, convened that body, on the receipt of the Declaration (which came by express in thirty-five days from Philadelphia), when they ordered it to be publicly read in front of the council-chamber. There, under a military escort, the council proceeded to the liberty-pole, where they were saluted by thirteen cannon-peals and small arms from the first Continental battalion, under Colonel M'Intosh. Proceeding to the battery, another salute of thirteen guns was fired. The people then partook of a dinner in a grove, where thirteen toasts were given. In the afternoon, there was a funeral procession, and the royal government was *buried*, with the customary ceremonies. In the evening, the town was brilliantly illuminated. – M'Call, ii., 90.

55 This was a small stockade, one hundred feet square, with a block-house in the center, and a bastion at each corner. It was situated upon the northeast side of Saltilla River, in the present Camden county.

56 Lachlin M'Intosh was born near Inverness, in Scotland, in 1727. He was the son of John M., who was at the head of the Borlam branch of the clan M'Intosh. He came to Georgia with General Oglethorpe in 1736, when Lachlin was nine years of age. His father being made a prisoner and sent to St. Augustine, Lachlin was left to the care of his mother at the age of thirteen years. His opportunities for education were small, yet his strong mind overcame many difficulties. Arrived at maturity, he went to Charleston, where, on account of his fine personal appearance and the services of his father, he commanded attention. He and Henry Laurens became friends, and he entered that gentleman's counting-room as clerk. He left commercial pursuits, returned to his friends on the Alatamaha, married, and engaged in the profession of a land surveyor. He made himself acquainted with military tactics, and when the War for Independence broke out, he was found, when needed, on the side of the Republicans. He was first appointed colonel, and in 1776 was commissioned a brigadier. He was persecuted by his rival, Button Gwinnett, until he could no longer forbear; and finally, pronouncing that gentleman a scoundrel, a duel ensued, and Gwinnett was killed.

M'Intosh afterward commanded in the Western Department, and led an expedition against the Indians. He returned to Georgia in 1779, and was at the siege and fall of Savannah. He was with Lincoln at Charleston, where he was made prisoner. After his release, he went with his family to Virginia, where he remained until the close of the war. When he returned to Georgia, he found his property nearly all wasted; and in retirement and comparative poverty, he lived in Savannah until his death, which occurred in 1806, at the age of seventy-nine. General M'Intosh, when young, was considered the handsomest man in Georgia.

57 Robert Howe was a native of Brunswick, North Carolina. History bears no record of his private life. He was in the Legislature in 1773. He appears to have been one of the earliest and most uncompromising of the patriots of the Cape Fear region, for we find him honored with an exception, together with Cornelius Harnett, when royal clemency was offered to the rebels by Sir Henry Clinton in 1776. He was appointed colonel of the first North Carolina regiment, and with his command went early into the field of Revolutionary strife. In December, 1775, he joined Woodford at Norfolk, in opposition to Lord Dunmore and his motley army. For his gallantry during this campaign, Congress, on the twenty-ninth of February, 1776, appointed him, with five others, brigadier general in the Continental army, and ordered him to Virginia. In the spring of 1776, British spite toward General Howe was exhibited by Sir Henry Clinton, who sent Cornwallis, with nine hundred men, to ravage his plantation near old Brunswick village. He was placed in chief command of the Southern troops in 1778, and was unsuccessful in an expedition against Florida, and in the defense of Savannah. His conduct was censured, but without just cause. Among others whose voice was raised against him, was Christopher Gadsden, of Charleston. Howe required him to deny or retract. Gadsden would do neither, and a duel ensued. They met at Cannonsburg, and all the damage either sustained was a scratch upon the ear of Gadsden by Howe's ball.*

---

* Major Andre wrote a humorous account, in rhyme, of this affair, in eighteen stanzas. Bernard Elliott was the second of Gadsden, and General Charles Cotesworth Pinckney, of Howe. The duel occurred on the thirteenth of August, 1778. After this affair, Howe and Gadsden were warm friends.

---

58 Colonel Elbert, who was stationed at Fort Howe, on the Alatamaha, early in the spring of 1778, went with three hundred men to Darien, where he embarked on board three galleys, accompanied by a detachment of artillery on a flat-boat, and proceeded to attack a hostile party at Oglethorpe's Fort. He was successful. A brigantine was captured, and the garrison, alarmed, fled from the fort to their boats, and escaped, leaving Elbert complete victor. On board of the brigantine were three hundred uniform suits, belonging to Colonel Pinckney's regiment, which had been captured while on their way, in the sloop Hatter, from Charleston to Savannah.

59 Soon after the return of Howe, some regulars and Loyalists had made a rapid incursion into Georgia, and menaced the fort at Sunbury, at the mouth of the Midway River. The little garrison was commanded by Lieutenant-colonel John M'Intosh (a brother of General M'Intosh). The enemy approached in two divisions, one with artillery, in boats, under Lieutenant-colonel Fuser; the other by land, under Lieutenant-colonel Mark Prevost, consisting of six hundred regulars. Fuser approached the fort and demanded its surrender. M'Intosh replied, *Come and take it!* The promptness and brevity of the reply indicated security, and Fuser withdrew, although he could easily have captured the fort. In the mean while, General Scriven, with others, were skirmishing with Colonel Prevost, who had been joined by a band of Tories, under M'Girth, in one of which the latter was mortally wounded. The invaders pressed forward until within three miles of Ogeechee Ferry, where they were confronted by Colonel Elbert and two hundred Continentals, at a breast-work thrown up by a planter named Savage. Unable to proceed further, they retraced their steps toward the Alatamaha, plundering and burning houses, and laying the whole country waste. Midway church was destroyed, rice barns were burned, and the people were made houseless.

60 These troops consisted of the 71st regiment of foot, two battalions of Hessians, four of provincials, and a detachment of the royal artillery.

61 From the landing-place (which was the nearest the ships could approach) a narrow causeway, with a ditch on each side, led through a rice swamp six hundred yards, to firm ground. The 71st regiment of royal Scots led the van across the causeway, and was attacked by some Americans. Captain Cameron and two of his company were killed, and five were wounded. The Highlanders were made furious, and, rushing forward, drove the Americans into the woods.

62 More clearly to understand the nature of the attack, defense, and result, it is necessary to know the position of the town at that time. It is situated upon a high bluff of forty feet altitude, and then, as now, was approachable by land on three sides. From the high ground of Brewton's Hill and Thunderbolt on the east, a road crossed a morass upon a causeway, having rice-fields on the north side to the river, and a wooded swamp, several miles in extent, on the south of it. It was approached from the south by the roads from White Bluff on Vernon River, and from the Ogeechee Ferry, which unite near the town; and from the westward by a road and causeway over the deep swamps of Musgrove's Creek, where, also, rice-fields extend from the causeway to the river on the north. From the western direction, the Central Rail-way enters Savannah. From the eastern to the western causeway was about three fourths of a mile.

63 Like credit can not be given to Commodore Parker. For want of other quarters the prisoners were placed on board of ships, where disease made dreadful havoc daily during the succeeding summer. Parker not only neglected the comforts of the prisoners, but was brutal in his manner. Among those confined in these horrid prison ships, was the venerable Jonathan Bryan, aged and infirm. When his daughter pleaded with Hyde Parker for an alleviation of the sufferings of her parent, he treated her with vulgar rudeness and contempt. The bodies of those who died were deposited in the marsh mud, where they were sometimes exposed and eaten by buzzards and crows. – See M'Call's *History of Georgia*, ii., 176.

64 About one hundred Americans were either killed in the action or drowned in the swamp, and thirty eight officers and four hundred and fifteen privates were taken prisoners. The fort, which only commanded the water, and was of no service on this occasion, with forty-eight pieces of cannon, twenty-three mortars and howitzers, eight hundred and seventeen small arms, ninety-four barrels of gunpowder, fifteen hundred and forty-five cannon shot, one hundred and four case ditto, two hundred shells, nine tons of lead, military stores, shipping in the river, and a large quantity of provisions, fell into the hands of the victors. The British lost only seven killed and nineteen wounded. The private soldiers who refused to enlist in the British army were confined in prison ships; the Continental officers were paroled to Sunbury.

65 Ramsay, ii., 4; Gordon. ii., 403; Marshall, i., 293; M'Call. ii., 168; Stedman. ii., 66.

66 Benjamin Lincoln was born on the third of February, 1733. He was trained to the business of a farmer, and had few educational advantages. He continued in his vocation in his native town (Hingham, Massachusetts) until past forty years of age, when he engaged in civil and military duties. He was a local magistrate, representative in the Colonial Legislature, and held the appointment of colonel of militia, when, in 1774, he was appointed a major general of militia. He was very active until the close of 1776, in training the militia for the Continental service, and in February, 1777, he joined Washington, at Morristown, with a re-enforcement. On the nineteenth of that month, Congress appointed Lincoln, with Lord Stirling, St. Clair, Mifflin, and Stephen, major general in the Continental army. He was active during the summer and autumn of that year in opposition to Burgoyne, while on his march toward Saratoga. He was severely wounded on the seventh of October, at Saratoga, which kept him from active service until August, 1778, when he joined

Washington. He was appointed to the chief command in the Southern department, in September, and arrived at Charleston in December. By judicious management he kept Prevost and his troops below the Savannah most of the time, until October the following year, when, with D'Estaing, he laid siege to Savannah. The effort was unsuccessful. In May following, he, with the largest portion of the Southern army, was made prisoner at Charleston by the British, under Sir Henry Clinton. He was permitted to return to Hingham on parole. In November he was exchanged, and the following spring he joined Washington on the Hudson. He was at the surrender of Cornwallis, and was deputed to receive that commander's sword. He was elected Secretary of War a few days after this event, which office he held for three years, and then retired to his farm. In 1786-7 he commanded the militia in the suppression of Shays's insurrection. He was elected lieutenant governor of Massachusetts in 1787. He was appointed collector of the port of Boston in 1789, which office he held for twenty years, when he was succeeded by General Dearborn. He died in Hingham, on the ninth of May, 1810, at the age of seventy-seven years. He lived with his wife fifty-five years. General Lincoln was temperate and religious. No profane word was ever heard uttered by his lips. A great part of his life he was a deacon in the Church.

67 The signature of Howe is from a letter written by him under date of "Verplanck's Point, July, 1779."

68 On one occasion two American galleys went down the Savannah and captured and destroyed two vessels belonging to the English. Prevost on another occasion, sent a party to surprise Beaufort, and capture stores there; and on the fourth of June, Colonel Cruger (who afterward commanded at Ninety-Six), with a party of Loyalists, while celebrating the kings birth-day at a plantation at Belfast, on the Midway, was captured by Captain Spencer. Cruger was afterward exchanged for Colonel John M'Intosh. On the south side of the Ogeechee, at a place called Hickory Hill, a party, under Colonel Twiggs, had a skirmish with some British soldiers, who attacked them. The enemy lost seven killed, ten wounded, and the remainder were taken prisoners. The Americans had two wounded. Major Baker, with thirty men, attacked and defeated a party of British soldiers near Sunbury, on the twenty-eighth of June, the same day when Twiggs had his engagement near the Ogeechee. These were Georgia Loyalists.

69 Count Casimir Pulaski was a native of Lithuania, in Poland. He was educated for the law, but stirring military events had their influence upon his mind, and he entered the army. With his father, the old Count Pulaski, he was engaged in the rebellion against Stanislaus, king of Poland, in 1769. The old count was taken prisoner, and put to death. In 1770, the young Count Casimir was elected commander-in-chief of the insurgents, but was not able to collect a competent force to act efficiently, for a pestilence had swept off 250,000 Poles the previous year. In 1771, himself and thirty-nine others entered Warsaw, disguised as peasants, for the purpose of seizing the king. The object was to place him at the head of the army, force him to act in that position, and call around him the Poles to beat back the Russian forces which Catharine had sent against them. They succeeded in taking him from his carriage in the streets, and carrying him out of the city; but were obliged to leave him, not far from the walls, and escape. Pulaski's little army was soon afterward defeated, and he entered the service of the Turks, who were fighting Russia. His estates were confiscated, himself outlawed. He went to Paris, had an interview there with Dr. Franklin, and came to America in 1777. He joined the army under Washington, and, as we have seen, was placed in command of cavalry. His legion did good service at the North. Early in the spring of 1778 he was ordered to Little Egg Harbor, on the New Jersey coast. His force consisted of cavalry and infantry, with a single field-piece from Proctor's artillery. While on his way from Trenton to Little Egg Harbor, and when within eight miles of the coast, he was surprised by a party of British, and a large portion of his infantry was bayoneted. Julien, a deserter from his corps, had given information of his position; the surprise was complete. His loss was forty men, among them Lieutenant-colonel Baron De Botzen. Pulaski was ordered to the South in February, 1779, and was in active service under Lincoln until the siege of Savannah, in October of that year, where he was mortally wounded. His banner was preserved, and carried to Baltimore. He was taken to the United States brig Wasp, where he died, and was buried under a large tree on St. Helen's Island, about fifty miles from Savannah, by his first lieutenant and personal friend, Charles Litomiski. Funeral honors were paid to his memory at Charleston, and, on the 29th of November, Congress voted the erection of a monument to his memory. Like other monuments ordered by the Continental Congress, the stone for Pulaski's is yet in the quarry. The citizens of Savannah reared this one in commemoration of the services of Greene and Pulaski.

70 Finding the French in possession of the only channel at the mouth of the Savannah which was navigable, when he arrived at Dawfuskie, Maitland, conducted by a negro fisherman, passed through a creek with his boats, at high water, and, concealed by a fog, eluded the French. D'Estaing, ignorant of the geography of the country about Savannah, had no idea that there was any other way than by the regular channel for boats to reach the town.

71 Lee, in his *Memoirs*, says, "Any four hours before the junction of Lieutenant-colonel Maitland was sufficient to have taken Savannah."

72 These remains are in the southeastern suburbs of the city, about half way between the Negro Cemetery and the residence of Major William Bowen, seen toward the right of the picture. The banks have an average height, from the bottom of the ditch, of about five feet, and are dotted with pines and chincapins or dwarf chestnuts, the former draped with moss. The ground is an open common, and although it was mid-winter when I was there, it was covered with green grass, bespangled with myriads of little flowers of stellar form. This view is from the direction of the town looking southeast.

73 Three thousand five hundred were French, a little more than six hundred were American regulars (chiefly North Carolinians), and about three hundred were militia from Charleston.

74 The Spring Hill redoubt was at the entrance of the Augusta road into the town, on the western side. The buildings of the rail-way station now cover its site.

75 The American standards were those of the second South Carolina regiment, embroidered and presented to them by Mrs. Susanna Elliott, three days after the battle at Fort Moultrie, in 1776, and were planted by Lieutenants Hume and Bush. The French standard was raised by one of D'Estaing's aids, who, with Hume and Bush, soon fell, mortally wounded, leaving their colors fluttering in the breeze. Lieutenant Gray of the South Carolina regiment, seeing his associates fall, seized the standards and kept them erect, when he, too, was prostrated by a bullet. Sergeant Jasper. whom we shall meet hereafter, sprang forward, secured the colors, and had just fastened them upon the parapet, when a rifle ball pierced him, and he fell into the ditch. He was carried to the camp, and soon afterward expired. Just before he died, he said to Major Horry, "Tell Mrs. Elliott I lost my life supporting the colors she presented to our regiment."

76 A sergeant of the Charleston grenadiers deserted during the night of the eighth, and communicated the general plan of attack, to Prevost. This gave the garrison a great advantage, for they strengthened the points to be attacked.

77 The whole force of the combined armies was four thousand nine hundred and fifty, of which two thousand eight hundred and twenty-three were French. The whole British force in Savannah, including a few militia, some Indians, and three hundred negroes, was two thousand eight hundred and fifty. The French lost, in killed and wounded, six hundred and thirty-seven men, and the Americans four hundred and fifty-seven. The whole loss of the British did not exceed one hundred and twenty. Lieutenant-colonel Maitland was attacked with a bilious disease during the siege, and died a few days afterward.

78 Ramsay, Gordon, Marshall, Moultrie, Stedman, M'Call, Lee.

79 Indescribable were the sufferings of the people of Savannah, particularly the families of the Whigs. The females were exposed to daily insults from the brutal soldiery, and many, reduced from affluence to poverty, unable to bear the indignities heaped upon them, traveled away on foot, some of them even without shoes upon their feet, and took refuge in the Carolinas.

80 James Jackson was born in the county of Devon, England, on the twenty-first of September, 1757. In 1772, he came to America, and began the study of the law in Savannah. At the age of eighteen, he shouldered a musket and prepared to resist British power. He was active in repulsing the British at Savannah in 1776. In 1778, he was appointed brigade major of the Georgia militia, and was wounded in the skirmish when General Scriven was killed. He participated in the defense of Savannah at the close of the year, and when it fell into the hands of Campbell, he was among those who fled into South Carolina, where he joined General Moultrie's command. While on his way, so wretched was his appearance, that some Whigs arrested, tried, and condemned him as a spy. He was about to be executed, when he was recognized by a gentleman of reputation from Georgia. Major Jackson was in the siege of Savannah in October, 1779. In August, 1780, he joined Colonel Elijah Clark's command, and was at the battle at Blackstocks. In 1781, General Pickens made Jackson his brigade major, and his fluent speech often infused new ardor into the corps of that partisan. He was at the siege of Augusta, and was left in command of the garrison after the expulsion of the British. He subsequently commanded a legionary corps, with which he did good service. He joined Wayne at Ebenezer, and was active with that officer until the evacuation of Savannah by the British. The Georgia Legislature gave him a house and lot in Savannah at the close of the war. He married in 1785; was made brigadier in 1786; and in 1788 was elected governor of Georgia, but modestly declined the honor on account of his youth and inexperience, being only about thirty years of age. He was one of the first representatives in Congress under the Federal Constitution. He was elected a major general in 1792, and during the three succeeding years was a member of the United States Senate. He was chiefly instrumental in framing the Georgia Constitution in 1798. From that year till 1801, he was governor of the state, when he again took a seat in the Senate of the United States. He held that office until his death, which occurred on the nineteenth of March, 1806. He was buried about four miles from Washington City. Subsequently, his remains were deposited in the Congressional burial-ground. The inscription upon the stone which covers them was written by John Randolph, his personal friend and admirer. There never lived a truer patriot or more honest man than General James Jackson.

81 General Clarke was governor of Canada in 1807.

82 Between the twelfth and the twenty-fifth of July, seven thousand persons, according to British accounts, left Savannah, consisting of twelve hundred British regulars and Loyalists, five hundred women and children, three hundred Indians, and five thousand negroes. Governor Wright, and some of the civil and military officers, went to Charleston; General Clarke and part of the British regulars to New York; Colonel Brown's rangers and the Indians to St. Augustine; and the remainder, under convoy of the Zebra frigate, the Vulture sloop of war, and other armed vessels, to the West Indies. It is estimated that nearly seven eighths of the slaves in Georgia were carried off now, and on previous occasions, by the British.

83 Colonel Jackson had a skirmish with some forces on Skidaway Island, below Savannah, on the twenty-fifth of July, and this was the last fought battle for independence, in Georgia.

84 This house is the third eastward from Drayton Street, and is said to be the oldest brick house in Savannah. Broad Street, upon which it stands, is a noble avenue, shaded by four rows of Pride-of-India Trees.

85 Lyman Hall, one of the signers of the Declaration of Independence, was chosen governor in January, 1784; George Walton, chief justice; Samuel Stirk, attorney general; John Milton, secretary of state; John Martin, treasurer; and Richard Call, surveyor general.

Chapter XX

There are but few remains of Revolutionary localities about Savannah. The city has spread out over all the British works; and where their batteries, redoubts, ramparts, and ditches were constructed, public squares are laid out and adorned with trees, or houses and stores cover the earth. Not so with the works constructed by the French engineers during the siege in the autumn of 1779. Although the regular forms are effaced, yet the mounds and ditches may be traced many rods near the margin of the swamp southeast of the city. These I visited early on the morning of my arrival in Savannah, after an instructive interview with the Honorable J. C. Nicoll, to whom I am indebted for a knowledge of the several historical localities in and near the city. After sketching General M'Intosh's house, I procured a saddle-horse and rode out to "Jasper's Spring," a place famous as the scene of a bold exploit, which has been the theme of history and song. **1** It is near the Augusta road, two and a half miles westward of the city. The day was very warm. The gardens were garnished with flowers; the orange-trees were blooming; blossoms covered the peach-trees, and insects were sporting in the sunbeams.

Jasper's Spring is just within the edge of a forest of oaks and gums, and is remarkable only on account of its historical associations. It is in the midst of a marshy spot partially covered with underwood, on the northern side of the road, and its area is marked by the circumference of a sunken barrel. Being the only fountain of pure water in the vicinity, it is resorted to daily by travelers upon the road. One of them, a wagoner, came, knelt, and quaffed when I opened my port-folio, and, as he arose from the spring I sketched him, as seen in the preceding picture. He knew nothing of the event which makes it famous.

After lingering for half an hour in the cool shade at the spring, I returned to Savannah. A slight haziness began to overspread the sky, which deepened toward evening, and descended in gentle rain when I left the city at eight o'clock in a steam-packet for Charleston. We passed the lights at Fort Pulaski at half past eight, and an hour later glided by the beacons of Tybee and breasted the rising waves of the Atlantic. Like Yellow Plush, I soon discovered the "use of basins," and at an early hour turned into my berth to prevent a turning out of my supper. During the night we passed through Port Royal entrance,

View at Jasper's Spring.

touched at Beaufort, stuck in the mud in the channel between Ladies' and St. Helena Islands, and at daylight emerged again into the Atlantic through St. Helena's Sound. The breeze was hourly stiffening, and every "landlubber" on board preferred the berth to breakfast, until we approached Charleston bar, when the wind died away, the sun gleamed through the breaking clouds, and upon the bosom of long, heaving swells, we were wafted into Charleston harbor. We landed at one o'clock, dined at two, and at three I called upon the Reverend Samuel Smythe, D. D., with a letter of introduction, with whom I passed the remainder of the afternoon in visiting places of interest upon the banks of the Cooper River, above the city. To the kind

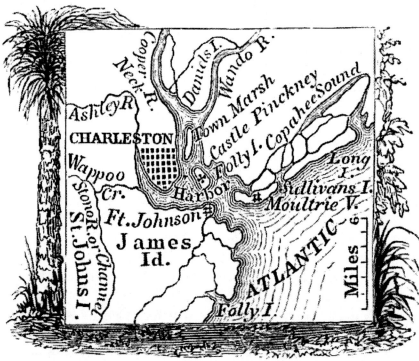

courtesy of Dr. Smythe I am indebted for much of the interest, pleasure, and profit of my visit at Charleston and vicinity. Here, upon the spot where the first permanent English settlement in South Carolina was accomplished, let us glance at the record of history.

In the Introduction to this work I have referred to the first attempt at permanent settlement on South Carolina soil, and the result. As it was only an *attempt* proved unsuccessful, and does not illustrate the growth of popular liberty, except so far as the *principles* of the Huguenots (those first emigrants) had influence in the political opinions of the people in after years, we will not stop to consider the details, but pass on to the period of permanent settlements.

For a hundred years after the first attempt at colonization in South Carolina was made, no settlements were undertaken, and no white man walked in her forests, except a few Spaniards, who penetrated the wilderness from St. Augustine in search of a fancied region of gold. At length the English, who had formed settlements on the Cape Fear and vicinity, turned their attention to more southerly regions.

In January, 1670, two ships, with materials for a permanent settlement, sailed from England, under the command of Sir William Sayle, who had previously visited and explored the South Carolina coast. He entered Port Royal, planted his colony upon Beaufort, and soon afterward died there. The jurisdiction of Sir John Yeamans, of the Northern colony, was then extended over this settlement, and in 1671 he was chosen their governor. The people were easily induced, "for the convenience of pasturage and tillage," to remove to the south bank of the Ashley River, further north, and there they laid the foundation of old Charlestown 2 (at present called Old Town, or the Landing); and there was planted the first fruitful seed of the commonwealth of South Carolina in 1671. The colony, in honor of Sir George Carteret, one of the proprietors, was called the *Carteret County Colony*. 3 Nine years afterward, the settlers abandoned this spot, and upon Oyster Point, nearer the sea, at the confluence of the Ashley and Cooper Rivers 4 (so called in compliment to Ashley Cooper, the Earl of Shaftesbury), a place more eligible, for commercial pursuits, they founded the present city of Charleston in 1680, and in the course of the year built thirty houses. 5 The city retained its original name of Charles *Town* until after the Revolution, when it was called Charleston. The general early history of South Carolina we have already considered in its connection with the North State; we have, therefore, only a few particular points to notice in its progress prior to the separation in 1729.

The beauty of the climate and the freedom which then prevailed made South Carolina a chosen refuge for the oppressed and the discontented of all lands. Several Dutch families of New York went to South

Carolina when that city passed into the hands of the English, and settled on the southwest side of the Ashley, near the English colony, from whence they spread over the state, and were joined by many from "fader-land." In 1679, Charles the Second sent quite a number of French Protestant refugees (Huguenots) thither; and when, in 1685, the Edict of Nantes was revoked, large numbers of the Huguenots crossed the Atlantic, and sought refuge in South Carolina from the fires of persecution about to be relighted in France. Ten years later in 1696, a colony of Congregationalists, from Dorchester, in Massachusetts, ascended the Ashley almost to its head, and founded the town of Dorchester, in the present parish of St. George, Dorchester. This was a village of considerable note during the Revolution, but it is now deserted, and little remains of the past but the primitive church and the graves around it.

Under various leaders, men of every creed and of various countries went to South Carolina; "and the Santee, the Congaree, the Wateree, and the Edisto now listened to the strange voices of several nations, who in the Old World had scarcely known each other, except as foes. There, for a while, they mingled harmoniously with the natives. The French Huguenot and the German Palatine smoked their pipes in amity with the Westo and the Serattee; and the tastes and habits of the Seine and the Rhine became familiar to the wandering eyes of the fearless warriors along the Congaree. It was not long before a French violinist had opened a school for dancing among the Indians on the Santee River." 6

For some time the colonists were obliged to depend, in part, upon the bounty of the proprietors for subsistence, and the calls of this dependence being generally answered, idle and improvident habits were begotten, highly inimical to the prosperity of a new state. The proprietors perceived the bad tendency of such indulgence, and in a letter to the colonists declared that they would "no longer continue to feed and clothe them, without expectation or demand of any return." This resolve, so unkind to the apprehension of the Carolinians, was of great benefit to the colonists. Ultimately the people, compelled to work or starve – to be provident or to be beggars – turned to their own resources, and their development began. Independence of action begat independence of thought and feeling, and in this first broken fallow, turned up to the vivifying influence of the sun and shower of free civil, political and religious life, the seed of Republican liberty, which subsequently bore such generous fruit in the Carolinas, was planted and took firm root.

In addition to the diseases incident to the climate, and the privations always attendant upon first settlement, the Carolinians were soon called upon to resist powerful foes – the Indian tribes upon whose hunting-grounds they were settling. These difficulties have been noted in the preceding chapter. The red men were hardly quieted before internal troubles menaced the colony with a more terrible blow. Food had become scarce, discontents were heard on every side, and an insurrectionary movement occurred. The rebellion was promptly suppressed, and some supplies just then arriving from England with some new settlers, the people were quieted and became loyal. This difficulty had just passed by, when the Spaniards menaced the English, and ships of war with land troops appeared. Before their arrival, vessels which had been sent to Virginia and Barbadoes for provisions and munitions of war reached the harbor of Charleston. Governor Yeamans at once acted on the offensive, and drove the Spaniards back to St. Augustine.

Yeamans left the colony in 1674, and was succeeded by Joseph West, a man of republican tendencies. He called the freemen of the colony together in convention at Charleston to make laws for their government. This was the first legislative assembly convened in South Carolina. It might have been an auspicious event, had not the jarring interests of classes and creeds, there represented, produced discord and confusion. Cavaliers and Puritans, Churchmen and Dissenters, each strenuous for the prevalence of their respective opinions, presented, in this first attempt at representative legislation, powerful arguments in favor of absolutism. Anarchy prevailed, and in the midst of the dissensions in Charleston, the Stono Indians swept along the frontiers of the settlements, and plundered a great quantity of grain and numerous cattle. The inhabitants armed themselves, defeated the Stonos in several skirmishes, took many of them prisoners, and sent them to the West Indies to be sold as slaves. After other obstinate conflicts, the Stonos were subdued and almost exterminated. They have never had a tribal existence since, and it is believed that they have no living representative upon the earth.

A Legislative Assembly met in Charleston in 1682, and enacted laws for the civil and military operations of the colony. The spirit of freedom had begun to work in the hearts of the people, and when the collection of rents, the great cause of discontent in the Northern colony, was pressed, they rebelled. The public records were seized, and the Assembly, assuming the functions of government, imprisoned the secretary of the province. The governor (Colleton) declared martial law. The exasperated people clamored for his impeachment. The Assembly complied, and he was banished from the province. Turbulence and misrule continued until the scheme of government of Locke and Shaftesbury was abandoned; a better day then dawned. John Archdale, the good Quaker, came, and his policy was like oil poured upon troubled waters. Only one great difficulty remained – the troubles arising from the antipathy of the English to the French. The general excellence of character possessed by the latter soon disarmed prejudices; their political disabilities were removed; they were no longer excluded from participation in governmental affairs, and the last fountain of disquietude was dried up. During the whole of Archdale's administration, and that of Blake, his successor, peace and prosperity prevailed.

James Moore succeeded Blake in 1700. He sent an expedition against the Spaniards at St. Augustine, in 1702, which proved unsuccessful. A subsequent expedition against the Apalachian Indians, undertaken by Moore, has been considered in a previous chapter.

Nathaniel Johnson, a pliant servant of Lord Granville, one of the proprietors, succeeded Moore in 1703, and, pursuant to a plan long cherished by that nobleman and his friends, he proceeded to the establishment of the Church of England in Carolina. This was the first budding of religious intolerance there. The Dissenters were excluded from the Colonial Legislature, and suffered other disabilities. They laid their grievances before the English Parliament. There they received encouragement, and the law of disfranchisement was soon repealed by the Colonial Assembly, but the Liturgy of the Church of England remained the established form of religion in the province until the Revolution.

England was now at war with France and Spain. Her enemies coalesced, and joined in an expedition against South Carolina in 1706. A squadron of five ships came from Havana and appeared before Charleston. The governor called upon the people to repel the invaders, and they cheerfully responded. The invading troops were compelled to fly to their ships, and these, in turn, being attacked by some vessels which had been speedily armed in the harbor, retreated in haste across the bar, and departed. This was the first *naval victory* of the South Carolinians. Of eight hundred of the enemy, almost three hundred were killed or taken prisoners.

In 1710 a speck of civil war appeared in Charleston, when two claimants to the office of acting governor, on the death of Tynte, the successor of Johnson, disputed for the honor. A compromise was effected, by referring the case to the proprietors for a decision. They wisely discarded both candidates, and appointed Charles Craven, brother of one of the proprietors, governor of the province. Under his administration the colony prospered, settlements extended, and the power of a dangerous Indian confederacy against the Carolinas was effectually broken. **7**

Craven was succeeded by Robert Johnson, a son of the former governor in 1717, and during his administration a revolution occurred in South Carolina which changed the government from a proprietary to a royal one. The remote causes of this change may be found in the desire of the people for a simple and inexpensive government responsible only to the crown, and not to be subjected to the caprices, avarice, and inefficiency of a Board of Control composed of private individuals, intent only upon personal gain. The immediate and ostensible cause was the refusal of the proprietors to pay any portion of the debt incurred by the Indian war so promptly suppressed by Governor Craven; and the severity with which they enforced the collection of rents. The people looked to the crown for relief, aid, and protection. A scheme for a revolution was secretly planned, and on the twenty-eighth of November, 1719, Governor Johnson was deposed. The people proceeded to elect James Moore governor. The militia, on whom Johnson looked for aid, were against him, and finding himself entirely unsupported, he withdrew to his plantation. Moore was proclaimed governor of the province in the king's name, and royal authority was established. During the administration of Francis Nicholson, the successor of Moore, and that of Arthur Middleton, acting governor, little of political importance occurred in relation to the colony, except the legal disputes in England concerning the rights of the proprietors. These were finally settled in 1729, by a royal purchase of both colonies from the proprietors, and during that year North and South Carolina became separate royal provinces.

The colony was now very prosperous, and from the period of the separation until the Revolution, nothing occurred to impede its general progress but the troubles with the Indians, detailed in preceding chapters, and difficulties with the Spaniards. Soon all alarm on account of the latter subsided, for Oglethorpe had established a barrier on the Southern border, by laying the foundation of the commonwealth of Georgia, and preparing means for keeping the Spaniards south of the St. John's. When this barrier was made secure, the treaties with the Indians were accomplished, the war with France ended, and universal peace reigned in the Carolinas. Emigration flowed thither in a broad and rapid stream. Immigrants came from all parts of Europe. Up the Pedee, Santee, Edisto, and Savannah Rivers, settlements spread rapidly, and soon the ax and the plow were plying with mighty energy upon the banks of the Wateree, the Broad, and the Saluda Rivers, and their tributaries. **8** At one time six hundred German settlers came in a body; and from the North of Ireland such numbers of the Protestant inhabitants (Scotch-Irish chiefly) departed for Carolina that the depopulation of whole districts was menaced. Immigrants came, too, from the other colonies. Within a single year (1764), more than a thousand families with their effects – their cattle, hogs, and horses – crossed the Alleghanies from the Eastern settlements, and pitched their tents in the bosom of Carolina. Far removed from the political power they had been taught to reverence, they soon became alienated. They felt neither the favors nor the oppressions of government, and in the free wilderness their minds and hearts became schooled in that sturdy independence which developed bold and energetic action when the Revolution broke out.

While the people of New England were murmuring because of Writs of Assistance and other grievances, the Carolinians were not indifferent listeners, especially those upon the seaboard; and before the Stamp Act lighted the flame of general indignation in America, leading men in South Carolina were freely discussing the rights and privileges of each colony, and saw in day-dreams a mighty empire stretching along the Atlantic coast from the Penobscot to the St. John's. Already their representatives had quarreled with the governor (William Boone), because he had presumed to touch, with official hands, one of their dearest privileges (the elective franchise), and refused to hold intercourse with him. In these disputes, Christopher Gadsden, Thomas Lynch, Henry Laurens, Charles Cotesworth Pinckney, the Rutledges, and other staunch patriots in the stormy strife ten years later, were engaged. A spirit of resistance was then aroused, which brought South Carolina early into the arena of conflict when the war began.

When intelligence of the Stamp Act came over the sea, the Assembly of South Carolina did not wait to consult the opinions of those of other colonies, but immediately passed a series of condemnatory resolves. When, soon afterward, the proposition for a Colonial Congress came from Massachusetts, a member of the Assembly ridiculed it, **9** others thought the scheme chimerical, yet a majority of them were in favor of it, and delegates were appointed to represent South Carolina in the Congress which was held at New York on October 7, 1765. The iniquitous character of the Stamp Act was freely discussed by the Carolinians, and as the day approached (November 1) when it was to go into operation, the people became more and more determined to resist it. When the stamps arrived in Charleston, no man was found willing to act as distributor, and Governor William Bull (who had succeeded Boone) ordered them to be placed in Fort Johnson, a strong fortress on James's Island, then garrisoned by a very small force. When the place of deposit became known, one hundred and fifty armed men, who had secretly organized, went down to the fort at midnight, in open boats, to destroy the stamps. They surprised and captured the garrison, loaded the cannons, hoisted a flag, and at sunrise proclaimed open defiance of the power of the governor. The captain of the armed ship which brought the stamps opened a parley with the insurgents, and agreed to take away the obnoxious articles, and "not land them elsewhere in America." **10** This was agreed to, and the men returned to the city. So universal was the opposition to the Act, that no attempt was made to arrest the men concerned in this overt act of treason.

Under a wide-spreading live oak, a little north of the residence of Christopher Gadsden – the Samuel Adams of South Carolina – the patriots used to assemble during the summer and autumn of 1765, and also the following summer, when the Stamp Act was repealed. There they discussed the political questions of the day. From this circumstance the green oak was called, like the great elm in Boston, Liberty Tree. **11** There Gadsden assembled some of his political friends after the repeal of the Stamp Act in 1766, and, while bonfires were blazing, cannons were pealing for joy, and the Legislature of South Carolina was voting a statue in honor of Pitt, **12** he warned them not to be deceived by this mere show of justice. **13** His keen perception comprehended the Declaratory Act in all its deformity, and while others were loud in their praises of the king and Parliament, he ceased not to proclaim the whole proceeding a deceptive and wicked scheme to lull the Americans into a dangerous inactivity. And more; it is claimed, and generally believed in South Carolina, that under Liberty Tree Christopher Gadsden first spoke of American Independence. How early is not known, but supposed to be as early as 1764. **14**

The people of Charleston cheerfully signed non-importation agreements in 1769 and 1770, and faithfully adhered thereto; and when the Continental Congress of 1774 adopted the *American Association*, its recommendations were very generally complied with in South Carolina. When tea was sent to America, under the provisions of a new act of 1773, the South Carolinians were as firm in their opposition to the landing of the cargoes for sale, as were the people of Boston. It was stored in the warehouses, and there rotted, for not a pound was allowed to be sold.

The closing of the port of Boston, by act of Parliament, on the first of January, 1774, aroused the indignation and sympathy of the South Carolinians, and substantial aid was freely sent to the suffering inhabitants of that city. When the proposition for a General Congress went forth, the affirmative voice of South Carolina was among the first heard in response. In an assembly of the people, held in Charleston, on the sixth, seventh, and eighth of July, 1774, it was declared that the Boston Port Bill was "most cruel and oppressive," and plainly showed that "if the inhabitants of that town are intimidated into a mean submission of said acts, that the like are designed for all the colonies; when not even the shadow of liberty to his person, or of security to his property, will be left to any of his majesty's subjects residing on the American continent." The same convention approved of the proposition for a General Congress, chose delegates to represent them in Federal Council, **15** and closed their proceedings by the appointment of a committee of ninety-nine, "to act as a general committee, to correspond with the committees of other colonies, and to do all matters and things necessary to carry the resolutions of the convention into execution." Henry Laurens was appointed chairman of this large committee, and it was agreed that twenty-one should constitute a business quorum. **16**

In defiance of the remonstrances and menaces of Lieutenant-governor Bull, a Provincial Congress of delegates, chosen by the people, met at Charleston on the eleventh of January, 1775. Charles Cotesworth Pinckney was chosen president. That Assembly approved of the proceedings of the General Congress, and appointed a committee of inspection and observation to see that its recommendations were complied with. **17** Now began those coercive measures of the Whigs which were often wrong and oppressive, but frequently necessary and salutary. The non-importation measures were rigorously enforced, and royal power was boldly defied. The people of Charleston formed themselves into volunteer companies to practice the use of fire-arms, and the boys, catching the spirit of the hour, banded together, and with mimic weapons imitated the discipline of their seniors.

On the nineteenth of April, 1775, the day when the first blow was struck for liberty at Lexington, the packet ship Swallow arrived at Charleston, bringing dispatches for the governors of the Southern colonies. Among others was a dispatch for the acting governor of South Carolina, William Bull. His disputes with the Committee of Safety and the Provincial Congress had risen to a high pitch of acrimony, and the public mind was greatly excited. Yet all hoped for reconciliation, and few could believe that civil war would actually ensue. The arrival of the Swallow extinguished these hopes, for a secret committee who had been appointed to seize the next mail that should arrive from England, performed their duty well. **18** On opening the dispatches to the governor, it was found that the British ministry had resolved to coerce the colonies into submission. The royal governors were ordered to seize the arms and ammunition belonging to the several provinces, raise provincial troops, if possible, and prepare to receive an army of British regulars to aid them. Gage and Dunmore, we have seen, acted upon these instructions, but the patriots of Lexington, Concord, and Williamsburg thwarted them; and the Charleston Committee of Correspondence, giving those of North Carolina and Georgia timely warning, enabled them to assume an attitude of defense before it was too late. A messenger, with these dispatches, was sent to the Continental Congress, and this was the first intelligence which that body had of the real intentions of the British ministry.

A few days after the discovery of this scheme, intelligence of the battle at Lexington arrived. Suspicion now yielded to demonstration; there was no longer any uncertainty; the mother was arming against her children; war was inevitable. While patriotism, gushing in full fountain from the hearts of the people, made them proclaim boldly, We are ready! sober reason saw the disparity in the strength of the oppressor and the oppressed. England was then among the first powers of the earth; the colonies were weak in material defenses. The savage tribes on their whole western frontier might be brought, like thirsty bloodhounds, upon them; they possessed not a single ship of war; they had very little money; at the South, the slaves, by offers of freedom, might become enemies in their midst; a large number of wealthy, influential, and conscientious men were loyal to the king; the governors, being commanders-in-chief, had control of the provincial military forces, and, if their thoughts had for a moment turned to the Continental powers of Europe for aid, they were pressed back by the reflection that republican principles were at variance with the dominant sentiments of the Old World. And yet they did not hesitate. Pleading the justice of their cause, they leaned for support upon the strong arm of the God of Battles.

Having resolved on rebellion, the people of Charleston were not afraid to commit acts of legal treason. They justly considered that "all statutes of allegiance were repealed on the plains of Lexington, and the laws of self-preservation left to operate in full force." **19** They accordingly concerted a plan, like their brethren in Savannah, to secure the arms and ammunition in the city, and on the night of the twentieth of April they seized upon all the munitions of war they could find. This was the first overt act of resistance, and at that hour began the Revolution, in earnest, in South Carolina.

A second session of the Provincial Congress commenced on the first of June. An association, drawn up by Henry Laurens, was adopted; **20** a permanent Committee of Safety was appointed; an issue of six hundred thousand dollars in paper money was ordered, and two regiments of infantry, of five hundred men each, and a battalion of cavalry or rangers, was directed to be raised. Some gentlemen were sent to the West Indies in a fast-sailing vessel to procure powder, and were fortunate enough to return with about ten thousand pounds.

After arranging military affairs, the attention of the Assembly was next turned to the organization of civil government. A Council of Safety was appointed to act during the recess of the Provincial Congress, to whom all the powers of that body were delegated. **21** They had the entire control of the army; were clothed with power to contract debts for the public service, and to issue coin and bills of credit. With this organization, civil government, upon a republican basis, was begun.

During the session of the Congress, Lord William Campbell, **22** who had been appointed governor, arrived at Charleston in July 1775, and was very courteously received. He professed great love for the people of the province, and assured them that he would use his best endeavors to promote the welfare of the inhabitants. Taught by experience to suspect the promises of royalty or its representatives, the people took measures to test his sincerity. The hollowness of his professions was proved, and turning their backs upon him, the patriots proceeded in their preparations for armed resistance. A vessel was fitted out by the Committee of Safety to attempt the capture of an English sloop laden with powder, then lying at St. Augustine. The expedition was successful, and fifteen thousand pounds of powder were brought safely into Charleston, though chased by cruisers sent out by Campbell. Part of this powder, which was sent to the Continental Congress for the use of the grand army, was used by Arnold and his men in the siege of Quebec at the close of 1775.

South Carolina Flag.

Early in September of 1775, Colonel Moultrie **23** proceeded to take possession of the fort on Sullivan's Island, in Charleston harbor. The small garrison made no resistance, but fled to the British sloops of war Tamar and Cherokee, then lying in Rebellion Roads, in front of Fort Sullivan. Lord Campbell, perceiving the storm of popular indignation against him daily increasing, particularly when it became known that he was endeavoring to incite the Indians on the frontier to lift the hatchet for the king, and was tampering with the Tories in the interior, also fled to these vessels for shelter, and thus "abdicated" royal power on September 14.

The Provincial Council now increased the defenses of the city, and organized a company of artillery. They also took measures for fortifying the harbor. Lieutenant-colonel Motte, accompanied by Captains Charles Cotesworth Pinckney, Bernard Elliot, and Francis Marion, took possession of Fort Johnson, on James Island, and on the same evening, Captain Heyward, with thirty-five of the Charleston artillery, went down and mounted three guns in the place of those spiked by the garrison when they fled. Three days afterward, the first Republican flag displayed at the South was floating over the main bastion of the fortress. **24**

Colonel Moultrie soon afterward mounted some heavy cannons upon Haddrell's Point, and all of the troops in and around Charleston were ordered on September 16, 1775 to hold themselves in readiness, for it was expected that the Tamar and Cherokee would, pursuant to Lord Campbell's menaces, open a fire upon the town or the forts. A magazine was built at Dorchester, and ten thousand pounds of powder were sent thither. A small fort was also erected upon the Cheraw Hills, on the Great Pedee, to give confidence to the Whigs in that region where Campbell's emissaries had been. In December, Moultrie, with a considerable force, took possession of Sullivan's Island and commenced the erection of a fascine battery. This advantage, and a few long shots from Haddrell's Point (where a battery had been erected), caused the Tamar and Cherokee to leave the harbor. Lord Campbell, despairing of maintaining his power, sailed to Jamaica. It was during these events upon the sea-board in the course of the autumn of 1775 that the organization of the Tories in Ninety-Six and other portions of the upper country occurred.

Colonel Gadsden assumed command of all the troops in Charleston early in 1776, and the Council of

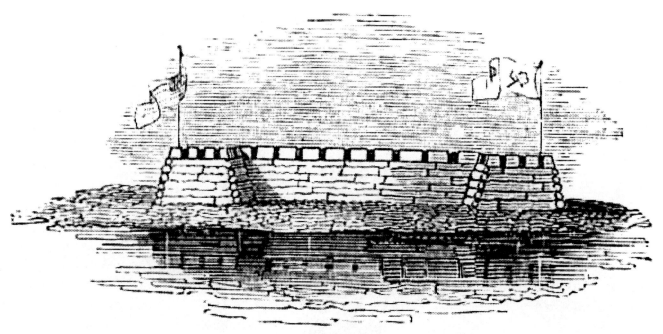

Fort Sullivan.

Safety commissioned him a brigadier. Colonel Moultrie was ordered in March 1776 to build a strong fort upon Sullivan's Island, large enough to accommodate one thousand men, and to take the command there. **25** This measure was considered necessary, for certain intelligence had arrived that a fleet and army were preparing to assail Charleston, and a fort at the point designated would be a key to the harbor, with the aid of Fort Johnson. The civil government was revised; a temporary Constitution was formed **26** (the first in the colonies); and the Legislature was called the General Assembly of South Carolina. It possessed all powers of supreme local government. John Rutledge **27** was chosen president, with the actual powers of governor; and other executive officers, with a privy and a legislative council, were elected by the new Assembly. **28** After passing a few necessary laws, the Assembly adjourned on April 11, 1776, the Council of Safety and General Committee were dissolved, and a constitutional government began. The president and privy council were vested with executive power to administer the government during the recess of the Legislature.

Under the efficient direction of President Rutledge, Charleston and vicinity were well prepared for defense in the spring of 1776. About one hundred pieces of cannon were mounted at various points around the harbor, and a strong battery was erected at Georgetown. Brigadier-general John Armstrong, of Pennsylvania, arrived in April, and took the general command; and early in June (June 4), Major-general Charles Lee reached Charleston. He had been sent by General Washington, after the expulsion of the British from Boston, to watch the movements of General Sir Henry Clinton, and to command the troops for the defense of the Southern sea-board. Lee's known experience, skill, and bravery gave the people great confidence, and the alarm which had prevailed since the appearance of a British squadron off Dewees Island, five days before, soon subsided. Lee was indefatigable in his preparations for the defense of Charleston, and was generally satisfied with all the arrangements of the

Sir Peter Parker.
From an
English Print.

local authorities. The garrison at Fort Sullivan worked day and night to complete it, and when the British fleet appeared, about thirty heavy pieces of cannon were mounted upon it. **29**

The British fleet bearing a land force, and both designed to act against the Southern colonies in the campaign of 1776, was commanded by Admiral Sir Peter Parker. Its approach was providentially discovered in time **30** to allow the Carolinians to prepare for defense, and for Washington to dispatch Lee and Armstrong, officers of experience, to aid them. Parker reached the Cape Fear early in May, where he was joined by Sir Henry Clinton, from New York, who assumed the chief command of all the land troops. On the fourth of June, the day when General Lee arrived, the fleet appeared off Charleston bar, and several hundred land troops took possession of Long Island, which lies eastward of Sullivan's Island, and is separated from it only by a narrow creek.

All was now activity among the patriots. The militia of the surrounding country obeyed the summons of Governor Rutledge with great alacrity, and flocked to the town. These, with the regular troops of South Carolina, and those of the Northern colonies who had come with Armstrong and Lee, made an available force of between five and six thousand men. Gadsden commanded the first regiment of South Carolina regulars at Fort Johnson, on James's Island, three miles from Charleston; Colonel Moultrie those at Fort Sullivan; and Colonel Thomson, the advanced post on the east end of Sullivan's Island. Thomson's troops were chiefly riflemen. There was also a strong force at Haddrell's Point, under the immediate command of General Lee. In the city, governor Rutledge, impelled by the necessities of the hour, and under the belief that an attempt would be made to pass the forts and land the troops in the city, pursued the rigorous course of martial law. Valuable stores on the wharves were torn down, and a line of defenses was made in their places. The streets near the water were barricaded, and, on account of the scarceness of lead, many window-sashes of that material were melted into bullets. He pressed into service seven hundred negroes with tools, who belonged to Loyalists; and seized, for the moment, the money and papers of the lukewarm. By these energetic measures the city was made strong in moral and physical material, and when the British fleet crossed the bar, all were ready to receive them.

While these preparations were in progress by the Republicans, Sir Henry Clinton was busy in arranging for a combined attack with the land and naval forces. He constructed two batteries upon Long Island, to confront those of Thomson upon Sullivan's Island, and to cover the passage of his troops in boats and in fording from the former to the latter, for Fort Sullivan, the main work in the harbor, was the devoted mark for the first blow. Its garrison consisted of only three hundred and forty-four regulars and a few volunteer militia, and its only aid was an armed sloop, with powder, which was anchored off Haddrell's Point, now Point Pleasant.

At half past ten o'clock on the morning of the twenty-eighth of June, Sir Peter Parker, on board his flag-ship, the Bristol, made the signal for attack. His fleet immediately advanced, and, with springs on their cables, anchored in front of Fort Sullivan. **31** The Active, Bristol, Experiment, and Solebay led to the attack, and anchored nearest the fort. At the moment of anchoring, the fort poured a heavy fire upon them, and each vessel returned the compliment by delivering a broadside upon the little fortress, but with almost harmless effect upon the spongy palmetto logs. **32** It was a little before eleven o'clock when the action began, and terrible to the people of Charleston who looked upon the contest from balconies, roofs, and steeples, was the roar of three hundred cannons. To the little garrison the peril seemed great, yet they maintained their fire with precision and coolness. Perceiving the unfinished state of the fort on the western side, toward Charleston, Parker ordered the Sphynx, Active, and Syren to take a position in the channel on that side, so as to enfilade the garrison. Had they succeeded, surrender or certain destruction must have been the alternative for the Americans. The three vessels advanced to execute the orders, when they all struck upon a shoal called the Middle Ground, and while thus entangled a very destructive fire was poured upon them from the fort. The Sphynx got off with the loss of her bowsprit, and the Syren without much injury, and withdrew to

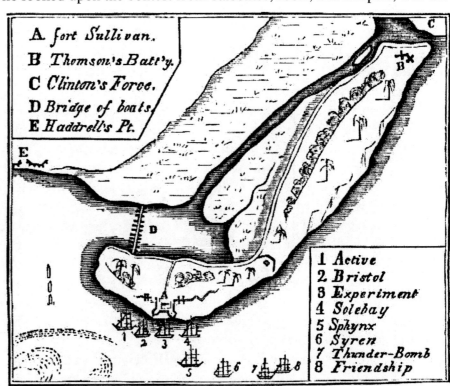

A. *fort Sullivan.*
B. *Thomson's Batt'y.*
C. *Clinton's Force.*
D. *Bridge of boats.*
E. *Haddrell's Pt.*

1. *Active*
2. *Bristol*
3. *Experiment*
4. *Solebay*
5. *Sphynx*
6. *Syren*
7. *Thunder-Bomb*
8. *Friendship*

Sullivan's Island and the British Fleet at the time of the attack.

another part of the harbor; but the Active was too thoroughly grounded to be moved. Simultaneously with the advance of the ships to the attack of Fort Sullivan, Clinton's batteries upon Long Island, and some floating batteries in the creek, opened upon those of Thomson; and a portion of the British land forces embarked in boats under cover of their artillery, to force their way to assail the fort on the west, where it was unfinished, or at least to prevent Lee from sending re-enforcements or ammunition from Haddrell's Point, across the bridge of boats which had now been constructed. Clinton's whole regular force on Long Island was about two thousand troops, and between five and six hundred seamen. Colonel Thomson had only two cannons, but his riflemen were among the best marksmen in the state. He allowed Clinton's flotilla to approach within musket shot, when he opened a destructive fire upon them from his battery and small arms. Several attempts to advance were made, and every time the sure marksmen of Carolina swept many from the boats, and Clinton was obliged to abandon his design. Lee, who had perceived the weakness of the fort on its western side, and penetrated the design of Clinton, observed this retrograde movement with joy; and when at about two o'clock, the garrison ceased firing, on account of the exhaustion of ammunition, he sent a sufficient supply from Haddrell's Point and a schooner, and the defensive cannonade was resumed.

The fire from the ships was almost incessant, and yet the patriots in the fort were firm. **33** Their shots were dreadfully effective, and the ships were severely battered and maimed. Anxiously the seamen and marines turned their eyes toward the East, expecting aid from Clinton, but it did not appear. For ten long hours, while the iron storm from the fort was beating their ships in pieces, and sweeping whole ranks from the decks, scarcely a ray of hope appeared for the seamen; and when the sun went down, its last gleams were upon the scarlet coats and burnished arms of the British, yet upon Long Island, and kept at bay by Thomson's batteries and sure-aimed riflemen. The contest continued without intermission until sunset, when it slackened, and at half past nine in the evening it entirely ceased. At eleven o'clock the shattered vessels slipped their cables and withdrew to Five Fathom Hole, about two miles northeastward of Fort Johnson, except the Active, which remained aground. Early the next morning the garrison fired a few shots at her, which were returned. At the same time, Clinton made another effort to cross from Long Island to Sullivan's Island, but Thomson confronted him with such hot volleys, that he was obliged to retreat behind his batteries. Perceiving further efforts to reduce the fort, especially in his crippled condition, to be futile, Parker ordered the crew of the Acteon to set fire to and abandon her. They did so, leaving the colors flying and guns loaded. When they had left, the Americans boarded her, secured her colors as a trophy, carried off the ship's bell, fired her guns at the Bristol, loaded three boats with stores, and set her on fire. Within half an hour after they left her, she blew up.

This battle was one of the severest during the whole war, and while it redounded to the military glory of the Americans, and greatly increased the patriot strength at the South, it was regarded by the British as peculiarly disastrous, aside from the actual loss of life and property in the action. **34** This discomfiture occurred at a time when the British were desirous of making the most favorable impression here and in Europe, for Lord Howe was then on his way as a *commissioner* to settle all disputes, or as a *commander* to prosecute the war. His course was to be determined by circumstances. This was the first time that the Americans had encountered a regular British fleet. The fact that it had been terribly shattered and driven to sea was very humiliating to the vanquished, and, at the same time, encouraging to the victors, at a moment when a brilliant act like this was of immense moment to the Republican cause.

On the morning after the battle, the British fleet left Charleston harbor, and proceeded to Long Island to recruit. Almost every vessel was obliged to remain for that purpose. On the thirtieth, General Clinton, with Cornwallis and the troops, escorted by the Solebay frigate, with Sir Peter Parker on board, sailed for New York with a heavy heart.

The joy of the Americans on account of this victory was unbounded, and the praises of the actors were upon all lips. On the day when Clinton sailed (June 30), the lady of Bernard Elliot **35** presented Colonel Moultrie's regiment with a pair of elegant colors. These were the standards which were afterward planted on the walls of Savannah by Bush, Hume, and Jasper. **36** They were afterward captured when Charleston fell, and were seen years after the war, among other British trophies, in the Tower of London. **37** The Legislature of South Carolina changed the name of the fort from Sullivan to Moultrie, in honor of its brave defender; and on the twentieth of July (1776), the Continental Congress passed a resolution of thanks to General Lee, Colonels Moultrie and Thomson, and the officers and men under their command. **38**

For three years after the repulse of the British from Charleston, South Carolina enjoyed comparative quiet while the war was raging at the North. Yet her sons were not idle listeners to the roar of cannons in New England, New York, and Pennsylvania, but flocked thither in hundreds, under brave leaders, to do battle for their common country. The patriots of that war were not divided by sectional interests. There was no line of demarkation over which men hesitated to pass. A desire for the happiness of the New England people was a twin sentiment with love for his own fireside, in the heart of the Carolinian and Georgian; and the bosom of the "Green Mountain Boy" heaved as strongly with emotions of joy when a blow for freedom was successfully dealt among the rice lands of the South, as when the shout of victory went up from the heights of Saratoga.

Upon the western frontiers of the South, the Indians, stirred up by Tory emissaries, gave the people some trouble; but from the day when the Declaration of Independence was read at Liberty Tree, **39** until, the opening of the campaign of 1779, the people of Charleston continued in quiet pursuit of lucrative commerce. Yet prosperity did not stifle aspirations for freedom, nor the accumulation of riches cause hesitation when danger drew nigh and demanded sacrifices. The spirit of liberty burned with a light as steady and eternal as the polar star, even amid the clouds and darkness of intensest sufferings which ensued.

I visited Sullivan's Island on the day of my departure from Charleston, on January 29, 1849, and sauntered for an hour upon the beach where the old Palmetto Fort once stood. Nothing of it now remains but a few of the logs imbedded in the drifting sand. The modern Fort Moultrie is not a large, but a well-constructed fortification. The island is sandy, and bears no shrub or tree spontaneously except the Palmetto,

View at Fort Moultrie. 40

and these are not seen in profusion. On the northwestern side of the island are the remains of an old causeway or bridge, extending to the main, nearly upon the site of a bridge of boats, which was used during the battle in 1776. It was constructed after that conflict, at the cost of Christopher Gadsden, and was called Gadsden's Bridge. The British, when they afterward possessed Charleston, used it to pass over to their lazaretto, which they erected on Sullivan's Island. This lazaretto was upon the site of the present Episcopal church in Moultrieville. A part of the old brick wall was yet standing when I visited the spot in 1849.

We have already considered the demonstration made by the British at the South, in the capture of Savannah at the close of 1778, and also the events in Georgia after the arrival of General Lincoln as commander-in-chief of the Southern army. Lincoln reached Charleston on the fourth of December (1779), and proceeded immediately to re-enforce the scattered army of Howe, after the fall of Savannah on April 25. On the first intimation of the designs of the British upon the South, North Carolina raised about two thousand men, and placed them under Generals Ashe and Rutherford. They did not arrive in time to aid Howe at Savannah, but helped to augment the small force of Lincoln. These had entered the state; and to the concentration of these troops, and the raising of South Carolina militia, Lincoln bent all his energies. He chose Major Thomas Pinckney **41** as his chief aid, and on the twenty-sixth of December, he marched from Charleston with about three hundred levies of that vicinity, and about nine hundred and fifty levies and militia of North Carolina, for the Georgia frontier. On the way, they met the flying Americans from the disastrous battle at the capital of Georgia, and on the third of January Lincoln established his head-quarters at Purysburg, on the north side of the Savannah River. He had been promised seven thousand men; he had only about fourteen hundred. He had been promised supplies, instead of which the new levies, and the militia conscripts who were brought to head-quarters, were destitute of tents, camp utensils, or lead, and had very little powder, and no field-pieces. The South Carolina militia, under Richardson, were insubordinate, and rapidly melted away by desertion, or became useless by actual refusal to be controled by any but their immediate commanders. Happily, their places were supplied by the arrival of General Ashe with eleven hundred North Carolinians at the close of January (January 31, 1779).

While Lincoln was recruiting and organizing an army near Purysburg, General Prevost joined Campbell at Savannah, with seven hundred regular troops from St. Augustine. Hoping to follow up Campbell's success by striking Charleston, he sent forward Major Gardiner with two hundred men, to take post on Port Royal Island, within about sixty miles of the capital of South Carolina. General Moultrie, with about an equal number of Charleston militia, and two field-pieces, attacked and defeated Gardiner on the morning of the third of February (1779). The British lost almost all of their officers, and several privates were made prisoners. The loss of the Americans was trifling. Gardiner, with the remnant of his force, escaped in boats and fled to Savannah, while Moultrie, crossing to the main, pressed forward and joined Lincoln at Purysburg.

Strengthened by a party of Creeks and Cherokees, for whom a communication with Savannah was opened by the defeat of General Ashe on Brier Creek, and informed that Lincoln, with his main army, was far up the river, near Augusta, Prevost determined to attempt the capture of Charleston. With about two thousand chosen troops, and a considerable body of Loyalists and Indians, he crossed the Savannah at Purysburg on April 25, and pushed forward by the road nearest the coast, toward Charleston.

When Lincoln was informed of this movement of Prevost, he considered it a feint to draw him from Georgia. With that view he crossed the Savannah, and for three days marched down its southern side, directly toward the capital of that state, hoping either to bring Prevost back or to capture Savannah. In the mean while, he detached Colonel Harris, with three hundred of his best light troops, to re-enforce Moultrie, who was retreating before Prevost, toward Charleston. Governor Rutledge, who had gone up to Orangeburg to embody the militia, advanced at the same time with six hundred men of that district, and when Lincoln recrossed the Savannah in pursuit of Prevost, the interesting spectacle was presented of four armies pressing toward Charleston. **42**

When Prevost commenced his invading march, Charleston was quite unprepared for an attack by land. The ferries of the Ashley were not fortified, and only some weak defenses guarded the Neck. Intelligence of the invasion aroused all the energies of the civil and military authorities in the city, and night and day the people labored in casting up intrenchments across the Neck from the Ashley to the Cooper, under the general direction of the Chevalier De Cambray, an accomplished French engineer. The Assembly, then in session, gave Rutledge power only a little less than was conferred upon him a few months afterward, when he was made dictator for the time, and the utmost energy was every where displayed. Lieutenant-governor Bee, with the council, aided the efforts to fortify the town by necessary legal orders. All the houses in the suburbs were burned, and within a few days a complete line of fortifications with abatis was raised across the Neck, on which several cannons were mounted. Colonel Marion, who commanded the garrison at Fort Moultrie, was re-enforced, and the battery on Haddrell's Point was well manned. These arrangements were effected before the arrival of Prevost, who halted, in hesitation, for three days at Pocataligo, on account of conflicting intelligence. This delay was fatal to his success, for it allowed the people of Charleston time to prepare for an attack.

Lincoln's distance from Charleston with the main army, the retreat of Moultrie, and the terror inspired by the torch of the invader, who went on plundering and burning, caused great numbers to remain on their plantations, and to take protection from Prevost. On the evening of the ninth of May (1779), he encamped on the south side of the Ashley River. On that and the following day, Moultrie, Rutledge, and Harris arrived with their respective forces. That of Moultrie had dwindled from one thousand men to about six hundred. He immediately took command of all the Continental troops, while Rutledge claimed the control of the militia. This produced some confusion, but no serious misunderstanding.

On the morning of the eleventh of May, Prevost, with nine hundred regulars, crossed the Ashley and appeared before the works on Charleston Neck. He left his main army and heavy baggage on the south side of the river, and approaching within cannon shot of the lines, summoned the garrison to surrender. During the forenoon, Count Pulaski, who was stationed at Haddrell's Point with his legion, crossed the Cooper

Charleston in 1780.
From a drawing by Leitch.

River and entered the town, and at noon he led his infantry to attack the British advanced guard. He was repulsed with great loss. A large portion of his infantry were killed, wounded, or made prisoners. The commander himself escaped with difficulty to the American lines, under cover of some discharges of cannon.

Prevost now advanced to within a mile of the American works, when his progress was checked by a sharp cannonade. He renewed his demand for a surrender, and the remainder of the day was spent in the passage of flags. Aware of the approach of Lincoln, the Americans desired procrastination, and asked time to deliberate. Prevost refused it, and the city was filled with consternation in expectation of an assault. The civil authorities, trembling in view of the horrors of a cannonade, sent a proposition to Prevost to guarantee the neutrality of South Carolina until the close of the war, and then allow it to follow the fate of its neighbors, on condition that the royal army should withdraw. Prevost rejected the proposition, and insisted that, as the garrison were in arms, they should surrender prisoners of war. To this Moultrie and the military objected, and every moment until past midnight a cannonade was expected. **43** Not an eye closed in slumber, and at three o'clock in the morning, at the solicitation of the civil authorities, Moultrie sent a message to Prevost, renewing the proposition of the previous day. It was rejected, and all anxiously awaited the dawn, expecting a terrible assault. The morning broke clear and serene, but the eyes of the sentinels upon the batteries, and of anxious watchers upon the house tops, could perceive no traces of a beleaguing army. For a moment it appeared as if all had been disturbed by a terrible dream, but as the sun arose, the scarlet uniforms and burnished arms of the invaders were seen south of the Ashley. The British host was crossing to James's Island. The mystery was soon solved. During the night, Prevost was informed that

Lincoln, with four thousand men, was pressing on toward Charleston, and he feared that his force, hardly sufficient to attack the town with hopes of success, would be annihilated if placed between two fires. **44** He prudently withdrew, and, perceiving his pathway of approach intercepted by Lincoln, he essayed to escape back to Savannah, by way of the islands along the coast.

Lincoln soon approached, and both armies encamped within thirty miles of Charleston, the Americans upon the main, and the British upon John's Island. **45** There they continued for a month, Prevost fearing to move forward, and Lincoln not feeling quite strong enough to pass over and attack him. Finally, an attempt to dislodge the British was made. They had cast up works at Stono Ferry, and garrisoned them with eight hundred men, under Colonel Maitland, the brave officer who died at Savannah a few months later. These were attacked on the morning of the twentieth of June by about twelve hundred of Lincoln's troops. The contest was severe, and for an hour and twenty minutes the battle was waged with skill and valor. A re-enforcement for Maitland appeared, and the Americans perceived it to be necessary to retreat. When they fell back, the whole garrison sallied out, but the American light troops covered the retreat so successfully, that all of the wounded patriots were brought off. The Americans lost in killed and wounded, one hundred and forty-six, besides one hundred and fifty-five missing. Of the killed and wounded twenty-four were officers. The British loss was somewhat less. Three days afterward, the British evacuated the post at Stono Ferry, and retreated from island to island, until they reached Beaufort, on Port Royal. After establishing a post on Ladies' Island, between Port Royal and St. Helena, they returned in boats to Savannah and St. Augustine. **46** The heat was now becoming intense, and Lincoln's army dispersed, with the exception of about eight hundred men, with whom he retired to Sheldon to prepare for the opening of another campaign in October. Thus closed, ingloriously to the invaders, the second attempt of the British to possess themselves of the capital of South Carolina.

Chapter XX
Endnotes

1 We have already met Sergeant William Jasper while securing the Carolina flags upon the parapet of the Spring Hill redoubt at Savannah, and there sealing his patriotism with his life's blood. Jasper was one of the bravest of the brave. After his exploits at Fort Moultrie, which we shall consider hereafter, his commander, General Moultrie, gave him a sort of roving commission, certain that he would always be usefully employed. Jasper belonged to the second South Carolina regiment, and was privileged to select from his corps such men as he pleased to accompany him in his enterprises. Bravery and humanity were his chief characteristics, and while he was active in the cause of his country, he never injured an enemy unnecessarily. While out upon one of his excursions, when the British had a camp at Ebenezer, all the sympathies of his heart were aroused by the distress of a Mrs. Jones; whose husband, an American by birth, was confined in irons for deserting the royal cause after taking a protection. She felt certain that he would be hanged, for, with others, he was to be taken to Savannah for that purpose the next morning. Jasper and his only companion (Sergeant Newton) resolved to rescue Jones and his fellow-prisoners. Concealing themselves in the thick bushes near the spring (at which they doubted not the guard of eight men would halt), they awaited their approach. As expected, the guard halted to drink. Only two of them remained with the prisoners, while the others, leaning their muskets against a tree, went to the spring. Jasper and his companion then leaped from their concealment, seized two of the guns, shot the two sentinels, and took possession of the remainder of the muskets. The guards, unarmed, were powerless, and surrendered. The irons were knocked off the wrists of the prisoners, muskets were placed in their hands, and the custodians of Jones and his fellow-patriots were taken to the American camp at Purysburg the next morning, themselves prisoners of war. Jones was restored to his wife, child, and country, and for that noble deed posterity blesses the name of Sergeant Jasper. That name is indelibly written on the page of history, and the people of Savannah have perpetuated it by bestowing it upon one of the beautiful squares of their city.

2 There were about fifty families who went from the Port Royal settlement to the Ashley River, and about the same number from the Northern colony accompanied Governor Yeamans thither.

3 Governor Yeamans caused a number of African slaves to be brought from Barbadoes, and in the year 1672 the slave system in South Carolina was commenced.

4 The Indian name for the Ashley was Ke-a-wah; for the Cooper, E-ti-wan. The city has a fine sheltered harbor, with the sea six miles distant.

5 The city of Charleston was laid out in 1680 by John Culpepper, who had been surveyor general of the Northern colony of the Carolinas, but was then a fugitive, on account of his participation in an insurrectionary movement there. The streets were laid out nearly at right angles, and the town site was completely inclosed with a line of fortifications. A plan of these fortifications, and of the city at that time, is published in Johnson's Traditions and Reminiscences of the Revolution, page 3.

6 Simm's History of South Carolina, page 64.

7 See page 356 in original text.

8 Previous to this period, some important settlements were made. Between the years 1730 and 1740, an Irish settlement was planted near the Santee, to which was given the name of Williamsburg township. At the same time, some Swiss emigrants, under John Pury, settled upon the northeast side of the Savannah, and founded the village of Purysburg. From 1748 to 1755, great numbers of Palatines (Germans) were introduced, and settled Orangeburgh and other places upon the Congaree and Wateree. After the battle of Culloden in 1745, many Scotch Highlanders came over. Some of them settled in South Carolina, but a larger portion located at Cross Creek (Fayetteville), in North Carolina. The greatest influx of settlement was after the treaty of Paris, in 1763.

9 "If you agree to the proposition of composing a Congress from the different British colonies," said the member, "what sort of a dish will you make. New England will throw in fish and onions; the Middle States flax-seed and flour; Maryland and Virginia will add tobacco; North Carolina pitch, tar, and turpentine; South Carolina rice and indigo; and Georgia will sprinkle the whole composition with saw-dust. Such an absurd jumble will you make if you attempt to form a union among such discordant materials as the thirteen British provinces." A shrewd country member replied, "I would not choose the gentleman who made the objection for my cook, but, nevertheless, I would venture to assert that if the colonies proceed judiciously in the appointment of deputies to a Continental Congress, they would prepare a dish fit to be presented to any crowned head in Europe." – Ramsay.

10 In a letter from Charleston, published in Weyman's New York Gazette, it is stated that on the morning of the nineteenth of October a gallows was discovered in the middle of Broad Street, where Church Street intersects (then the central part of the town), on which were suspended an effigy representing a stamp distributor, and another to impersonate the devil. Near by was suspended a boot (Lord Bute), with a head upon it, covered by a blue Scotch bonnet. To these effigies labels were affixed. Upon one was the warning, "Whoever shall dare to pull down these effigies had better been born with a mill-stone about his neck, and cast into the sea." At evening they were taken down, and paraded through the street by about two thousand persons, until they came to the house of George Saxby, in Tradd Street, an appointed stamp distributor, where they made a great noise, and injured his windows and other portions of his house, to "the value of five pounds sterling." No other riotous feelings were manifested. Nine days afterward, Saxby and Caleb Lloyd made oath at Fort Johnson that they would have nothing more to do with the stamps.

11 This tree stood within the square now bounded by Charlotte, Washington, Boundary, and Alexander streets. This continued to be the favorite meeting-place until the Revolution was in full progress. Beneath that tree the Declaration of Independence was first read to the assembled people of Charleston. Its history and associations were hateful to the officers of the crown, and when Sir Henry Clinton took possession of the city in 1780, he ordered it to be cut down, and a fire lighted over the stump by piling its branches around it. Many cane heads were made from the remains of the stump in after years. A part of it was sawed into thin boards and made into a neat ballot-box, and presented to the " '76 Association." This box was destroyed by fire, at the rooms of the association, during the great conflagration in 1838.

12 This statue was of marble, and stood at the intersection of Broad and Meeting Streets. During the siege of Charleston, in April, 1780, a British cannon-ball from James's Island passed up Meeting Street, struck this statue, and broke off its left arm. Several years after the war, the statue, being considered an obstruction, was rudely pulled down by some workmen employed for the purpose, when the head was broken off, and it was otherwise mutilated. Good taste would have restored the arm, and kept the statue in its place until this day.

13 The following are the names of the Sons of Liberty of Charleston, who met with Gadsden, under Liberty Tree, in 1766, and with linked hands pledged themselves to resist when the hour for resistance should arrive. They are published by Johnson from the original record of George Flagg, one of the party: General Christopher Gadsden, William Johnson, Joseph Verree, John Fullerton, James Brown, Nathaniel Libby, George Flagg, Thomas Coleman, John Hall, William Field, Robert Jones, John Lawton, Uzziah Rogers, John Calvert, Henry Bookless, J. Barlow, Tunis Tebout, Peter Munclear, William Trusler, Robert Howard, Alexander Alexander, Edward Weyman, Thomas Searl, William Laughton, Daniel Cannon, and Benjamin Hawes. The last survivor, George Flagg, died in 1824.

14 Christopher Gadsden was born in Charleston in 1724. He was educated in England, where he became accomplished in the learned languages. He returned to America at the age of sixteen, and entered the counting-house of a merchant in Philadelphia, where he remained until he was twenty-one years of age. He then went to England, and on his return engaged in mercantile pursuits in Charleston. He was successful, and was soon able to purchase all of the property known as Ansonborough, which his father lost in play with Lord Anson. His house was upon the lot now (1848) owned by Mrs. Isaac Ball, and the kitchen is yet standing on the lot at the northeast corner of East Bay and Vernon Streets. Mr. Gadsden was one of the earliest opponents of Great Britain in South Carolina, and, as the Revolution advanced, was one of its firmest supporters. He was a delegate in the first Continental Congress in 1774, and his name is attached to the American Association agreed to by that body. In 1775, he was elected senior colonel and commandant of three South Carolina regiments, and was subsequently made a brigadier. He was in the engagement at the siege of Charleston in 1776. He was one of the framers of the Constitution of South Carolina, adopted in 1778. He resigned his commission in 1779, and when Charleston was taken by Clinton, in 1780, he was lieutenant governor; as such, he signed the capitulation. Three months afterward, he was taken, with others, and cast into the loathsome prison at St. Augustine (an act in open violation of the terms of capitulation), because he would not submit to indignity at the hands of Governor Tonyn. There he suffered for eleven months, until exchanged in June, 1781, when he sailed to Philadelphia with other prisoners. He returned to Charleston, and was a member of the Assembly convened at Jacksonburg in the winter of 1782. He opposed the confiscation of the property of the Loyalists, and thereby won their esteem. He was elected governor of the state in 1782, but declined the honor, and went into the retirement of private life. He died on the twenty-eighth of August, 1805, at the age of eighty-one years.

15 Henry Middleton, John Rutledge, Christopher Gadsden, Thomas Lynch, and Edward Rutledge, were appointed delegates.

16 Ramsay's History of South Carolina, i., 18; Moultrie's Memoirs, i., 10. The place of meeting was at a large tavern on the northeast corner of Broad and Church Streets, commonly called, at that day, "The Corner."

17 The following gentlemen composed the Charleston committee: Christopher Gadsden, Isaac Huger, William Gibbes, William Parker, Aaron Locock, Roger Smith, Maurice Simons, John Poang, Thomas Legare, Sen., Edward Simons, Edward Blake, Samuel Prioleau, Jr., Hugh Swinton, John Champneys, William Host, John Brewton, Alexander Chisholme, Alexander Chovin, William Livingston, and John Baddeley.

18 This committee consisted of William Henry Drayton, John Neufville, and Thomas Corbett. After the mail was carried to the post-office, and before it could be opened, this committee went thither, and demanded it from Stevens, the postmaster, in the name of the Provincial Congress. Stevens allowed them to take it, under protest. It was then carried to the State House and opened. The packages for the governors were retained and opened; the private letters, with seals unbroken, were returned to the post-office.

19 Ramsay, i., 30.

20 The core of this document consisted in the declaration of those who signed it, that they were "ready to sacrifice life and fortune to secure the freedom and safety of South Carolina; holding all persons inimical to the liberties of the colonies who shall refuse to subscribe to the association."

21 This council consisted of Henry Laurens, Charles Pinckney, Rawlins Lowndes, Thomas Ferguson, Miles Brewton, Arthur Middleton, Thomas Heyward, Jr., Thomas Bee, John Huger, James Parsons, William Henry Drayton, Benjamin Elliott, and William Williams.

22 Lord Campbell was the third brother of the Duke of Argyle. He had married Sarah Izard, the sister of Ralph Izard, who belonged to the richest family in the province. The residence of Lord Campbell was on Meeting Street, now (1851) owned and occupied by Judge D. E. Huger. Soon finding his residence in Charleston unsafe, he escaped to a British vessel in the harbor, leaving his family behind. Lady Campbell was treated with great respect, but finally she too went on board the vessel, and was landed at Jamaica. The next year (1776), Campbell was on board the Bristol in the attack upon Charleston, and, while fighting on the quarter-deck, he was wounded. He died from the effects of his wounds, two years afterward.

23 William Moultrie was a native of South Carolina. He was born in 1730. We find him first in public service as an officer, in the expedition against the Cherokees in 1760. He was also in subsequent expeditions against that unhappy people. When the Revolution broke out, he was among the earliest in South Carolina to take the field on the Republican side. His defense of the fort on Sullivan's Island in 1776, gave him great eclat, and he was promoted to brigadier. He gained a battle over the British near Beaufort in 1779, and in May, 1780, was second in command when Charleston was besieged. He went to Philadelphia while a prisoner of war, and did not return to South Carolina until 1782. He was several times chosen governor of the state, and retired from public life only when the infirmities of age demanded repose. He published his Memoirs of the Revolution, relating to the war in the South, in two volumes, in 1802, printed by David Longworth, of New York. Governor Moultrie died at Charleston on the twenty-seventh of September, 1805, at the age of seventy-five years.

24 Moultrie, in his Memoirs, says, "As there was no national flag at the time, I was desired by the Council of Safety to have one made, upon which, as the state troops were clothed in blue, and the fort was garrisoned by the first and second regiments, who wore a silver crescent on the front of their caps, I had a large blue flag made, with a crescent in the dexter corner, to be in uniform with the troops. This was the first American flag displayed in the South." – Vol. i., p. 90.

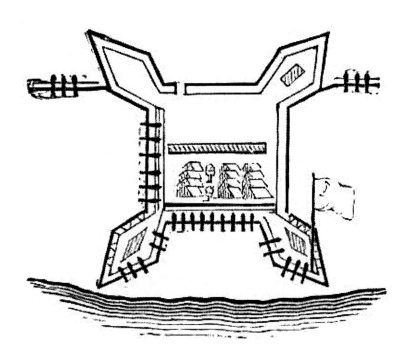

25 This fort was constructed of palmetto logs, in sections, and filled in with sand. The merlons were sixteen feet thick, and sufficiently high to cover the men from the fire that might be directed upon them from the tops of the British vessels. It was first called Fort Sullivan, being upon the island of that name, but was named Fort Moultrie, after its gallant defense by its commander, in June, 1776. When I visited its site (a portion of which is covered by the modern strong works of Fort Moultrie) in 1849, some of the palmetto logs were visible, imbedded in the sand. The annexed engraving shows the plan of the fort when attacked in June, 1776, before it was completed. The drawing of the fort is from a large plan by an English engineer, who was attached to the British fleet.

26 This Constitution was to remain in force until October of the same year.

27 John Rutledge was a native of Ireland, and came to America with his father in 1735. He studied law at the Temple in London, and returned to Charleston in 1761. He espoused the Republican cause at an early period of the dispute, and was a member of the first Continental Congress in 1774. When the temporary Constitution of South Carolina was adopted in the spring of 1776, he was appointed president and commander-in-chief of the colony. When the new and permanent Constitution was established two years later, he refused his assent, because he thought it too democratic. His prejudices yielded, however, and in 1779 he was chosen governor under it, with the temporary power of a dictator. He took the field at the head of the militia, and with great skill and energy managed the affairs of the state until the fall of Charleston in May, 1780. After the war, he was made judge of the Court of Chancery, and in 1789 a judge of the Supreme Court of the United States. He was appointed chief justice of South Carolina in 1791, and in 1796 was elevated to the seat of chief justice of the United States. He died in July, 1800.

28 Henry Laurens was elected vice-president; William Henry Drayton, chief justice;* Alexander Moultrie, attorney general; John Huger, secretary; Hugh Rutledge, judge of the admiralty; and James Parsons, William H. Drayton, John Edwards, Charles Pinckney, Thomas Ferguson, and Rawlins Lowndes, members of the Privy Council.

---

* In April, about a month after his appointment, Chief-justice Drayton delivered an able charge to the Grand Jury on the subject of independence. Its effects were powerful, salutary, and extensive. In South Carolina its arguments convinced the dubious, and its boldness, both of reason and expression, strengthened the feeble and upheld the wavering. It was published in all of the Whig papers of the Northern colonies; was commented upon by the London press, and received the warmest expressions of approbation from the friends of the colonists every where.

---

29 General Moultrie says that Lee ordered a bridge of boats to be constructed for a retreat. There were not boats enough, and empty hogsheads, with planks across, were tried, but without success. Lee was very anxious on this point, and felt that in case of attack, the garrison must be sacrificed. "For my part," says Moultrie, "I never was uneasy on not having a retreat, because I never imagined that the enemy could force me to that necessity."

30 Early in April, Lord Dunmore sent a boat to Annapolis, with dispatches for Governor Eden, from Lord Dartmouth. James Barron, then cruising in the Chesapeake, captured this boat and conveyed the papers to Williamsburg. Germain's communication revealed the whole plan of operations. It was dated December 23, 1775.

31 The British vessels brought into action were the Bristol and Experiment, of fifty guns each; the frigates Active, Solebay, Acteon, Syren, and Sphynx, of twenty-eight guns each; the Thunder-bomb, and Ranger, sloop, each of twenty-eight guns; and the Friendship, an armed vessel of twenty-two guns.

32 The palmetto is peculiar to the low sandy shores of the Southern States. It grows from twenty to forty feet in height, without branches, terminating in a large tuft of very long leaves. The wood is very porous, and a bullet or cannon-ball, on entering it, makes no extended fracture. It becomes buried, without injuring adjacent parts.

33 Burke, in his Annual Register, gave the following graphic account of the naval engagement and the fort: "While the continued thunder from the ships seemed sufficient to shake the firmness of the bravest enemy, and daunt the courage of the most veteran soldier, the return made by the fort could not fail of calling for the respect, as well as of highly incommoding the brave seamen of Britain. In the midst of that dreadful war of artillery, they stuck with the greatest firmness and constancy to their guns, fired deliberately and slowly, and took a cool and effective aim. The ships suffered accordingly; they were torn to pieces, and the slaughter was dreadful. Never did British valor shine more conspicuous, and never did our marines, in an engagement of the same nature with any foreign enemy, experience as rude an encounter. The springs of the Bristol's cable being cut by the shot, she lay for some time exposed in such a manner to the enemy's fire as to be most dreadfully raked. The brave Captain Morris, after receiving a number of wounds, which would have sufficiently justified a gallant man in retiring from his station, still with a noble obstinacy disdained to quit his duty, until his arm being at length shot off, he was carried away in a condition which did not afford a possibility of recovery. It is said that the quarter-deck of the Bristol was at one time cleared of every person but the commodore, who stood alone, a spectacle of intrepidity and firmness which have seldom been equaled, never exceeded. The others on that deck were either killed or carried down to have their wounds dressed. Nor did Captain Scott, of the Experiment, miss his share of the danger or glory, who, besides the loss of an arm, received so many other wounds, that his life was at first despaired of."

34 The loss on board of the ships was frightful. Every man stationed on the quarter-decks of the vessels, at the beginning of the action, was either killed or wounded. The commodore suffered a slight contusion. Captain Morris soon afterward died of his wounds. Forty men were killed and seventy-one wounded, on board the Bristol. The Experiment had twenty-three killed and seventy-six wounded. Her commander, Captain Scott, lost an arm. Lord William Campbell, the last royal governor of the province, who served as a volunteer, was badly wounded at the beginning of the action. The whole loss of the British, in killed and wounded, was two hundred and twenty-five. The Bristol had not less than seventy balls put through her. When the spring of her cable was cut, she swung round with her stern toward the fort, and instantly every gun that could be brought to bear upon her hurled its iron balls upon her. At the beginning of the action, Moultrie gave the word, "Mind the commodore and the fifty gun ships!" These were the principal sufferers. Although the Thunder-bomb cast more than fifty shells into the fort, not one of them did serious damage. There was a large moat, filled with water, in the center of the fort, which received nearly all of the shells, and extinguished the fusees before the fire reached the powder. Others were buried in the sand, and did no harm. Only ten of the garrison were killed and twenty-two wounded. Most of these were injured by shots which passed through the embrasures. Moultrie says that, after the battle, they picked up, in and around the fort, twelve hundred shot of different calibre that were fired at them, and a great number of thirteen inch shells.

During the action, Sergeant William Jasper, whom we have already met at the Spring, near Savannah, and witnessed his death while planting the South Carolina flag upon the parapet of the British works, at the siege of that town, performed a daring feat. At the commencement of the action, the flag-staff was cut away by a ball from a British ship, and the Crescent flag of South Carolina, that waved opposite the Union flag upon the western bastion, fell outside, upon the beach. Jasper leaped the parapet, walked the length of the fort, picked up the flag, fastened it upon a sponge staff, and in the midst of the iron hail pouring upon the fortress, and in sight of the whole fleet, he fixed the flag firmly upon the bastion. Three cheers greeted him as he ascended to the parapet and leaped, unhurt, within the fort. On the day after the battle, Governor Rutledge visited the fort, and rewarded Jasper for his valor by presenting him with his own handsome small sword which hung at his side, and thanked him in the name of his country. He offered him a lieutenant's commission, but the young hero, who could neither read nor write, modestly refused it, saying, "I am not fit to keep officer's company; I am but a sergeant."

35 Mrs. Elliot is represented as one of "the most busy among the Revolutionary women, and always active among soldiers." She was a niece of Mrs. Rebecca Motte, the patriot widow of Orangeburg, and during the whole war was a useful co-worker with her republican husband. The wife of Charles Elliot, brother of Bernard Elliot, was also a glorious Whig. Her wit and repartee often scathed the proud feelings of the British officers, when the royal army occupied Charleston. On one occasion, Colonel Balfour was walking with her in her garden, when, pointing to a chamomile flower, he asked its name. "The rebel flower," she replied. "And why is it called the rebel flower?" asked the officer. "Because," replied Mrs. Elliot, "it always flourishes most when trampled upon."

36 See page 217 in original text.

37 Moultrie, i., 182. One of them was of fine blue silk, and the other of fine red silk, richly embroidered.

38 Journals, ii., 260.

39 Johnson relates that on that occasion (fifth of August, 1776) the people of Charleston, young and old, of both sexes, assembled around Liberty Tree with all the military of the city and vicinity, drums beating and flags flying. The ceremonies were opened with prayer. The Declaration was then read by Major Bernard Elliot (whose lady presented the flags), and were closed by an eloquent address by the Reverend William Percy, of the Protestant Episcopal Church. It was a hot day, and Mr. Percy's black servant held an umbrella over his head and fanned him during the delivering of his address. Alluding to this, a British wag wrote:

"Good Mr. Parson, it is not quite civil
To be preaching rebellion, thus fanned by the devil."

40 This view is from the southwestern angle of Fort Sullivan, looking toward James's Island. That angle, with cannons, a portion of the barracks, and the flag-staff, are seen on the right. The small building toward the left marks the center of the old Palmetto Fort. In the distance is seen Fort Sumter, and in the extreme distance, close by the angle of the fort, is seen the village upon the site of old Fort Johnson. Charleston bar, at the entrance of the harbor, is about six miles from the city. The width of the inner harbor, at its mouth, is about a mile wide. This is guarded by Forts Moultrie, Sumter, and Johnson, and by Castle Pinckney, a handsome work in front of the city, within the inner harbor.

41 Thomas Pinckney was born at Charleston on the twenty-third of October, 1750. His early years were passed in England. At the close of his studies there, he returned to Charleston, and, with his brother, Charles Cotesworth Pinckney, was among the earliest and most efficient military patriots in the provincial regiment raised there. Assured of his talents and worth, Lincoln appointed him his aid, and in that capacity he served at the siege of Savannah by the Americans and French in October, 1779. He distinguished himself in the battle at Stono Ferry. He was aid-de-camp to General Gates in the battle near Camden, where he was wounded and made a prisoner. When sufficiently recovered, he was sent to Philadelphia. In 1787, Major Pinckney succeeded General Moultrie as governor of South Carolina; and in 1792, was appointed by Washington, Minister Plenipotentiary to the Court of St. James. In November, 1794, he was appointed Envoy Extraordinary to the Spanish court, and repaired to Madrid the following summer. He effected a treaty by which the free navigation of the Mississippi was secured to the United States. He returned to Charleston in 1796. At the beginning of the war of 1812, President Madison appointed him to the command of the Southern division of the army, and it was under General Pinckney that General Andrew Jackson distinguished himself. After the war, General Pinckney retired into private life. He died on the 2d of November, 1828, aged seventy-eight years. He married the daughter of Rebecca Motte.

42 Rutledge, with the men of Orangeburg; Moultrie pursued by Prevost; Prevost pursued by Lincoln; and Colonel Harris with his corps of light troops.

43 During the evening, an unfortunate accident deprived the state of the life and services of a brave officer. Having discovered a breach in the abatis, Governor Rutledge, without the knowledge of the garrison, sent out Major Benjamin Huger* and a small party to repair it. The garrison had lighted tar barrels in front of their lines to prevent a surprise, and by their light Huger and his men were discovered, and believed to be a party of the enemy. Immediately a fire of cannons, muskets, and rifles ran along almost the whole line, and poor Huger and twelve of his men were slain. The folly of having two commanders was perceived, and all military authority was immediately given to Moultrie. The cannonade alarmed the town, it being regarded as a prelude to something more dreadful.

---

* Benjamin was one of the five patriot brothers, who were active in revolutionary scenes. He was the gentleman who first received La Fayette on his arrival at Georgetown in 1777. His brother Isaac was a

brigadier in the army under Greene; John was Secretary of the State of South Carolina; Daniel was a member of the Continental Congress; and Francis K. was quartermaster general of the Southern Department. Major Huger's son, Francis K., married a daughter of General Thomas Pinckney, and was that officer's adjutant general during the war of 1812.

---

44 According to an imperfect estimate, the number of American troops in the city was three thousand one hundred and eighty; the British force numbered about three thousand three hundred and sixty.

45 This island is separated from the main land by a narrow inlet, which is called Stono River. Over this, at a narrow place, there was then (and is still) a ferry, where the British cast up defensive works.

46 On their retreat across the fertile islands, on the Carolina coast, the British committed the most cruel depredations. The people hid their treasures, but the negroes, who had been promised freedom, repaired in great numbers to the British camp, and informed the soldiers where their master's property was concealed. It is believed that in this incursion three thousand negroes were carried out of the state, many of whom were shipped to the West Indies and sold. Hundreds died of camp fever upon Otter Island, and for years afterward their bleaching bones strewed the ground thereon. The whole loss was more than four thousand, valued at two hundred and eighty thousand dollars. Houses were stripped of plate, jewelry, clothing, money, and every thing of value that could be carried away. Live-stock was wantonly slaughtered, and in a few cases females were violated by the brutal soldiery.

CHAPTER XXI

The season of repose enjoyed by Charleston after the invasion of Prevost was brief. When the hot summer months had passed away, both parties commenced preparations for a vigorous autumn campaign – the British to maintain their position and extend their conquests, if possible; the Americans to drive the invaders from the Southern States, or, at least, to confine them to the sea-ports of Savannah and St. Augustine. The fall of Savannah was a disastrous event. It was the initial step in those strides of power which the royal army made a few months later, when Charleston fell, when the patriot army of the South was crushed, and when the civil institutions of South Carolina and Georgia, established by the Republicans, were prostrated at the feet of the conquerors.

During the winter preceding the siege of Charleston, Lincoln's army had dwindled to a handful, chiefly on account of the termination of the enlistments, and the hesitation of the militia when called to service, because of the defeat at Savannah and the apparent hopelessness of further resistance. The prison-ships at Savannah were crowded with the captives of the Georgia regiments, and the heel of British power, planted firmly upon the patriots of that state, made the Loyalists bold and active. All along the Southern frontier of South Carolina the voice of rebellion was subdued to a whisper, and a fearful cloud of hostile savages, gathered by the emissaries of the crown, frowned sullenly and threatening upon her western borders; while within her bosom, bands of unprincipled Tories, encouraged by others more respectable but passive, were endeavoring, by menaces and promises, to sap the foundation of Republican strength. Such was the condition of South Carolina when a British fleet, under Admiral Arbuthnot, bearing five thousand land troops, commanded by Sir Henry Clinton, **1** appeared off Edisto Inlet, within thirty miles of Charleston, toward the close of the winter of 1780 (February 11, 1780). They came to subjugate the whole South, the chief feature in the programme of operations for that year.

The Assembly of South Carolina was in session when the enemy appeared. Governor Rutledge was immediately clothed with the powers of supreme dictator, and with judgment and vigor he exercised them for the defense of the capital. Yet he did not accomplish much, for the militia were tardy in obeying his call to hasten to the city. If Clinton had marched directly upon Charleston when he landed his troops upon John's Island, he might have conquered it within a week after his debarkation. **2** More cautious than wise, he formed a depot at Wappoo, on James's Island, and tarried more than a month in preparations for a siege.

General Lincoln was in Charleston with about fourteen hundred troops, a large portion of them North Carolina levies, whose term of service was almost expired. The finances of the state were in a wretched condition. The paper money was so rapidly diminishing, that it required seven hundred dollars to purchase a pair of shoes; and in every department, civil and military, the patriots were exceedingly weak. Lincoln's first

Sir Henry Clinton
From an English Print

impulse was to evacuate the city, retire to the upper country, collect a sufficient army, and then return and drive the invaders from it. The tardy plans of Clinton changed Lincoln's views. Hoping for re-enforcements, then daily expected, and also aid from the Spanish West Indies, **3** he resolved to maintain a siege. His first care was to strengthen the works upon Charleston Neck, cast up the previous year when Prevost menaced the town. Rutledge ordered three hundred negroes to be brought from the neighboring plantations to work upon the fortifications, and within a few days cannons and mortars were mounted; a trench, filled with water, stretched across the Neck from the Ashley to the Cooper, and two rows of *abatis* protected the whole. Fort Moultrie, the redoubts at Haddrell's Point and Hobcaw, the works at South Bay, Hospital Point, and all along the city front, were strengthened and manned. **4** Charles Cotesworth Pinckney **5** was placed in command of the garrison at Fort Moultrie. Captain Daniel Horry was sent to Ashley Ferry to watch the approach of the enemy, and General Moultrie went southward to gather the militia, direct the movements of the cavalry, and annoy the enemy on his approach.

The little flotilla of Commodore Whipple, then in the harbor, was ordered to oppose the passage of the British fleet over the bar, but his vessels were small and thinly manned, and little reliance was placed upon them. The inhabitants viewed the gathering dangers with increasing alarm. Knowing the weakness of Lincoln's army, and desirous of saving it, as their only hope for the future, the citizens advised an evacuation before it should be too late. Lincoln, hourly expecting re-enforcements, was hopeful, and expressing a belief that he might maintain a siege, or leave at a future time, if necessary, he resolved to remain, at the same time taking measures for keeping open a communication with the country toward the Santee.

On the twenty-eighth of March the royal army crossed the Stono, marched to the Ashley, at Old Town (the site of ancient Charleston), and there crossed that stream toward evening. They had strengthened Fort Johnson, cast up intrenchments along the Ashley to confront those of the Americans upon the opposite shore, and galleys were in motion to enter the harbor and anchor in the Ashley. The army moved slowly down the Neck, and on Sunday morning, the first of April, broke ground within eleven hundred yards of the American works, then defended by about eighty cannons and mortars. They were annoyed all the way by a party of light horsemen under Lieutenant-colonel John Laurens, and lost between twenty and thirty men in the skirmishes.

Admiral Arbuthnot entered the harbor on the twentieth of March with his smaller vessels and transports, and drove Whipple with his little fleet from Five Fathom Hole to the

C C Pinckney

immediate vicinity of the town. On the ninth of April he left his anchorage, and, though exposed to an enfilading fire from Fort Moultrie, 6 halted under the guns of Fort Johnson, within cannon shot of the town. Pinckney hoped that Whipple would retard the British vessels, and allow him to batter them, as Moultrie did four years before; but the commodore, with prudent caution, retreated to the mouth of the Cooper River, and sunk most of his own and some merchant vessels between the town and Shute's Folly (marked boom on the map below), and thus formed an effectual bar to the passage of British vessels up the channel to rake the American works upon the Neck. Clinton advanced to Hamstead Hill on April 5, 1780, and in the face of a sharp fire erected a battery and mounted twelve cannons upon it. He now demanded an immediate surrender of the town and garrison. Brigadier Woodford had just arrived with seven hundred Virginians, and reported others on their way. The citizens urged Lincoln to maintain a siege, for rumors had come that large numbers

were pressing forward from the North to the relief of the city. Thus strengthened by fresh troops 7 and public opinion, Lincoln assured the besiegers that he should continue his defense until the last extremity. Forty-eight hours elapsed, when Clinton opened his batteries upon the town and fortifications, and a terrible cannonade from both parties was kept up from that time until the twentieth.

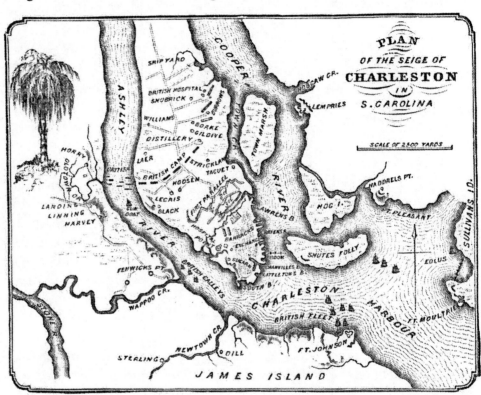

When the British were about to open their batteries, Governor Rutledge, leaving the civil power in the hands of his lieutenant, Gadsden, went into the country, between the Cooper and Santee Rivers, to arouse the militia and keep a communication open with the town in that direction. Lincoln sent his cavalry (about three hundred men), with General Isaac Huger in command, to watch the country in the vicinity of the head waters of the Cooper River. Led through the woods by a negro, Tarleton, with his legion cavalry, fell upon Huger at Biggin Bridge, near Monk's Corner, at dawn on the fourteenth of April, and scattered his troops, who were unsuspicious of danger. Twenty-five Americans were killed; the remainder fled to the swamps. Tarleton secured almost three hundred horses, and then scouring the country between the Cooper and Wando, returned in triumph to the British camp.

Four days after the surprise of Huger (April 18, 1780), Cornwallis arrived at Charleston with three thousand troops from New York. Thus strengthened, Clinton enlarged the area of his operations. Detachments were sent into the country, and drove the Americans back. Governor Rutledge was compelled to flee higher up the Santee; Haddrell's Point was taken possession of and fortified; supplies from the surrounding country were cut off, and every avenue for escape seemed closed. Lincoln called a council of war on April 21, and an attempted retreat to the open country was proposed. The inhabitants objected, because they feared the invading army was too exasperated by the obstinate defense already made, to spare them in person and property. With rapine and pillage before them, they implored Lincoln to remain. Terms of capitulation, which allowed the army to withdraw to the interior, and the property of the citizens to be undisturbed, were agreed upon and proposed to Clinton. Clinton would not acquiesce, and the terrible work of siege went on. The Americans made but one sortie, and that did not seriously damage the British or impede their progress, **8** and on the sixth of May **9** the besiegers completed their third parallel, and in the face of a heavy fire raised redoubts nearer and nearer the American lines. **10**

Now fully prepared to storm the town by sea and land, Clinton and Arbuthnot again demanded a surrender. The situation of the Americans was deplorable. The garrison consisted of less than three thousand men, a large portion of them raw militia; provisions of all kinds were becoming scarce, and the Loyalists in the city were fomenting disaffection among the distressed inhabitants. The engineers asserted that the lines could not be defended ten days longer, and that they might be carried by assault in ten minutes. Bombs and carcasses were falling in every part of the city with destructive effect, killing women and children, and setting houses on fire; and the town militia, in utter despair, had thrown down their arms. Further resistance seemed foolish and inhuman, for success was hardly possible, and lives and property were hourly sacrificed. The citizens, appalled by the destructive agencies at work around them, worn out by want of sleep and anxiety, and coveting any condition other than the one they were

Marriott Arbuthnot

enduring, now expressed their willingness to treat for a surrender. A flag was sent out, and Clinton's ultimatum was received. He demanded the surrender of the garrison and the citizens as prisoners of war, with all the forts and other works, and their appliances, together with the shipping that remained in the harbor. He would promise nothing except that the town property of those within the lines should remain unmolested, and that all prisoners should be paroled. A truce until the next day (May 9, 1780) was asked by the besieged, and was allowed, when Lincoln again refused compliance with Clinton's demands. At eight o'clock in the evening the firing commenced again. It was a fearful night in Charleston. The thunder of two hundred cannons shook the city like the power of an earthquake, and the moon, then near its full, with the bright stars, was hidden by the lurid smoke. Shells were seen coursing in all directions, some bursting in mid air, others falling upon houses and in the streets, and in five different places the flames of burning buildings simultaneously shot up from the depths of the city. "It appeared," says Moultrie, alluding to the bomb-shells, "as if the stars were tumbling down. The fire was incessant almost the whole night; cannon-balls whizzing and shells hissing continually among us; ammunition chests and temporary magazines blowing up; great guns bursting, and wounded men groaning along the lines; it was a dreadful night!" The cannonade was continued all the next day and part of the night, and many Americans were killed by the passage of balls through the embrasures of their batteries. Sand-bags were freely used for protection, but these were swept away, until at several points the besieged were obliged to abandon their works and withdraw. Arbuthnot now prepared to bombard the town from the water, and the batteries at Fort Johnson and at Wappoo hurled round shot into the streets. **11**

At two o'clock on the morning of the eleventh (May 1780), Lieutenant-governor Gadsden, the council, and many leading citizens, requested Lincoln to signify his agreement to Clinton's proposed terms of surrender, if better could not be obtained. A signal was given, the firing ceased, and before dawn all the guns were quiet. Articles of capitulation were agreed to, and signed by the respective commanders, and by Christopher Gadsden in behalf of the citizens. **12** Between eleven and twelve o'clock on the twelfth of May, the Continental troops marched out with the Turk's march, and laid down their arms, after a gallant and desperate defense of about forty days. General Leslie immediately marched in and took possession of the town.

Great skill and courage were brought to bear upon the patriots during the siege, and never was a defense more obstinate and heroic, and yet it was not a bloody one. The loss on both sides in killed and wounded was nearly equal; that of the Americans, exclusive of the inhabitants of the town not bearing arms, was ninety-two killed, and one hundred and forty-eight wounded. The British lost seventy-six killed, and one hundred and eighty nine wounded. The number of prisoners, including the inhabitants of the town, was between five and six thousand. About four hundred cannons were a part of the spoils of victory. Thirty houses were destroyed during the siege. **13**

The fall of Charleston, and loss of Lincoln's army, paralyzed the Republican strength at the South, and the British commanders confidently believed that the finishing-stroke of the war had been given. Lincoln suffered the infliction of unsparing censure, because he allowed himself to be thus shut up in a town; but had he repulsed the enemy, or the siege been raised, as at one time contemplated, **14** the skill and wisdom of his course would have exceeded all praise.

Sir Henry Clinton now proceeded to re-establish the civil power of Great Britain in South Carolina. In proclamations, he made many promises of benefits to the obedient, and menaced the refractory with the miseries of confiscation of property and personal punishments. Finally, on June 1, 1780, he offered pardon to all who should submit and crave it, and promised political franchises such as the people had never enjoyed. Lured by these promises, the timid and lukewarm flocked to Charleston, took protection, and many entered the military service of the king. Two hundred and ten influential citizens in Charleston agreed to an address of congratulation on the restoration of order and the ancient bond of union between the province and Great Britain. This movement, with the hasty retreat northward of troops marching to the relief of Charleston, and the destruction of Buford's command on the Waxhaw, almost effaced every lineament of resistance in the South. As we have seen, garrison's were posted in the interior, and the voice of rebellion was hushed.

Clinton and Arbuthnot sailed for New York on the fifth of June, leaving Cornwallis in chief command of the British troops at the South. Before his departure, Clinton issued a proclamation, declaring all persons not in the military service, who were made prisoners at Charleston, released from their paroles, provided they returned to their allegiance as subjects of Great Britain. So far, well; but not the sequel. All persons refusing to comply with this requisition were declared to be *enemies and rebels, and were to be treated accordingly.* And more; they were required to enroll themselves as militia under the king's standard. This flagrant violation of the terms of capitulation aroused a spirit of indignant defiance, which proved a powerful lever in overturning the royal power in the South. Many considered themselves released from all the obligations of their paroles, and immediately armed themselves in defense of their homes and country, while others refused to exchange their paroles, for any new conditions. The silent influence of eminent citizens who took this course was now perceived by Cornwallis, and, in further violation of the conditions of capitulation, he sent many leading men of Charleston as close prisoners to St. Augustine on August 27, 1780, **15** while a large number of the Continental soldiers were cast into the loathsome prison-ships, and other vessels in the harbor. There they suffered all the horrors of confined air, bad food, filth, and disease. It was to these that the mother of President Jackson came, as an angel of mercy, with materials of alleviation for the sufferers. But the camp and typhoid fevers, and dysentery, swept off hundreds before the cruel hand of the oppressor relinquished its grasp. Maddened by torture, and almost heart-broken on account of the sufferings of their families, more than five hundred of the soldiers who capitulated at Charleston agreed to enroll themselves as royal militia, as the least of two present evils, and were sent to do service in the British army in Jamaica. Of nineteen hundred prisoners surrendered at Charleston, and several hundreds more taken at Camden and Fishing Creek, only seven hundred and forty were restored to the service of their country. **16**

A brief lull in the storm of party strife and warring legions in South Carolina succeeded the blow which smote down Republicanism; but when the trumpet-blasts of the conqueror of Burgoyne were heard upon the Roanoke, and the brave hearts of Virginia and North Carolina were gathering around the standard of Gates, the patriots of the South lifted up their heads, and many of them, like Samson rising in strength, broke the feeble cords of "paroles" and "protections," and smote the Philistines of the crown with mighty energy. Sumter sounded the bugle among the hills on the Catawba and Broad Rivers; Marion's shrill whistle rang amid the swamps on the Pedee; and Pickens and Clarke called forth the brave sons of liberty upon the banks of the Saluda, the Savannah, the Ogeechee, and the Alatamaha. The noble deeds of these partisans; the efforts and defeat of Gates; the successes of Greene and Morgan; and the brilliant achievements of "Legion Harry Lee," the strong right arm of the Southern army in the campaigns of 1781, we have considered in former chapters. Let us here, from this commanding point of view, note those daring exploits of Marion and his men not already considered, and also of their brave compatriots in their warfare in the vicinity of the sea-coast.

Marion was elected a captain in Moultrie's second South Carolina regiment, and, with his friend Peter Horry, received his commission on the twentieth of June, 1775. These young officers, in new uniforms and helmet-shaped leather caps, decorated with silver crescents inscribed "Liberty or Death!" went out immediately upon the recruiting service on the Black River and the Pedee, and every where excited the enthusiasm of the people. Brave young patriots flocked around them, and in Fort Sullivan, when its cannons shattered the fleet of Sir Peter Parker in 1776, these stout hearts and hands received their first practical lessons in defensive warfare. Already, as we have seen, they had been efficient in capturing Fort Johnson, on James's Island on September 14, 1775, but here they participated in the severer duties of vigorous conflict.

Fortunately for the Republican cause, an accident **17** prevented Marion being among the prisoners when Charleston fell, and he was yet at liberty, having no parole to violate, to arouse his countrymen to make further efforts against the invaders. While yet unable to be active, he took refuge in the swamps upon the Black River, while Governor Rutledge, Colonel Horry, and others, who had escaped the disasters at Charleston, were in North Carolina arousing the people of that state to meet the danger which stood menacing upon its southern border. Marion's military genius and great bravery were known to friends and foes, and while the latter sought to entrap him, the former held over him the shield of their vigilance. "In the moment of alarm he was sped from house to house, from tree to thicket, from the thicket to the swamp." **18** As soon as he was able, he collected a few friends and started for North Carolina to join the Baron De Kalb, then marching southward with a small Continental army. On the way, he was joined by his old friend Horry and a few of his neighbors, and these formed the "ragged regiment" who appeared before General Gates, the successor of De Kalb. It was while in the camp of Gates that Governor Rutledge, who also was there, commissioned Marion a brigadier, and he sped to the district of Williamsburg, between the Santee and Pedee, to lead its rising patriots to the field of active military duties. They had accepted the protection of British power after Charleston was surrendered, in common with their subdued brethren of the low country; but when Clinton's proclamation was promulgated, making active service for the crown or the penalty for rebellion an alternative, they eagerly chose the latter, and lifted the strong arm of resistance to tyranny. They called Marion to be their leader, and of these men he formed his efficient brigade, the terror of British scouts and outposts. Near the mouth of Lynch's Creek he assumed the command, and among the interminable swamps upon Snow's Island, near the junction of that stream with the Great Pedee, he made his chief rendezvous during a greater portion of his independent partisan warfare.

Marion's first expedition after taking command was against a large body of Tories, under Major Gainey, an active British officer, who were encamped upon Britton's Neck, between the Great and Little Pedee. He dispersed the whole party without losing a man in August, 1780. Flushed with victory, Marion was again in motion within twenty-four hours. Informed that Captain Barfield and some Tories were encamped a few miles distant, he sped thither, fell upon and scattered them to the winds. These two victories inspired his followers with the greatest confidence in their commander and reliance upon themselves. These sentiments, acted upon with faithfulness, formed a prime element of that success which distinguished Marion's brigade.

Marion now sent Colonel Peter Horry, with a part of his brigade, to scour the country between the Santee and Pedee, while with the remainder of his command he proceeded to attack the British post near Nelson's Ferry. Striking his blows in quick succession, and at remote points, Marion excited the alarm of the British commander-in-chief, and he ordered Tarleton to endeavor to entrap and crush the "Swamp Fox." Colonel Wemyss, whom Sumter afterward defeated on the Broad River, was first sent after him with a strong force. With untiring industry he followed Marion in the direction of the Black River, and often fell upon his trail. But the wary patriot never suffered himself to be surprised, nor allowed his men to fight when almost certain destruction appeared inevitable. Wemyss was too strong for Marion, so the latter fled before him, and with sixty trusty followers he thridded his way through interminable swamps and across deep streams into North Carolina. It was a grievous necessity, for it left Williamsburg District, the hot-bed of rebellion, exposed to the fury of the pursuers. Marion first halted on Drowning Creek on August 30, 1780; then pushing further on, he encamped near Lake Waccamaw, whence he sent back scouts to procure intelligence. Soon, he was swiftly retracing his steps, for Wemyss had relinquished pursuit, and had retired to Georgetown, leaving the sad marks of his desolating march over a space of seventy miles in length and fifteen in breadth. The injured inhabitants hailed Marion's return with joy, and his little army, seldom exceeding sixty men, soon had the appearance of a brigade. They were desperate men. Cruel wrongs gave strength to their arms, fleetness to their feet, power to their wills, and with joy they followed Marion toward the Black Mingo, fifteen miles below Georgetown, where a body of Tories were encamped. They fell upon them in two divisions, at midnight. An obstinate resistance was made, but the patriots were victorious. Marion lost but one man killed; the enemy were almost annihilated. This victory dispirited the Tories throughout the low country, and for some time Marion's brigade enjoyed needful repose upon the banks of the Santee, except during a brief period when Tarleton, who succeeded Wemyss in attempts to smite Marion, came in pursuit. He scoured the country southward from Camden, between the Santee and the Black Rivers, in search of the partisan, and, like Wemyss, spread desolation in his path. Tarleton exerted his utmost skill and energy, but could never overtake the vigilant Marion. Sometimes he would be within a few miles of him, and feel sure of securing him before to-morrow's sun, when at the same moment Marion would be watching the movements of the Briton from some dark nook of a morass, and at midnight would strike his rear or flank with a keen and terrible blow.

In October, Marion proceeded toward Lynch's Creek to chastise Harrison, the lieutenant of Wemyss, who was encamped there with a considerable body of Tories. On his way toward Williamsburg, he fell upon Colonel Tyne, who, with two hundred Tories, was encamped at Tarcote Swamp, on the forks of Black River, in fancied security. It was midnight on October 25, 1780 when he struck the blow. While some slept, others were eating and drinking; a few were playing cards; but none were watching. The surprise was complete. Some were slain, twenty-three were made prisoners, but a large portion escaped to Tarcote Swamp, from which some soon appeared and joined the ranks of the victor, upon the High Hills of the Santee, where he encamped a short time after the action. Marion did not lose a man.

Informed that Harrison had moved from Lynch's Creek, Marion collected some new recruits, and with his bold followers pushed forward to assail the British post at Georgetown, where only he could procure what he now most needed, namely, salt, clothing, and powder. He knew a surprise would be difficult, and an open assault dangerous. He chose the former method, but when he approached, the garrison was on the alert. A severe skirmish ensued within a short distance of the town, and Marion, discomfited, retired to Snow's Island, where he fixed his camp and secured it by such works of art as the absence of natural defenses required. In this skirmish, Gabriel Marion, a nephew of the general, was made a prisoner, and murdered on the spot. After that, "No quarter for Tories!" was the battle cry of Marion's men.

From Snow's Island **19** Marion sent out his scouts in every direction, and there he planned some of his boldest expeditions. Re-enforcements came, and at the close of 1780, Marion felt strong enough to confront any British detachment then abroad from head-quarters.

While Greene's army was approaching the Pedee early in 1781, Marion was very active abroad from his camp, at which he always left a sufficient garrison for its defense. Here and there he was smiting detachments of the British army; and when Lee, who had been sent by Greene to join him with a part of his legion, sought for Marion, it was with great difficulty that he could be found, for his rapid marches were in the midst of vast swamps. As soon as the junction was consummated in January 1781, these brave partisans planned an expedition against the British post at Georgetown, then garrisoned by two hundred men. Although the British works were strong, and our partisans had no cannons, they felt confident of the success of their plan, which was to attack the town and fortifications at two separate points. One division went down the Pedee in boats, the other proceeded cautiously by land. The attack was made at midnight, but nothing was effected beyond the capture of Campbell (the commandant) and a few privates, and slaying some stragglers from the garrison, who could not escape to the stockade. Yet the enterprise was not fruitless of good to the patriot cause. The audacity of the attempt had a powerful effect upon the minds of the British officers at the South, and the contemplated movement of a large portion of their forces from the sea-board to the interior, was abandoned. Thus was begun a series of movements to keep Cornwallis from Virginia until a sufficient force could be collected in Carolina to oppose him, which was the object of earnest efforts on the part of Greene.

After resting a few hours, Marion and Lee moved rapidly up the north bank of the Santee, toward Nelson's Ferry, to surprise Colonel Watson, who had taken post there. That officer, informed of his approach, placed a small garrison in Fort Watson, five miles above, and with the remainder of his force hastened on toward Camden. At this time Greene was commencing his famous retreat, and summoned Huger and his troops at Cheraw, and Lee with his whole legion, to meet him at Guilford. The events which ensued in that quarter have been detailed in preceding chapters. **20**

The departure of Lee, with his legion, greatly weakened Marion's force. Yet he was not less active than before, and his enterprises were generally more important and successful. He sent out small detachments to beat up Tory camps and recruiting stations, where ever they might be found. His subordinates caught his spirit and imitated his example, and were generally successful. The brothers Captain and Major Postelle greatly annoyed the British and Tories beyond the Santee, in the direction of Charleston, early in 1781. Like Marion, his subordinates never lingered upon the arena of victory to be surprised, but, when a blow was struck, they hastened away to other fields of conflict. The great partisan never encumbered himself with prisoners – he always paroled them.

Toward the last of January 1781, we find the blacksmiths of Kingstree forging saws into rough broadswords for a corps of cavalry which Marion placed in command of Colonel Peter Horry. In February, Horry is observed eastward of the Pedee battling with Tories and British regulars. Soon afterward he is engaged in a bloody conflict of eight hours, near Georgetown, slaying almost one half of his adversaries, and winning the victory. Every where the name of Marion was feared, and the presence of his men was dreaded by the opponents of the patriot cause.

In the spring of 1781, Colonel Watson was sent with a select corps of five hundred men to attempt the destruction of Marion's brigade. He moved with caution, evidently afraid of the partisan, for he was then striking successful blows at different points, in rapid succession, and appeared to be possessed of ubiquitous powers. **21** Marion observed him, and concentrated his force on Snow's Island, whence he sallied forth as occasion required. He sped with rapid foot to the path of Watson's approach, and at Wiboo Swamp, nearly opposite the present Santee Canal, he confronted him. The advanced guards of Marion and Watson (the former under Horry, the latter under Richboo, a Tory colonel) met unexpectedly, and a severe skirmish ensued. Other portions of the two armies engaged in the fight. The field-pieces of Watson gave him great advantage, and Marion was obliged to fall back in the direction of Williamsburg. At a bridge over the Black River, below Kingstree, he checked his pursuers by well-aimed rifle-balls and the destruction of the bridge by fire. Down the stream, upon opposite sides, the belligerents marched nearly ten miles, skirmishing all the way. Darkness terminated the conflict, and both parties arranged their flying camps for rest, near each other. For ten days Watson remained stationary, continually annoyed by Marion, until he was obliged to choose between certain destruction in detail there, or attempt boldly to fight his way to Georgetown. He decided upon the latter course, and at midnight he fled. Marion pursued, fell upon him at Sampit Bridge, near Georgetown, and smote down many of his wearied soldiers. Watson escaped to Georgetown with the remnant of his army, complaining that Marion would not "fight like a gentleman or a Christian!"

Sad intelligence now reached Marion. The Tory colonel, Doyle, had penetrated to his camp on Snow's Island, dispersed the little garrison, destroyed his provisions and stores, and then marched up Lynch's Creek. He pursued the marauder until he was informed that Doyle had destroyed all his heavy baggage, and had the advantage of a day's march on the road to Camden. Marion wheeled, and hastened, through the overflowed swamps, to confront Watson, who was again in motion with fresh troops, and had encamped upon Cat-fish Creek, near the present Marion Court House. Our partisan encamped within five miles of him, and there he was joined by Lee on the fourteenth of April (1781). This junction alarmed Watson. He destroyed his heavy baggage, wheeled his field-pieces into Cat-fish Creek, and fled precipitately by a circuitous route toward Georgetown. Soon after this, we find Marion in May, 1781, hanging upon the rear of Lord Rawdon on his retreat from Nelson's Ferry toward Charleston; and from that time until the siege of Ninety-Six, he was often with Sumter and Colonel Washington, watching the enemy's movements near the Santee and Edisto, and cutting off intelligence and supplies from Cruger.

In June (1781) Marion took possession of Georgetown, the garrison fleeing down Winyaw Bay after a slight resistance. He could not garrison it, so he moved the stores up the Pedee to his old encampment on Snow's Island, and demolished the military works. Informed that the Loyalists of Charleston had organized, and under Colonel Ball were about to ravage the country south of the Santee, he anticipated them. He drove off the cattle, removed the provisions to a place of safety, laid waste the country, and left nothing but barrenness and desolation in the district menaced by the enemy.

We have observed that soon after Greene abandoned his design of attacking Rawdon at Orangeburg, and retired to the High Hills of Santee, he detached Sumter, with Marion, Lee, and other active partisans, to beat up the British posts in the direction of Charleston, drive these hostile detachments to the gates of the city, and cut off all convoys of supplies for the British troops on the Edisto. The chief object to be gained was to cause Rawdon to abandon Orangeburg and hasten to the relief of Charleston. Sumter was the commander-in-chief of this expedition. As he approached Monk's Corner, he divided his little army into separate detachments. Among the subordinate commanders of these were Horry, Mayham, Taylor, the Hamptons, and James. The garrison at Dorchester, first attacked, made no resistance to Colonel Lee, who also captured, at about the same time, all the wagons and wagon horses belonging to a convoy of provisions; while Colonel Wade Hampton pressed forward to the very lines at Charleston, captured the patrol and guard at the Quarter-house, five miles from the city, and spread terror through the town. He also took fifty prisoners (mounted refugees) at Strawberry Ferry, and burned four vessels laden with valuable stores for the British army.

At Biggin's, near Monk's Corner, where Huger's cavalry were surprised more than a year before, was a strong force of about five hundred infantry, one hundred and fifty horse, and a piece of artillery, under Colonel Coates of the British army. Biggin Church, and a redoubt at Monk's Corner, about a quarter of a mile distant, composed the defenses of the garrison. Against these Sumter, Marion, and Lee proceeded. They halted at sunset within a short distance of Coates's camp, with the intention of attacking him early in the morning. Coates, alarmed by the intelligence brought by his patrols, that one half of Greene's army, with all the partisan officers of the South, were upon him, decamped during the night, set fire to Biggin Church, so as to destroy stores which he could not carry away, and crossing the head waters of the Cooper River on the eastern side, retreated rapidly toward Charleston. When the blaze of the church was perceived in the American camp, Sumter called his troops to arms and hotly pursued the fugitives. Within a short distance of

Quimby's Creek Bridge, eighteen miles from Monk's Corner, the cavalry of Lee and Marion overtook the rear-guard of the flying troops. Dismayed at the near approach of horsemen, they cast down their arms without firing a gun, and begged for quarter. Coates had crossed the bridge with his main body, and was waiting for the passage of his rear-guard, with the baggage, to destroy the bridge. The planks were already loosened, and every thing was in readiness for its demolition when the American cavalry approached. The brave Armstrong, with a section of Lee's horsemen, dashed across the bridge and fell upon the British guard with a howitzer stationed there for its defense, and drove the artillerists from the gun. The place of contest was a narrow causeway and lane leading to the bridge, and for a short time a close and deadly conflict ensued. Many of the British fled, and Coates and some of his officers were left to fight alone, defended only by a wagon. Another section of the cavalry, under Carrington, followed close upon Armstrong, and leaping the chasm formed by the casting down of some loose planks by the hoofs of Armstrong's horses, joined in the close combat with the enemy. Lee had now gained the bridge, where Captain O'Neil, with the third section, had halted. Captain Mayham, of Marion's cavalry, dashed by them, when his horse was shot under him. The chasm had been widened by the passage of Carrington's troops, and all Lee's efforts to repair the breach were ineffectual. The stream was too deep to ford, and the shores too muddy to land if the horses had swam it, and, consequently, a victory so nearly secured had to be abandoned. Coates, with his recaptured howitzer, retreated to a strong two-story house and other buildings a little further up the stream, into which many of his soldiers had fled at the first attack. There he was assailed by Sumter and Marion, between three and four o'clock in the afternoon, and a severe battle was waged for three hours. Darkness, and the failure of the powder of the patriots, terminated the contest. Fifty of Marion's brigade were killed or wounded, and seventy of the British fell. Coates held his position, and Sumter, informed of the approach of Rawdon, collected his own immediate forces, crossed the Santee, and joined Greene upon the High Hills, while Marion remained lower down upon the river to watch the movements of the enemy.

It was at about this time, while the army of General Greene was in repose near the Wateree, that the execution of Colonel Isaac Hayne, a leading Whig of South Carolina, took place at Charleston; an event which, in the opinion of the Americans, and of just men in Europe, marked the character of the British officer in command at Charleston with the foul stain of dishonor and savage cruelty. 22 The patriots were greatly exasperated by it, and General Greene gave the British commander notice that he would retaliate when opportunity should offer, not by the sacrifice of misguided Tories, but of British officers. He soon had power to exhibit terrible retribution, but happily, actuated by a more humane policy, Greene hesitated; the beams of peace soon appeared in the horizon, and bloody human sacrifices were prevented.

Here let us resume the general narrative of events in the South not already related, from the time of the encampment of Greene upon the High Hills of Santee, in 1781, until the evacuation of Charleston by the British the following yea.r.

We have noticed that Greene's camp upon the Hills was broken up on the eighteenth of November, and the remnants of his diminished army were put in motion toward Charleston. Already intelligence of the surrender of Cornwallis at Yorktown had reached him, and the day of its arrival (October 30) was made jubilant by the army. In the mean while, Marion was operating with vigor. He suddenly disappeared from the Santee upon one of his secret expeditions, and as suddenly was seen sweeping across the country in the direction of the Edisto, on his way to relieve Colonel Harden, who was closely pressed near Parker's Ferry, a few miles above Jacksonborough, in Colleton District, by a British force of five hundred men, under Major Fraser. That officer's camp was at the ferry. Marion prepared an ambuscade, and then sent out some of his swiftest horses with experienced riders to decoy his enemy into the snare. Fraser, with his cavalry, fell into the ambuscade in a narrow place, and was terribly handled on August 30, 1781. The sure rifles of Marion's men thinned his ranks, and had not their ammunition failed them, they would have accomplished a complete victory. For the want of powder, they were obliged to retire at the moment when the palm was offered to them. The loss of the British was severe, while Marion was not bereft of a man. He had succeeded in rescuing Harden, and as we have seen, obedient to the call of Greene, hastened toward the Santee and joined the American army at Laurens's plantation on September 7, 1781, when pressing on toward Eutaw. After the great battle at that place, and his pursuit of Stewart, Marion encamped in the deep recesses of a cane-brake on Santee River Swamp, and awaited an occasion again to go forth to action.

The British commander, ignorant of the weakened condition of Marion's brigade, **23** and the great diminution of Greene's army, was alarmed when he was informed that the latter had crossed the Congaree, and was again pressing on toward Eutaw. He struck his tents and hastened toward Charleston. Perceiving this movement, Greene left his army while on its march from the Santee Hills, and at the head of two hundred cavalry and as many infantry moved rapidly toward Charleston. The garrison at Dorchester, more than six hundred strong, advised of his approach, went out to meet him. But so sudden and vigorous was the charge of Colonel Hampton, of the advance, that the enemy wheeled and fled in great confusion to their camp. Believing the whole army of Greene to be near, they destroyed all the public property, cast their cannons into the Ashley, and then fled toward Charleston, closely pursued. At the Quarter-house they were joined by Stewart's forces, retreating by another road, and all hastened to the city gates. Terror spread through the town. The bells were rung, alarm guns were fired, and every friend of the crown was called to the defense of the city. Greene's object was accomplished; the British outposts were driven in, and he hastened to join his army, now encamped at Round O, not far from the Four Holes' Creek, forty or fifty miles from the city. Marion and his men lingered around the head waters of the Cooper to watch the enemy, and prevent his incursions beyond Charleston Neck. St. Clair had driven the British from Wilmington, and only Charleston and Savannah, with their respective dependencies, now remained in undisputed possession of the Royalists.

Governor Rutledge, with his accustomed energy, now prepared to re-establish civil government. He first offered conditional pardon to Tories and others who should join the American army. Hundreds came from the British lines and eagerly accepted the governor's clemency. Writs for an election of representatives were issued, and in January, 1782, a Republican Legislature convened at Jacksonborough, on the Edisto, thirty-five miles below Charleston.

Hope dawned upon the future of the South, and the bowed head of Republicanism was lifted up. General Leslie, the chief commandant in Charleston, perceived the change in the aspect of affairs, with alarm, and sent out proclamations, filled with promises and menaces, to counteract the movements of the patriots. It was too late. The people perceived the waning of British power as the area of its action was diminished, and promises and threats were alike unheeded. The army of Greene drew near to Jacksonborough, and encamped upon the Charleston road, six miles below the town. Thus protected, the Legislature acted freely and judiciously, and from that time the civil power met with no obstructions.

John's Island was yet occupied by the enemy, under the command of Major Craig, who had been driven from Wilmington. Greene resolved to expel them. An expedition for the purpose was intrusted to Lieutenant-colonel Laurens, a son of Henry Laurens, who had lately come from the field of victory at Yorktown. Lee was his second in command. An attempt was made, on the night of the thirteenth of January (1782), to surprise and capture the garrison of five hundred men, but the miscarriage of a part of their plan deprived them of their anticipated victory. Yet the design was not abandoned. A large body of Greene's army moved forward, and Craig, taking counsel of his fears, abandoned the island, and fled, with his troops, to Charleston. A few prisoners, and provisions and stores of the camp, were the spoils of victory. Still further secure, the Legislature now labored industriously and without fear. Confiscation laws were enacted; the currency was regulated; general laws for the future government of the state were adopted; and a bill was originated for presenting to General Greene, in consideration of his services, the sum of ten thousand guineas. **24** They closed their labors by electing John Matthews governor.

From this time until the evacuation of Charleston, military operations were confined to attempts on the part of the British to procure supplies from the country, and opposition thereto by the patriots. In these operations, Marion's brigade was conspicuous. Elected to a seat in the Assembly at Jacksonborough, he left it in command of Colonel Horry. Previous to his departure, he had a severe skirmish, near Monk's Corner, with three hundred regulars and Loyalists, who came up from Charleston to surprise him. He repulsed them, but soon afterward, while he was absent, a larger force, under Colonel Thompson (the celebrated Count Rumford, subsequently), attacked his brigade near the Santee. Fortunately, he arrived during the engagement, but not in time to prevent the defeat and partial dispersion of his beloved troops. The remnant of his brigade rallied around him, and he retired beyond the Santee to reorganize and recruit.

The main armies continued quiet. Each felt too weak to attempt to disturb the other. Leslie's condition was far worse than Greene's. Confined within the city, provisions soon became scarce, while the flight of Tories to the town increased the demand. Greene had ample provisions, and moving forward, encamped near the head of the Ashley, within twenty miles of the enemy's lines. Unable to damage the Americans in warfare, the British employed stratagem and bribery to weaken their power. Emissaries came into camp, and a mutinous spirit was engendered. A scheme was planned to abduct Greene, and convey him to Charleston. It was discovered twenty-four hours before it ripened, and was crushed. The conspirators were of the Pennsylvania line. Gornell, the leader, was executed, and four of his known companions in crime were sent, guarded, up to Orangeburg. The demon of discord was seen no more, and the British made no further attempts to arouse it.

Early in April, Marion, with a considerable force, was sent to "keep watch and ward" over the country between the Cooper and Santee Rivers. A Scotchman, pretending to be a deserter, came out from the city, visited Marion, and passed on unsuspected toward the Scotch settlements on the Pedee. Soon an insurrection appeared in that quarter, and Marion was informed that Major Gainey, for the third time, was gathering the Tories. The pretended deserter was a spy, and, by false representations of the power of the British and weakness of the Americans, he called the Highlanders to arms. The spy was caught and hanged while returning to Charleston, and before Gainey could organize his recruits, Marion fell upon him. More than five hundred Loyalists laid down their arms, and Gainey, thoroughly humbled, joined the ranks of Marion. 25

While the theater of war was thus narrowing, British statesmen of all parties, considering the capture of Cornwallis and his army as the death-blow to all hope for future conquests, turned their attention to measures for an honorable termination of the unnatural war. General Conway, the firm and long-tried friend of the Americans, offered a resolution in Parliament in February (1782), which was preliminary to the enactment of a decree for commanding the cessation of hostilities. It was lost by only *one vote*. Thus encouraged, the opposition pressed the subject warmly upon the attention of the House of Commons and the nation, and on the fourth of March, Conway moved "That the House would consider as enemies to his majesty and the country all those who should advise, or by any means attempt, the further prosecution of offensive war on the Continent of North America." The resolution was carried without a division, and the next day the attorney general introduced a plan for a truce with the Americans. Lord North, after an administration of affairs, as prime minister, for twelve years, finding himself in the minority, resigned the seals of office on March 20, 1782. Orders for a cessation of hostilities speedily went forth to the British commanders in America, and preparations were soon made for evacuating the cities of Savannah and Charleston.

When General Leslie was apprised of these proceedings in Parliament, he proposed to General Greene a cessation of hostilities in the South. That officer, like a true soldier, refused to meddle in civil affairs, and referred the matter to the Continental Congress, the only competent tribunal to decide. Of course there must be a delay of several weeks, and while no important military movement was made by the main army of either party, each was as vigilant as if an active campaign was in progress.

On the thirteenth of August, Leslie, in general orders, declared his intention of evacuating Charleston, and sent a flag to Greene with a request that he might be allowed to receive and purchase supplies from the planters. 26 Greene refused his acquiescence, for it would tend to nourish a viper, perhaps yet disposed to sting. Leslie replied that he should obtain supplies by force, for it was necessary to have them before putting to sea. This menace gave activity to the camp of Greene, for he resolved to oppose with spirit every attempt of the enemy to penetrate the country. General Gist, with a strong force, was advanced to the Stono, and spread defensive corps, under good officers, southward to the Combahee, while Marion was instructed to keep watch over the region of the Lower Santee. Rapidly, and in wide circuits, that partisan, with his cavalry, scoured the region between the Sampit and the Santee, and sometimes he would sweep down the country, all the way to Cainhoy and Haddrell's Point. Some warm skirmishes occurred, but he effectually kept the enemy at bay in that quarter.

Anxious to leave Charleston, where famine stood menacing the army and civilians, Leslie resolved to make a bold effort to penetrate the country by the Combahee, for little could be effected in the region guarded by Marion. He accordingly sent a large party thither in armed boats and schooners, where they arrived on the 25th of August, and passed up directly toward the head of the stream. Gist, with about three hundred cavalry and infantry, hastened to oppose the invaders, leaving Colonel Laurens with a guard near Wappoo, to watch the movements of the enemy in Charleston. Laurens, burning with a desire for active service, left a sick-bed and followed Gist. He overtook him upon the north bank of the Combahee, near the ferry, and at his earnest solicitation he was detached to the extreme end of Chehaw Neck, to garrison a small redoubt cast up there for the purpose of annoying the British when they should return down the river. With fifty light infantry, some matrosses, and a howitzer, Laurens moved down the river on August 26, 1782, and halted at the house of Mrs. Stock, within a short distance of the point. At three o'clock in the morning he resumed his march. He had proceeded but a short distance, when a picket of the enemy was perceived, and at the same moment a large detachment, which lay concealed in the high fennel grass, arose and delivered a murderous fire. They had been informed of the march of Laurens, and landing on the north shore of the Combahee, concealed themselves in ambush by the road side. Laurens saw the danger of a retreat, and had no alternative but to surrender or fight. His brave spirit could not brook the former, and leading the way, he made an energetic charge upon the foe. The step was fatal to the young commander; he fell at the first fire. Captain Smith of the artillery was also slain, the howitzer was seized by the enemy, and the whole American force turned and fled in confusion. The fugitives were pursued a short distance, when Gist, with a considerable force, confronted the victors. They recoiled for a moment, but soon recovered, and a severe combat ensued. The British fell back to their boats, and the field of strife was the field of victory for the Americans; yet it was dearly won. Many unnamed patriots fell, and in the death of Laurens the country lost one of its most promising men. **27** The British succeeded in carrying off a large quantity of provisions and plunder from the Combahee, and from Beaufort and the neighboring islands. They made no other attempt to procure supplies, but applied themselves diligently to preparations for leaving Charleston. Kosciuszko, who was placed in command of Laurens's corps, watched Charleston Neck, and detachments guarded the passes of the Stono. In this latter service the last blood of the Revolution was shed. **28**

The evacuation of Charleston took place on the fourteenth of December (1782). **29** Leslie had leveled the walls of Charleston and demolished Fort Johnson, and on the morning of the thirteenth, the American army crossed the Ashley, and slowly approached the city, according to previous arrangements with Leslie. At daylight the next morning the British marched to Gadsden's Wharf, and embarked. At eleven o'clock an American detachment took formal possession of the town, and at three in the afternoon General Greene escorted Governor Mathews and other civil officers to the Town Hall. From windows, balconies, even housetops, the troops were greeted with cheers, waving of handkerchiefs, and cries, "God bless you, gentlemen! Welcome! welcome!" Before night the British squadron (about three hundred sail) crossed the bar, and the last speck of canvas of that hostile array glittered far out upon the ocean in the parting beams of the sun that evening. The cool starry night which succeeded was one of great joy to the people, and the dawn of the morrow was that of a long and bright day for the emancipated state. Generosity succeeded revengeful feelings; confiscation acts were repealed; Loyalists were forgiven, on repentance, and those who had adhered to royal rule as the least of two evils, rejoiced in the glories of the happy days of freedom and prosperity which succeeded.

Here let us close the chronicles of the war in the Southern States, and depart for the North.

On the morning of the day when I departed from Charleston (January 29, 1849), the sun came up from the sea bright and unclouded, and I could not have wished for a lovelier day to visit places of note in Charleston and vicinity. I had already been out to the Lines, and the old ship-yard and magazines on Cooper River, with Reverend Dr. Smythe. The scars of the former are yet visible in several places upon the Neck, and a portion of the citadel, a remnant of the "horn work," survives the general wreck of the military works about Charleston. It was just at sunset when we passed through a beautiful avenue of live oaks, draped with moss, to view the ruins of the magazines and officers' quarters among thick shrubbery and tangled vines near the banks of the river, about four miles above the city. A little to the northwest of these ruins is an ancient burial-ground, on the verge of a deep morass. The tall trees, pendent moss, silent ruins, and deep shadows of night fast hovering over the scene, gave the place a tinge of romance, thrilling and sad. On our way to this interesting spot we turned aside, about a mile and a half nearer the town, to view a venerable and lordly magnolia, under whose spreading branches tradition avers General Lincoln held a council of officers during the siege in 1780. Incredible as it may appear, the owner of the land, and of the house shaded by the tree wherein he and his mother were born, had just felled it for fire-wood. Instead of being its destroyer, who, in like circumstances, would not have been its defender? and when rude hands were laid upon it, would not have exclaimed,

"Woodman, spare that tree!
Touch not a single bough!
In youth it sheltered me,
And I'll protect it now.
'Twas my forefather's hand
That placed it near his cot;
There, woodman, let it stand,
Thy ax shall harm it not!"
– MORRIS.

The Council Tree.

I sketched the venerable house near by, the property of Colonel William Cummington during the Revolution, and marking the position of the stump of the magnolia, preserved for posterity a sketch of what tradition calls the Council Tree, with its surroundings.

It was on the bright and balmy day of my departure that I visited Sullivan's Island. From thence I crossed over to Haddrell's Point (now Point Pleasant), and after passing an hour there, where so many of the brave patriots of South Carolina suffered a long imprisonment, I returned by steam-boat to the city. There are no remains of Revolutionary fortifications at Point Pleasant, and it is now famous in the minds of the citizens of Charleston only as a delightful summer resort.

At three o'clock in the afternoon I left Charleston for home, in a steam-packet bound to Wilmington, bearing with me many mementoes of the war for independence at the South, and filled with pleasing recollections of a journey of several weeks among the inhabitants of that sunny land where I had enjoyed the hospitality and kindness of true Republicans, keenly alive to the reflected glory of their patriot fathers, and devotedly attached to the free institutions of our common country, the fruits of a happy union.

The waters of the harbor were unruffled by a breeze, and I anticipated a delightful voyage to the Cape Fear; but as the city and fortifications receded, and we crossed the bar to the broad bosom of the Atlantic, we found it heaving with long, silent undulations, the effects of the subsiding anger of a storm. Sea-sickness came upon me, and I went supperless to my berth, where I remained until we were fairly within the mouth of the Cape Fear, at Smith's Island, on the following morning. The low wooded shores of Carolina approached nearer and nearer, and at eight o'clock we landed at the ancient town of Wilmington, on the eastern side of the Cape Fear.

I contemplated spending a day at Wilmington, but circumstances requiring me to hasten homeward, I was there only during the hour while waiting for the starting of the rail-way cars for the North. I had but little opportunity to view the town, where Republicanism was most rife on the sea-board of North Carolina before and during the Revolution; but by the kindness of friends there, especially of Edward Kidder, Esq., I am enabled to give, traditionally and pictorially all that I could have possibly obtained by a protracted visit. Already I have noticed many stirring events here during the earlier years of the war; it now remains for me to notice only the British occupation.

When, toward the close of 1780, Cornwallis prepared to move from his encampment at Winnsborough, toward North Carolina, he directed Colonel Balfour, at Charleston, to dispatch a sufficient force to take possession of Wilmington, that he might have a sea-port for supplies, while in that state. Major James H. Craig (who was governor general of Canada in 1807) was sent with four hundred regulars to perform that service. He took possession of the town without much resistance, toward the close of January, 1781. He immediately fortified himself, using the Episcopal church, a strong brick edifice (of the front of which the engraving is a correct view), for a citadel. **30** Craig held undisturbed possession of Wilmington until the arrival of Cornwallis, on the seventh of April, after his battle with Greene, at Guilford. He remained in Wilmington, with his shattered army, eighteen days, to recruit and to determine upon his future course. His residence was on the corner of Market and Third Streets, now (1852) the dwelling of Doctor T. H. Wright. Apprised of Greene's march toward Camden, and hoping to draw him away from Rawdon, then encamped there, Cornwallis marched into Virginia, and joined the forces of Arnold and Phillips at Petersburg. The subsequent movements of the earl, until his surrender at Yorktown, have been detailed in former chapters.

Major Craig held possession of Wilmington until the autumn of 1781, when, informed of the surrender of Cornwallis, and the approach of St. Clair on his way to join Greene, he abandoned Wilmington and fled to Charleston. This was the only post in North Carolina held by the British, and with the flight of Craig all military operations ceased within its borders. **32**

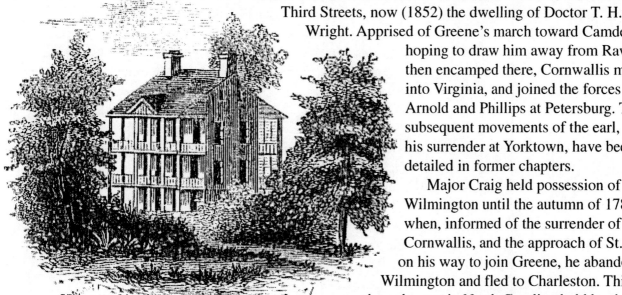

Cornwallis' Head-Quarters. 31

The rail-way from Wilmington to Weldon, on the Roanoke, a distance of one hundred and sixty-two miles, passes through a level pine region, where little business is done, except gathering of turpentine and the manufacture of tar. It was a dreary day's ride, for on every side were interminable pine forests, dotted with swamps and traversed by numerous streams, all running coastward. We crossed the Neuse at Goldsborough, eighty-five miles north of Wilmington, and the Tar at Rocky Mount, forty miles further. At sunset we passed Halifax, **33** near the falls of the Roanoke, and arrived at Weldon at dark. The morning was uncomfortably warm; the evening was damp and chilly; and when we arrived at Richmond the next morning, two hundred and forty miles north of Wilmington, a cold rain was falling, and every thing was incrusted with ice. I tarried a day at Richmond, another at Washington City, and on the fourth of February (1849) I sat by my own fireside in the city of New York, after an absence of about eleven weeks, and a journey of almost three thousand miles. There my long and interesting tour ended, except an occasional "journey of a day" to some hallowed spot in its vicinity. God, in his providence, dealt kindly with me, in all that long and devious travel, for I did not suffer sickness for an hour, and no accident befell me on the way.

Chapter XXI
Endnotes

1 Henry Clinton, K. B., was a son of George Clinton, governor of New York in 1743, and grandson of the Earl of Lincoln. He served in the British army on the Continent, during the Seven Years' War, and came to America with General Howe in the spring of 1775, bearing the commission of a major general. He was distinguished at the battle of Bunker Hill; commanded in New York, and operated against the forts among the Hudson Highlands in 1777; and in 1778, succeeded Sir William Howe in the supreme command. After he evacuated Philadelphia, he went to New York, where he continued his head-quarters until he left the country, in 1782. He was appointed governor of Gibraltar in 1795, and died there on the twenty-second of December, the same year.

2 On the voyage from New York, one vessel, carrying heavy ordnance for the siege, foundered and was lost, and nearly all the horses belonging to the artillery and cavalry perished at sea. Immediately after landing, Lieutenant-colonel Tarleton was ordered to obtain a fresh supply of horses. This service he soon performed, by seizing all that fell in his way on the plantations upon the islands and the main, some of which were paid for, and some were not. The Whigs were not considered entitled to any pay. Having mounted his cavalry, Tarleton joined a body of one thousand men, under General Patterson, whom Clinton had ordered from Savannah to re-enforce him.

3 Spain was now at war with Great Britain, and willingly became a party in our quarrel, with the hope, like France, of crippling English power. When the approach of the British fleet was made known, Lincoln dispatched a messenger to Havana to solicit material aid from the Spanish governor. Direct assistance was refused, but the Spaniards indirectly aided the Americans. When Clinton was preparing to march upon Charleston, Don Bernardo de Galvez sailed from New Orleans to reduce Fort Charlotte, an English post at Mobile. It surrendered to the Spaniards on the fourteenth of March, 1781, and on the ninth of May, Pensacola also bowed to Spanish domination. These successes placed the two Floridas in possession of the Spaniards, except the strong fortress of St. Augustine.

4 The lines of intrenchments were on the ridge of land whereon St. Paul's Church, the Orphan House, the "Citadel" (a part of the old works), and the Presbyterian church now stand.

5 Charles Cotesworth Pinckney was born in Charleston on the twenty-fifth of February, 1746. At the age of seven years, be was taken to England with his brother, Thomas, by their father (Chief-justice Pinckney), where he was educated, and also studied law. In 1769 he returned to Charleston, after visiting the Continent. In England he took part against the Stamp Act with its opposers there, and, on reaching his native country, he eagerly espoused the cause of the patriots. He commenced the practice of law in 1770, and soon became eminent. When a regiment was formed in Charleston in 1775, of which Gadsden was colonel, Pinckney was appointed a captain, and was at Newbern for a while on recruiting service. He was active in the defense of Charleston in 1776. In 1778, he accompanied General Howe in his expedition to Florida. He assisted in the repulse of Prevost in 1779, and in the defense of Charleston in 1780. When the city fell, he became a prisoner, and suffered much from sickness and cruel treatment. He was exchanged in February, 1782, when the war was almost ended. He was soon afterward raised to the brevet rank of brigadier. On the return of peace, he resumed the practice of his profession. He was a member of the convention which formed the Constitution of the United States. Washington offered him a seat in his cabinet, which he declined, and in 1796 he accepted the appointment of minister to the French Republic. There he had a delicate duty to perform, and while in the midst of personal peril in the French capital, he uttered that noble sentiment, "Millions for defense, not one cent for tribute." In 1797, Mr. Pinckney was appointed the second major general in the army under Washington, and for many years he was an active politician. For about twenty-five years he lived in elegant retirement, in the enjoyment of books and the pleasures of domestic happiness. He died on the sixteenth of August, 1825, in the eightieth year of his age.

6 In this passage the British lost twenty-seven seamen killed, and a transport which ran aground and was burned by its crew.

7 Woodford had marched five hundred miles within twenty-eight days. On the day of his arrival the terms of enlistment of about seven hundred North Carolinians expired, and they all went home at an hour when they were most needed.

8 At daybreak on the twenty-fourth of April, a party under Lieutenant-colonel Henderson made a sortie, surprised a British picket, and with the bayonet killed about twenty of them. Twelve were made prisoners. Captain Moultrie, a brother of the general, was killed, and two other Americans were wounded.

9 This day was marked by disasters to the Americans. On that morning, Colonel Anthony Walton White, of New Jersey, with the collected remnant of Huger's cavalry, had crossed the Santee and captured a small party of British. While waiting at Lanneau's Ferry for boats to recross the river with his prisoners, a Tory informed Cornwallis of his situation. Tarleton was detached with a party of horse to surprise White, and was successful. A general rout of the Americans ensued. About thirty of them were killed, wounded, or captured, and the prisoners were retaken. Lieutenant-colonel Washington, with Major Jamieson and a few privates, escaped by swimming the Santee. Major Call and seven others fought their way through the British cavalry, and escaped. At noon on the same day, the British flag was seen waving over Fort Moultrie, the little garrison, under Lieutenant-colonel Scott, having been obliged to surrender to Captain Charles Hudson, of the British Navy.

10 Clinton's nearest battery in making this approach was on the lot in Mary Street, formerly used as the lower rail-way depùt, and long known, according to Johnson, as the Fresh-water Pond. This redoubt was several times demolished by the American cannons, and rebuilt during the siege. – Johnson's *Traditions*, &c., 248.

11 One of these shots demolished an arm of Pitt's statue.

12 The terms of the capitulation were partly honorable and partly humiliating. The town, fortifications and shipping, artillery and stores, were to be given up; the Continental troops and sailors were to be conducted to some place to be agreed upon, there to remain prisoners of war until exchanged; the militia to be permitted to return home, as prisoners of war, on parole, and to be secured from molestation as long as they did not violate these paroles; the arms and baggage of the officers and their servants were to be retained by them; the garrison were to march out, and lay down their arms between the works and the canal, the drums not to beat a British march, nor the colors to be uncased; the French consul, and French and Spanish residents should be unmolested, but considered prisoners of war; and that a vessel should convey a messenger to New York, that he might carry dispatches to General Washington.

13 Gordon, Ramsay, Moultrie, Marshall, Stedman, Lee, Tarleton.

14 During the siege, Arbuthnot was informed that Admiral De Ternay was approaching with a French fleet, direct from Newport, to aid Lincoln; and on the very day when terms of surrender were agreed upon, the fear of being blockaded in the harbor of Charleston made Arbuthnot resolve to put to sea immediately. Ternay was certified of the surrender of Lincoln while on his way, by the capture of a pilot-boat, bearing Clinton's dispatches to Knyphausen, then in command at New York. These dispatches informed Knyphausen of the fall of Charleston. Had Lincoln held out another day, his army might have been saved, but he was not aware of the approach of Ternay.

15 Lieutenant-governor Gadsden and seventy-seven other public and influential men were taken from their beds by armed parties, before dawn on the morning of the twenty-seventh of August, hurried on board the Sandwich prison-ship, without being allowed to bid adieu to their families, and were conveyed to St. Augustine. The pretense for this measure, by which the British authorities attempted to justify it, was the false accusation that these men were concerting a scheme for burning the town and massacring the loyal inhabitants! Nobody believed the tale, and the act was made more flagrant by this wicked calumny. Arrived at St. Augustine, the prisoners were offered paroles to enjoy liberty within the precincts of the town. Gadsden, the sturdy patriot, refused acquiescence, for he disdained making further terms with a power that did not regard the sanctity of a solemn treaty. He was determined not to be deceived a second time. "Had the British commanders," he said, "regarded the terms of capitulation at Charleston, I might now, although a prisoner, enjoy the smiles and consolations of my family under my own roof; but even without a shadow of accusation preferred against me, for any act inconsistent with my plighted faith, I am torn from them, and here, in a distant land, invited to enter into new engagements. I will give no parole." "Think better of it," said Governor Tonyn, who was in command; "a second refusal of it will fix your destiny – a dungeon will be your future habitation." "Prepare it, then," replied the inflexible patriot. "I will give no parole, so help me God!" And the petty tyrant *did* "prepare it;" and for forty-two weeks that patriot of almost threescore years of age, never saw the light of the blessed sun, but lay incarcerated in the dungeon of the Castle of St. Augustine. All the other prisoners accepted paroles, but they were exposed to indignities more harrowing to the sensitive soul than close confinement. When, in June, 1781, they were exchanged, they were not allowed to even touch at Charleston, but were sent to Philadelphia, whither their families had been expelled when the prisoners were taken to the Sandwich. More than a thousand persons were thus exiled, and husbands and wives, fathers and children, first met in a distant state, after a separation of ten months.

The Continental prisoners kept at Haddrell's Point suffered terribly. Many of them had been nurtured in affluence; now, far from friends and destitute of hard money, they were reduced to the greatest straits. During thirteen months' captivity, they received no more than nine days' pay. They were not allowed to fish for their support, but were obliged to perform the most menial services. Cornwallis finally ordered Balfour, the commandant of Charleston, to send them to one of the West India islands. The general exchange of prisoners which soon afterward took place alone prevented the execution of this cruel order.

16 Gordon, iii., 226.

17 At the beginning of the siege, Marion was at a house in Tradd Street, and the host, determined that all of his guests should drink his wine freely, locked the door to prevent their departure. Marion would not submit to this act of social tyranny, and leaped from a second story window to the ground. His ankle was broken, and before the communication with the country toward the Santee was closed he was carried to his residence, in St. John's parish, on a litter. He was yet confined by the accident when the capitulation was signed. See Simm's Life of Marion, page 96.

18 Simms.

19 This island is at the confluence of Lynch's Creek and the Pedee. It is chiefly high river swamp, dry, and covered with a heavy forest filled with game. The lower portions are cane-brakes, and a few spots are now devoted to the cultivation of Indian corn. Here was the scene of the interview between Marion and a young British officer from Georgetown, so well remembered by tradition, and so well delineated by the pen of Simms and the pencil of White. The officer who came to treat respecting prisoners was led blind-folded to the camp of Marion. There he first saw the diminutive form of the great partisan leader, and around him in groups were his followers, lounging beneath magnificent trees draped with moss. When their business was concluded, Marion invited the young Briton to dine with him. He remained, and to his utter astonishment he saw some roasted potatoes brought forward on a piece of bark, of which the general partook freely, and invited his guest to do the same. "Surely, general," said the officer, "this can not be your ordinary fare!" "Indeed it is," replied Marion, "and we are fortunate, on this occasion, entertaining company, to have more than our usual allowance." It is related that the young officer gave up his commission on his return, declaring that such a people could not be, and ought not to be subdued.

20 At about this time, Colonel Harden, a gentleman of Beaufort, who, with a large number of the Whigs of his district, had joined Marion in Williamsburg, marched with seventy of the most resolute of his comrades to visit their homes. A few others from Georgia, under Colonel Baker, accompanied them, and in the face of the foe, then in possession of the country upon the Lower Santee and Edisto, they ravaged the region from Monk's corner to the Savannah River. Like Marion, Harden made rapid and excentric marches, and always baffled pursuit. He crossed and recrossed the Savannah as often as circumstances required, and soon his force amounted to two hundred men. The name of Harden became as terrible to the Tories of Beaufort, Barnwell, and Colleton, as that of Marion beyond the Santee. He had several skirmishes with British detachments, and finally, on the twelfth of April, 1781, he surprised and captured a redoubt and garrison called Fort Balfour, at ancient Pocataligo, below the Combahee. Having awed the Tories in that section of the state, Colonel Harden and his detachment joined the forces under General Pickens, higher up on the Savannah.

21 At this time, Major M'Ilraith, with a force about equal to that of Marion's, was met by the latter in a swamp near Nelson's Ferry. They prepared for battle, when M'Ilraith, who was a humane man, made the chivalric proposition that twenty picked men of each army should meet and fight for victory. It was agreed to; the forty men were drawn up in line and approached each other, when those of M'Ilraith's party fell back. The sun went down, and yet they lingered; and at midnight, M'Ilraith doubtless considering prudence the better part of valor, decamped, leaving his heavy baggage behind. He was pursued by Colonel Horry early in the morning, but without effect.

22 Isaac Hayne was a highly respected and well-beloved citizen of South Carolina. He was among the early patriots of that state who took the field, and at the siege of Charleston, in 1780, he served in a company of mounted militia, and at the same time was a member of the State Legislature. His corps was not in the city, but operated in the open country, in the rear of the besiegers, consequently it was not included in the capitulation. After that event his command was dispersed, and he returned to his family and estate, near the Edisto. Believing that the wisest policy for him to pursue was to go to Charleston, surrender himself a prisoner, and take his parole like others, he repaired thither. He was too confiding in the honor of the conquerors, for, knowing him to be a man of influence, the commandant refused the privilege, and told him that he must either become a British subject or submit to close confinement. He would gladly have endured imprisonment, but he could not bear the thought of leaving his family exposed to the insults of marauders, and the pestilence of small-pox, then spreading over the lower country. He consulted his friend, Dr. Ramsay, the historian, who was himself a prisoner in Charleston, and, influenced by family affection, he accepted a British protection upon the humiliating terms proposed by Clinton in his second and cruel proclamation, and took the oath of allegiance. He was assured by Patterson, the deputy British commandant in Charleston, that he would not be called upon to take up arms for the king, "For," he said, "when the regular forces of his majesty need the aid of the inhabitants for the defense of the province, it will be high time for them to leave it."

Colonel Hayne was often called upon by subordinate officers to take up arms for the king, but steadily refused. When, in 1781, Greene approached with a Continental army, and the partisan troops had swept royal power from almost every place where it had planted its heel of military subjugation, Colonel Hayne felt released from his oath of allegiance, because its conditions were such that its obligations ceased when royal rule should be suppressed. When again summoned (as he was peremptorily, while his wife was upon her dying bed) to repair, with arms, to the British camp at Charleston, he again refused. He did more; he buckled on his armor, repaired to the American camp, and, forswearing his forced allegiance to the British crown, he pledged his life to the defense of his country. With a troop of horse, accompanied by Colonel Harden, he scoured the country toward Charleston, and captured General Andrew Williamson, a former efficient patriot, but now active in the British service. When intelligence of the event reached the city, a troop of cavalry was sent in pursuit of Hayne. A battle ensued, and the patriot was made a prisoner and conveyed to Charleston. Colonel Nesbit Balfour, a proud, vain, and ambitious man, was then the commandant. He knew that the surest road to distinction was rigor toward the rebels. He chose to consider Hayne a traitor, because he had signed an oath of allegiance, and then took up arms against the king. Here was an opportunity for Balfour to distinguish himself, and Hayne was cast into the provost prison, and kept there until Rawdon arrived from Orangeburg. He was then taken before a court of inquiry, where neither the members nor the witnesses were sworn. The whole proceeding was a mockery, for Rawdon and Balfour had prejudged him worthy of death. Without even the form of a trial, he was condemned to be hung. No one, not even the prisoner, supposed that such cruelty was contemplated, until the sentence was made public, and he had but two days to live! The men of the city pleaded for him; the women signed petitions, and went in troops and upon their knees implored a remission of his sentence. His sister, Mrs. Peronneau, with his orphan children (for his wife was in her grave), clad in deep mourning, knelt in supplication before his judges, but in vain. Rawdon and Balfour were inexorable, and on the thirty-first of July, 1781, one of the purest patriots and most amiable of men was hung upon a gibbet. Like Andre, he asked to be shot as a soldier, but this boon was denied him. Thirty-two years afterward, Lord Rawdon, in a letter to General Henry Lee (see his *Memoirs*, page 459), attempted to excuse his want of humanity, by pleading the justice of the sentence. But the denunciations of the Duke of Richmond at the time, in the House of Lords, and the truth of history, have given the whole transaction the stamp of barbarism.

23 After the battle at Eutaw, Marion was re-enforced by detachments of mountain men, under Colonels Shelby and Sevier, the heroes of King's Mountain, and with them he confidently took the field. He attacked the British outpost at Fairlawn, while the main body, under Stewart, were encamped behind redoubts at Wappetaw and Wantoot. The attack upon Fairlawn was successful. The garrison, and three hundred stand of arms, with provisions and stores, were the spoils of victory. Encouraged by this success, Marion prepared for other enterprises, when the Mountaineers, after about three weeks' service, suddenly left him and returned to the upper country. No satisfactory reason for this movement has ever been given.

24 This example was imitated by the Legislatures of North Carolina and Georgia. The former voted him five thousand guineas, and the latter twenty-four thousand acres of land.

25 Among the insurgents was the notorious David Fanning, a Loyalist of North Carolina. He was one of the most desperate and brutal of the Tory leaders, and at one time had command of almost a thousand marauders like himself. He became a terror to the people of central North Carolina. He captured many leading Whigs, and took them to Craig, at Wilmington. On the thirteenth of September, 1781, he and his associate, Hector M'Neil, with their followers, entered Hillsborough, carried off the governor, Thomas Burke,* and other prominent Whigs, and hastened with them toward Wilmington. They were intercepted by a party under General Butler, and a severe skirmish ensued at Lindley's Mill, on Cane Creek. Fanning was wounded, but successfully retreated with his prisoners to Wilmington. After the defeat here mentioned, on the Pedee, Fanning went to Charleston, and accompanied the Tories who fled to Nova Scotia, where he died in 1825.

---

* Thomas Burke was one of the purest patriots of the South. He was a native of Ireland; came in early life to Virginia, and in 1774 settled as practicing lawyer, in Hillsborough, North Carolina. He was one of the earliest Republican legislators in the state. He was a member of the Provincial Congress at Halifax in 1776, and of the Continental Congress, from 1777 till 1781, when he was chosen governor of his state. After his capture by Fanning, he was sent to Charleston, and kept closely guarded, upon John's Island, when Craig commanded there. He escaped, and in 1782 resumed his official duties. He died at Hillsborough in 1783.

---

26 Greene's army now covered a fertile district, where wealth abounded, and prevented foraging and plundering where the enemy had generally found the best supplies. Perceiving their homes thus secured, many of the families returned from exile, and every where the board of hospitality was wide spread to their deliverers. The rugged features of war were soon changed by the refinements of social life, and the soldiers, who had been battling for years among desolated homes or the dark wilderness, felt that a paradise was gained. The wife of General Greene reached his camp at the close of March, and was every where caressed. The officers were greeted at numerous social gatherings, and the charms of many a fair daughter of the sunny South subdued hearts which never quailed before an enemy. In the district occupied by the army, were many wealthy, beautiful, and accomplished women, and "many," says Johnson, in his Life of Greene, "were the matrimonial connections to which this period gave rise between the officers of the army and the heiresses of Carolina and Georgia."

27 John Laurens was a son of Henry Laurens, president of the Continental Congress in 1777. He joined the army early in 1777, and was wounded in the battle at Germantown. He continued in the army (with the exception of a few months), under the immediate command of Washington, until after the surrender of Cornwallis, in which event he was a conspicuous participant as one of the commissioners appointed to arrange the terms. Early in 1782, he was sent on a special mission to France, to solicit a loan of money and to procure arms. He was successful, and on his return received the thanks of Congress. Within three days after his arrival in Philadelphia, he had settled all matters with Congress, and departed for the army in the South, under Greene. There he did good service, and was killed on the Combahee, on the twenty-seventh of August, 1782, when he was but twenty-nine years of age. Washington, who made him his aid, loved him as a child. He declared that he could discover no fault in him, unless it was intrepidity, bordering on rashness. "Poor Laurens," wrote Greene, "has fallen in a paltry little skirmish. You knew his temper, and I predicted his fate. The love of military glory made him seek it upon occasions unworthy his rank. The state will feel his loss." He was buried upon the plantation of Mrs. Stock, in whose family he spent the evening previous to his death in cheerful conversation. A small inclosure, without a stone, marks his grave.

28 Captain Wilmot, a brave young officer, who commanded a company detailed for the purpose of covering John's Island, impatient of inaction, often crossed the river to harass British foraging parties on the island. While engaged in one of these excursions, in company with Kosciuszko, he fell into an ambuscade and was killed. This occurred in September, 1782, and was, it is believed, the last life sacrificed in battle.

29 Preparatory to the evacuation, commissioners were appointed to make arrangements to prevent the carrying away of slaves on the departure of the British. All was made satisfactory; but the promises of the enemy were shamefully violated. Moultrie says that more than eight hundred slaves, employed on the works in the city, were sent to the West Indies and sold. It has been estimated that between the years 1775 and 1783 the state of South Carolina was robbed of twenty-five thousand negroes, valued at about twelve million five hundred thousand dollars.

30 This church was demolished in 1841, and upon its site a new Protestant Episcopal church now stands.

31 This is from a pencil sketch, by Mr. Charles Burr, of Wilmington.

32 At Elizabeth, higher up on the Cape Fear, in Bladen county, quite a severe battle was fought in July, 1781, between a few refugee Whigs, under Colonel Thomas Brown, and a body of Tories. The Whigs forded the Cape Fear after dark, and before midnight were in deadly conflict with the Tories. The surprise was complete, and the victory quite easy. This bold act crushed Tory ascendency in that section of the state. I received from the venerable Dr. De Rosset, of Wilmington, an interesting account of a gallant affair on the part of the Americans at a place called "The Oaks," near Wilmington, in which he, though a lad, participated. I regret the want of space that precludes the possibility of giving the narrative here. Like many other similar details, the local historian must make the record. Dr. De Rosset is a son, I believe, of the mayor of that name. I have also received (too late for insertion), from the venerable A. M. Hooper, of Crawford, Alabama, an interesting sketch of the public life of William Hill, an active patriot of Cape Fear, of whom Josiah Quincy in his journal (1773), said "though a crown officer, a man replete with sentiments of general liberty, and warmly attached to the cause of American freedom."

33 Here the Provincial Congress of North Carolina met on the fourth of April, 1776, and took precedence of all similar assemblies in action favorable to independence. It was at Halifax that Cornwallis crossed the Roanoke while on his march to Virginia, in May, 1781.

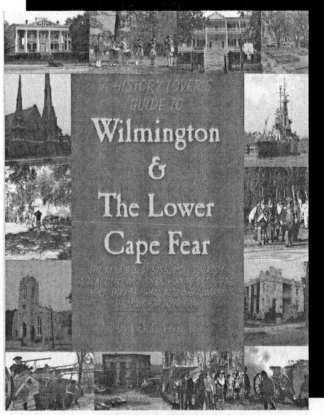

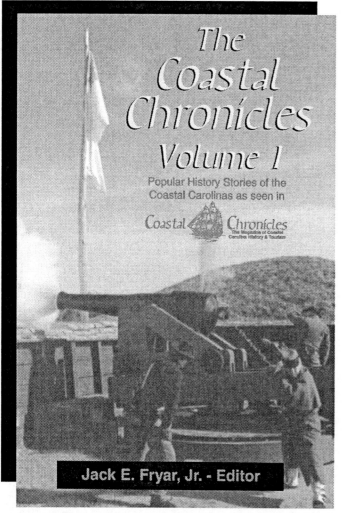

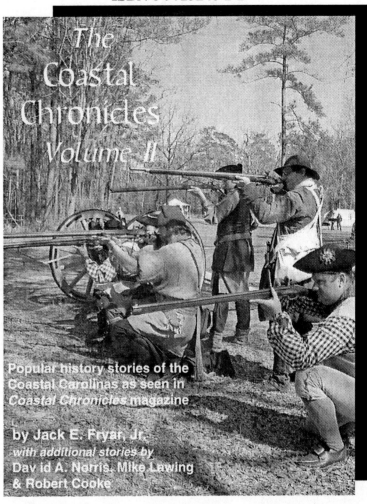

Printed in the United States
26493LVS00001B/83-118